Writing the History of
SOMERSET

Family, Community, and Religion

Essays in Honour of Robert Dunning

Edited by
Adrian J. Webb and Andrew F. Butcher

HALSGROVE

First published in Great Britain in 2018

British Library Cataloguing-in-Publication Data
A CIP record for this title is available from the British Library

ISBN 978 0 85704 329 0

HALSGROVE
Halsgrove House,
Ryelands Business Park,
Bagley Road, Wellington, Somerset TA21 9PZ
Tel: 01823 653777   Fax: 01823 216796
email: sales@halsgrove.com

Part of the Halsgrove group of companies
Information on all Halsgrove titles is available at: www.halsgrove.com

Printed and bound by Parksons Graphics, India

Contents

Acknowledgements 5

Abbreviations 6

Foreword 8

1. Introduction 9

2. The Saints of Medieval Somerset 15

3. St Lawrence in Somerset 28

4. The Urban Estate of the Vicars Choral of Wells: a Study in
   Bad Management? 43

5. Thoughts on Martin Renger, a 16th-century Somerset Potter 60

6. Kingston Iuxta Yeovil in 1633 67

7. A Somerset Gentleman & Landowner: Thomas Smyth of
   Ashton Court, Long Ashton 1609-1642 84

8. A Sequestrator's Lot is Not a Happy One: Edward Curll,
   Sequestrator of Catsash Hundred 100

9. Dr Westover of Wedmore, Physician and Farmer, 1686-1705 107

10. Thomas Carew of Crowcombe: the Pecuniary Problems
    of an 18th-century Gentleman 123

11. New Light on William Day of Blagdon, Land-Surveyor,
    Cartographer and Linen Draper 138

12. Were Somerset Parish Churches Physically Neglected in
    the 18th Century? An Examination of the Evidence in
    Edmund Rack's Survey of Somerset 161

13. Monastic Revival in Somerset: Benedictine Monasticism from
    the Henrician Dissolution to the Second Vatican Council 177

    Bibliography of Robert W. Dunning's Works to 2017 192

    Index of Personal Names 204

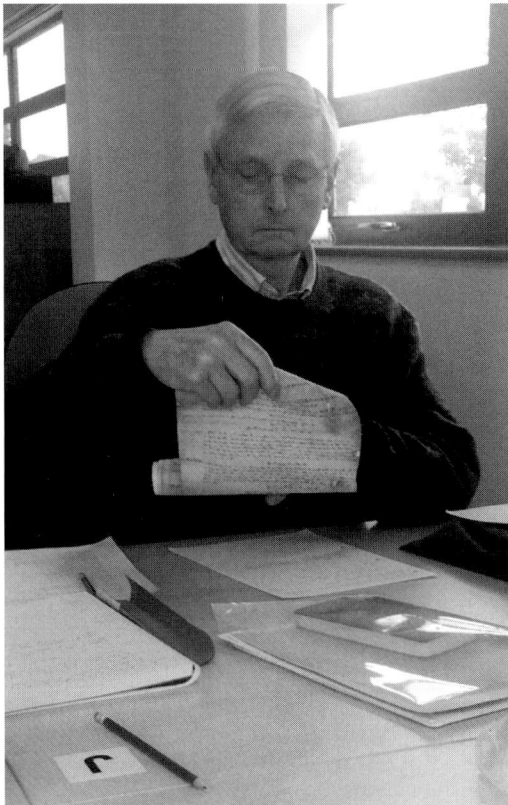

Robert Dunning.

Acknowledgements

The editors are grateful to the following for their assistance and support in the production of this volume: Anton Bantock, Sue Berry, Michael Blandford, David Bromwich (SANHS Honorary Librarian), Robert Browning (Senior Strong-Room Controller, South West Heritage Service), Anne Buchanan (Local Studies Librarian, Bath Central Library), Michael T. Clanchy (London University), Matt Coles (Bristol Record Office), Michael Costen, Ann Crawford (former Archivist of Wells Cathedral), John d'Arcy (Archivist at Mells), Wilf Deckner (Somerset Studies Librarian, South West Heritage Service), Emma Down (The National Archive), Anne Dunning, Graeme Edwards (Senior Archivist, South West Heritage Service), Jenny Gaschke (Bristol Museum and Art Gallery), Liz Grant (Archivist, South West Heritage Service), Gail Griffith, Teresa Hall, William Hancock, Max Hebditch (former President of the United Kingdom Museums Association), Sophie Hippisley (Search Room Assistant, South West Heritage Service), Esther Hoyle (Senior Archivist, South West Heritage Service), Hazel Hudson, Kate Iles (Bristol City Museum and Art Gallery), Graham Jones, Amal Khreisheh (Curator, South West Heritage Service), Simon Jones (Assistant Strong-Room Controller, South West Heritage Service), Margit Kaye (Beinecke Library), Sue Isherwood Lane, Kim Legate (Hestercombe), Rob Lutton (Lecturer, University of Nottingham), George Miles (Beinecke Library), Lynn Moore, Frances Neale, The Earl of Oxford (Mells), Kate Parr (Archives and Local Studies Supervisor, South West Heritage Service), Steven Pugsley, Andy Playle (Search Room Assistant, South West Heritage Service), Mervyn Richens (Senior Conservator, South West Heritage Service), Anna Riggs (Archivist of Bath Abbey), Jim Skeggs, Lindsay Stainton, Drew Westerman (Bath Record Office), Chris Webster (South West Heritage Service), Andy White (Taunton), Philip White (Hestercombe), and Ben Whitworth (Hestercombe).

Special thanks are due to the two anonymous donors who kindly supported this publication financially, along with the Trustees of the Somerset Record Society, the Trustees of the Somersetshire Archaeological and National History Society and the Trustees of the Fairfield Trust.

Abbreviations

Arch. Journ.	Archaeological Journal
BAR	British Archaeological Report
BIHR	Bulletin of the Institute of Historical Research
B&GAST	Bristol & Gloucester Archaeological Society Transactions
BM	British Museum
BA	Bristol Archives (formerly Bristol Record Office)
BRS	Bristol Record Society
CalChRolls	Calendar of Charter Rolls
CPL	Calendar of Papal Letters
CalPapReg	Calendar of Papal Registers
CRS	Catholic Record Society
D&CRS	Devon & Cornwall Record Society, New Series
DRO	Dorset Record Office
ECA	Exeter Cathedral Archive
HMC, Cal Mss D & C Wells	Historical Manuscripts Commission, Calendar of Manuscripts of the Dean & Chapter of Wells
JWEH	Journal of Welsh Ecclesiastical History
Med. Arch.	Medieval Archaeology
ODNB	Oxford Dictionary of National Biography
Post-med. Arch.	Post-medieval Archaeology
Proc. Hug. Soc. London	Proceedings of Huguenot Society London
PSANHS	Proceedings of the Somerset Archaeological and Natural History Society
R&TDevon Assoc.	Reports & Transactions of the Devonshire Association
SANHS	Somerset Archaeological and Natural History Society
SDNQ	Somerset and Dorset Notes and Queries
SHC	Somerset Heritage Centre
SHER	Somerset Historical Environment Record

SM	Somerset Magazine
SRO	Somerset Record Office
SRS	Somerset Record Society
Surrey Arch. Soc. Res.	Surrey Archaeological Society Research
SWCH	South Western Catholic History
TAMS	Transactions of Ancient Monuments Society
TNA	The National Archives
TRHS	Transactions of the Royal Historical Society
VCH	Victoria County History
WA&NHM	Wiltshire Arts & Natural History Magazine
WCA	Wells Cathedral Archives
WEHS	Welsh Ecclesiastical History Society
WHR	Welsh History Review
WRS	Wiltshire Record Society
WSA	Wiltshire & Swindon Archives
WSRO	West Sussex Record Office

Foreword

Like many people, I was impressed immediately by Robert Dunning when in the late 1960s he took up the post of editor of the Victoria County History of Somerset. From that point onwards he became the indisputable guide to the heritage of the County, and this book attests to the depth and breadth of his interests and the originality and significance of his written contributions, both in the VCH and elsewhere. As an academic he is peerless and he is an inspiring and tireless lecturer. I well remember the lectures he gave for the University of Bristol Extra-mural Department in towns and villages across the County, where he would not only impart information but, in a friendly and attentive way, was prepared to gather the historical wisdom of his audience: this is a tremendous gift.

However, it is right in honouring his work interpreting and memorialising the past in Somerset, we should also pay tribute to his commitment to the wider community. His involvement in Church affairs has been decades long – as a Lay Reader, and as a lay leader within his parish, deanery and diocese. He has held many positions which have been far from sinecures, including Chairman of the Trustees of Glastonbury Abbey. Above all, he served with distinction as a Deputy Lieutenant of the County. This office speaks of the historical importance of the locality within our Nation, but also, practically, embodies leadership and encouragement of others in the contemporary world. These have been the touchstones of Robert Dunning's life and career.

All of the essays in this volume bear witness to the honour the contributors feel due to Robert Dunning and the esteem in which he is held. They also betray something rather rarer: genuine affection, in which I am sure all of us who have known Dr Dunning these many years share to the full.

Lady Gass DCVO

1. Introduction:
Robert W. Dunning,
the Making of a Historian

RALPH GRIFFITHS

Robert Dunning is the pre-eminent historian of Somerset for this generation. Anyone with only a passing acquaintance with the long history of the county – or of the diocese of Bath and Wells which practically coincides with it – soon encounters his name. Not only was he the editor of the *Victoria County History* for Somerset from 1967 to 2005, but county and diocese are fortunate in that he has readily placed his unrivalled historical knowledge and expertise at the disposal of their communities, their institutions and their visitors – and continues to do so. The friends and colleagues who have contributed essays to this book, and the subjects they have chosen in the sure expectation that he will enjoy reading about them, represent a far wider constituency and reflect his broad historical interests. The West Country, and in particular Somerset where generations of his family have lived and farmed, is in his DNA. For him, life and art, conversation and writings, have been focussed on this region throughout his career, and he has become one of the foremost interpreters of Somerset's history to the rest of provincial Britain.

No one who has spent any length of time in Robert Dunning's company comes away thinking of him other than as Bob. The University of Bristol turned him into a professional historian with a special interest in the Middle Ages. There he was taught by the redoubtable David Douglas, a distinguished Anglo-Norman historian and biographer of William the Conqueror; by Margaret Sharp, daughter and collaborator of T. F. Tout, the outstanding medieval historian of an earlier generation (and with roots in Somerset's soil to boot); and, of a younger generation, by Charles Ross who would later excel as the foremost historian of Yorkist England. While Bob was a student, Ross published his edition of the Cartulary of St Mark's Hospital, Bristol, and was also preparing his *Cartulary of Cirencester Abbey* (whose original volume he would occasionally show to students when he had it under his desk!). It was Charles Ross who supervised Bob's postgraduate research, on a subject congenial to both of them: 'The administration of the diocese of Bath and Wells' under five notable bishops with high profiles in the English church and the state in the fifteenth century. His doctoral thesis was examined and approved by E. F. Jacob of Oxford University, one of the country's leading ecclesiastical historians. This was impeccable training in medieval history and the foundation of Bob's later work on both the Middle Ages and on modern history too. The close relationship with Charles Ross was expressed in the invitation to contribute an essay to the tribute-volume for him in 1986.

Historians are trained to identify influences in society, and influences are crucial to a historian's development. As with many a young scholar, Bob's inspiration and experience came from several quarters, enabling him to extend his historical interests while, at the same time, enriching his knowledge of the West Country. As a researcher with the History of Parliament Trust, he joined a small, talented group of young scholars studying the parliaments of Richard II, Henry IV and Henry V, under the direction of J. S. Roskell, historian of the medieval parliaments. Bob's remit was right up his street: to write the histories of the county and borough constituencies of Somerset, Devon and Cornwall, and their MPs, a task that broadened his knowledge from the ecclesiastical and the administrative to the political, social and personal, focussing on the market towns of the region and identifying some of the local families which sent members to the Commons. Although Bob had left the Trust by the time the four authoritative volumes of the *History of Parliament* from 1386 to 1421 were published in 1992, his was an essential contribution – especially on Somerset and its representatives. And friendships and associations among colleagues while he was 'a parliamentary historian' have been of lasting importance to him and them.

A warm West Country inspiration came independently from the writings of John Betjeman, later to be Britain's poet laureate, who in the 1950s moved west from his native London and eventually made Cornwall his home. Betjeman's wit and humour, his fascination with provincial life and ordinary people, and with places, their names and religious buildings, both medieval and Victorian, appealed to Bob who soon had what must have seemed a golden opportunity to pursue very similar interests as a full-time historian with the whole of Somerset's history as his canvas. Seemingly reserved and yet sociable and practical, unflappable and patient with a passion for Somerset cricket, he has proved generous with his time and knowledge; his wry sense of humour and a fund of telling anecdotes make him an entertaining lecturer, to judge by frequent reports of satisfied audiences, which also appreciate the lightness of touch and earthiness of his writing. Had they met, Betjeman might have recognised a soul-mate.

In 1967, Bob was appointed editor of the recently revived *Victoria County History* of Somerset which had been suspended following the First World War. He now needed to develop the talents required of a historian who could range widely across the county's entire history. On a trip to South Cadbury camp while still a student, he impressed fellow students by announcing that he had tramped its extensive earthen banks as a boy and had no need to do so again. But a much closer acquaintance with archaeology was required of the new editor of the VCH: this was provided, along with expert introduction to the fine building traditions of some of the county's towns, in the course of an enduring friendship with (amongst others) W. J. (Bill) Wedlake, whose major excavations at Camerton, south-west of Bath, had just been completed, and Peter Greening of the Bath Preservation Trust, who first introduced Bob to Glastonbury as a town as well as an abbey. The evolution of the humane landscape and the importance of topography would have a central place in

Bob's published work in later years.

The far-sighted and generous sponsorship of the VCH by Somerset County Council and the University of London (which hosts the VCH for the whole of England) was prompted by the Somerset Archaeological and Natural History Society, one of the country's earliest such societies. It flourishes still and, in return for its vision, Bob has played a prominent part in its activities. Each county's VCH volumes share a common approach, parish by parish, town by town: encompassing landownership and economic life, local government and administration, the church and nonconformity, education and 'charitable bodies'. If sometimes the universal structure of the VCH appears to be restrictive, this has not prevented Somerset's editors from addressing historians' more recent concerns, among them cultural activities in local communities, social structure at all ranks, migration and (a subject hitherto relatively neglected) to treat the Bristol Channel as an avenue of connection with southern Wales and beyond rather than as a boundary. Bob and his two assistant editors, Robin Bush (to 1978) and then Mary Siraut, were responsible for seven magisterial volumes covering a swathe of central Somerset, and since retirement he has contributed to subsequent volumes under the editorship of Mary Siraut. These authoritative volumes are notable not simply for their detailed reliance on national and local public archives but also on many private sources to which Bob and his colleagues have gained access.

In the course of this work, Bob has done more than anyone else to establish the VCH as one of the pillars of the historical 'establishment' in the county, with all the implications they now have for public awareness of its heritage, the historical meaning of its landscape, and the attraction of its buildings and countryside to visitors and tourists. Since returning to Somerset, Bob has staunchly supported the Somerset Archaeological and Natural History Society, as it supported the VCH, serving successively as its honorary editor, chairman of its council and its president. For almost as long as he has been the VCH editor, he has been general editor of the Somerset Record Society, one of Britain's long-established learned societies that has regularly published major documentary sources across the entire span of the county's history. Fresh from his researches at the History of Parliament Trust, where he wrote the biography of Robert Hill (or Hylle) of Spaxton, MP for Somerset in Henry V's reign, his appointment as editor coincided with his edition of the *Hylle Cartulary* for the Record Society, one of the relatively few secular cartularies of deeds and other memoranda known to exist in Britain. Soon afterwards, he found himself the Society's general editor, a post he has occupied ever since, seeing more than twenty-five volumes through the press. Bringing the original work of others to the point of publication is an invaluable (if often thankless) service. In 1983, as the Society approached its centenary, Bob pointedly noted that it had not published any source written after 1700, with the exception of two valuable historic maps; that gap has now been repaired.

The Church of England occupies an important place not only in Bob's writings but also in his life and that of his family, his wife Anne and their children Christy and

Jeremy. Though at university he joined the Methodist Society ('Methsoc'), which had one of the liveliest and most congenial fellowships among the student societies, at Taunton he quickly found his spiritual home at St George's church, Wilton. Its medieval foundation appealed to the ecclesiastical historian and he and Anne have since served the church (and the diocese) in countless ways. In this, he stands in a tradition of the writing of history in provincial England that stretches back to the eighteenth century and beyond. When Oxford University Press planned its new edition of *The Dictionary of National Biography* (published in 2004), Bob was invited to contribute twelve essays to it, all of them in one way or another concerned with Somerset and the West Country. They reflect his mastery of the region's medieval history and his appreciation of the work of its earlier antiquarians and historians: four of the essays are on abbots (or priors) of Bath and Glastonbury abbeys, two are on bishops of Bath and Wells, three on the Luttrell and Mohun families of Dunster, and, interestingly, three on Richard Locke of Burnham-on-Sea, local agriculturist and antiquary, his contemporary the Revd John Collinson, the eighteenth-century antiquary whose *The History and Antiquities of the county of Somerset* was reprinted in 1983 with Bob's introduction, and, finally, William Hunt of Bristol, a notable historian who was secretary of the Somerset Archaeological and Natural History Society in the 1870s, president of the Royal Historical Society before the First World War – and one of Bob's predecessors as editor of the Somerset Record Society.

Bob's professional reputation among historians has three strands which extend over the range of Britain's history. He is a medieval ecclesiastical historian who took on the medieval and modern history of Somerset, and he regards it as his mission to appeal to an inclusive range of audiences throughout Somerset and across its borders. Witness David Bromwich's tally of publications at the conclusion of this volume: it lists from the 1960s onwards Bob's contributions to learned journals and academic volumes that advance our knowledge by placing the West Country experience in the context of the history of the later medieval church, culminating in essays for the volumes in honour of F. R. H. DuBoulay (1985), distinguished historian of society and the economy in the see of Canterbury in the Middle Ages, and in tribute to Charles Ross (1986), Bob's own supervisor. These essays – on Cleeve Abbey and on Athelney, 'the Abbey of the Princes' – shed a more nuanced light than had been customary on the difficulties and resilience of some of England's monasteries before they faced sudden dissolution by Henry VIII. Along the way, Bob's work on Glastonbury abbey in the course of preparing the VCH volumes is of equal significance, while his essay on patronage and promotion in the late medieval church (1981) draws on the archives of the Courtenay earls of Devon and ranges as far as the bishopric of St David's to which Hugh Pavy of Bristol was appointed in 1485. These writings and the steady publication of the VCH volumes explain the frequency with which Bob is consulted on all things relating to Somerset by academics in Britain and North America. His professional standing was recognised by his early election to the fellowship of both the Royal Historical Society and the Society of Antiquaries of London.

At the same time, Bob has long had a commitment to explain the history of the West Country beyond the ranks of specialist historians, and this commitment has become stronger as the decades have passed. Beginning with his connection with extra-mural departments at the Universities of Bristol and Exeter, and his link with the Local Studies Centre at Exeter, he makes an immense contribution to the wider culture of the region by his readiness to lecture to interested groups and to give his advice to anyone who seeks it, as well as through a score of more popular and accessible books on Somerset's history – its castles, churches, towns, landscape and buildings. All of them – from the first, an innovative book, sponsored by Somerset Education Committee, on *Christianity in Somerset* (1975) for teachers and students in schools and colleges, via *The Concise History of Somerset* (1983), to the recent, beautiful books on Wells Cathedral and its buildings – are underpinned by his own original scholarship. Two features of these books stand out. They show a growing awareness of the visual sources of history – photographs, drawings, maps and paintings – which enable buildings, portraits and landscapes to add their perspective to the fundamental stories that documentary research and earlier antiquarians tell. Bob has established himself as a master of both. Secondly, it has been an article of faith with him that the range of available sources for the study and writing of Somerset's history should be made available to his readers: most of his books – even those that might find their way on to coffee-tables – end with ample guidance to further information about castles, country houses and families, churches and monasteries. His account of the county's castles (1995), with its gazetteer to aid the visitor, is comprehensive, though only in the 'follies and fantasies' section could he indulge his interest in the families who lived in them. By contrast, his companion book on Somerset's twenty-eight monasteries (2001) rescues the names of monks whose world was turned upside down in 1536-9, drawing especially on Glastonbury's records (and not forgetting some monks of Welsh origin). Both books are scholarly and yet successfully aimed at a broad readership.

Two of most famous chapters in West Country history have been examined by Bob with a combination of sensitivity and objectivity for the general reader: the Battle of Sedgmoor, near Bridgewater, where in 1685 the duke of Monmouth led the last popular rebellion in England; and 'the quest for King Arthur' and its links with Cadbury camp (the *legendary* Avalon) and Glastonbury (the *supposed* burial place of Arthur and Queen Guinevere). There are, too, several novel approaches in his armoury. The books on Bridgwater and Glastonbury combine history with detailed walking tours which highlight little noticed buildings that must surely be as much a revelation to their residents as to visitors. Others are personal rather than anodyne histories: *his* selection of 30 country houses (in 1991), *his* 50 churches (in 1996) and *his* 34 significant Somerset families (in 2005) – yet none the worse for that. His sense of humour even extends to his 50 churches, some of which are characterized with a wry (even irreverent) phrase: 'Defying the bishop' at Beckington St George, where a seventeenth-century rector and his parishioners stood up to a wrathful bishop; and 'a dignity of rectors' elevating the reputation of the rectors of St John the Evangelist at Weston-super-Mare. Hardly a more appropriate person could have been chosen to serve, at various times, as chairman of the Trustees of Glastonbury abbey, chairman of the Friends of Wells Cathedral and a Trustee of the Friends of Somerset Churches and Chapels.

In the course of a successful career as a county historian, Bob's advice has been sought in both Devon and Cornwall on how to revive an authoritative county history – so far with uncertain results in Devon, but in 2002 the VCH in Cornwall re-emerged as if a phoenix. He was, moreover, the ideal person to submit an innovative proposal in 2001 on behalf of the Victoria County History for the 'England's Past for Everyone' national project. It secured the support of the Heritage Lottery Fund in 2005 and the work began, in collaboration with Exmoor National Park Authority. In several ways this was a new departure for the VCH, but not for Bob: the subject was dictated by landscape and history rather than by county boundaries, it was executed in a multidisciplinary fashion, and *Exmoor*, published in 2009 (after Bob's retirement), is directed towards schools, colleges and the public at large – it might even entice Devon to resurrect its VCH.

On occasion he has ventured further afield, though the paths have usually started in Somerset and betray his interest in the history of people and their faith. In 1991 he collaborated with John Bickersteth, formerly bishop of Bath and Wells and clerk of the closet in the royal household, to produce an elegant monograph on the arcane-sounding office ('the closet') which manages the Chapel Royal of HM The Queen, to whom the book is dedicated. With Bob's experience as a succinct biographer, they identified the 55 known clerks and their role in the Chapel Royal since the reign of Henry VI, the spiritually-minded monarch who instituted the post in 1437 and whom Bob had studied years earlier as an undergraduate. Most recent of all, and on an even wider front of social history, is his analysis of the deaths, burials and commemorations of almost 1,450 peers of the realm in the 800 years before the early twentieth century: from Bob's pen it is unlikely to be as cheerless a story as it sounds. I, for one, look forward to this book, and to the future writings of (to appropriate Bob's description of an earlier Somerset worthy) this 'Sage of Somerset'.

2. The Saints of Medieval Somerset

NICHOLAS ORME

From Roman times to the Reformation, Christians in England remembered and honoured the saints. Their images stood in churches; their names were recalled through the year. There were hundreds of them: far more than most people knew. Everyone was familiar with Mary whose statue flanked the high altar of every church and whose prayer ('Ave Maria') was known by everyone and said by many each day. On the other hand, early Roman martyrs like Abdon and Sennen, although in all church calendars, were scarcely remembered outside the liturgy in which the clergy mentioned them on 30 July. And there were saints like Wulfric of Haselbury who were chiefly honoured in a single district or even, like Dubricius at Porlock and the saint of Culbone nearby, at one sole church.

In theory one could list every instance of every saint recorded or venerated in medieval Somerset, but the task would be almost impossible to achieve. The present author attempted it for Cornwall in 2000, but that county is distinguished by a large number of unusual and local saints which helped to vary the task.[1] Even so, the listing of sites dedicated to Mary ran into eight columns without including every altar image and Lady chapel that must have existed, and the survey did not take full account of church calendars and their large number of saints who were remembered without having a concrete local presence. In consequence, the present article can provide only a brief tour of the subject. It aims to trace how the cults of saints throw light on the history of the Church in Somerset and on religion as it was understood and practised by local people. It focuses on cults that had a site in the county – church, chapel, altar, shrine, or image – rather than those that existed and were known of elsewhere, or those celebrated only in the liturgy. The reader must bear in mind that Somerset people also made prayers or pilgrimages to saints outside the county, like Mary of Walsingham and Thomas of Canterbury. Equally, saints in calendars were a regular part of the yearly routine of the clergy and more important to them, at least, than their absence of sites may suggest.[2]

Christianity came to Somerset during the Roman period. After 313, at the latest, it was possible to build churches whose worship would have included the veneration of

---

[1] N. Orme, *The Saints of Cornwall* (Oxford, 2000).
[2] J. Armitage Robinson, 'The Medieval Calendars of Somerset', in B. Schofield, ed., *Muchelney Memoranda*, SRS 42 (1927), pp. 143-83.

Mary, the apostles, and the early Christian martyrs. That veneration has left no discernible traces, however. Nor does much more survive from the period between about 400 and about 650 when the county was under the control of Celtic, or more accurately Brittonic, rulers who were also Christians. 'Brittonic' mean the ancient British language and culture, which remained in Wales, Cornwall, and Brittany. Here we encounter the difficult matter of Brittonic saint dedications, particularly those of churches. It will be necessary first to lay out the evidence and then to attempt to assess it.

There are several traditions linking Brittonic saints with sites in Somerset. The earliest may be a charter attributed to Bishop Hædde of Winchester in the late seventh century, granting land to the church of Glastonbury at *Lantokay*: a place which that church later identified with Leigh-on-Street.[3] *Lantokay* means 'church site of Kea', the name of a Brittonic saint venerated in Cornwall and Brittany.[4] A second such figure, Congar, was the principal saint of the church of Congresbury by the late ninth century,[5] and a third, Carantoc, is implied as being the patron of one of the two parish churches in Carhampton by the end of the twelfth.[6] Decuman was the church saint of St Decumans near Watchet by about the same date (figure 6).[7] Two other non-English figures are attested only just before the Reformation. The saint of Kitnor (a place now known as Culbone) is recorded as St *Cullanus* (perhaps a mistranscription of *Culbanus*) in 1527 and as Culbone in 1532, while Dubritius (the Welsh *Dyfrig*) is described as the patron of Porlock in 1527.[8]

Beyond these certain cases there are more difficult ones. The church of Glastonbury claimed by about the year 1000 to have been visited by St Patrick in the fifth century, and displayed his supposed tomb and shrine.[9] It also asserted, by then or soon afterwards, the presence of two other Irish saints: Indract, said to have been martyred at Shapwick, and Benignus, a hermit of Meare, both allegedly buried in the church.[10] Close to Glastonbury, a chapel dedicated to the Irish saint Bridget existed at Beckery by the twelfth century, and one of the Brittonic historian Gildas at Street by the thirteenth.[11] Glastonbury tradition asserted that Gildas died at Glastonbury and

---

[3] L. Abrams, *Anglo-Saxon Glastonbury: church and endowments* (Woodbridge, 1996), pp. 153-4. The attribution could be mistaken, however. There is a similarly named place, Landkey, in north Devon, but it seems too far west for a donation of land to Glastonbury at that date.

[4] Orme, *Saints of Cornwall*, pp. 156-8.

[5] Mentioned by Asser in about the 890s: see S. Keynes and M. Lapidge, eds., *Alfred the Great: Asser's Life of King Alfred and other contemporary sources* (Harmondsworth, 1983), p. 97.

[6] F. M. R. Ramsey, ed., *English Episcopal Acta*, vol. x: *Bath and Wells* (Oxford, 1995), p. 55; L. Toulmin Smith, ed., John Leland, *Itinerary*, 5 vols (London, 1908-11), i, p. 167.

[7] *VCH Somerset*, v, p. 165.

[8] F. W. Weaver, ed., *Somerset Medieval Wills*, 3 vols, SRS 16, 19, 21 (1901-5), ii, p. 268 (*Cullanus*; original text in The National Archives, PROB 11/23/239); iii, p. 14 (Culbone); and ii, p. 268 (Dubritius). Dr O. J. Padel observes that Culbone looks Irish rather than Brittonic (private information).

[9] M. Winterbottom and M. Lapidge, eds., *The Early Lives of St Dunstan* (Oxford, 2012), pp. 19-21; J. P. Carley, ed., *The Chronicle of Glastonbury Abbey* (Woodbridge, 1985), pp. 16-17.

[10] J. Scott, ed., *The Early History of Glastonbury* (Woodbridge, 1981), p. 61; M. Winterbottom and R. M. Thompson, eds., *Saints' Lives* (Oxford, 2002), pp. 371-81.

[11] *VCH Somerset*, ix, pp. 57, 191.

that Bridget lived for a time at Beckery, but as with the other Irish saints the asser-
tion is not supported by firm evidence.[12] At some point Bridget also inspired the dedication of two more parish churches: Brean and Chelvey. A further Brittonic saint cult
has been posited at Kewstoke, from the conjecture that the element 'Kew' might
relate to Kewa, the saint of St Kew in north Cornwall. This view has some merit,
because the earliest reference to the place as *Chiwestoch* in the Exchequer version of
Domesday Book (1086) suggests a pronunciation with a K rather than Ch as in Chew
Stoke in the Mendips, although in later times the church at Kewstoke was dedicated
to Paul.[13] As for the Welsh saint Cadoc, who is sometimes associated with the island
of Steep Holm, his linkage was in fact with the neighbouring Flat Holm which lay in
Wales not Somerset.[14]

How should we interpret this evidence? The traditional belief about post-Roman
Church history in western Britain, which can be traced back as far as Breton hagiog-
raphy in the eighth century, was that Brittonic saints brought Christianity from
Wales to the south-west of England and to Brittany in the fifth and sixth centuries,
after the end of the Roman Empire. This belief is not supported by contemporary
evidence. The earliest life of such a saint (that of Samson) may have been written in
the 8th century, as long as 150 years after his death, and the others at even greater
lapses of time. There is no sign that the writers of the lives had access to any sources
other than folk tradition. The lives conform to a pattern in which a saint comes to
his or her final resting place from Wales or Ireland, and personally founds the church
in which he or she was subsequently commemorated.[15] There is no compelling
support for such events in Somerset. True, Dubritius was a Welsh saint with numerous dedications in south-east Wales and the Marches, but his church at Porlock may
date from no earlier than the tenth century when parish churches became common.
It would thus be an outlier of his Welsh cult at that time, not a sign of his influence
in the early Christian centuries. The same applies to the dedications to Bridget,
which are found quite widely in Britain.

Rather, the Brittonic evidence turns out to be more complicated. If *Lantokay* was
really Leigh-on-Street, it might point to a saint cult coming not from Wales but
from Cornwall, which appears to have held Kea's principal church at Old Kea,
whence perhaps his cult also spread to Brittany.[16] Similarly, the most important
church of Carantoc of Carhampton was the minster church of Crantock in Cornwall:
the term 'minster' being used here to mean a major church staffed by a body of
clergy, either monks or more worldly clerks or canons. Kewa's chief church was that
of St Kew in the same county. Kea had an additional Welsh church at Landygai in
Caernarfonshire and Carantoc one at Llangrannog in Ceredigion, but these places

---

[12] Scott, ed., *Early History of Glastonbury*, pp. 55, 61.
[13] C. and F. Thorn, eds., *Domesday Book*, viii: *Somerset* (Chichester, 1980), p. 263, 42,1. I am grateful to
Dr O. J. Padel for advice on this point.
[14] Orme, *Saints of Cornwall*, p. 81.
[15] On this subject, see *ibid.*, pp. 27-9.
[16] *Ibid.*, pp. 156-8.

look too remote to have inspired dedications in Somerset.[17] The county also appears to have had two indigenous Brittonic saints: Congar and Decuman. Both had churches in the county which were minsters and are more likely to have been the centres of their cults, from which other churches or chapels were founded in Cornwall and Wales, than to have been colonies from some other point of origin.[18] Indract too, whose cult seems to have originated in Somerset, managed to inspire a chapel dedication in Cornwall.[19] The Glastonbury evidence about saints like Patrick, Indract, and Gildas is late, and indicates that Glastonbury adopted the hagiographical tradition of saints coming to England from Wales or Ireland, rather than proving that such a coming happened. As for Culbone, the name of the saint is recorded so late that we cannot even be sure of its original form; there is no warrant for interpreting it as Beuno, as is sometimes done. The same applies to a mysterious 'St Erne' with a well in Weare parish, recorded in 1602 and recently suggested as a Brittonic saint,[20] with the rider than one of the alleged analogous names (of a saint in Cornwall) is not compatible.[21] On the whole, the Brittonic evidence points to Somerset receiving and sending saint cults from various directions, to which we must add the even stronger likelihood of interchange with Roman Britain further east. There is nothing definite to show that a classic age of saintly journeys from Wales to the South-West of England took place in the fifth and sixth centuries, let alone that the saints then established the churches named after them.

By the middle of the seventh century, Somerset was passing under the rule of the kings of the West Saxons who, by this time, were becoming Christians. There followed the establishment of Anglo-Saxon minsters of monks or, from the eighth century onwards, of clerks or canons, along with the likely reorganisation of similar older Brittonic churches at Congresbury, Glastonbury, and St Decumans. Over twenty such minsters are documented or may be proposed up to the Norman Conquest, but most of what is known about their saint cults is restricted to their dedications. These came from a fairly small list. Mary was chosen at Bruton, Glastonbury (figure 7), Ilminster, and Stogumber, while Peter or Peter and Paul were adopted at Athelney, Bath, Muchelney, South Petherton, and Taunton, with Mary and Peter at North Petherton. Andrew, Peter's brother, became the patron of Aller, Banwell, Ilchester (Northover), and Wells, and eventually co-patron of Congresbury. A few minsters had a less usual saint: John the Baptist (Bedminster and Frome), John the Evangelist (Milborne Port), and Bartholomew (Crewkerne), along with the survival of Congar and Decuman.[22]

---

[17] *Ibid.*, pp. 83-5.

[18] On Congresbury as a minster, see Keynes and Lapidge, eds., *Alfred the Great* (1983), p. 97. A field near St Decumans church was called the 'Old Minster', and the church had a dean in the twelfth century (*VCH Somerset*, v, p. 165).

[19] Orme, *The Saints of Cornwall*, pp. 145-7.

[20] Orme, *Saints of Cornwall*, p. 161; M. D. Costen, 'A Celtic Saint at Weare', *SDNQ*, 30 (1974-9), pp. 219-20.

[21] *I.e.* Erney, correctly Terney (*ibid.*, p. 244).

[22] For the evidence, see N. Orme, 'The Medieval Church Dedications of Somerset', *PSANHS*, 160 (2017), pp. 83-94.

In the tenth century, lesser churches staffed by a single clergyman began to proliferate in England, and the historic system of parish churches with fairly small territories came into being. The evidence for their dedications comes mostly from wills after 1400, but there seems to have been little change in this matter during the previous five hundred years, so that the evidence can reasonably be read back to the origins of the churches concerned. Table 1 lists the known dedications of parish churches and major chapels which functioned as chapels of ease with parochial functions:

Table 1

Numbers of Documented Church Dedications in Somerset before 1550
In cases of double dedications, each saint is counted separately.
Information in brackets relates to chapels.

Cult	*Parish Churches*	*Selected Major Parochial Chapels*	*Total*
Mary	71	10	81
All Saints	43	4	47
Michael	30	3	33
Andrew	30	1	31
Peter (often with Paul)	30	1	31
John the Baptist	19	4	23
Nicholas	14	4	18
Paul (usually with Peter)	17	-	17
Leonard	10	1	11
Mary Magdalene	8	1	9
Martin	8	-	8
James the Great	5	4	9
George	7	1	8
Laurence	5	2	7
Giles	3	3	6
Margaret	5	1	6

Saints with between 2 and 5 dedications: Augustine 3, Bartholomew 3, Benignus 2, Bridget 2, Catherine 2 + (1), Congar 2, Dunstan (1), Gregory (2), Holy Cross 2, John Evangelist 2, Thomas Becket 1 + (1), Trinity 4 + (1).

Saints with single dedications: Aldhelm, Barnabas, Carantoc, Culbone, Cuthbert, Cyricus, Decuman, Dubritius, Edmund (1), Edward (probably the Martyr), Gildas, Julietta, Luke (1), Matthew, Olave, Petroc, Philip, Salvin (or Saviour), Stephen, Swithun, Vincent.

The dedications, most of which probably arose by 1100, show that the Anglo-Saxons usually chose the saints of their parish churches from the same short list that they used for their minsters. It also consisted of Mary, All Saints, Michael, Andrew, and Peter (sometimes with Paul). English saints were few: a mere one or two each of Aldhelm, Cuthbert, Dunstan, Edmund, Edward the Martyr, and Swithun, although some of these may have been honoured by unrecorded altars or images within parish churches.[23]

The history of the choice of church saints is still obscure. In most cases we do not know when the churches themselves were founded let alone why a particular saint was selected. Of the most popular ones, George was venerated in England by the late Anglo-Saxon period, before the Crusades with which he is sometimes associated. Exeter had a church in his name by 1066, and Somerset's first known, at Dunster, was in place by about 1090.[24] Martin had a church in Canterbury by 597, and he was certainly present in Somerset by the mid twelfth century.[25] John the Baptist, Nicholas, and Leonard became quite common too, although it is hard to say when. Giles looks likely to be post-Conquest, since he was pre-eminently a French saint, while Thomas Becket certainly came late to the scene. He is only authentically linked with churches founded after 1170 or chapels similarly founded that became parish churches. A few Brittonic saints clung on, but with some difficulty. Carantoc's church at Carhampton was eventually eclipsed by its neighbour, dedicated to John the Baptist. Congar had to share Congresbury with Andrew, and Gildas at Street was eventually confused with Giles.[26]

Somerset did not produce many saints of its own. One was Indract, already mentioned, although he was believed to have been Irish and his alleged martyrdom at Shapwick cannot be confirmed historically.[27] Benignus appears to have originated at Meare as Beonna and to have been more likely an Anglo-Saxon. His relics were moved to Glastonbury in 1091, and he became the patron of a new church there as well as retaining a share of the patronage of Meare.[28] By the twelfth century the abbey of Athelney honoured a saint called Athelwin(e) who was believed to have belonged to the royal family of Wessex in the seventh century: at a time when the abbey has left no record of its existence![29] His cult does not appear to have spread beyond this one place. A little more popularity was achieved by Wulfric, anchorite of Haselbury Plucknett (died 1155), who was visited during his life by King Stephen, and received popular canonisation after his death. A Life was written in his

---

[23] For the evidence, see *ibid.*

[24] W. Hunt, ed., *Two Chartularies of the Priory of St Peter at Bath*, SRS 7 (1893), ii, pp. 169-70.

[25] A chapel at Marchey in Meare parish (*VCH Somerset*, ix, p. 136). A charter of 725 mentioning the chapel is reckoned to be spurious.

[26] Orme, 'Medieval Church Dedications in Somerset', *PSANHS*, 160 (2016), pp. 83-94.

[27] Scott, ed., *Early History of Glastonbury*, p. 61; Winterbottom and Thompson, eds., *Saints' Lives*, pp. 371-81.

[28] Scott, ed., *Early History of Glastonbury*, p. 63; Winterbottom and Thompson, eds., *Saints' Lives*, pp. 344-55.

[29] Alison Binns, *Dedications of Monastic Houses in England and Wales* (Woodbridge, 1989), p. 62.

honour and miracles were said to be done by him in the thirteenth century, but he came too late to have parish churches named after him.[30]

Although we think of churches as dedicated to one saint, or two at most, the formula of dedication was usually to God (or the Trinity or Christ), Mary, one or more saints, and All Saints.[31] Within a church, additional saints would be commemorated through relics, images, and calendar observances. Few places in Somerset would have done more in this respect than Wells Cathedral, whose elaborate liturgy marked many saints' days during the year. The cathedral had a collection of relics of saints, a keeper to look after them, and a practice of displaying them to worshippers from time to time.[32] The chapels within its structure were dedicated to Christ (Corpus Christi) and to various saints: Calixtus, John the Baptist, Katherine, Martin, Mary (with two chapels), and Stephen. The high altar honoured Andrew who had a second altar at the entrance to the choir, while there were additional altars to Edmund, Holy Cross, Katherine (a second altar in the cloisters), Margaret, Mary (a third altar by the choir entrance), Mary Magdalene, Nicholas, and the Saviour. By the end of the Middle Ages there were also images of Anne, Christopher, David, Erasmus, George, Leonard, Michael, Sythe, Thomas Becket, and William (presumably William of York).[33]

Unlike cathedrals such as Canterbury, Durham, St Paul's, and Winchester, Wells had no ancient saint of its own whose body lay in a shrine and formed an attraction to pilgrims. In the later Middle Ages, attempts were made to remedy this lack, as they were at Exeter which was similarly disadvantaged.[34] These attempts centred on bishops of the diocese, reflecting a wider national feeling, perceptible from the Conquest to the fifteenth century, that bishops were holy men and sometimes came close to sanctity. The first such bishop to be honoured at Wells was William Bitton II (died 1274), whose tomb in the south aisle drew worshippers and offerings. His cult remained in being for the next two hundred and fifty years, and a collection box by the tomb received modest but consistent levels of offerings. Miracles were recorded, particularly relief from toothache.[35] A second cult grew up around the tomb of William of March (died 1302), to such an extent that, in 1324, the dean and chapter of Wells applied to the papal court for a formal canonisation. But this, although supported by two English kings and their bishops, was not successful, apparently due to the bureaucracy that attended canonisation by this time.[36] A third bishop, Ralph Shrewsbury (died 1363), also came to be venerated at his tomb in front of the high altar, but here the devotion appears to have declined or disappeared

---

[30] Dom M. Bell, ed., *Wulfric of Haselbury*, SRS 47 (1933).

[31] See, for example, N. Orme, *The Churches of Medieval Exeter* (Exeter, 2014), p. 24. Meare church was dedicated to Mary, All Saints, and Benignus in 1323, Rt Rev. Bishop Hobhouse, ed., *Calendar of the Register of John de Drokensford, Bishop of Bath and* Wells (A.D. 1309-29), SRS 1 (1887), p. 219.

[32] See the references in W.H.B. Bird and W. Paley Baildon, eds., *Calendar of the Manuscripts of the Dean and Chapter of Wells*, 2 vols (London, Historical Manuscripts Commission, 1907-14), ii. p. 935.

[33] For references, see *ibid.*, ii. p. 925-8.

[34] N. Orme, *Exeter Cathedral: the first thousand years* (Exeter, 2009), pp. 64-7.

[35] *Oxford Dictionary of National Biography*, article by D. G. Shaw.

[36] *Ibid.*, article by H. M. Jewell.

by the end of the century (figure 8).[37] Only that to William Bitton remained in being until the Reformation.

Glastonbury, which was the second wealthiest religious house in England in the early sixteenth century, rivalled Wells in terms of its saints; indeed, in its own opinion, it far outranked the cathedral in this respect. By the twelfth century, it claimed the bodies of several famous men and expanded its claims in the next two hundred years.[38] By the fourteenth, it proclaimed its church to contain twelve disciples of the Apostle Philip, led by Joseph of Arimathea who had allegedly founded the abbey. They were accompanied by Patrick of Ireland, Benignus his so-called disciple, and Benignus's follower Pincius. These lay in the church along with Aidan, David of Wales, Dunstan, Gildas, Indract, and Pope Urban I, some of whom were definitely or more plausibly buried elsewhere.[39] As well as these claims, the abbey boasted a large collection of relics of which lists were made. They included portions or possessions of Christ, Mary, Old Testament figures, apostles, martyrs, confessors, and virgins from both England and the wider Christian world.[40] From England, there were allegedly relics of the early missionaries like Augustine and Paulinus, Anglo-Saxon figures such as Oswald, Bede, and Hilda of Whitby, and some more recent figures. The latter included Edmund of Abingdon, Hugh of Lincoln, and the rare saint Walter of Cowick: a Benedictine monk of Exeter.[41]

The parish churches of Somerset could not match the saint collections of Wells and Glastonbury. All, however, were required to have images of their patron saints north of the high altar and Mary south of it. Most came to acquire additional chapels, altars, and images to Mary and other saints. Wills are important sources for this matter, because their makers often left small sums of money to the images or altars in their parish churches. Bridgwater's church, for example, contained altars dedicated to the Holy Cross, Erasmus, George, Gregory, Katherine, Mary, and the Trinity.[42] Dulverton's housed images of Blaise, Christopher, Erasmus, George, Katherine, Mary, Michael, and Peter.[43] Turning to more rural places, Brompton Regis had images of Mary, Mary 'of pity' holding the body of Christ, Maurice, Michael, and Sunday.[44] Cutcombe contained John the Baptist, Anthony, Katherine, Laurence, Mary, and Sunday.[45] 'Sunday' was a wall painting of Christ wounded by

[37] *Ibid.*, article by David N. Lepine.
[38] Scott, ed., *Early History of Glastonbury*, pp. 61-83.
[39] J.P. Carley, ed., *Chronicle of Glastonbury Abbey*, pp. 16-19.
[40] Scott, ed., *Early History of Glastonbury*, pp. 61-83; J.P. Carley, ed., *Chronicle of Glastonbury Abbey*, pp. 16-19; T. Hearne, ed., *Chronica sive Historia de Rebus Glastoniensibus*, 2 vols (Oxford, 1726), i, pp. 18-29; ii, pp. 445-54. On Glastonbury's saints, see J. P. Carley, *Glastonbury Abbey* (Woodbridge, 1988), pp. 87-119, and on its relics, pp. 120-31.
[41] N. Orme, 'Saint Walter of Cowick', *Analecta Bollandiana*, 108 (1990), pp. 1-7.
[42] F. W. Weaver, ed., *Somerset Medieval Wills*, i. p. 246; F. W. Weaver, ed., *Wells Wills* (London, 1890), p. 14.
[43] Weaver, *Wells Wills*, pp. 73-5.
[44] *Ibid.*, p. 31.
[45] A. J. Monday and M. Siraut, eds., *Somerset Wills*, SRS 89 (2003), p. 167.

the tools and games of those who violated the sanctity of the Lord's day.[46]

Such images were not merely part of the decoration. They were venerated and the fact can be established from the wills, which mention three kinds of organisations in parish churches devoted to Christ or the saints. These were stores, guilds, and companies.[47] A store consisted of money (or sometimes sheep or bees) which funded a light before an image and the cost of beautifying it. Stores might have wardens to administer them, but were not strongly social organisations. Guilds also honoured a cult but were less common. They were societies with officers and members who held meetings and feasts, and conveyed benefits to those of their members in need. Finally, many parish churches had companies of wives, young men, and maidens, the two latter groups being aged between puberty and marriage. These held social functions too, raised money for the church, and might have a particular devotion to an image: wives, for example, to the Virgin Mary.

Behind the institutional framework of saint veneration existed people's personal preferences. We rarely know of these because there was probably a sense of duty in leaving legacies in wills to parish images and stores. Only occasionally do will-makers mention the saints to whom they were devoted. William Carent of Henstridge, in 1516, commended himself to 'the good saints that I have had mind and prayers most unto, that is to say St Nicholas, St George, St John the Baptist, St Christopher, St Mary Magdalene, St Gabriel, St Erasmus, St Fabian, [and] St Sebastian'. He had previously mentioned Christ and Mary as was the standard practice.[48] James Hadley of Withycombe, in 1532, expressed his preferences differently by leaving money to various shrines, because 'I have been negligent to visit holy places and in going of pilgrimage'. He gave small sums to places both local and distant: Our Lady of Cleeve (to be mentioned presently), St Saviour of Porlock, St Culbone, three other images of the Saviour at Taunton, Bradford, and Bridgwater, St Joseph of Arimathea at Glastonbury, King Henry VI and Master John Shorn (both at Windsor Chapel), the Holy Blood of Hailes Abbey (Gloucs.), Our Lady of Walsingham (Norfolk), and St Thomas of Canterbury.[49] This reminds us that worshippers were aware of national saints and their shrines as well as Somerset ones.

Time is an important consideration in the study of saint cults. It manifests itself in the lack of evidence about parish churches before about 1400, so that we have little knowledge of what profusion of cults there may have been up to that date. The abundance evident thereafter need not have been new. Time also matters because of changes in the structures within which cults operated and in the appearance of new cults in the later Middle Ages that had not been in being previously. A structural change came with the appearance of large numbers of free-standing chapels alongside the parish churches. These were founded from the twelfth century until the eve

---

[46] A. Reiss, *The Sunday Christ: Sabbatarianism in English medieval wall painting* (Oxford, 2000).

[47] This important point is confused in K. L. French's study of Somerset, *The People of the Parish* (Philadelphia, 2001), which calls many stores 'guilds' when they were not (pp. 196, 211-27).

[48] Weaver, *Somerset Medieval Wills*, ii, p. 186.

[49] *Ibid.*, iii, p. 14.

of the Reformation and Somerset had some hundreds of them, although they have not yet been counted.[50] Some were private foundations in the houses of the gentry and senior clergy, or for the use of guilds. Others were public, these dividing into what became known as 'chapels of ease' to serve outlying communities, and cult chapels founded to promote the veneration of Mary, Michael, or some other saint (figure 5). Many chapels honoured the major figures of Christianity like the parish churches, but whereas the latter were virtually all in existence by 1200, the chapels founded later were able to give themselves wholly to the new religious fashions of their day.

A second structural change was a shift of popular interest from relics, so important in Anglo-Saxon and Norman times, to images: the favourite forms of the fifteenth and early sixteenth centuries. Relics were hard to come by and raised problems of authentication, already an issue by Chaucer's day.[51] Images were easier to get. Every parish church could acquire them, and a representation of the Saviour on the Rood or of Mary might develop a reputation for miracle working. This could happen not only in a church but in a chapel: indeed it might happen more easily in a chapel which did not suffer the restrictions imposed by parish incumbents and congregational worship. A good example of this phenomenon is the chapel of St Mary at Cleeve, built before 1320 on the sea shore near the modern Blue Anchor.[52] The chapel was already notable as a place of miracles, probably linked with a statue of the Virgin, when it was destroyed by a falling cliff in 1452 except for the statue and altar which were miraculously spared. A new chapel was then built further inland at the modern Chapel Cleeve, to which indulgences were granted on the grounds that Christ had 'deigned to work signs of miracles and numberless recoveries of health by the merits of his glorious mother'.[53] When the Tudor antiquary John Leland visited the area in 1542, he heard that the resort of pilgrims had been so great and evidently so wide that 'a goodly inn all of stone' had been provided for their lodgings.[54] In 1536 the offerings at the chapel were reckoned to total £9 3s. 4d. per annum.

Religious cults were not necessarily as long lasting as this. Some might decline and disappear. As has been mentioned, Gildas at Street became confused with Giles, and the same happened to Cyricus (or Quiricus) of Tickenham who was referred to in writing by the 1530s, if not in practice, as the different saint Sythe.[55] Should one

---

[50] On chapels, see N. Orme, 'Church and Chapel in Medieval England', *TRHS*, 6th series, 6 (1996), pp. 75-102; and *idem*, 'The Other Parish Churches: Chapels in Late Medieval England', in *Parish Churches in Late Medieval England*, ed. C. Burgess and E. Duffy (Donington, 2006), pp. 78-94. *VCH Somerset*, vol. iii and onwards, provides information about them in specific parishes.

[51] *E.g.* L. D. Benson, ed., Chaucer, 'The Canterbury Tales', in *The Riverside Chaucer*, 3rd ed. (Oxford, 1988), I (A) 695-700, VI (C) 347-388.

[52] On what follows, see T. Hugo, 'On the Charters and other Archives of Cleeve Abbey', *PSANHS* 6 (1856), pp. 41-5; F. W. Weaver, 'Cleve Abbey', *ibid.*, 52 (1907), pp. 9-12; and *VCH Somerset*, v, p. 52.

[53] H.C. Maxwell-Lyte and M.C.B. Dawes, eds., *The Register of Thomas Bekynton, Bishop of Bath and Wells, 1443-65*, SRS 49 (1934), pp. 178-9.

[54] Leland, *Itinerary*, i, p. 165.

[55] Weaver, *Wells Wills*, pp. 172-3.

have visited a medieval church, one might have encountered old images largely ignored by worshippers besides those well maintained and honoured with constant burning lights. Even a traditional cult might be imagined in new ways. In the fifteenth century, the devotion to Christ as the Saviour on the Cross came to be accompanied by one to the Name of Jesus, in which the Holy Name was written on walls and pronounced as a devotion. Cults of the Name of Jesus are mentioned at Middlezoy, Wedmore, Wincanton, St Cuthbert (Wells), and Yeovil.[56] There was a chapel of the Holy Ghost at Charlton Adam by 1348 – another cult rarely found before the later Middle Ages.[57] The veneration of Mary also branched into different forms. As well as her 'standard image' as the mother of Christ holding the baby Jesus, she could be painted or modelled with Gabriel in the Annunciation, with Elizabeth in the Visitation, in childbed (this was the image of Mary *in gisina* possessed by Wells Cathedral), holding the dead body of Christ (Our Lady of Pity), or ascending to heaven in her Assumption.[58]

There were new saints in the later Middle Ages, not known in earlier ages. One was Anne, mother of Mary, who became widely popular. An important chapel in her honour existed at St Anne's in Brislington by the late fourteenth century, where the pilgrims included Henry VII himself.[59] The college of chantry priests founded at Wells Cathedral in 1401 was dedicated to her,[60] and her images stood in many churches including Portbury, Stogursey, St Mary Magdalene (Taunton), and Wedmore.[61] Other newcomers were Roch (died *c.*1380), a Provençal saint venerated for protection from the plague, and Sythe or Zita (died 1272), patroness of servants and helper in finding lost objects, hence her emblem of keys. Images of Roch are recorded at Skilgate and of Sythe at Beckington as well as in Wells Cathedral.[62] A fourth late arrival was that of Wilgefortis or Uncumber, a bearded female whose cult apparently originated in Flanders during the fourteenth century. She was believed to relieve women of their husbands, and there was an image of her in Chew Stoke church by 1530.[63]

Even these do not exhaust the variety of what existed or was known about. By about the 13th century two chapels on Windwhistle hill between Chard and Crewkerne celebrated the rare women saints Reine and White, the latter buried at

[56] E. Green, ed., *The Survey and Rental of the Chantries, Colleges, and free Chapels, Guilds, Fraternities, Lamps, Lights, and obits in the County of Somerset, 1548,* SRS 2 (1888), pp. 65, 71, 127, 139; Weaver, *Somerset Medieval Wills,* ii, 107.

[57] T. Scott Holmes, ed., *The Register of Ralph of Shrewsbury, Bishop of Bath and Wells, 1329-63,* SRS 10 (1896), p. 557.

[58] On Wells, see *Calendar of the MSS of Wells,* ii, pp. 93, 131, 195.

[59] K. Taylor, *The Holy Well and the Chapel of St Anne in the Wood, Brislington* (Bristol, 2014).

[60] H. C. Maxwell-Lyte, ed., *The Registers of Robert Stillington, Bishop of bath & Wells, 1466-91 and Richard Fox, Bishop of Bath & Wells, 1492-94,* SRS 52 (1937), p. 196.

[61] Weaver, *Wells Wills,* pp. ix, 148, 159; E. Green, ed., *The Survey and Rental of the Chantries* (etc), SRS 2 (1888), p. 69

[62] Weaver, *Wells Wills,* p. 140; Weaver, *Somerset Medieval Wills,* ii, p. 351.

[63] Weaver, *Wells Wills,* p. 52.

Whitchurch Canonicorum in Dorset.[64] By 1321, the parish of Cheddar contained a chapel dedicated to the Irish saint Columbanus,[65] and by 1493 its parish church possessed an altar of the north Devon and Cornish saint Nectan. The latter appears to have been due to the Fitz-Walter family who were linked with a part of Cornwall where Nectan had a chapel.[66] A chapel of St 'Gonthal' in Wedmore church or nearby, mentioned in 1503, presumably commemorated the Spanish saint Gonzalo, bishop of Mondoñedo near Compostella: perhaps the cult was imported through a pilgrimage.[67] In 1525 a man of Yeovil bequeathed 6s. 8d. to a chapel of St Juthwara, a female saint first heard of in the late Anglo-Saxon period: the chapel may have been her original church at Halstock in Dorset.[68] In 1513, a will-maker even left money for a pilgrimage to St Edward at Tewkesbury.[69] This was Edward, prince of Wales, son of Henry VI, who was killed after the battle there in 1471 and buried in the abbey. The victory of Henry VII in 1485, the heir of his family, made it possible for him to be venerated by those who supported his cause.[70]

Two antiquaries journeyed through Somerset while the cults were still in being or remembered. The first of them was William Worcester, traveller and tireless collector of assorted historical data, who came that way in 1478. Worcester was interested in saints.[71] His travels were planned to take him to Cornwall where he noted many of its unusual ones, but he seems to have viewed Somerset as a normal English county in this respect and did not set out to collect its saints systematically. Nevertheless, his interests were so wide and his note-taking so obsessive that he wrote down some relevant facts that came to his notice. Glastonbury had the body of Joseph of Arimathea, and Worcester recorded a prayer to him. St Indract, martyr and confessor, lay at 'Shepton', a misunderstanding of information that the saint had been martyred at Shapwick. Bishop William Bitton of Wells was 'distinguished by many miracles', and his festival day of 4 December was recorded in the martyrology of the Franciscan friary at Bridgwater. The same martyrology included the feast of the Blessed Thomas of Lancaster, a political martyr of 1322 and a saint otherwise little mentioned in Somerset. Finally, Worcester noted the chapels of Reine and White near Crewkerne, and a chain of chapels of St Michael including Glastonbury Tor, a place in the neighbourhood of Crewkerne, and Montacute, with others further west in Devon and Cornwall.[72]

---

[64] *VCH Somerset*, iv, pp. 33 and see 141.

[65] Hobhouse, ed., *Calendar of the Register of John de Drokensford, Bishop of Bath and Wells (A.D. 1309-29)*, SRS 1 (1887), pp. 22, 194.

[66] J. Coleman, 'St Nectan in Somerset', *SDNQ* 10 (1907), pp. 114-15.

[67] Weaver, *Somerset Medieval Wills*, ii, p. 43.

[68] *Ibid.*, ii, p. 238

[69] *Ibid.*, ii, p. 173.

[70] Queen Elizabeth of York made a donation to his shrine in 1502 (N. H. Nicolas, *Privy Purse Expenses of Elizabeth of York* [London, 1830], p. 3).

[71] On this subject, see N. Orme, 'William Worcester and Saint Collecting in Medieval England', in *Saints and Cults in Medieval England*, ed. S. Powell (Donington, 2017), pp. 199-216.

[72] J. H. Harvey, ed., William Worcester, *Itineraries* (Oxford, 1969), pp. 15, 73, 79, 81, 129, 297, 299.

Worcester's journeys took place while the cults of saints were still at their height. The next traveller, John Leland, arrived in 1542 when they were in decline, following the prohibition of the veneration of images in royal injunctions of 1538. Moreover, Leland came as a servant of Henry VIII: entrusted with gathering historical information but careful to accord with the official disapproval of superstition. In consequence, he wrote little about saints as such. He noted a number of chapels: of Mary Magdalene at Bath, the Saviour by the harbour of Bridgwater, and Carantoc – formerly a parish church – at Carhampton. He also recorded the chapel of Our Lady of Loretta, which Abbot Bere of Glastonbury had built on the north side of the nave: perhaps a replica or a memorial of the 'holy house of Nazareth' which was claimed by the church of Loretta in Italy. He mentioned only two saint cults, and firmly placed them both in the past. Chapel Cleeve 'was' a place of offering to Our Lady, and its inn used 'late' by pilgrims, while the tomb of William Bitton at Wells was that of someone 'whom the people formerly worshipped for a saint'.[73]

Leland's notes are a testimony that saint cults were beginning to fade. In 1536 indulgences were suppressed: incentives that had often helped to bring pilgrims and their offerings, particularly to chapels. Two years later the veneration of saintly relics and images was forbidden, and within two further years all the religious houses in Somerset had been closed, apart from the cathedral. Even that last redoubt did not maintain its saintly observances much longer. In 1549, the new Book of Common Prayer removed all saints from the calendar apart from those mentioned in the New Testament, and this was shortly followed by the removal of the altars and images at which they had been commemorated. A long period elapsed of nearly two hundred years, in which even the saints of the parish churches were not spoken of or remembered except in towns where one church needed to be distinguished from another. It was not until about 1730 that curiosity about identifying church saints returned, to be followed by a wider interest in religious cults following the Oxford Movement of the nineteenth century.

We have now recovered a great deal about the saints of medieval Somerset, but our gains are matched by even greater losses. It is salutary to consider how much we depend on casual references to reconstruct the cults that existed. Knowledge of them often relies on a single document, and if one could assemble every possible source, it would still fall short of doing justice to the complexity of the subject. As for how people related to them – with how much devotion and surely at times indifference or even hostility – that is an even more intricate matter to probe.

---

[73] Leland, *Itinerary*, i, pp. 139, 155-8, 162, 165, 167, 290, 293.

3. St Lawrence in Somerset

BARRY LANE†

Editor's preface

*S*adly, Barry Lane died in March 2017 before he could develop his arguments fully. In *deference to his wishes, David Dawson and Teresa Hall, in collaboration with Barry's widow, Sue Isherwood Lane, have prepared this paper for publication. We have tried to remain faithful to Barry's intentions and express them in his voice, in so far as we are able to discern them, from the material he left us and from our limited discussions with him on the subject. We are conscious that some parts, particularly the discussion of the topographical interpretation of individual churches in their setting, which requires much more extensive documentary and archaeological work, are presented as the germ of his ideas and must be left to others to develop. He explained his approach with reference to Lewis-Williams: 'The intertwining of numerous strands of evidence is a method of constructing explanations that philosophers of science recognize as being closer to what actually happens in daily scientific practice than formal, sequential testing of hypotheses, the method about which researchers frequently talk. … some arguments are like chains: they follow link after logical link; if one fails through lack of evidence or faulty logic, the whole argument breaks down. Archaeologists overcome this problem by intertwining multiple strands of evidence as in a cable or rope. Each strand is both sustaining and constraining, but if one strand is broken, the whole is not. This is the process presented here where the historical and archaeological evidence is exiguous'.[1] Barry very much admired the work of the Victoria County History and of Robert Dunning and was adamant that he would contribute to this volume.*

Introduction

During 2016, members of the Westbury Society were excavating an early 12th-century first floor hall house at Court House Farm in Westbury-sub-Mendip, which Dr Robert Dunning suggested had been built by John of Tours, first Bishop of Bath and Wells (1088-1122) at the same time that he was creating the deer park in the parish. Each Wednesday morning a glance at the nearby church clock tower, to check if it was yet time for coffee, would start speculation about who was St Lawrence, the dedicatee of the church, and when and how did that happen (figure 9). Team member Nicky Amos focused thoughts by raising questions about saints' relics and associated matters. It brought to mind an important lecture, given in 2005 by Dr Graham Jones entitled *Church dedications 'west of Selwood'*. His support, advice and encouragement for this essay has been invaluable. Dr Michael Costen has

---

[1] D. Lewis-Williams, *The Mind in the Cave* (London, 2014), pp. 102-103.

also generously shared his Somerset research, particularly his sources and database of dedications to St Lawrence in the county.

The significance of relics

Miracles and the relics of saints, that is either fragments of a saint's body or an object closely associated with them, were essential tools in the early phases of the conversion of the Irish, British and Anglo-Saxons to Roman Christianity. Bede makes many references to relics and miracles in his *Ecclesiastical History of the English People* written about 731. His first story concerns Germanus of Auxerre's visit to Britain about 429 to combat the heresy of Pelagianism and how he cured a young girl of blindness with a little bag, containing relics of saints, that he kept hanging around his neck.[2]

When, shortly afterwards, Pope Celestine sent the Roman deacon Palladius to be the first bishop of the Irish in 431, it is quite likely that he also sent with him those relics of Peter, Paul, Stephen and Lawrence, which were treasured by the church of Armagh two or three hundred years later.[3] Church dedications to these four saints are common during the first few centuries of the conversion of Britain .[4] The Second Council of Nicaea, held in Turkey in 787, promoted the canon that every altar should contain a relic and relics were central to the rite of consecration of a church, of which dedication in its patron saint's honour was part, carried out by a bishop. Relics were frequently deposited in a cavity in the high altar slab. The ceremony remains the case in modern Catholic and Orthodox regulations.[5]

Augustine brought with him relics, as well as 'all such things as were generally necessary for the worship and ministry of the Church',[6] when he was sent by Pope Gregory to Britain to convert the Anglo-Saxons. Part of Pope Gregory's instructions to Augustine included the passage, '… the idol temples of that race should by no means be destroyed, but only the idols in them. Take holy water and sprinkle it in these shrines, build altars and place relics in them'.[7]

Following the Reformation, dedications are just a name, with little or no meaning. Joe Bettey illustrated this well by reproducing a letter from Richard Layton, one of Thomas Cromwell's agents in the West Country, written on 7 August 1535 to his employer, showing his contempt for the monks and his scorn of their superstitious reverence for relics.[8]

---

[2] L. Shirley-Price, trans., *Bede: A History of the English Church and People* (Harmondsworth, 1967), i., pp. 18, 59.

[3] K. Hughes, 'The Celtic Church and the Papacy', in C. H. Lawrence, ed., *The English Church and the Papacy in the Middle Ages* (Stroud, 1999), p. 5.

[4] W. Levison, *England and the Continent in the Eighth Century* (Oxford, 1946), p. 264.

[5] Canon VII.

[6] L. Shirley-Price, *Bede*, i., p. 29.

[7] L. Shirley-Price, *Bede*, i., pp. 30, 107.

[8] J. Bettey, *The Suppression of the Monasteries in the West Country* (Gloucester, 1989), pp. 170-1.

Who was St Lawrence?

A well-known legend has persisted from earliest times. As deacon in Rome, St Lawrence was charged with the responsibility for the material goods of the Church and the distribution of alms to the poor. St Ambrose of Milan relates that when St Lawrence was asked for the treasures of the Church he brought forward the poor, among whom he had divided the treasure as alms. 'Behold in these poor persons the treasures which I promised to show you; to which I will add pearls and precious stones, those widows and consecrated virgins, which are the church's crown.'[9] The prefect was so angry that he had a great gridiron prepared, with coals beneath it, and had Lawrence's body placed on it. After the martyr had suffered the pain for a long time, the legend concludes, he made his famous cheerful remark, 'I'm well done. Turn me over!' Lawrence was in fact more than a simple deacon, the lowliest step on the stairway to ordination. He was Archdeacon of Rome and adjutant to Pope Sixtus II, handpicked by the pontiff and noted for his devotion to his master, as well as his charitable management of the church's wealth.[10] He died in 298 and is not to be confused with the St Lawrence who was St Augustine's successor at Canterbury.[11]

The importance of Lawrence's feast day of 10th August in the heat of the summer, was underlined by three privileges not extended to the offices of other martyrs: his feast was preceded by a vigil, it had an octave, and the repetition of antiphons. The first two exceptions add to the seasonal significance of Lawrence as a dedicatee of churches, since the vigil marks the status of the commemoration, while vigil, feast and octave together embrace the even greater feast of the Assumption of Mary the mother of Jesus on 15th August.[12]

Down the centuries, Lawrence has been the most popular choice among the martyrs for the titular patronage of churches in Britain: 222 in England, 24 in Scotland, and seven in Wales, about two per cent of the whole. Ten per cent of the English parochial dedications are found in the area from around Worcester and Gloucester, stretching as far as Huntingdon.[13]

Northumbria and the rise of Wilfrid

This story starts with king Oswiu of Northumbria (642-670) and his queen Eanflaed planning their Easter celebrations, only to find that they had different dates in their diaries! Oswiu was a devoted Christian raised in the Celtic tradition of much of the Irish world, while Eanflaed was a Kentish princess brought up a Roman Christian with St Augustine's manual for calculating the dates for Easter. Oswiu's answer was

---

[9] This quotation and the tradition seem to be based on Ambrose, Prudentius and other accounts and taken from a composite life of St Lawrence such as A. Butler, *The Lives of the Fathers, Martyrs and Other Principal Saints* (Dublin, 1866), p. 8.

[10] G. Jones, *Church Dedications and Landed Units of Lordship and Administration in the pre-Reformation Diocese of Worcester* (forthcoming).

[11] D.H. Farmer, *The Oxford Dictionary of Saints* (Oxford, 1978), pp. 237-9.

[12] G. Jones (forthcoming).

[13] G. Jones, *Saints in the Landscape* (Stroud, 2007), pp. 35,114.

to convene the Synod of Whitby in 664 when Wilfrid was delegated to make the case for Roman Christianity against the Celtic church, with the proper method for calculating the date of Easter being the main issue.

Wilfrid was a Northumbrian nobleman who entered religious life as a teenager and studied at Lindisfarne. About 653-4 he, with Benedict Biscop, was among the first Anglo-Saxons to make the pilgrimage to Rome.[14] In the words of his biographer, 'After the lapse of a few years, it came into the heart of this same young man, by promptings of the Holy Spirit, to pay a visit to the see of the Apostle Peter, the chief of the Apostles, and to attempt a road hitherto untrodden by any of our race. By so doing he believed that he would cleanse himself from every blot and stain and receive the joy of divine blessing'. In Rome, he learned the Roman method of calculating the date of Easter and studied the Roman practice of relic collecting.[15] Bede records that 'on his way to Rome Wilfrid stayed with the saintly Willibrord, archbishop of the Frisians, and often heard the archbishop describe the miracles which happened in that kingdom at the relics of the most reverend king'.[16] In their lifetimes, Benedict Biscop visited Rome six times and Wilfrid made the journey three times and, after each visit, returned with books, paintings, vestments and unspecified relics.[17]

At the conclusion of the Whitby debate, Oswiu opted to change his ways, to adopt Roman Christianity, and he made Wilfrid bishop of York.[18] Not long afterwards Oswiu, and king Egbert of Kent, sent gifts and wrote to the Pope asking him to nominate someone suitable to become archbishop in Britain. No doubt rather flattered, Pope Vitalian replied that he was not able immediately to recommend a fit person but 'We have received the gifts sent by your Highness to the blessed chief of the apostles to be a lasting memorial of you. ... we have directed that the blessings of the saints, in the form of relics of the apostles St Peter and St Paul and of the holy martyrs Laurence, John and Paul, as well as Gregory and Pancras, should be given to your messengers who are bearers of this letter to be directed to your Highness. To your wife, our spiritual daughter, we send by the same bearers a cross with a golden key, made from the holy fetters of the apostles St Peter and St Paul.'[19]; relics could be as much objects associated with a saint as corporeal remains. Bury St Edmunds claimed to have 'the coles that Saint Laurence was tosted withall'.[20]

[14] B. Colgrove, *The Life of Bishop Wilfrid by Eddius Stephanus* (Cambridge, 1927), pp. 9-13; P. Sims-Williams, *Religion and Literature in Western England 600-800* (Cambridge, 1990), p. 194.

[15] G. Hardin Brown, 'Royal and ecclesiastical rivalries in Bede's History', *Renascence*, Vol.52, Issue 1, Fall 1999, p. 29.

[16] L. Shirley-Price, *Bede*, iii, pp. 12-13, 253.

[17] L. Shirley-Price, *Bede*, v, p.7, n. 2; J. F. Webb and D.H. Farmer, *The Age of Bede* (Harmondsworth, 1970), pp. 140, 167.

[18] B. Colgrove, *The Life of Bishop Wilfrid by Eddius Stephanus* (Cambridge, 1927), pp. 21-5.

[19] L. Shirley-Price, *Bede*, iii, pp. 321, 29

[20] J. Crook, *Architectural Settings of the Cult of Saints in the Early Christian West c.300-c.1200* (Oxford, 2000), p. 6.

By 674, Benedict Biscop, with Wilfrid's help, had founded the minster at Monkwearmouth, Sunderland, where Biscop became abbot and Bede later received his early education. The church there was dedicated to St Peter and had a chapel or 'oratorium' dedicated to St Lawrence.[21] Presumably the saints' relics had been provided by Oswiu and Wilfrid.

Wessex: the roles of Wilfrid (c.633-709) and Aldhelm (639-709)

After king Oswiu's death in 670, his son Ecgfrith defeated Wulfhere, king of the Mercians, who 'ruled in peace over a wider realm'.[22] Wilfrid moved south to the sub-kingdom of Mercia known as the Hwicce and more or less equivalent to the pre-Reformation diocese of Worcester, an area relatively rich in dedications to St Lawrence.[23] During this time, up to about 678, Wilfrid was at his height of power and influence.

A monastery at Bath was founded by Osric, sub-king of the Hwicce and with the consent of Aethelred, king of Mercia, in 675. Wilfrid was a signatory to the foundation charter and it has been suggested that Wilfrid was responsible for instigating the use of incarnational dating on the charter.[24] A medieval cartulary of Bath Priory records scores of relics of their saints, including two of St Laurence, '*Item vest. Sancte Marie et de Sanguine Sanct Laurentii, et de Cruce St Andree Apostoli... item de Sancto Laurencio*' – possibly the first relics of the saint in Somerset.[25]

In *c.*676, Centwine became king of Wessex. Shortly afterwards, he made the first known grant of six hides of land to Glastonbury Abbey to one of the early Saxon abbots, Haemgisl. About the same time, Centwine is said to have granted Wilfrid the large estate of 70 hides at Wedmore and one hide at Clewer.[26] Wilfrid may have subsequently granted these estates to Glastonbury Abbey when he was restored to his former see in Northumberland in 686. Alternatively, Centwine's successor may have rescinded the original gift because of Wilfrid's return north. Wilfrid was clearly a charismatic and powerful figure, and made friends and enemies equally fast. About 677, Wilfrid was banished from his post in Northumbria by king Ecgfrith, persuaded by his wife, Iurminburh, whom Wilfrid had offended, and Abbot Aldhelm wrote an impassioned defence of Wilfrid to his abbots.[27] Following this episode, Wilfrid set out again for Rome to obtain the pope's support.[28]

Aldhelm was a contemporary of Wilfrid. He was born of the royal house of

---

[21] W. Levison, *England and the Continent,* p. 264.

[22] B. Colgrove, *The Life of Bishop Wilfrid,* p. 43.

[23] G. Jones, 'Church dedications and landed units of lordship and administration in the pre-Reformation diocese of Worcester', unpublished PhD, University of Leicester, 1996, pp.152-154, 162, 164. Jones notes that none of the St Lawrence dedications can be dated to before 950, p.153.

[24] N. Brooks, 'Anglo-Saxon charters: the work of the last twenty years', *Anglo-Saxon England*, December 1974, pp. 211-231, at p. 225).

[25] W. Hunt, ed., *Two Chartularies of the Priory of St Peter at Bath*, SRS 7 (1893), lxxv.

[26] L. Abrams, *Anglo-Saxon Glastonbury; Church and Endowment* (Woodbridge, 1996), pp. 90-2.

[27] M. Lapidge and M. Herren, *Aldhelm: The Prose Works* (Ipswich, 1979), pp. 168-70.

[28] B. Colgrove, *The Life of Bishop Wilfrid,* pp. 49-67.

Wessex and William of Malmesbury reported that he received his first education with the Irish monk Maelduib at Malmesbury. He also studied at Canterbury with Theodore of Tarsus and Hadrian. He appears to have been a close friend and godfather to Oswiu's second son Aldfrith, and had probably assisted in arranging Aldfrith's marriage to Cuthberg, sister of king Ine of Wessex. Lapidge has suggested that Aldhelm received his early education at Iona, where he was fostered along with Aldfrith.[29]

According to William of Malmesbury, Aldhelm was made abbot of Malmesbury in c.675[30] and a St Lawrence dedication is recorded there. Aldhelm also founded or refounded a daughter house at Bradford-on-Avon where there was an 'ecclesiola' to St Lawrence[31] About the same time, William of Malmesbury records that Aldhelm also founded another daughter house *juxta fluvium qui vocatur From,* which most scholars identify as Frome in Somerset, only 30 miles south of Malmesbury.[32]

Centwine abdicated in 687/6 to become a monk. He was succeeded by Caedwalla, who immediately summoned Wilfrid to Wessex where he was made 'supreme counsellor over the whole kingdom' and Caedwalla 'rewarded him with innumerable pieces of land and other gifts'.[33] Caedwalla's reign was short and his successor was the successful and long reigning Ine, king of Wessex from 688- 726, associated with the foundation or building of stone churches. Aldhelm's sole visit to Rome may have been as a companion to Caedwalla who died there. He returned with privileges for Malmesbury, relics and a marble altar.[34]

Bishop Haedde of Winchester died an old man in 705 and the opportunity was taken to divide the unwieldy and westward-growing diocese, by creating Aldhelm to be bishop of the new diocese 'west of Selwood' with his see based at Sherborne. At the same time Aldhelm was persuaded to remain as abbot of Malmesbury. After establishing a new base in Sherborne itself, Aldhelm's first obligations would be to attend to the ecclesiastical needs of his diocese, including his main churches, which he partly accomplished by bringing saintly relics and, with Ine's support, building some of the first stone churches. These actions are frequently described in charters

[29] M. Lapidge, 'The career of Aldhelm', *Anglo-Saxon England* 36 (2007), pp. 15-69, at pp.15, 22.

[30] D. Preest, ed., *The Deeds of the Bishops of England (Gesta pontificum Anglorum) by William of Malmesbury* (Woodbridge, 2002), p. 262.

[31] W. Levison, *England and the Continent*, p. 264; the ascription of the dedication of St Lawrence to the present pre-Conquest chapel and, therefore, its often presumed association with Aldhelm dates from the building's discovery and publication by Canon Jones, 'Bradford-upon-Avon' *Wilts. Arch. and Nat. Hist. Mag.,* 5 (1859), pp. 1-88, 210-55, 352-90; recent architectural analysis and archaeological work suggests the structure was erected in the 11th century as a temporary refuge to house the body of King Edward the Martyr before his return to Shaftesbury, see E. Fernie, *The Architecture of the Anglo-Saxons* (London, 1983), pp. 145-50 and D. A. Hinton, 'Recent work at the chapel of St Laurence, Bradford-on-Avon, Wiltshire' *Arch. Journ.,* 166 (2009), pp. 193-209; as an alignment of free-standing chapels was common at this date, it is likely that the *ecclesiola* lies under the present parish church of the Holy Trinity, if that is the site of the Saxon minster church, or elsewhere in the surrounding precinct [eds.].

[32] D. Preest, *The Deeds of the Bishops*, pp. 235-6, 252, 259.

[33] B. Colgrove, *The Life of Bishop Wilfrid*, p. 85.

[34] D. Preest, *The Deeds of the Bishops*, pp. 248-54.

and other documents as 'founding churches' although in some cases they could be 'refounding' earlier British Christian centres.

Like Wilfrid, Aldhelm was committed to persuading the British church to adopt the Roman way of calculating Easter. Archbishop Theodore also called together the Synod of Hertford in 672 which had again dealt with the contentious issue of the date of Easter, and, at this Synod, Aldhelm was instructed to write to Geraint, the king of Dumnonia (Devon & Cornwall) to persuade him and his bishops to adopt the Roman date.[35]

Malmesbury abbey held relics of St Lawrence and it is possible that Aldhelm obtained these from either Aldfrith, king of Northumbria or bishop Wilfrid, if they were not amongst those that he himself brought back from Rome. The two contemporaries, Wilfrid and Aldhelm, both visited Rome and returned with relics including, in the case of Wilfrid, relics of St Lawrence. It is argued that both used these relics in their campaigns of proselytization. In particular, following Jones's suggestion, the dedication to St Lawrence was appropriate for 'converted temples and other pre-existing sacred sites'.[36]

St Lawrence in Somerset

The starting point for this study of dedications to St Lawrence is a preliminary list of earliest references kindly compiled by Michael Costen. This list appears in the table below where it has been correlated with recently published work by N. Orme.[37]

Batcombe	Spargrove	chapel	1390	*Cal.Pap.Reg.* iv, 338	Orme 92; 1403	*CPL* v, 523
Bath		fair	1304	Chapman 29		
Bath		bridge chapel	1718	Cunliffe 85		
Charlcombe	Lansdown	chapel	1923	Horne 18		
Congresbury	Wick St Lawrence	chapel	1326	SRS 1, 251	Orme 94; 1450	SRS 49, 137
Cucklington		parish church	1519	SRS 19, 203	Orme 89; 1468	SRS 52, 15
Cutcombe		light	1531	Weaver 69		
Dunster		chantry	1548	SRS 2, 42		
East Harptree		parish church	1730		Orme 89; 1730-40	
Glastonbury		Abbey relic				

---

[35] A. W. Haddon and W. Stubbs, eds., *Councils and Ecclesiastical Documents relating to Great Britain and Ireland, Vol III the English Church 595-1066* (Oxford, 1871), pp. 268-73.

[36] G. Jones, *Saints in the Landscape* (Stroud, 2007), p. 114.

[37] N. Orme, 'Medieval Church Dedications in Somerset', *PSANHS* 160 (2016), pp. 83-94. There is a presumption that a dedication is to St Lawrence the Deacon and Martyr rather than St Lawrence of Canterbury. The chapel on the hill above Milton Clevedon was subsequently added (figure 10).

Lydeard St Lawrence		parish church	1530	Weaver 97	Orme 91; 13th	SRS 14, 178
Middlezoy		parish church	c.1220	Hulbert 82	Orme 91; e 13th	SRS 63, 501
Rode		parish church	1421	SRS 16,105	Orme 92; 1421	SRS 16, 105
Stanton Prior		parish church	1736		Orme 92; 1530	SRS 55, 64
Stratton-on-Fosse		parish church	-		Orme 93; c.1730-3	
Wellington		chapel	1184-5			
Westbury-sub-Mendip		parish church	-		Orme 93; 1742	
Westbury-sub-Mendip	Priddy	chapel	1449			
Woolavington		parish church	1906			

Sources: M. Chapman, 'Bath Fairs', *The Survey of Bath and District* 12 (1999), pp. 26-32; B. Cunliffe, *The City of Bath* (Stroud, 1986); Dom E. Horne, *Somerset Holy Wells and other named wells* (London, Somerset Folk Press 1923); N. F. Hulbert, 'A survey of Somerset fairs', *PSANHS* 82 (1936), pp. 83-159; F. W. Weaver, ed., *Somerset Medieval Wills* (Gloucester, 1983).

Conclusion

This essay is an attempt to raise questions about the origins of the numerous dedications to St Lawrence in the county of Somerset. Barry Lane argued strongly that there is a pattern and a process that can be discerned. It stems from the importance of relics in spreading and consolidating the hold of Roman orthodoxy in Britain by the insistence, institutionalised at the Second Council of Nicaea in 787, that every new church or rededication had to be accompanied by the physical installation of an altar consecrated by the incorporation of relics of a saint. Under papal instruction, a steady supply of relics arrived from Rome to feed the demand of proselytisation led in this part of the country by Wilfrid and Aldhelm. They worked from firmly established centres – Bath, Glastonbury, Frome and Bruton – and that spread in the 8th century can be seen in the enduring links of ownership between these centres and places with dedications to St Lawrence. As can be seen in the following gazetteer, Barry had started the process of considering the evidence relating to each individual dedication. It must be acknowledged that there are weaknesses in the chain of evidence: some dedications, for example the bridge chapel at Bath, are clearly later, offset by others that have been superseded like that of Stratton-on-the-Fosse, for others such as Westbury-sub-Mendip there is a gap in the evidence, others do not fit the pattern such as Lydeard St Lawrence and may be later. It is strange that in all his prolific writings and commentaries on specific saints Aldhelm never refers to St Lawrence, neither in his prose works or in his poetic works,[38] but then given the size of his proselytisation programme he must have deployed the relics of many other saints.

Conscious of the need to draw upon topographical evidence, Barry had made preliminary visits and had started to compile a group of comparative maps of the sites with St Lawrence dedications. He was experimenting with the possibility that the sites may have had similar rectilinear layouts. Barry was pursuing the idea that the St Lawrence dedications may have been used at British Christian sites that were taken over and absorbed into the post-Whitby English church. However, this work was still in its early stages, and he had not been able to undertake the necessary map regression associated with such an exercise. His maps of the sites have been reproduced here, along with the notes he was putting together for each site. They must be seen as a work in progress (figure 11).

The gazetteer of sites (figure 10)
A. Dedications associated with Bath Priory

Bath Priory

The 675 foundation of the minster at Bath was created by a grant of a large estate of 100 hides, within which are a number of St Lawrence dedications. The relics held by the monastery at Bath have been referred to above, and it is possible that they led to the dedications of a chapel on one of the bridges across the Avon and of the chapel at Lansdown in Charlcombe. Bath also held an annual fair on the saint's day, 10 August, each year in Barton. The parish church at Stanton Prior is also dedicated to the saint, and this church belonged to Bath at the time of the Domesday survey.[39]

St Lawrence's Bridge and Gate in Bath

The Somerset historian the Revd John Collinson mentions that St Lawrence's Bridge and Gate in Bath took their names from a small chapel or oratory that was built on the bridge over the Avon at Southgate in the late twelfth or early thirteenth century and demolished during or shortly after the Civil War.[40] It is shown by Joseph Gilmore on his 1696 map of Bath and in a watercolour by Bernard Lens of 1718.[41]

Lansdown chapel, Charlcombe

It is likely that the small village of Charlcombe, with its free chapel of St Lawrence, was within the area of the 100 hide grant to the Priory.[42] The present St Lawrence chapel, now converted to Chapel Farmhouse opposite the Blathwayt Arms, is only

[38] M. Lapidge and M. Herren, *Aldhelm The Prose* Works (Ipswich, 1979); M. Lapidge and J. Rosier, *Aldhelm the Poetic Works* (Cambridge, 1985).

[39] C. Thorn and F. Thorn, *Domesday Book* (Chichester, 1980), 7.3.

[40] J. Collinson, *History and Antiquities of the County of Somerset* (Bath, 1791), pp. 35, 53.

[41] B. Cunliffe, *The City of Bath* (Gloucester, 1986), p. 86.

[42] F. R. Thorn, 'That most famous *monasterium* at Bath', its hundred hides and its estates viewed from South Stoke', *PSANHS* 153 (2010), pp. 13-53.

50m from Bronze age barrows and 100m from a spring to the east (ST 727 687) (figure 11). The topography of the chapel strongly parallels several similar locations of Priddy and Lamyatt Beacon. There is a reference to a chapel at Lantesdon in 1344.[43]

Robert de Cloppecote became prior of Bath in 1303 and the following year King Edward granted to him the liberty of holding two fairs annually, one in the manor of Lyncombe, the other in the manor of Barton. This fair became known as the Prior's Fair and took place over two days, the vigil and feast of St Lawrence (9-10 August). The manorial centre of Barton is situated just to the west of the city centre in the area now occupied by Barton Street, but its lands extended far onto Lansdown, where the fair was held. The fair seemed to have quickly gained in popularity and usefulness, for in 1335 Edward III, on the petition of the Prior and Convent, extended the time to eight days by adding four days before the feast and one after.[44] The Prior's Fair continued its existence after the Reformation had swept away its original owner and was recorded in the lists of 1729, but seems to have ceased by 1801.

Stanton Prior parish church

The parish church of Stanton Prior, just 8 miles southwest of Bath, may be located within the original 100 hide estate, if it extended into Somerset. Many of the charters grant estates to the Priory from the area to the south and west of the city. Stanton Prior was granted to the Priory in 965 by king Edgar to abbot Aescwig, the first abbot of the reformed Benedictine monastery.[45] The dedication to St Lawrence is first mentioned in 1530.[46]

Dunster, chantry to St Lawrence

There are two far west Somerset St Lawrence dedications, one at Dunster and the other at Cutcombe. At the Norman conquest William the Conqueror took over the large hundred of Carhampton and out of it took just one half hide of land at Dunster to give to William de Mohun as the new Sheriff of Somerset, together with fifty six other manors in Somerset and Dorset to form the Honour of Dunster. The half hide of land would have been the castle mound and probably no more than another 100 acres on which he could create the new borough with the market in High Street.

About 1090-1100 William de Mohun granted the church of Dunster and other lands to the church of St Peter at the Priory of Bath, in order that the monks should rebuild the church and establish a small priory.[47] A later agreement, made in 1254,

---

[43] W. Hunt, ed., *Two Chartularies of the Priory of St Peter at Bath*, SRS 7 (1893), pp. 172, 861.

[44] *Cal. Ch. Rolls, vol. IV, 1327-41*, 30 June 1335, p. 341.

[45] S. E. Kelly, ed., *Charters of Bath and Wells* (London, 2007), pp. 121-7.

[46] N. Orme, 'The Medieval Church Dedications of Somerset', *PSANHS* 160 (2016), p. 92.

[47] H. C. Maxwell-Lyte, *A History of Dunster and the families of Mohun and Luttrell* (London, 1909), pp. 383-4.

between Reginald de Mohun and the monks of Bath, mentions a chapel of St Lawrence in the Priory which was in or next to the south transept.[48] The dedication may have been inspired by the relics at Bath.

B. Dedications associated with Glastonbury Abbey

Glastonbury Abbey

Relics of St Lawrence being owned by the Abbey are first recorded in 1340-42[49] and are described at about the same time: '*De Sancto Laurencio unum magnum os. De costa eiusdem,. De carne et sanguine eiusdem. Particula una de craticula ferre super quam fuit assatus*'.[50]

Within its estates, a chapel at Spargrove in the parish of Batcombe and the parish church of Middlezoy are both dedicated to St Lawrence.[51] In addition Domesday notes that Stratton on Fosse, which also has a St Lawrence dedication, formerly belonged to the Abbey.[52] In all three cases, a likely explanation is that the dedications were created by the abbey in the late Saxon/early Norman period in order to strengthen its historical narrative.

Spargrove chapel, Batcombe

Batcombe was probably originally part of the *parochia* of the minster at Bruton. At the time of the Domesday survey, GlastonburyAbbey held 20 hides at Batcombe, of which Roger of Courselles held 2 hides which 'Wulfwy held them before 1066: he could not be separated from the church'.[53] (fn. 54. DB 8.24). These two hides have been identified as Spargrove.[54] Batcombe appears to have been granted to the abbey in about 940 when king Edmund gave the land to Aelfsige, his relative and official and from him it seems to have passed to Aelfheah, the ealdorman of Hampshire, and so to his wife, Aelswith. At her death, it passed to Glastonbury in the 10th century.[55]

The chapel of St Lawrence at Spargrove lay beside the river Alham and was demolished in 1560.[56] Its dedication is recorded in 1390.[57]

Middlezoy parish church

Middlezoy was a chapel of Westonzoyland in the early 13th century when its dedi-

[48] J. Jordan, *The History of Dunster Church and Priory* I (Wellington, 2007), pp. 11-13.

[49] J. P. Carley and M. Howley, 'Relics of Glastonbury Abbey in the Fourteenth Century: an annotated edition of British Library, Cotton Titus D.vii, fols. 2r-13v', in J. P. Carley, ed., *Glastonbury Abbey and the Arthurian Tradition* (Woodbridge, 2001), pp. 576, 611.

[50] J. P. Carley, ed., 'John of Glastonbury Cronica', *BAR* 47 (1978), vol. I, p. 29.

[51] pers.comm. Michael Costen.

[52] C. Thorn and F. Thorn, *Domesday Book Somerset*, 5.88.

[53] C. Thorn and F. Thorn, *Domesday Book Somerset* 8.24.

[54] S. C. Morland, 'Further notes on Somerset Domesday', *PSANHS* 108 (1963-4), p. 96.

[55] L. Abrams, *Anglo-Saxon Glastonbury: church and endowment* (Woodbridge, 1996), p. 55.

[56] SHER 23106.

[57] M. Costen, pers.comm. see table.

cation to St Lawrence was mentioned in a deed.[58] The estate of Sowy, which included both, had been granted to Glastonbury by king Ine in 705.[59] Since the 1540s, the parish church has been dedicated to the Holy Cross.

Stratton on the Fosse parish church

Queen Aelfthryth (964-975) gave the 6 hides of Stratton to Glastonbury.[60] Domesday book records that the manor was held by the Bishop of Coutances; but also that 'Alfwold held it before 1066 from Glastonbury Church; he could not be separated from it.' After the Bishop of Coutances' death in 1093 Stratton passed to a Norman family called *de Sancto Vigore*, after the town near Bayeux called Saint-Vigeur-le-Grand, where a monastery was founded in the early 6th century by St Vigor to whom the parish church is now dedicated. However, there is a record of 1734 giving the dedication as St Lawrence.[61]

C. Dedications associated with the minster at Frome

Aldhelm founded a daughter house *juxta fluvium qui vocatur From,* which most scholars identify as Frome in Somerset, only 30 miles south of Malmesbury.[62]

The dedication to St John has been proudly maintained as it was mentioned in Domesday, but any subsidiary dedications that would certainly have been derived from the relics brought back from Rome did not survive the Reformation.[63] Yet there is indirect evidence that would support a St Lawrence dedication having been present in one of the chapels or at one of the altars.

Woolverton and Rode parish churches

The early large *parochia* of Frome Hundred extended at least 13km to the east and included the later parishes of Woolverton and Rode. They are small villages sited on either side of the river Frome and close to Aldhelm's minster at Frome itself. Woolverton (earlier -ington) is one of a group of place-names around the minster centre of Frome which are of the type 'personal name + *ing* + *tun*' indicating their foundations as a grant to fighting men in the 9th or 10th century.[64] Michael McGarvie provides evidence from a Rental of 1392, annotated apparently around 1556, that parts of Rode were still held by military service from Frome, and that

---

[58] A. Watkins, *The Great Chartulary of Glastonbury Abbey* Vol. 2, SRS 63 (1952), p. 501; pers.comm. Michael Costen.

[59] L. Abrams, 'A single-sheet facsimile of a diploma of king Ine for Glastonbury Abbey', in L. Abrams and J.P. Carley, eds., *The Archaeology and History of Glastonbury Abbey: essays in honour of the ninetieth birthday of C.A. Ralegh Radford* (Woodbridge, 1991), p.120.

[60] J. Scott, *The Early History of Glastonbury* (Woodbridge, 1981), pp. 128-31.

[61] J. A. Robinson, 'Some doubtful dedications of Somerset Churches', *PSANHS* 73 (1927), pp. 70-9; N. Orme, 'Medieval Church Dedications in Somerset' *PSANHS* 160 (2016), p. 93.

[62] D. Preest, *The Deeds of the Bishops* (2002), pp. 236-7, 252, 259.

[63] C. Thorn and F. Thorn, *Domesday Book Somerset*, 1.8.

[64] M. Costen, *Anglo-Saxon Somerset* (Oxford, 2011), pp. 42-3.

both Rode and Woolverton also owed payment of burial rites to Frome.[65] From the date of the creation of these sub-infeudated estates to the lay lords, any dedication of their parish churches would have been vetted by the bishop of the diocese of Sherborne. Both have St Lawrence dedications which may have been derived from the relics at Frome.

D. Dedications associated with Bruton Abbey

Bruton Abbey

William of Malmesbury records that king Ine founded a church dedicated to St Mary to which he gave the altar which Aldhelm had brought back from Rome. He also notes that in Ine's day there was a second larger church dedicated to St Peter which he attributed to Aldhelm.[66]

It is notable that two other St Lawrence dedications have been found in the Bruton/Lamyatt Beacon area — the chapel at the nearby manor of Spargrove (see above) and the chapel on the hill above Milton Cleveden.

Chapel above Milton Clevedon

At a crossroads on the ridge about 800m north of Lamyatt Beacon stood a chapel founded in about 1200 and dedicated to St Lawrence.[67] This probably lay within the *parochia* of Bruton. At Lamyatt Beacon, archaeological excavations found burials associated with what may well have been a sub-Roman chapel on the site of the temple.[68]

Cutcombe parish church

James Savage recorded in 1830 that there was a wake held in Cutcombe on St Lawrence's Day, and that this had probably given rise to the notion that the church was dedicated to that saint.[69] It was certainly dedicated to St John in 1831 as it is today.[70] Michael Costen also records a 'light' in 1531.[71] The church stands high on the eastern slopes of the Forest of Exmoor, just 6 miles up the River Avil from Dunster. For the sake of his soul, William de Mohun granted the church of Cutcombe to the Augustinian canons of the Priory of Bruton by 1291.[72]

---

[65] SHC, DD/SAS C258, 6, no 39; ex inf. Michael McGarvie.

[66] D. Preest, *The Deeds of the Bishops* (2002), p. 254; Aldhelm is commemorated in the great west window installed in memory of the Bennett family in 1888 see J. Bishton, *St Mary the Virgin, Bruton: a brief history* (Bruton, Friends of St Mary the Virgin Church, 2011).

[67] *SHER* 25386.

[68] R. Leach, 'The excavation of a Romano-Celtic temple and later cemetery on Lamyatt Beacon, Somerset', *Britannia* 17 (1973), pp. 259-328.

[69] J. Savage, *History of the Hundred of Carhampton* (Bristol, 1830), pp. 212-3.

[70] N. Orme, 'The Medieval Church Dedications of Somerset', *PSANHS* 160 (2016), p. 89.

[71] See Table.

[72] W. Page, ed., *A History of the County of Somerset II* (London, Victoria County History, 1911), pp. 134-9.

E. Dedications associated with Wells Cathedral

Wells Cathedral

There is a tradition that there was a minster here in Aldhelm's time which later served as the cathedral for the newly founded diocese established in *c.*909.[73] There is no record of the minster owning any relics of saints.

Westbury-sub-Mendip parish church and Priddy chapel

The current dedication of the parish church at Westbury-sub-Mendip is to St Lawrence though there seems to be no record of this before 1742.[74] Westbury church also had a chapel at Priddy, at least by the 13th century, although the dedication is not recorded until 1449.[75]

F. Other foundations

Congresbury, Wick St Lawrence chapel

The dedication of Wick St. Lawrence is in keeping with the area's colonisation in the late pre-Conquest or immediately post-Conquest period, it often being found in areas of reclamation and colonization away from the primary settlement areas.[76] There was a chapelry of Congresbury and the dedication is first recorded in 1326.[77]

Cucklington parish church

The dedication is first recorded in 1468.[78] No link can be found with Aldhelm.

East Harptree parish church

Not mentioned in Barry Lane's notes.

Lydeard St Lawrence parish church

Appropriated to Taunton Priory fair, 10 August, but said to be dedicated to St Lawrence of Canterbury! The church dedication is first mentioned in 13th century.[79]

Wellington chapel of St Lawrence

It was located adjacent to the parish church.[80] This may be an example of the connec-

---

[73] W. Rodwell, *Wells Cathedral: excavations and structural studies 1978-93* (London, English Heritage, 2001), p. 2.

[74] N. Orme, 'The Medieval Church Dedications of Somerset', *PSANHS* 160 (2016), p. 93.

[75] M. Costen pers.comm..

[76] S. Rippon, *Landscape, Community and Colonisation* (York, Council for British Archaeology Research Report 152, 2006), p. 105.

[77] M. Costen pers.comm., see table.

[78] N. Orme, 'The Medieval Church Dedications of Somerset', *PSANHS* 160 (2016), p. 89.

[79] N. Orme, 'The Medieval Church Dedications of Somerset', *PSANHS* 160 (2016), p. 91.

[80] M. Aston and R. Leach, *Historic Towns in Somerset: Archaeology and Planning* (Bristol, Committee for Rescue Archaeology In Avon, Gloucestershire and Somerset, 1977), p. 143.

tion between the dedication of St Lawrence and ecclesiastical lordship estates.[81]

Acknowledgements

The subject of this essay arose from discussions with members of the Westbury Society while excavating a 12th-century first floor hall house within 100m, under the shadow of Westbury church, dedicated to St Lawrence. Dr Graham Jones has been a support throughout and Dr Michael Costen was generous in making his list of 30 or so St Lawrence dedications in the county available as the basis of this work. One more dedication was uncovered during the research; that of the chapel in the parish of Milton Clevedon. A great debt is also due to the many local historians and professional academics including Anna Riggs, the Archivist of Bath Abbey.

The editors are grateful to Chris Webster who generated the maps in figures 10 and 11 from Barry's notes, to Sue Isherwood-Lane for her support and guidance and to Dr Graham Jones and Dr Michael Costen for their invaluable assistance and advice.

---

[81] G. Jones, 'Church dedications and landed units of lordship and administration in the pre-Reformation diocese of Worcester', unpublished PhD, University of Leicester, 1996, p. 160.

4. The Urban Estate of the Vicars Choral of Wells: A Study in Bad Management?

ANTHONY J. SCRASE

Introduction

Over the last twenty years, considerable attention has been paid to the Vicars Choral of our cathedrals, building on Orme's extensive work on Exeter.[1] Attention has been focused also on Wells[2] and York.[3] Hill studied the estate management of the Wells vicars in the early modern period (1591-1866) concluding that their properties were not well managed. This is a view to which this author has also subscribed, arguing that, at this time, the Vicars Choral chose not to defray their limited revenues on costly administration.[4] Hill, however, explained the problem as due to the continued use of 'outdated medieval methods' attributing this to a lack of expertise intensified by an administrative system in which the vicars' main officers served for only a single year.[5]

This chapter attempts to examine matters in more depth by focusing on the properties the Vicars Choral held within Wells. This enables us to look back into the Middle Ages and see how difficulties were built into the origins and early development of the estate. It also allows consideration of the vicars' properties as part of a wider property market, making comparisons with other institutional owners,

---

[1] R. Hall and D. Stocker, eds., *Vicars Choral at English Cathedrals: Cantate Domino: History, Architecture, and Archaeology* (Oxford, 2005); N. Orme, *The Minor Clergy of Exeter Cathedral 1300-1584* (Exeter, 1980); N. Orme, 'The medieval clergy of Exeter Cathedral, I: the vicars and annuellars', *R&T Devon Assoc*, vol. 113 (1982), pp. 79-102; N. Orme, *Exeter Cathedral: the first thousand years* (Exeter, 2009); N. Orme, ed., *The Minor clergy of Exeter Cathedral biographies, 1250-1548*, D&CRS, New Series, vol. 54 (Exeter, 2013).

[2] R. G. Hill, 'The Somerset Estates of the Vicars Choral of Wells', *PSANHS* 142 (1998), pp. 287-309; W. Rodwell and F. Neale, "Begun while the Black Death raged ...' The Vicars Close at Wells', in R. Hall and D. Stocker, ed., *Vicars Choral at English Cathedrals*, pp. 112-37; A. J. Scrase, 'Who were the Vicars Choral of Wells c.1200-1380?', *PSANHS* 158 (2015), pp. 29-43; A. Crawford, *The Vicars of Wells* (Wells, 2016); A. J. Scrase, 'Coping with change: the sixteenth century vicars choral of Wells', *PSANHS* 160 (2017), pp. 95-105.

[3] S. Rees Jones, 'God and Mammon: the role of the city estate of vicars choral in the religious life of York Minster', in Hall and Stocker, eds., *Vicars Choral at English Cathedrals*, pp. 192-9.

[4] A. J. Scrase, *Wells: the anatomy of a medieval and early modern property market* (Bristol, 1993), p. 133.

[5] R. G. Hill, 'The Somerset Estates of the Vicars Choral of Wells', *PSANHS* 142 (1998), p. 304.

notably the dean and chapter, the town authority and Bubwith's Almshouse. The Wells estate must, indeed, have been the most apparent to the vicars. They would have been familiar with their properties as they moved about the city and its suburb of East Wells. If they had any doubts, all were within a short walk whereas questions concerning rural properties might involve sending a senior member on a journey of investigation. Also, some vicars had sufficient means themselves to own or lease property in the town, so they might know intimately how the market operated. Their management in Wells might, therefore, be expected to have been better than elsewhere.

The origins of the estate

Bishop Ralph of Shrewsbury obtained corporate status for the vicars simultaneously with setting up their hall and close in 1348. Thereafter, they could own properties collectively. The main donors were characteristically other churchmen. They were granted partly to gain prayers for the donor's soul, whether in an annual obit, a more regular commemoration or in a chantry. Here of 30 properties held in 1535 the origins of 21 are clear and only two were gifts by laymen. However, the geographical distribution is different from that of the York vicars. Rees Jones describes their estates as forming an outer zone around the cathedral close, often on land that had formed part of prebendal estates.[6] The Wells holdings are more scattered, with some at a distance from the cathedral liberty in Southover and Tucker Street, where they formed part of the wider urban property market. The main benefactors were Canon John Hwysch, Canon John Wareyn, Dean Pempel and sub-dean Nicholas Pontesbury. The motives of one of the lay donors, Nicholas Matrevers, who gave modern 61-65 St Thomas Street, are unclear.[7] The gift of the other lay donor, John le Roper, was part of a set of benefactions to the local religious institutions and was one of his lesser donations. The largest was to establish a chantry in St Cuthbert's, whereas the legacy to the vicars was known as the 'Backhouse'. This was because it occupied the rear portion of the modern Sun, Union Street. Its rent yield was low, being 6s. 8d. p.a. in 1649 when the Commonwealth surveyors suggested that it might be improved by £1. The frontage property across the street, however, which Roper left to the chapter, paid 10s p.a. with a greater suggested possible improvement of £2.[8]

---

[6] R. Jones, 'God and Mammon', Hall and Stocker, eds., *Vicars Choral*, pp. 193-4. It should be recognised that the size of the vicars' estate in York grew from about 80 city properties in the early 14th century to over 240 by the end of the century, making the vicars one of the largest landowners in the city. The city of Wells and the vicars' estate were notably smaller than that of York. For description of the size and structure of Wells in the middle ages see D. G. Shaw, Ch. 2, 'The Size of a small Town', *The Creation of a Community. The City of Wells in the Middle Ages* (Oxford, 1993).

[7] W. P. Baildon, ed., *Historical Manuscripts Commission, Calendar of Manuscripts of the Dean & Chapter of Wells*, vol. II (1914), Ch. 667 683; L. S. Colchester, ed., *Registers of the Vicars Choral of Wells 1393-1534* (Wells, n.d. 1980s), p. 19.

[8] W. H. B. Bird, ed., *Historical Manuscripts Commission, Calendar of Manuscripts of the Dean & Chapter of Wells*, vol. I (1907), pp. 279-80; SHC, DD/CC 116013 17, DD/CC 111733-5.

By chance, the vicars received one property after the Reformation. In 1526, Walter Stride, burgess, assigned the vicars two leases he had received from Bishop Cornish. They were the Antelope Inn (held of the chapter) and a garden east of 1 The Liberty held on a 99-year lease from Wells Hospital. They were granted in return for commemorative services for Stride, Cornish and John Lugwardyn. Then, in 1566, John Ayleworth, who held a lease of the estates of the former hospital, granted a further 300-year lease of the garden. This limit was forgotten. In 1591, the Royal Charter did not list it as part of the vicars' properties. But in 1649, it was included as part of the freehold estate.[9]

Despite the vicars' corporate status, many properties were not granted to them collectively but to a group of vicars or sometimes to two canons and a group of vicars. The last survivors then passed the property on to another group. This procedure was in keeping with the vicars' approach to sharing tasks. It also avoided the need to purchase a mortmain licence from the government. The arrangements can be seen most clearly with the Wareyn estate for which there survives the original establishment and transfers in 1415, 1467 and 1519.[10] Such arrangements did not persist so long for Moniers Lane where, in 1453, the last two survivors of a group transferred it to the vicars' principals. By that time, the lane was reduced to gardens and detailed management was not needed.[11] Elsewhere, the practice was still being used. The Matraver's property was initially granted to two vicars and then, in 1477, the survivor, Richard Burnell, transferred it to the two principals and four other vicars.[12] As we shall see, this method was still used in the sixteenth century.

One may infer similar arrangements for Hwysch's bequests. One group of rents was to support obits for members of the Hwysch and Fisher families. Such commemorations, however, cannot be found in the cathedral escheator's records. Perhaps the responsibility fell on the vicars or a group of them. It may be significant that the first known transaction after Hwysch's will involves a group of five vicars and, later in 1534, four vicars were in charge of the property.[13]

The origins of two significant blocks of property may be suggested in the absence of documentation. The vicars owned 18-22 Chamberlain Street by 1575. It is known that the knight, John Chideok, left rents of £1 5s. from Chamberlain Street houses to provide a chantry for his soul. Record of such a responsibility, once again, was not found in the escheator's accounts. So, it is possible that the four vicars who sang the service were in charge. The arrangement seems to have been relatively informal as a

[9] W. P. Baildon, ed., HMC, Cal Mss D & C Wells, vol. II (1914), Ch. 744 699, Ch. 794 708; SHC DD/CC 116013 26.

[10] W. P. Baildon, ed., HMC, Cal Mss D & C Wells, vol. II (1914), Ch. 472 647, Ch. 479 648, Ch. 483 649, Ch. 538 659, Ch. 675 684-5, Ch. 742-3 699.

[11] A. J. Scrase, 'A French Merchant in Fourteenth-Century Wells' PSANHS 133 (1989), pp. 134-5; Cal. ii Ch. 644 680.

[12] W. P. Baildon, ed., HMC, Cal Mss D & C Wells, vol. II (1914), Ch. 667 683, Ch. 701-2 690; Colchester, Registers, p. 19.

[13] W. P. Baildon, ed., HMC, Cal Mss D & C Wells, vol. II (1914), Ch. 366 626, Ch. 448 643, Ch. 752 701.

cathedral record of 1386 mentions one vicar passing the duty to another.[14] No other vicars' or chapter properties are unaccounted for in Chamberlain Street so it is likely that this block was Chideok's bequest.

The other block was 22a-28 St Thomas Street. This group had chapter property to its west and south, forming a large unit running back to the stream. This may have originally included the later vicars' holding and was left to secure Nicholas Selbourne's obit. It was subdivided several times with parts being used to house canons for whom a canonical house was unavailable, vicars or chantry priests.[15] By about 1420, fewer canons wished to take up residence and both the vicars and annuellars were housed. It is likely, therefore, that it was transferred to the vicars at about that time. We know that a house site in College Street was given to the vicars about 1433/4 for an obit rent of 1s. p.a., compared with the 3s. it should have secured.[16]

If these conjectures are correct, it leaves only one Southover cottage and two Tucker Street houses unexplained. But these speculations suggest something about the vicars' management. They may not have taken good care of potentially important records. In contrast, surviving records of the town, chapter and Bubwith's Almshouse all contain abundant early transactions for properties they came to own and presumably formed their title deeds.[17] The vicars only preserved such runs for Sub-dean Pontesbury's[18] and the Matraver's bequests.[19] Dean Pempel's legacy of Moniers Lane is more patchy. Surviving documents have much concerning Peter le Monier's acquisition of the site and what was there before. Again, they show how the ownership passed to Pempel. What is missing is Pempel's will and how Dean Ralph Tregision of Exeter became involved. Part of what was required is apparent from the escheator's accounts as first £1 and then 13s. 4d. was paid to him. His accounts refer to an indenture between the vicars and Dean Tregision's executor 'still remaining in the possession of the vicars'. Presumably, that is the surviving charter of 1417.[20]

The situation was worse for other properties. For example, only two transactions

[14] A. Watkins, ed., *Dean Cosyn and Wells Cathedral Miscellanea,* SRS 56 (1941), p. 17; W. H. B. Bird, ed., *HMC, Cal Mss D & C Wells*, vol. I (1907), p. 300.

[15] W. H. B. Bird, ed., *HMC, Cal Mss D & C Wells*, vol. I (1907), *p.* 217; W. P. Baildon, ed., *HMC, Cal Mss D & C Wells*, vol. II (1914)*, Ch. 268 607, Ch. 354 624, Ch. 419 637; L. S. Colchester, ed., *Wells Cathedral Escheator's Accounts 1369-1600* (Wells, 1988), pp. 6, 31-2, 77-8.

[16] Colchester, *Escheator's Accounts*, pp. 5, 100, 116.

[17] A. J. Scrase and J. Hasler, eds., *Wells Corporation Properties* SRS 87 (2002), pp. 3-7; A. J. Scrase, 'Wells Almshouse Records and Topographic Reconstruction,' *SDNQ* xxxii, Part 329, pp. 738-46; A. J. Scrase 'The urban estate of Bubswith's Almshouse,' *SDNQ* xxxv, Part 357, pp. 216-27.

[18] W. P. Baildon, ed., *HMC, Cal Mss D & C Wells*, vol. II (1914), Ch.76 561, Ch. 88 564-5, Ch. 155 580, Ch. 173 585, Ch. 241 600, Ch. 293 612, Ch. 345 622, Ch. 389 631, Ch. 392 631, Ch. 523 652; WCA, AD/E 9.

[19] W. P. Baildon, ed., *HMC, Cal Mss D & C Wells*, vol. II (1914), Ch. 198 591, Ch. 202 592, Ch. 223 596-7, Ch. 459 645, Ch. 474 647, Ch. 623 674, Ch. 667 683, Ch 701-2 690; Colchester, *Registers*, p. 19.

[20] A. J. Scrase 'A French Merchant', p. 133-4; see W. P. Baildon, ed., *HMC, Cal Mss D & C Wells*, vol. II (1914), Ch. 550 661 for the terms.

survive concerning the Hwysch properties from before his will. They concerned the southernmost of four cottages in Union Street.[21] They probably survived because one related to the party wall with 40 High Street. The vicars would have faced serious difficulties if many of their ownerships had been challenged.

One consequence of the vicars' inefficient management, furthermore, was that they lost track of rent charges on properties they did not own (a problem that also afflicted the cathedral escheator). Certainly, John Hwysch's will included mention of a Mill Lane site that cannot be traced.[22] Wareyn's donation included a rent from modern 53 High Street that was subsequently lost.[23] Another rent is listed amongst the vicars' properties in the 1591 Royal Charter and that too had disappeared by 1649.

Medieval management

Successful management of Wells Cathedral in the middle ages was mutually dependent upon the provision of adequate musicians and of administrators of sufficient legal and financial competence. The demand for such people was apparent before the vicars were incorporated. From the mid-thirteenth century, they were drawn into the requirements of the diocese and cathedral. Bishops could call on the services of two vicars by 1335 but far more roles were required in the cathedral. Vicars regularly served as communar, escheator, warden (or keeper) of the fabric and sub-treasurer. The communar controlled funds supporting the residential canons and vicars. The escheator initially administered holdings that reverted to the chapter by death or surrender but came to deal with most obit rents. The warden disbursed the funds for maintenance of the cathedral fabric. The sub-treasurer is a more shadowy role but presumably aided the treasurer with accounts. These posts offered rewards to the ambitious; certainly more money but also a chance of advancement. Nationally, vicars had only remote opportunities of joining the ranks of the canons. At Wells, however, there were more chances and (apart from nepotism under Bishops Bitton and Burnell) the surest route was through administration. Suitable persons might occupy these posts for many years. There were also lesser roles, assisting the four or in particular tasks such as surveying buildings.[24]

The vicars' incorporation added a new set of officers. They had two principals, two receivers or bursars (of whom the more significant was the receiver general who had to be backed by two sureties), three auditors and a steward. The principals, five seniors (who assisted the principals in selecting new officers), the receiver general and auditors were selected annually. Further appointments, as principal or auditor, were common but everybody was expected to take their turn as receiver general.

In the rotation of the performance of the offices of steward and receiver general, we seem to see the principle of a sharing of the burdens of administration and this

---

[21] W. P. Baildon, ed., *HMC, Cal Mss D & C Wells*, vol. II (1914), Ch.195 590.

[22] W. P. Baildon, ed., *HMC, Cal Mss D & C Wells*, vol. II (1914), Ch. 366 626.

[23] W. P. Baildon, ed., *HMC, Cal Mss D & C Wells*, vol. II (1914), Ch. 472 647, Ch. 483 649.

[24] A. J. Scrase 'Who were the Vicars Choral of Wells, c. 1200-1380?', pp. 38-41.

principle may underlie the allocation of property management to small groups of vicars, a practice not necessarily intended primarily to establish expertise in property management. It was only in 1435, when John Knocston was added to the Moniers Lane group (having been one of the administrators of the Wareyn properties from 1415), that any common membership appeared. A fall in the number of vicars may have necessitated an increase in individual responsibilities, and such a division of responsibilities may have adversely affected the successful control of significant documentation, causing it to be dispersed and mislaid. And such a loss of control may have resulted in the loss of a single, coherent management regime for the estate.

The early phases of the vicars' incorporation coincided with the impact of the Black Death, which was to transform the economy. Initially, some towns did quite well, as surviving peasants and labourers obtained higher wages and purchased more or better goods and rents held up well, despite early signs of decline. Some disadvantaged sites were hard to let or abandoned, notably, in Wells, in the northern part of New Street, modern Market Street and Moniers Lane. Then from *c.*1420 property markets collapsed. The difficulties with Moniers Lane are shown by two transactions of 1425. In the first, the managers leased a burgess, a toft (building plot) at 6*d. p.a.*, described as having a toft to its north. In the second, John Frome, who held 28 High Street from the town authority, was let the southern 28m (93 ft.) of the lane and a rear access to his High Street property for 1*s. p.a.*.[25]

Prior to the 1420s, the vicars had done a little to improve their holdings. In 1402 they granted a rebuilding lease for 7 Southover. The takers were to rebuild half of the house within two years and the remainder within a further two. In return, they were to pay a nominal rent of a rose for four years and then 4*s. p.a.*[26] By 1407, it appears, 35 High Street (the best of Hwysch's legacy) had become the Christopher or New Inn, evidence for which survives not in the vicars' records but in record of an abuttal of 33 High Street that gives the neighbouring occupier as John Stokes, taverner.[27]

The other institutional owners took action. The town authority's 1427/8 rental shows that they had undertaken a comprehensive review of rents, reducing them to realistic levels. Over all their income fell by nearly 15%. The rental shows that problems now reached the heart of the town. On High Street, 18 rents were reduced while two properties were described as derelict and one as a toft. Abuttals mention another toft and a void plot.[28] The town and the chapter (in the forms of the communar and escheator, who controlled separate properties) tried to address the problems. All issued building leases with no rent or a much-reduced rent for the period of

[25] W. P. Baildon, ed., *HMC, Cal Mss D & C Wells*, vol. II (1914), Ch. 582 667-8 (abuttal from original); L. S. Colchester, ed., *Documents 1348-1600 of the Vicars Choral of Wells* (Wells, 1986), Ch. 4 4-5.
[26] W. P. Baildon, ed., *HMC, Cal Mss D & C Wells*, vol. II (1914), Ch. 511 654.
[27] D. Shilton and R. Holworthy, eds., *Wells City Charters*, SRS 46 (1932), pp. 8-10.
[28] A. J. Scrase and J. Hasler, *Wells Corporation Properties*, SRS 87 (2002), pp. 30-2.

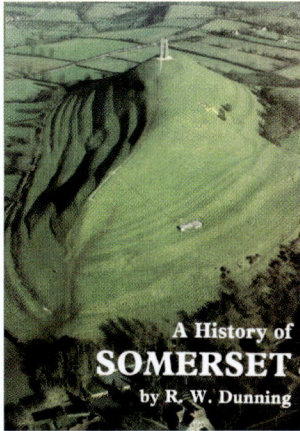

Above left: 1. An illustration of rural Somerset in the 1930s from 'A study in rural settlement in Somerset' by Beatrice M. Swainson. (S.H.C., D/P/lanf 23/4.) *Centre:* 2. The cover of Robert Dunning's *A history of Somerset*, published in 1987, using a photograph taken by the late Professor Aston. (S.A.N.H.S., Aston Collection.) *Right:* 3. The interior of Culbone church by Samuel Griffiths Tovey (1808-1873). (S.A.N.H.S., Braikenridge Collection.)

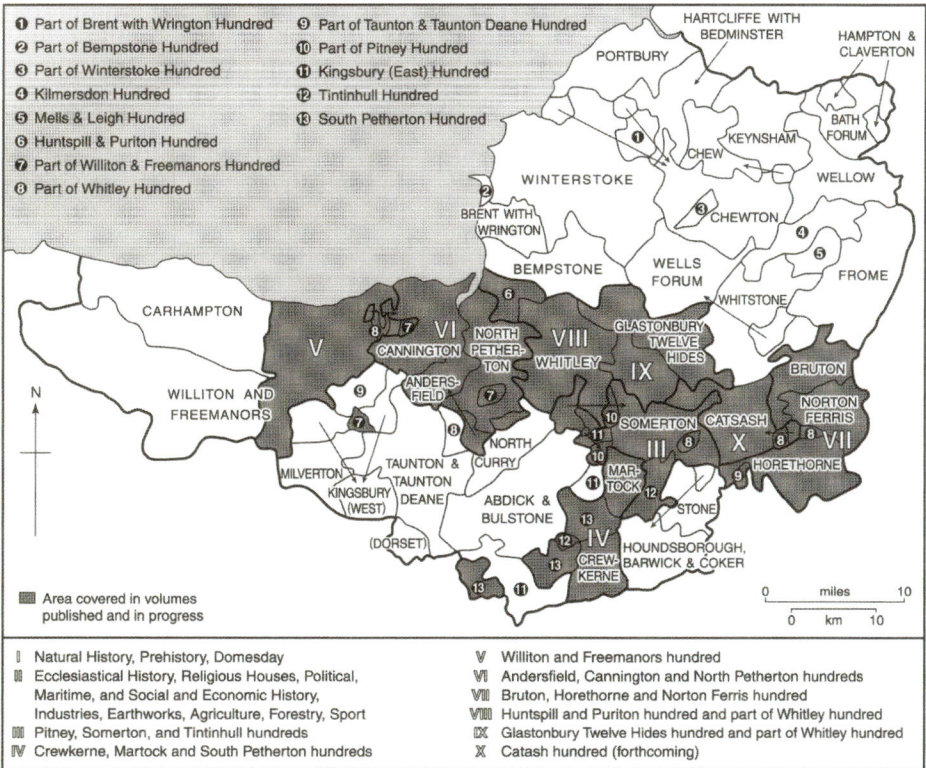

❶ Part of Brent with Wrington Hundred
❷ Part of Bempstone Hundred
❸ Part of Winterstoke Hundred
❹ Kilmersdon Hundred
❺ Mells & Leigh Hundred
❻ Huntspill & Puriton Hundred
❼ Part of Williton & Freemanors Hundred
❽ Part of Whitley Hundred
❾ Part of Taunton & Taunton Deane Hundred
❿ Part of Pitney Hundred
⓫ Kingsbury (East) Hundred
⓬ Tintinhull Hundred
⓭ South Petherton Hundred

Area covered in volumes published and in progress

I Natural History, Prehistory, Domesday
II Ecclesiastical History, Religious Houses, Political, Maritime, and Social and Economic History, Industries, Earthworks, Agriculture, Forestry, Sport
III Pitney, Somerton, and Tintinhull hundreds
IV Crewkerne, Martock and South Petherton hundreds
V Williton and Freemanors hundred
VI Andersfield, Cannington and North Petherton hundreds
VII Bruton, Horethorne and Norton Ferris hundred
VIII Huntspill and Puriton hundred and part of Whitley hundred
IX Glastonbury Twelve Hides hundred and part of Whitley hundred
X Catash hundred (forthcoming)

4. A map showing the extent of the work Robert Dunning was involved in whilst head of the Victoria County History of Somerset (reproduced from volume IX in that series).

5. A view of the 'Burrough chapel' (Burrow Mump) at Lyng engraved by Samuel Sparrow and published in 1785. (© S.A.N.H.S., Braikenridge Collection.)

6. A sepia and grey watercolour and pencil drawing of St Decuman's church, Watchet, from the south-east by W.W. Wheatley, 1845. (© S.A.N.H.S., Braikenridge Collection.)

7. The Lady Chapel at Glastonbury, 2009. (© Nilfanion, 2009.)

8. The tomb of Ralph of Shrewsbury in Wells Cathedral. (Photograph by Michael Blandford, © Dean & Chapter of Wells, 2017.)

9. The parish church of St Lawrence, Westbury-sub-Mendip, in May 2009. (© David Dawson.)

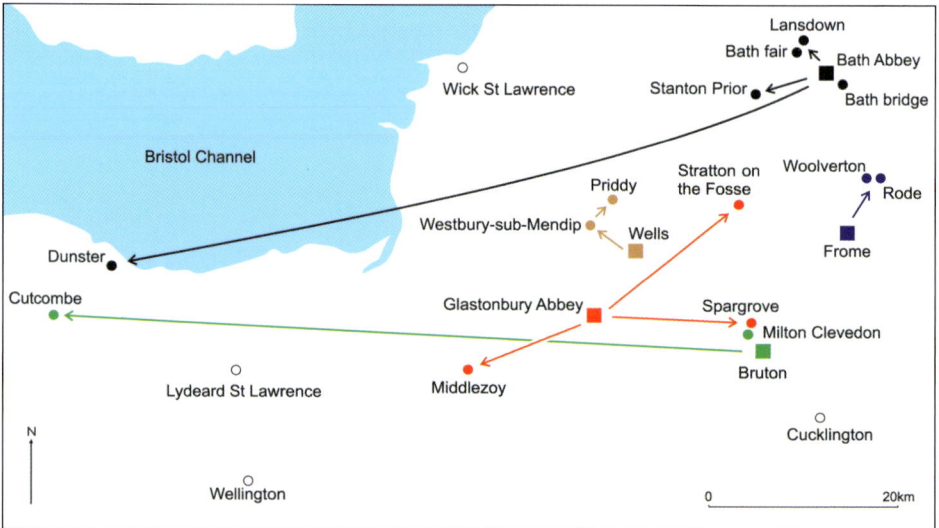

10. A map showing the locations of places mentioned in the gazetteer of sites associated with St Lawrence. (Map designed by Chris Webster.)

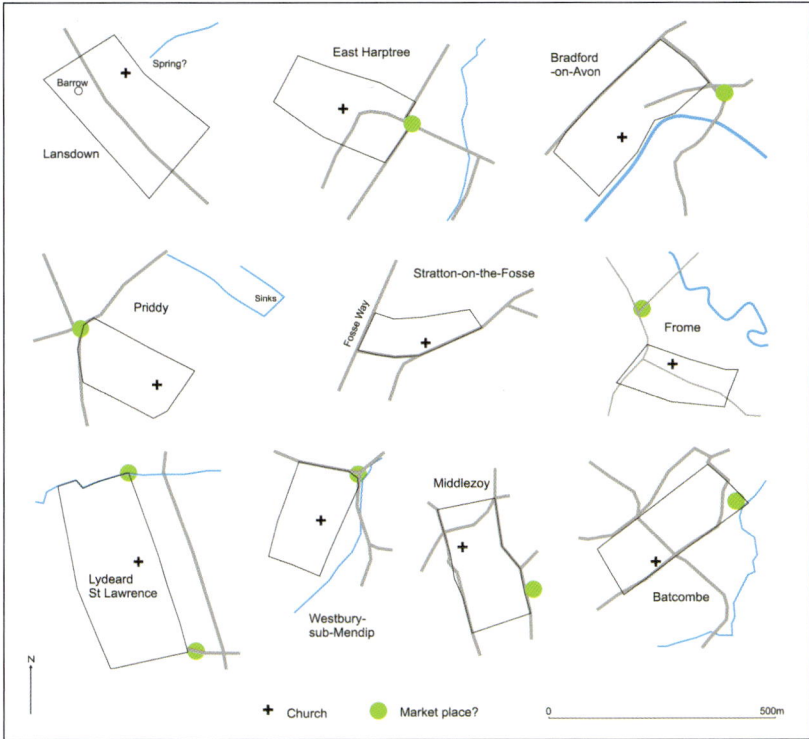

11. Sketch plans of settlements associated with St Lawrence. (Redrawn to scale from Barry Lane's notes by courtesy of Chris Webster.)

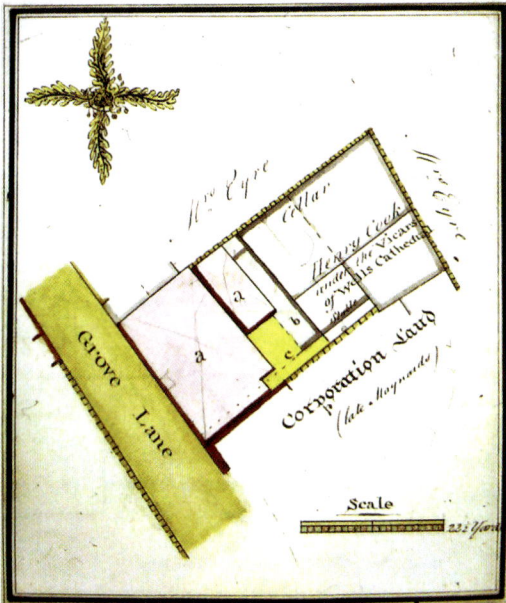

12. The Sun Inn, Union Street, Wells, from the 1821 Corporation Survey. The front portion (labelled a, b and c) was owned by the Corporation while the rear, as is indicated, belonged to the Vicars Choral being the medieval Backhouse. The fact that the illustration is drawn from the town archives is a comment on the vicars' estate management. They alone of the institutional owners did not commission accurate plans of their properties in the early-19th century. (Wells City Archives.)

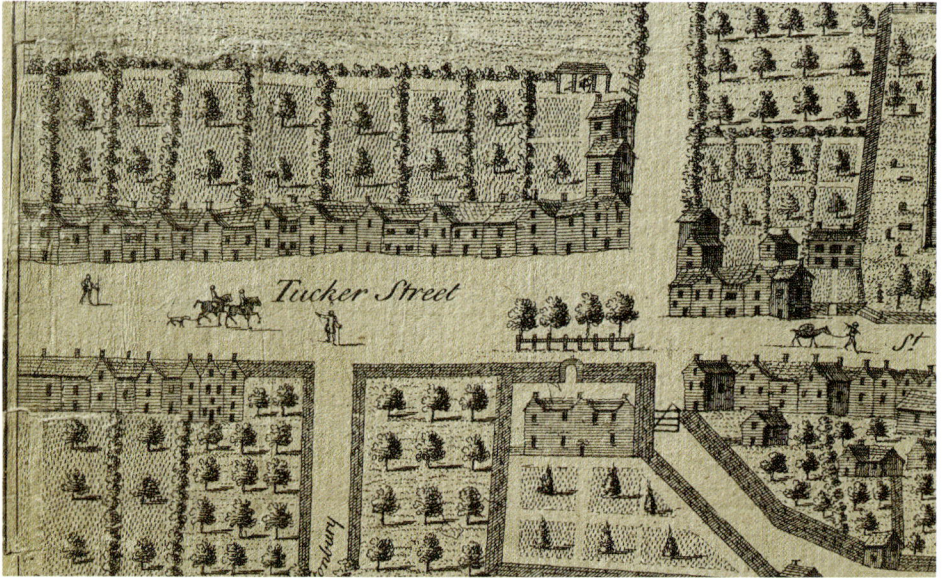

13. Tucker Street from Symes' Birds-eye Plan of Wells, 1735. This shows the vicars' property on the south side of Tucker Street. It was the only house on that side between West Street and Market Street. (S.A.N.H.S.)

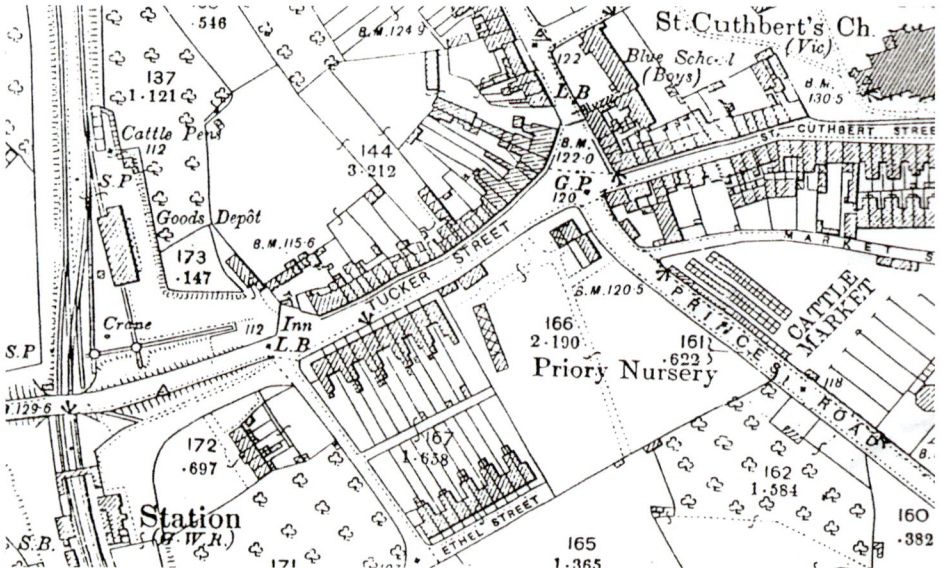

14. Tucker Street in 1886. The same area as illustrated by the first edition Ordnance Survey 1:2,500 of 1886. Despite the requirement to rebuild in the 1835 lease the site was undeveloped on the Tithe Map of 1837/8 when it had been thrown into a parcel called the Mermaid Ground. In 1886 it was part of Priory Nursery and was only finally redeveloped late in the twentieth century. (A.J. Scrase collection.)

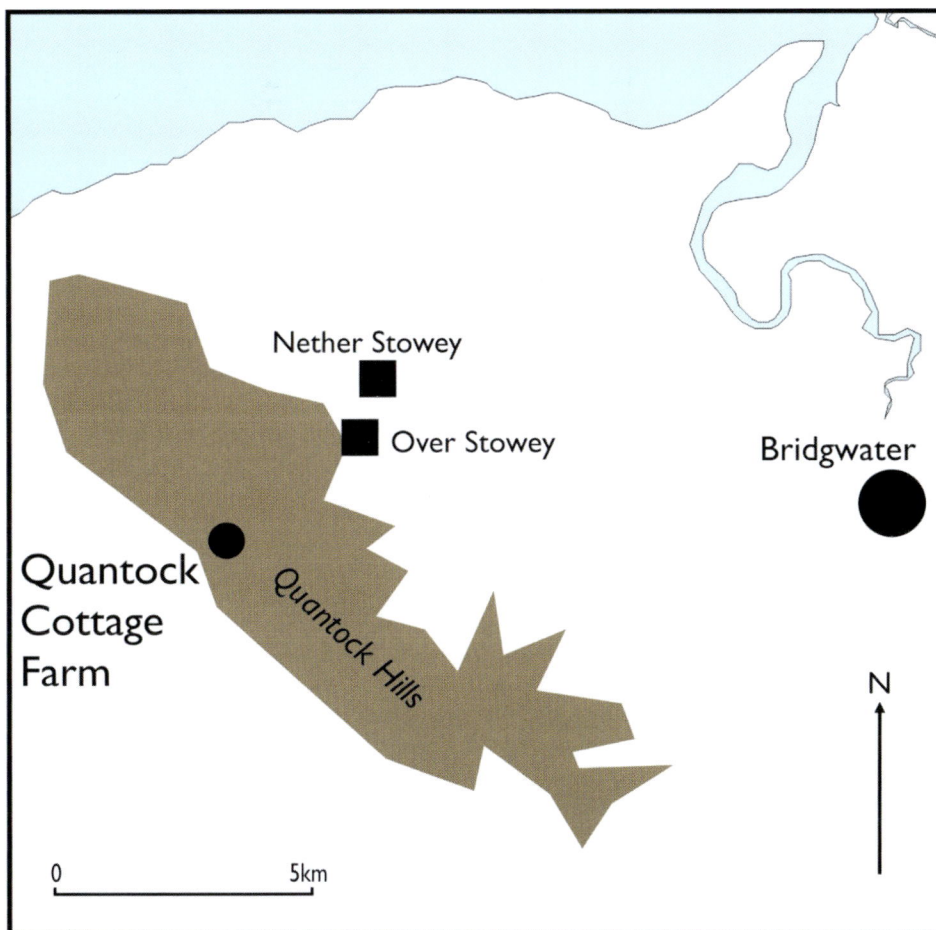

Above: 15. Map showing the location of the potteries at Nether and Over Stowey in relation to Quantock Gate and Bridgwater. (Reproduced by kind permission of Chris Webster.)

Left: 16. An example of a bucket-handled jar from St Clements' Dock found during excavations at Narrow Quay, Bristol; height 250mm. This particular vessel though very similar to West Somerset-made pieces, can be confidently ascribed to the potteries of East Somerset. (Reproduced by kind permission of Bristol City Museum and Art Gallery.)

17. An assemblage of pottery deposited in the reredorter of Cleeve Abbey *c*.1536 as reconstructed by the late Richard Coleman-Smith advised by John Allan.
(Reproduced from *Proceedings of the Somerset Archaeology and Natural History* volume 142 by kind permission of John Allan.)

building, often followed by a low rent for the remainder of the lease. As an added incentive, the town sometimes even provided building materials.[29] Penalties were also tried. Forfeiture, higher rents or deferred fines might be threatened. Tenants were also pursued about repairs. The communars alone attempted redevelopment. In 1445-6, the 'large Cheleworth burgage', at 11-13 High Street, was divided into two new tenements.[30] In 1497, the 'Barliche' tenement in Sadler Street was redeveloped. It was supposed to pay 16s. but had produced only 10s. for over a century. It was now rebuilt as an inn, the Hart's Head (later the White Hart) with two smaller houses on what is now the yard to its south. The rents rose to £2 18s. 8d.[31] Both of these entrepreneurial communars were vicars! Between these events, the communar's income had experienced an enormous boost with Beckington's gift of 15 new properties.

In comparison with the communars, the vicars seem to have failed to find the means to manage their limited estate in such a way as to resist decline. By 1448, they appear to have given up on Moniers Lane. One of their number, Roger Martyn, had been granted a tenement there for 6s. 8d. p.a. plus repairs. In 1443, he was granted an elm from Easton for repairs. But, in 1448, nothing had been done and his executors were instructed to make a vault beneath the tower instead. Thereafter, the lane produced at best £1 p.a. of which two-thirds was given to the escheator. The remainder could not pay for the masses and distributions they were contracted to provide.[32]

The attitude of the vicars may reflect the fact that they were receiving further properties and felt less need to improve the existing estate in contrast to succeeding communars. This idea may have been reinforced by events in 1469. The abbey of Muchelney had owned 23 The Liberty since the thirteenth century. Now, as they suffered falling income, they were unable to maintain it, surrendering the property to the dean and chapter. The cathedral treasurer rebuilt it, at his own expense, and issued ordinances for its use, to benefit the vicars and the chaplain of St Saviour's Chantry. Perhaps he understood the vicars' needs better than they did.[33] Finally, in 1485, the vicars agreed a second building lease with one of their number, Ralph Gardener. It was for 28 St Thomas Street, then described as a toft now ruinous with a garden. It was for 99 years at 5s. p.a. (subsequently the rent was 13s. 4d.) and he was to build a house.[34] Perhaps this was an effort by an affluent vicar to help his fellows.

The medieval period ended, therefore, with the vicars' estate in a poor condition

---

[29] D. G. Shaw, *Creation of a Community: The City of Wells in the Middle Ages* (Oxford, 1993), pp. 49-51.

[30] L. S. Colchester, ed., *Wells Cathedral Communar's Accounts 1327-1600* (Wells, 1986), pp. 105-8.

[31] W. P. Baildon, ed., *HMC, Cal Mss D & C Wells*, vol. II (1914), p. 269; Colchester *Communar's Accounts*, pp. 168.

[32] W. P. Baildon, ed., *HMC, Cal Mss D & C Wells*, vol. II (1914), Ch. 550 662; Colchester *Registers*, pp. 4, 13; L. S. Colchester, ed., *Act Book 1541-1593 of the Vicars Choral of Wells* (Wells, 1986), p. 28.

[33] W. P. Baildon, ed., *HMC, Cal Mss D & C Wells*, vol. II (1914), Ch. 691 688, Ch. 694 688-9.

[34] W. P. Baildon, ed., *HMC, Cal Mss D & C Wells*, vol. II (1914), Ch. 711 692.

in a generally depressed market. There may have been problems with fragmented management both between groups controlling properties and between regularly changing officers. Perhaps it had become difficult for anyone take an overview or systematically pursue arrears and repairs over a period, or, as those with sufficient ability to tackle the problems were drawn into the service of the chapter and often retained in their posts for many years, it may have proved an increasingly impossible task.

Early modern management to 1645

The sixteenth century began with an intensification of previous trends. The numbers of vicars continued to decline as did real income, exacerbated by increasing inflation. In the short term, the obvious difficulty was to find sufficient vicars for key administrative roles. This is illustrated by the career of Richard Pomeroy. When the century started, he had been keeper of the fabric since 1488/9 and he continued as such until 1502/3. In 1502, he was one of the vicars' principals and in September the chapter recognised the burdens placed on him by excusing him from night-time services for 'good and diligent service'. This was usually a concession for old and ailing vicars. He must have been about 60 but his health seems to have been good and he lived to 1523. In 1503, the chapter also accepted his excuses about serving as communar, from 1506, he returned as keeper. In addition, he had been, from 1467, one of the group of vicars managing the Wareyn properties. In 1477, he also became one of a new group set up for 61-65 St Thomas Street.[35] Problems were made worse by the actions of the chapter. They were also suffering from falling numbers and income. They therefore tried to shift tasks on to the vicars. In the past, the role of organist had sometimes been held by vicars but was occasionally an independent appointment. When Richard Bramston returned to Wells by 1516, he was appointed organist and master of the choristers. These roles were thereafter combined with that of vicar. Bramston was merely allocated a house in the close whereas his predecessor Richard Hygons had been given a house in the New Works rent free. When Bramston, uniquely, also took on the role of clerk of works, in return only for extra vacations, the chapter must have been delighted.[36]

With so many tasks for the able, it is unsurprising that improvements to the maintenance and yield of the estate were given little attention. There was one improvement. The 1508/9 escheator's accounts note that there was now a cottage on the site in College Street that the chapter had passed to the vicars in 1433.[37] No other records survive to show whether this was a collective enterprise by the vicars or an initiative by an individual vicar or tenant. Certainly, the other institutional owners were now being helped by wealthier members. Firstly, in 1501, the chapter

[35] W. P. Baildon, ed., *HMC, Cal Mss D & C Wells*, vol. II (1914), pp. 113, 170, 173, 195, Chs. 701-2 690 Ch. 732 697.

[36] W. P. Baildon, ed., *HMC, Cal Mss D & C Wells*, vol. II (1914), Chs. 749-50 700-1.

[37] Colchester, *Escheator's Accounts*, p. 239.

granted Thomas Cornish, suffragan bishop and chancellor of Wells, and John Lugwardyn, the succentor, the Antelope at 2 Chamberlain Street for 80 years at a reduced rent of 4s. provided they rebuilt it. As mentioned, the lease was assigned to the vicars in 1526.[38] Then, in 1515, Canon Peter Carsleygh took a 20-year lease of 15 New Street at 6d *p.a.* It had been noted as burned down since 1408/9, with a resultant loss of 5s.[39] In 1511, the town guild tried a less voluntary variation when incoming councillors were required to contribute towards the redevelopment of a High Street tenement.[40]

The vicars lacked the resources of the canons but they did include those from affluent families or those who managed independently to accumulate funds. However, most of these did not make the vicars' properties a priority. Richard Pomeroy preferred to improve the vicars' hall, while Richard Bramston left legacies to the cathedral fabric and loans for town burgesses.[41] It was over 20 years after the chapter and town estates gained in this way that a single vicar followed these examples. He was William Capron, who had served as communar for a decade from 1503, so he would have been well-aware of the Antelope redevelopment. He was responsible for redeveloping the Christopher around 1533. The result was not entirely happy as his executors got into a dispute with four vicars managing the property. Both parties and the wider body of vicars had to agree to an arbitration. But, in the long term, the benefits were clear. In 1361, Hwysch left the future Christopher and various other properties to yield £3 4s. 10d. In 1562, the vicars leased the Christopher for £6.[42]

Dramatic changes followed from Henry VIII's break with Rome but the initial impact was slow and took the form of by-products of the dissolution of the monasteries. In 1545, the vicars lost 23 The Liberty when the Earl of Hertford (subsequently Protector Somerset) seized it on the basis of his possession of 'the late monasterye of Mochilney'. On his fall, it became part of the Crown estates.[43] When the cathedrals with monastic chapters were re-established, they were given a staff of singing men who, unlike Vicars Choral, did not have to be in holy orders. By the 1550s, lay vicars were appearing at Wells. Now allowed to marry, the nature of the close began to change, and also the living expenses of vicars.[44]

The major transformation came after Edward VI's accession. In 1547, prayers for the dead were abolished. The vicars gained slightly as an institution. They kept the

[38] W. P. Baildon, ed., *HMC, Cal Mss D & C Wells*, vol. II (1914), pp. 165, 175-6, Ch. 744 699; Colchester, *Communar's Accounts*, pp. 175, 182.

[39] Colchester, *Escheator's Accounts*, pp. 71, 271, 275, 280.

[40] A. Nott and J. Hasler, eds. *Wells Convocation Acts Books, 1589-1665,* SRS 91 (2004), p. 264; D. G. Shaw, *The Creation of a Community* (Oxford, 1993), p. 53.

[41] F. W. Weaver, ed., *Somerset Medieval Wills 1531-58,* SRS 21 (19050, pp. 19, 154; Crawford, *The Vicars of Wells*, pp. 35-6.

[42] W. P. Baildon, ed., *HMC, Cal Mss D & C Wells*, vol. II (1914), Ch. 366 626, Ch. 752 701; Colchester, *Act Book*, p. 19.

[43] W. P. Baildon, ed., *HMC, Cal Mss D & C Wells*, vol. II (1914), p. 260.

[44] Colchester, *Act Book* 11, pp. 15-6.

bequests from Wareyn, Hywysch, Penpel and Pontesbury but no longer had the expense of the commemorations. Individual vicars, however, lost far more. They had been paid for these services and a large number of others. The cycle of services in the cathedral began to change, a process completed in 1549. Until this time, services were held at the eight canonical hours, supplemented by a Marian mass in the Lady Chapel, and a varying number of other masses at the chantries and altars around the cathedral. Now there would be only three services, Matins, Communion and Evensong, and Communion was only to be held once or twice a month. Vicars were now required part-time. They could thus look for other employment to boost their income. This was even more necessary as another change of 1549 allowed priests to marry.

The accession of Mary led to a total reversal. The incoming bishop, Gilbert Bourne, seems to have realised that a return to near continuous services meant that the vicars had to have more resources. In 1554, he leased them an 18-acre close in his park called Waterleaze, which adjoined Southover. It was leased for a fine of £30, compared with a market value of £50, and they were to pay him rent of £1 13s. 4d. *p.a.* According to customary practice, the vicars then put its management into the hands of four of their number. They initially let it, with the Christopher, for £7 *p.a.* but this had been increased to £13 by 1649. This beneficial arrangement was to last until the Ecclesiastical Commissioners took over in 1866.[45]

Mary's changes prove temporary. The accession of her half-sister Elizabeth saw a return to Protestantism. Again, there were only two services on a typical day. The vicars were once more part-timers and short of money, both as an institution and individuals. This compelled some attention to the estate. In 1561, they were able to grant their own lease of the Antelope for the final 20 years of their interest. It was let together with Monday's Mead, their own meadow to the north of Chamberlain Street.[46] They received £3 *p.a.* for the inn and £5 for the field. In 1563, they regained 23 The Liberty. In what must have been a pre-arranged sequence, on successive days, the Crown granted it to Cecily Pyckerell of Norwich, she conveyed it to Richard Robertz, her heir, and he granted it to the vicars' principals, Thomas Fudge and Thomas Hooper. Both principals had been vicars when the house was lost. They followed standard practice and transferred it to a group of four of their colleagues.[47] Next, in about 1570, something was done about Moniers Lane. The land to the east of the lane was used to create two frontage plots on Chamberlain Street.[48] Nothing survives to show who took the initiative. The profitable experience of sub-

[45] W. P. Baildon, ed., *HMC, Cal Mss D & C Wells*, vol. II (1914), Ch. 799 706; L. S. Colchester, ed., *Documents 1348-1600 of The Vicars Choral of Wells* (Wells, 1986), Ch. 15 7, Ch. 22a 12; Colchester, *Act Book*, p. 19; SHC, DD/CC 115825-33, DD/CC 116013 68-9, DD/CC 13202 no. 181, DD/CC 31526 140; WCA, VC/E/3/6 nos.70, 217, 223.

[46] Colchester, *Act Book*, p. 17.

[47] W. P. Baildon, ed., *HMC, Cal Mss D & C Wells*, vol. II (1914), Ch. 791 708, Ch. 799 709; WCA, DC/E/14/3(a), DC/E/14/3(b).

[48] Colchester, *Act Book*, p. 33; Colchester, *Documents,* Ch. 22 11, Ch. 33 15.

leasing Waterleaze and the Antelope led them to an innovation not attempted by any other Wells estate. They rented another property to sublet. In 1586, they leased 11 St Thomas Street from St John's Hospital, Bath paying them 7s. 2d. but subletting for 14s p.a.[49] The vicars had a pond and physick (or herb) garden at the north end of Tor Street. In the 1591 Royal Charter, it is described as a pond or building plot let to one of their number, John Clarke junior. Shortly afterwards, he built a row of small cottages on the site. In later leases, he is described as both vicar and gentleman, probably a man of independent means.[50]

The second quarter of the century saw a more problematic trend. Several senior or principal vicars took leases of properties. Most were reversions, so they were either acting over the heads of sitting tenants or taking advantage of knowledge that they would not renew their lease. They did not do it to improve the property and paid the usual rent but we do not know whether the fine was standard. The obvious purpose seems to have been to provide for kin. In 1557, Thomas Hooper took the reversion of three closes of pasture. One of the lives was Elizabeth Hooper *alias* Lyte (presumably a sister or niece). In 1562, he was granted two more closes on the northern portion of College Street. In 1575, Walter Cely was granted a cottage in Union Street for the lives of himself and his two brothers. Soon after, Matthew Naylor was granted the reversion of one of the new Chamberlain Street houses for the lives of his wife, their daughter and the latter's first-born.[51]

The circumstances of the Wells vicars encouraged a greater mobility as the more talented at either music or administration moved away. As regards musical ability, Walter Nowell moved to Salisbury cathedral and Elway Bevan first to Bristol and then the Chapel Royal. Walter Cely, an able administrator, was given an ultimatum by the chapter. He preferred his work at St Cuthbert's and what he could earn as a notary and left. Such changes showed the weakness of the group management system for administering properties. In 1583, Nowell was the sole survivor of the four controlling Waterleaze and messages to Salisbury were necessary to arrange the reassignment of the leasehold interest. In the same year, Cely (now 'sometime vicar choral') had to participate in a transfer of 23 The Liberty.[52] Thereafter, this system fell out of use.

With the exception of John Clarke's activities, attention to the estate faded in the late-1580s. This was the result of other pressures. Both vicars and chapter were suffering from the shortage of suitable personnel for key tasks. In addition, there was friction over control of appointment of new vicars. One result was the grant of Royal Charters to both the chapter and vicars in 1591. The vicars' charter confirmed their right to own property and listed their estate. It also specified their minimum

---

[49] Colchester, *Documents*, Ch. 22b 12; SHC, DD/CC 116013 65-7.
[50] SHC, DD/CC 116013 15, 19, 23.
[51] Colchester, *Act Book*, pp. 15-6, 19, 32, 33.
[52] W. P. Baildon, ed., *HMC, Cal Mss D & C Wells*, vol. II (1914), Ch. 799 709; Colchester, *Documents*, Ch. 21a 9-11; Colchester, *Act Book*, pp. 38-9; Crawford, *The Vicars of Wells*, p. 45.

number as 14, having been running at 12 or 13 in the previous years. However, the Charters did not solve all difficulties. A major crisis occurred in 1592. The chapter had had to accept that vicars could no longer provide keepers of the fabric or communars. The former were now canons but they had to hire lawyers for communars and their fees were high. They, therefore, seemed to have determined to make a stand on two remaining roles, the escheator for administration and the tabular for help in conducting services. In October, they tried to force these roles on John Clarke, senior, and Nicholas Clunn, threatening them with deprivation. When one principal, Thomas Welstead, attempted a legal challenge he was ordered to withdraw his 'inhibition'. He returned with his fellow principal, Humphrey Bayley, and they stated 'that neither they nor the rest of the vicars choral aforesaid doe intend to doe any service in the said Cathedral Church'. They were accused of rebellion and conspiracy but next day second thoughts had prevailed. The principals apologised for their bearing and expressed their intention to celebrate divine office. The posts were again offered to Clarke and Clunn and, when they declined, other volunteer vicars were appointed. The implications of this were explored for some time and, when the Act Book breaks off for 20 years, another dispute was underway about use of priest vicars in baptisms and weddings in the cathedral.[53]

The Stuart kings proved more supportive of the church, abandoning the Tudors' willingness to use it as an unfailing source of resources. There were no more absentee, lay deans at Wells. Churches were also encouraged to rationalise leases so properties were not alienated for long periods. The chapter switched mainly to three-life leasehold but preferred 40-year terms for better properties such as the New Works. Unusually, the vicars were in the forefront and switched their Wells properties to three-lives, except for 11-14a Tucker Street that was leased for 20-year terms until 1748.[54] In contrast, the town on this occasion was the slow one. They ordered a survey of their properties in 1605 to investigate the falling income from fines. It revealed a jumble of terms of years and lives and it took them to about 1640 to settle to the pattern of three-life leasehold.[55]

However, the vicars did not study their leases once made. The longest running lease the Parliamentary surveyors found amongst the ecclesiastical estates at Wells in 1649 belonged to the vicars. It was a South Street property, leased for three lives in 1587 and still held by one surviving life, although assigned to a third party.[56] A more active management would have approached Thomas Salmon, the assignee, and suggested a new lease and, if he was not interested, have offered the reversion elsewhere. This was just the sort of opportunity that had attracted Thomas Hooper and Matthew Naylor in the previous century. But the vicars now had other things to occupy them.

---

[53] Colchester, *Act Book*, pp. 53-9.
[54] SHC, DD/CC 115628, DD/CC 116018 8.
[55] A. J. Scrase and J. Hasler, *Wells Corporation Properties*, pp. 11, 43.
[56] Colchester, *Documents*, Ch. 24 12; SHC, DD/CC 116013 20.

The key issue was the growing crisis that culminated in the Civil War. The townsfolk and the chapter were split between Puritans and others.[57] Although they have not been studied in the same way, it is easy to see similar fault lines in the vicars. Those of a Puritan disposition proclaimed themselves by insulting the bishop in his palace, insulting the dean in both the cathedral and deanery, and in various disruptive activities in services.[58] Estate management was not a priority.

Management from 1660

This part of the story can be told more briefly. A list of 1664 reveals that five vicars were survivors from before the Commonwealth (and the organist John Oker had lived until 1662). Another two were kin of these survivors while a third was kin of a deceased vicar.[59] This was not a group likely to be seeking radical new ways. All the ecclesiastical owners had copies of the Commonwealth survey of 1649, showing how their rents lagged behind market values. None of them chose to change their ways although, in fairness, all had much else to attend to and were faced by a rush to renew long-running leases or replace doubtful ones issued under the Commonwealth. The vicars granted their first post-Restoration lease on 21st September 1660. Within a year they had granted 35 spread over all their lands.[60]

Nevertheless, a great opportunity was lost. In fact, the vicars were unique in improving any rent - for the Christopher. In 1649, it was yielding £7 4s. p.a. and the surveyors suggested an improvement of £12 16s. It was now increased but to £11 4s. This needs to be seen in the context of other owners increasing the rents of inns while rents otherwise remained constant. Thus, between 1550 and 1662 the corporation increased the rent of the Swan by stages from £1 16s. 8d. to £10 and the Ash in the Well from £1 6s. 8d. to £6 2s. 6d. Moreover, the Christopher's increase was not as great as it seemed. The new rent included a row of small shambles in front of the inn. These had previously been separately let at 16s which the surveyors thought should be worth £3 more.[61]

There was a sharp contrast between the chapter and vicars in the use of fines after 1660. The former devoted much of this income to restoring and repairing the cathedral. The vicars seem to have treated fines as a sort of bonus to be divided between them, yielding a good sum some years and nothing in others. Meanwhile their hall and houses needed attention. In 1663, they petitioned the bishop, asking for help in their desperate condition.[62]

---

[57] A. Nott, 'Poxe, Puncke and Puritans', *History Round Wells*, 4 (2001), pp. 2-16; Nott, *Under God's Visitation* (Westbury-sub-Mendip, 2010), pp. 29-38.

[58] W. P. Baildon, ed., *HMC, Cal Mss D & C Wells*, vol. II (1914), pp. 390-1, 393, 395, 396-7, 411, 413, 417.

[59] W. P. Baildon, ed., *HMC, Cal Mss D & C Wells*, vol. II (1914), p. 433.

[60] WCA, VC/E/3/4 95-148.

[61] SHC, DD/CC 116013 16, 22, DD/TD Box 23/3, DD/TD Box 40/76, DD/SAS c/238 (53); A. J. Scrase and J. Hasler, *Wells Corporation Properties*, pp. 37, 50, 51, 177, 180.

[62] Crawford, *The Vicars of Wells*, pp. 61-4.

The nature of the vicars began to change in the years that followed. Recruits were more likely to be graduates or drawn from musical families. Many of the vicars were keen musicians playing instruments. They were a mainstay of Claver Morris' music society that met in their hall until Morris quarrelled with the vicars over a claimed right of way through the close. Disciplinary matters now mainly concerned either absenteeism or undergraduate-style excesses often rooted in drink. Thus, in 1684, Gabriel Green and John Cooper confessed that they had insulted William Piers, son of Canon Piers, and attacked his man in his room at the Mitre. Similarly, in 1688, Robert Hodge confessed he had been in the company of persons who broke windows in the city and liberty. He was warned on future conduct but two years later he had 'gone off'.[63]

This frequent absenteeism or departure of vicars probably reflects their poverty and increased workload. The chapter had by the eighteenth century largely withdrawn from day-to-day cathedral services. The burden fell on the vicars particularly the priest vicars. Crawford entitled her chapter on this period 'Stagnation and complacency?'. This phrase certainly encapsulates their estate management.[64]

Provided they received the usual income, the vicars took no further interest. In *c.*1720, George Hamilton improved his Chamberlain Street mansion, extending its grounds westward, clearing the vicars' properties there and setting it within high walls. He also demolished houses opposite to create a rural view. The vicars continued to lease the sites of Moniers Lane and its two neighbours to him in the usual way. In contrast, the chapter imposed covenants to protect their interest when their house was cleared to open the view and required a lease renewal every 14 years.[65] Similarly, the vicars were willing to trade urban properties for farmland paying the same sum. When Charles Tudway wished to build stables for his new mansion in 1756, the vicars agreed to swap their College Street site for land at Easton. In 1762, they exchanged Chamberlain Street houses for land in Torfield and Dinder.[66]

---

[63] W. P. Baildon, ed., *HMC, Cal Mss D & C Wells*, vol. II (1914), pp. 452-3, 463-4, 466.

[64] Crawford, *The Vicars of Wells*, pp. 69-80, p. 75. The question mark which terminates Crawford's title to Chapter 5 is significant. Whatever the shortcomings of the canons and the vicars, she writes, 'they are not necessarily the whole story ...' and 'if some of the vicars were lackadaisical about performing their duties, others served both the college and cathedral diligently and did their best, within limited means, to maintain their ancient college buildings.' As for the management of the estates, Crawford draws attention to the vicars' survey of their estates carried out in April 1754, using the 1649 Commonwealth Survey as a basis, providing a valuable critical assessment of its implementation. Little, she notes, was done to increase rent values as opportunities arose but 'It was clear that some of the tenants at least, were struggling to pay even the customary ones ... Most ... were subsistence farmers faced with agricultural depressions brought about by severe weather or cattle plagues, who often found it difficult to pay their rents, and were not in a position to take advantage of periods of agricultural prosperity or the advances in farming techniques. Whether the expense of a court action was justified and the vicars were able to collect the arrears is undocumented.'

[65] SHC, DD/DN 92, DD/SAS c/151, DD/TD Box 40/76; WCA, a67, A330, B324; S. Bailey, *Wells Manor of Canon Grange* (Gloucester, 1985), p. 180.

[66] SHC, DD/TD Box 41/3, DD/CC 116014.

For many years, the key estate document remained the Commonwealth survey. When it became worn and difficult to read it was copied into a ledger without updates.[67] Eventually, a new list was made in 1753/4. Hill wondered about this.[68] It was certainly needed where properties had been divided or garden land shifted to a neighbour but the key reason was that the bishop and communar had just done something similar but more elaborate.[69] Then, in the new century, institutional owners in Wells began to commission surveys, in the sense of plans. Bubwith's Almshouse was the pioneer in 1809 with a volume of plans illustrating each house. The chapter followed in c.1815 with a single map. This was less useful as the scale was not sufficient to show minor alterations and it needed an inset for the small properties on Sadler Street. Next, in 1821, the corporation commissioned a volume of plans (figure 12). Finally, in 1828, the precentor also commissioned a volume.[70] The vicars, however, did nothing, relying on written lists.

A final example shows the continuing lack of interest in properties, provided the usual income arrived. They owned an isolated house on the south side of Tucker Street. In 1835, it was leased to the owners of surrounding land. The lessees were to rebuild the house 'lately taken down'.[71] Three years later the Tithe map shows the site thrown in with the adjoining land. The site was not built on again until the late-twentieth century (figures 13 and 14).

Yields

The vicars suffered from two problems in exploiting their Wells properties. Firstly, they operated in a market where rents were fixed by custom and remained constant for centuries. Most institutional rents were fixed by 1600 and many were of medieval origins. The best chance for change was in 1660 but the ecclesiastical owners stuck to old ways. So pervasive was the system that gentry families, the Tudways and Sherstons, who accumulated Wells property and new charities were all constrained to lease for three-lives and if their rents were initially more realistic they were soon outpaced by inflation.

Secondly, the vicars were relative latecomers. By 1348, patterns of benevolence to the cathedral, parish church, town guild and hospital were well established. In the aftermath of the plague the hospital particularly benefited. Furthermore, the borough was then at its most prosperous and a succession of major merchants built up substantial holdings. There were fewer houses readily available to be given to the vicars. What was obtainable was often small or situated in poorer areas such as Southover.

The best rents were found in Market Place, Sadler Street and High Street. Here the vicars had only one full-size burgage, the Christopher. It was supplemented by

---

[67] WCA, VC/E/1/1.
[68] SHC, DD/CC 116014. See also Hill, *PSANHS* 142 (1998), p. 304.
[69] SHC, DD/CC 114081, DD/CC 13202.
[70] WCA, AH/E/553; SHC, DD/CC 5060, DD/CC 10878.
[71] WCA, VC/E/3/10 no. 256.

the small shambles at its front and beyond that a small property in the middle row. The Commonwealth survey gives a unique overview. The Wells properties yielded £23 11s. 8d. which could have been increased to £99 3s. 8d. This is an increase of 320%. But the problems of the holding with its small or badly placed properties is illustrated by comparisons. Improvements of 453% were suggested for the chapter's holdings and 598% for the precentor's 10 well-placed properties. The vicars' average rent also compares badly. At 13s. 1d. it was well behind the chapter's 17s. 6d. and the precentor's 14s. 8d.[72]

This lack of realistic rents benefited others. In 1757, Clement Tudway was assigned the lease of the Christopher. He immediately sublet it for a year for £50.[73] Elsewhere, a rentier class emerged. The Southover tenements were taken by a range of people, farmers from the surrounding area, gentlemen, wealthy widows and more affluent townsfolk. They did not intend to live there but sublet for a good profit. By the nineteenth century better descriptions make it clear that Southover properties had been subdivided. The common form was a frontage house and a number of cottages in a court approached by a side passage or arch. The resultant shortfall in rent in theory should have been covered by the fine. However, both Hill looking at the vicars' estates overall and this present writer, considering the total Wells property market, are agreed that fines remained stable until the nineteenth century.[74]

Conclusion

The vicars were not good estate managers but the other institutional owners were only slightly better. All were constrained by a very traditional market. Some of the others did demonstrate for a time a more active approach. The town authority from 1420 to 1645 was better at reviewing its estate overall and adjusting rents and leases. From 1440 to 1550 the chapter did well in promoting redevelopment of sites. The vicars were prompt in the switch to three-life leases but generally they lagged behind best practice by one or two decades.

There were obvious reasons for the problems. They were primarily selected as singers and not administrators. The major town burgesses and the cathedral canons were more likely to have acquired managerial skills and also funds that sometimes might be invested to help. Such administrative talent as the vicars possessed was often drawn off to help the cathedral. Their own system of administration may have militated against being able to take a long-term overview. Also, in Wells, their properties did not have much potential. When they acquired the garden in The Liberty they leased it for 16s. p.a., a sum the Parliamentary commissioners found (uniquely) to be correct.[75] Only three of their rents for the Christopher, Moniers Lane and 23 The Liberty exceeded that sum.

---

[72] A. J. Scrase, *Wells: anatomy of a property market*, pp. 218-22.
[73] SHC, DD/TD Box 40/76, DD/SAS c/238 (53).
[74] A. J. Scrase, *Wells: anatomy of a property market*, pp. 63-73; Hill, 'The Somerset estates of the Vicars Choral of Wells', pp. 302-4.
[75] SHC, DD/CC 116013 26.

We should beware of applying modern standards retrospectively. In their approach to fines and money from sales when the Act to Redeem the Land Tax began to encourage these there was a total failure to distinguish capital and income. This was true, however, of all the other Wells institutions and such concepts would have been alien. If the vicars failed by the standards and best opportunities of their own day, moreover, it should be recognised that they faced considerable difficulties adapting legal and administrative practices to cope with contemporary demographic, economic, and institutional change.

5. Thoughts on Martin Renger, a 16th-century Somerset Potter

DAVID DAWSON

Robert Dunning is a tireless supporter of the practice of archaeology in the county of Somerset. He has participated in many projects to encourage activity which provided very different kinds of evidence of the history of the county than that commonly held to be the province of the historian. His preface to *The Archaeology of Taunton* epitomises his enthusiasm for the significance of evidence from archaeological fieldwork and excavation in the context of understanding the development of a particular community and our wider understanding of the development of society.[1] It is not surprising then to find that his work as editor of the Victoria County History for Somerset was imbued with current archaeological thought.

'A potter living in the parish [of Over Stowey] in 1591 and probably originating in Flanders may have been responsible for introducing a particular continental style into south-west England'.[2] This paper explores the possible activities of Martin Renger, the potter in question, his relationship with his contemporary West Country potters and their relationship with the wider world.[3] One difficulty noted by many trying to trace the activities of immigrants is the habit of anglicising their surname – Renger to Raineare/Rayneare to Ranger, Jansen to

---

[1] R. Dunning, 'Preface' in P. Leech, ed., *The Archaeology of Taunton* (Bristol, Western Archaeological Trust, 1984), p. iv.

[2] C. R. Elrington, ed., *The Victoria County History of the Counties of England*, R.W. Dunning, A.P. Baggs, and M.C. Siraut, eds., *A History of the County of Somerset*, vol. VI, Andersfield, Cannington, and North Petherton Hundreds (Bridgwater and Neighbouring Parishes) (Oxford, 1992), A.P. Baggs and M.C. Siraut, 'Over Stowey: Economic History', in R.W. Dunning and C.R. Elrington, eds., *A History of the County of Somerset: Volume 6, Andersfield, Cannington and North Petherton Hundreds (Bridgwater and Neighbouring Parishes)* (London, 1992), pp. 165-168.

[3] In the document cited in the VCH as SHC, D\B\bw/1305, his name can be read as Martine Raineare, Martine Rayneare and Martyen Renyer or Renger. The author is aware that Robert Dunning found other possible references to him, one of which, as Andrew Butcher has kindly pointed out, appears as Martin Rayner, 'An Alyante 4d', living in the tything of Byncombe, straddling the parishes of Nether Stowey and Over Stowey in A.J. Webb, *Two subsidy assessments for the county of Somerset in 1558 and 1581-2*, SRS 88 (2002), p. 115.

Johnson.[4]

The concept of the post-medieval revolution in ceramic production, as identified by Graham Dawson in 1979 and reviewed by Ken Barton in 1992, that is the great explosion in the types of pottery in circulation and the technology used to make them, was further refined by David Gaimster in his review in 1997.[5] Gaimster suggests that it is useful to divide the revolution into two phases: the Age of Transition *c.*1450-1550 and the Pre-Industrial Pottery Market *c.*1550-1660. The first phase is characterised by the dominance of imports from mainland Europe particularly the Low Countries and the Rhineland; the second by the making of many of these new wares in England, either by indigenous potters or by potters who have moved across from these areas. Martin Renger fits neatly into this second phase.

The period 1550-1650 is also marked by immigration from the Low Countries and elsewhere on mainland Europe. The skills which the newcomers brought with them were very varied. As ever, the motives that impelled individuals to move to Protestant England are complex but the disruption and devastation visited on those who refused to adhere to Roman Catholicism was a strong motive for many.[6]

Material evidence of immigrant communities is hard to find. One striking piece of albeit circumstantial evidence became apparent in reworking the pottery from Glastonbury Abbey. A substantial group of early to mid 16th-century red earthenwares which consists of jugs from the South Somerset potteries around Donyatt and pans from the East Somerset potteries around Wanstrow and Nunney together with a large quantity of fine imported wares, appears to be associated with the Abbot's Lodging.[7] The implication is that these vessels are associated with the establishment in 1550 of a community of French and Walloon clothworkers with the intention of introducing the art of worsted weaving to the south-west of England under the patronage of the Lord Protector, Edward Seymour, Duke of Somerset.[8] Their endeavours were cut short by the accession of Queen Mary and the suppression of all Protestant activity.

---

[4] K. Tyler, I. Betts, and R. Stephenson, *London's Delftware Industry: the tin-glazed pottery industries of Southwark and Lambeth* (London, Museum of London Archaeology Service monograph 40, 2008), p. 9.

[5] G. Dawson, 'Excavations at Guy's Hospital 1967', *Sur Arch Soc Res*, Volume 7, 1979, pp. 27-65; K. Barton, 'Ceramic changes in the western European littoral at the end of the Middle Ages: a personal view', in D. Gaimster and M. Redknap, eds., *Everyday and Exotic Pottery in Europe c.600-1500: essays in honour of John Hurst* (Oxford, 1992), pp. 246-55; D. Gaimster, 'The post-medieval ceramic revolution in Southern Britain' in G. Egan and R. L. Michael, eds., *Old and New Worlds* (Oxford, 1999), pp. 214-25.

[6] See N. Goose and L. Luu, eds., *Immigrants in Tudor and Stuart England* (Brighton, Sussex Academic Press, 2005) for a full discussion of these issues.

[7] J. Allan, D. Dawson and O. Kent, 'Post-medieval pottery' in R. Gilchrist and C. Green, *Glastonbury Abbey: archaeological investigations 1904-1979* (London, The Society of Antiquaries of London, 2015), pp. 267-9.

[8] H. J. Colwell, 'The French-Walloon church at Glastonbury, 1550-1553', *Proceedings of the Huguenot Society London* 13, 1923-29, pp. 483-515; R. W. Dunning, *Glastonbury: history and guide* (Stroud, 1994), pp. 37-40.

Evidence of attracting potters from the Low Countries to tap into new technology is expressed by Henry VIII's unsuccessful attempt to entice the tile-maker, Guido Andries of Antwerp (otherwise known as Guido di Luca Savino of Castel Durante) to set up a workshop in this country.[9] His sons, Jasper, Joris and Lucas together with Jacob Jansen, did however found at Norwich the first manufactory of tin-glazed ware in England.[10] Tin-glazed ware, commonly known as delftware, demanded new technology and the application of new techniques. The distinctive opalescent opaque white glaze which could so readily be decorated with colorants, primarily rich cobalt blue, producing an effect similar to Chinese export porcelains, became much in demand in the 17th and 18th centuries. It relies on a small percentage of tin oxide being added to opacify a normally translucent lead glaze. Its making also demanded twice firing: first to biscuit, then to firing on the decoration and the glaze. New types of kiln furniture were required to protect and separate vessels in the gloss firing and a new design of kiln.[11] Jasper and Jacob went on to found a successful pottery at Aldgate in London in 1571 but it was to fail c.1617 because they did not recruit locally. It was left to Christian Wilhelm from the Palatinate to re-establish the industry in Southwark from where the technology spread by 1658 to Brislington in Somerset and thereafter to other places in Britain.[12]

In coming to a view on Martin Renger, it is useful to examine a particularly well-documented instance of the changes in an already established earthenware industry brought about by direct involvement from the Low Countries: the case of the potteries of the Blackwater valley on the border between Surrey and Hampshire as researched by Jacqui Pearce and Peter Tipton.[13] Evidence that waste pottery from Farnborough Hill which includes a variety of new forms can be linked to the potter Herman Reynolds (Herman Raignold) who was recorded as an alien in the 1586 Lay Subsidy Rolls for Farnborough.[14] It is evident through archaeological discoveries in the city of London that these new wares found a ready market. It is also evident through the will of another potter, Richard Dee, who owned works in Farnborough and Lambeth and who died in 1593 that a number of other immigrant potters were beneficiaries. Dee's output seems to have included specialist metal working vessels derived from Hessian originals.

---

[9] F. Britton, *London Delftware* (London, 1987), p. 20.

[10] R. Esser, 'Immigrant cultures in Tudor and Stuart England', in N. Goose and L. Luu, eds., *Immigrants in Tudor and Early Stuart England* (Brighton, Sussex Academic Press, 2005), p. 170.

[11] D. Dawson and O. Kent, 'The development of the bottle kiln in pottery manufacture in Britain', *Post-medieval Archaeology,* 42/1 (2008), pp. 211-12.

[12] R. Esser, 'Immigrant cultures in Tudor and Stuart England', in N. Goose and L. Luu, eds., *Immigrants in Tudor and Early Stuart England* (Brighton, Sussex Academic Press, 2005), p. 170; K. Tyler, I. Betts, and R. Stephenson, *London's Delftware Industry: the tin-glazed pottery industries of Southwark and Lambeth* (London, Museum of London Archaeology Service monograph 40 (2008), p. 9.

[13] J. Pearce and P. J. Tipton, 'How technology transfer from the Continent transformed English ceramic manufacture in the 16th century', *English Ceramic Circle Transactions* 22 (2011), pp. 179-213.

[14] J. Pearce, *Pots and Potters in Tudor Hampshire; excavations at Farnborough Hill Convent 1968-72* (Guildford, Guildford Museum and Museum of London Archaeology Service, 2007) pp. 13-16, 194-201.

What of Somerset? The major visible technical change was the ubiquity of iron-rich red-firing earthenwares using a fine fabric in pottery in everyday use. Analysis of the red earthenwares of this date from the three main centres of production, West between Nether Stowey and Wrangway, South around Donyatt and East Somerset between Nunney and Wanstrow, demonstrates how the amount of temper added to the clay matrix has been reduced from 15% and higher to less than 10% and in some cases nearing 1%.[15] Apart from the iron-enriched black-glazed wares, most ware has been reoxidised to red producing glossy brown to green glazes and yellow over white slip.[16] This is in contrast to earlier wares that are much more highly tempered, tend to be reduced grey and have external green glazes. It should be noted that so far there has been no evidence for twice firing of red earthenwares in Somerset (as needed for tin-glazed ware). This was a technique commonly employed on the Continent for making slip-decorated wares and was used by the potters of North Devon. Alison Grant has argued this as one factor to suggest the immigration of potters working in Bideford for example.[17]

The other noticeable change was in the enormous expansion in the range of forms. Before the 15th century the majority of vessels were either coarse open jars or fine glazed jugs. By the 16th century the range included a wide variety of storage jars and cisterns, heavy pancheons, dishes, cups, cooking vessels such as posnets, dripping trays and chafing dishes as can been seen in figure 17.

Although there is no waste pottery yet found at Over Stowey which could possibly be linked to Renger, there is waste from Quantock Cottage Farm at Crowcombe and from nearby Nether Stowey which may give some clue as to what kind of pottery Renger distributed. The waste from Crowcombe may have been dumped as hard-core from over the hill (figure 15). There is no direct dating evidence for this group but the forms of pottery seem to belong to the early 16th century, possibly the late 15th. The kiln furniture includes the kind of cylindrical prop used *c.*1500 at Hemyock, Devon.[18] Unfortunately the range of forms, which includes dishes, pancheons, bowls and jars, mostly unglazed, seems to be incomplete as jugs and cups could be expected. Though probably too early for Renger's work, the group demonstrates that the second phase of the ceramic revolution was underway in Somerset in the early 16th century. The waste from Nether Stowey is late 17th/18th century in date and was published in limited form by Richard Coleman-Smith and Terry Pearson.[19] However by matching the fabric, both visually and chemically, it is possi-

---

[15] J. Andersen, D. Dawson, and G. Rollinson, 'Mineralogical Report on Ceramics' in C. J. Webster, *Taunton Castle* (SANHS, 2016), pp. 285-300.

[16] For an explanation of the process of the oxidised-reduced-reoxidised firing cycle see D. Dawson and O. Kent, 'Reduction fired low-temperature ceramics', *Post-medieval Archaeology* 33 (1999), pp. 164-178.

[17] A. Grant, *North Devon Pottery* (Appledore, 2005), p.39.

[18] Crowcombe is awaiting publication; D. Dawson and O. Kent, 'Evidence of kiln furniture, kiln setting and the structure of kilns', in C. Smart, *Excavations at Churchill's Farm, Hemyock, Devon, 2008,* forthcoming.

[19] R. Coleman-Smith and T. Pearson, *Excavations at Donyatt and Nether Stowey, Somerset* (Southampton: Donyatt Research Group, 1970), pp. 6-7.

ble to identify 16th-century pottery made at Nether Stowey from excavations at Cleeve Abbey and Narrow Quay in Bristol.[20] The group from the reredorter at Cleeve Abbey which seems to have been dumped there at the time of the dissolution in 1536 is a little early to be associated with Renger but in the reconstruction drawing by Richard Coleman-Smith in collaboration with John Allan is a perfect illustration of the kinds of pottery which was in circulation at that time.[21] Partially glazed red earthenwares matched with Nether Stowey waste (jug 20, chafing dishes 22 & 23, cups 25 & 26, pan 28, jars 29 & 31) vie with similar wares from South Somerset (Donyatt) and the odd vessel from North Devon (pan 21) and are accompanied by an assortment of imports typical of an assemblage of this period (from Merida 14 & 15 and Beauvais 16, tin-glazed ware from Italy 17, south Netherlands 18 and Isabella polychrome from Spain 40, and stoneware from Raeren in the Rhineland 41 (figure 16).

The best contemporary example is a much larger group of wares which was ascribed by Terry Pearson to production at Nether Stowey. This was recovered together with red earthenwares from East Somerset and imported fine wares in excavations at Narrow Quay, Bristol, in 1978-9.[22] Of particular interest is the pottery from what has been interpreted as St Clement's Dock (BAC pit 10) which the excavator suggests was backfilled shortly after the launch of the *Minion* in 1581.[23] The assemblage is large and instructive. Of 1,443 sherds identified to an English origin, 50% derive from the West Somerset potteries *i.e.* Nether Stowey. The range of vessels from this source included a minimum of 26 storage jars, 24 bowls, 17 chafing dishes, 15 cisterns, 15 pancheons, 11 jars, 11 sgraffito-decorated dishes, 7 colanders, 5 pipkins and 3 each of dripping pans, costrels and cucurbits. The only form that is missing from West Somerset is the cup. All the cups from this context were supplied from other sources. Storage jars, chafing dishes (a term which covers a variety of very similar but different vessels which function as plate warmers to miniature braziers[24] and pancheons are present at Cleeve Abbey (figure 17, nos 31, 22 & 23, and 28). The cucurbit is a form associated with its matching vessel, the alembic. Distilling apparatus like this is not common but its distribution does seem to be fairly widespread. The underlying use of such apparatus is uncertain though before the Dissolution they are often associated with monastic houses.[25] Eight of the jars are of the distinc-

---

[20] J. Allan, 'Cleeve Abbey: the pottery', *PSANHS* 142 (1998), pp. 41-75; G. L. Good, 'The excavation of two docks at Narrow Quay, Bristol, 1978-9', *Post-medieval Archaeology* 21 (1987), pp. 25-126.

[21] J. Allan, 'Cleeve Abbey: the pottery', *PSANHS* 142 (1998), p. 45, figure 4.

[22] G. L. Good, 'The excavation of two docks at Narrow Quay, Bristol, 1978-9', *Post-medieval Archaeology* 21 (1987), pp. 25-126.

[23] *Ibid.*, p. 34.

[24] P. Brears, 'Culinary artefacts in West Country Households, 1550-1700: form, function and nomenclature', in N. Alcock, J. Allan, and D. Dawson, eds., *West Country Households 1500-1700* (Woodbridge, 2015), pp. 258-9.

[25] S. Moorhouse, 'Medieval distilling apparatus of glass and pottery', *Medieval Archaeology*, 16/1 (1972), pp. 79-121; O. Kent, 'Ceramic finds from archaeological excavations at Glastonbury Abbey, 1901-1979', *PSANHS* 140 (1996), pp. 90-3.

tive bucket-handled form which was a type commonly found in Somerset potteries at this date (figure 16). This particular vessel, though very similar to West Somerset-made pieces, can be confidently ascribed to the potteries of East Somerset (photograph reproduced by kind permission of Bristol City Museum and Art Gallery). The pipkin or more correctly the posnet[26] is a three-legged pot usually with a single handle that forms part of the range of new cooking vessels which accompany the changes in food-preparation in early post-medieval society. Finally, for the first time, we have a securely dateable context for the early appearance of sgraffito ware.[27] The technique which came to be employed in North Devon and at Buckley (Flintshire) and much later at Ewenny in the Vale of Glamorgan, became a distinctive hall mark of the Somerset tradition of pottery-making through to the 19th century.[28] The decoration is made by scratching through a layer of white slip to expose the body underneath. When fired the glaze will assume a yellow colour over the slip but the line will assume a contrasting brown or green appearance depending on the state of the firing when the glaze matured.[29] The border patterns are derived from those found on tin-glazed wares of the period. A commonly used motif in the centre of a dish is the cockerel (figure 18). The feet of the cockerel forming the central motif survive (photograph reproduced by kind permission of Bristol City Museum and Art Gallery). Whilst the use of white firing slip for decoration can be found much earlier in the medieval period and occasionally as at Glastonbury Abbey with scratched decoration,[30] how the technique of sgraffito decoration came to be used in England, in this more expressive way, is a matter of debate. Mary Wondrausch has suggested the pottery of Beauvais was the inspiration.[31] However, Renger, if indeed he was a Fleming, would have been familiar with the technique as sgraffito wares were being produced in the Low Countries and widely distributed earlier in the 16th century.[32] Indeed, a perusal of any late 16th-century assemblage of ceramics from the

---

[26] P. Brears, 'Culinary artefacts in West Country Households, 1550-1700: form, function and nomenclature', in N. Alcock, J. Allan and D. Dawson, eds., *West Country Households 1500-1700* (Woodbridge, 2015), pp. 257-8.

[27] G. L. Good, 'The excavation of two docks at Narrow Quay, Bristol, 1978-9', *Post-medieval Archaeology* 21 (1987), pp. 45-7, catalogue numbers 37-44).

[28] See R. Coleman-Smith and T. Pearson, *Excavations in the Donyatt Potteries* (Chichester, 1988), pp. 152-4, 174-182, 276-306.

[29] D. Dawson and O. Kent, O., 'Reduction fired low-temperature ceramics', *Post-medieval Archaeology* 33 (1999), p. 167.

[30] O. Kent, 'A late medieval jug with lettering from Glastonbury Abbey Somerset', *Medieval Archaeology* 39 (1995), pp. 176-178.

[31] M. Wondrausch, *Mary Wondrausch on Slipware* (London 1986), pp. 57-9.

[32] J. G. Hurst, D. S. Neal, and H. J. van Beuningen, *Pottery Produced and Traded in North-West Europe 1350-1650* (Rotterdam: Museum Boymans-van Beuningen, Rotterdam Papers VI, 1986), pp. 150-3; for an example see J. Gavronski, ed., *Amsterdam Ceramics: a city's history and an archaeological ceramics catalogue 1175-2011* (Amsterdam, Bureau Monumenten & Archeologie, 172 (2012), catalogue number 327). Ultimately the technique can be traced back through Italy to the 11th-century Byzantine empire – D. Papanikola-Bakirtzi, ed., *Byzantine Glazed Ceramics: the art of sgraffito* (Athens, Archaeological Receipts Fund, 1999), pp. 18-20.

Low Countries illustrates affinities in the forms of vessels between what was being produced in Somerset and the earthenwares of that region of mainland Europe.

The document that triggered Dunning's comment and this paper is a lease dated 1591 for a shop and chamber above in the Flesh Shambles in Bridgwater taken in the name of Martine Raineare or Regneare of Over Stowey, potter.[33] It was a shrewd move. The archaeological evidence is clear that over the next two hundred years pottery made in West Somerset was widely traded in the Bristol Channel region.[34] Can one discern a presence in the sparse archaeological record that can be attributed to Martin Renger? The second phase of the ceramic revolution may have been under-way by the time Renger began working. There cannot be absolute certainty that Renger did hale from the Low Countries but as the surname is found there and he belongs to a time when Flemish potters were working in England it must remain a probability. His presence working in this part of Somerset must have boosted changes in the local production of red earthenwares which was clearly influenced by wares made in the Low Countries.[35] Perhaps most intriguing is the coincidence that from the infilling of St Clement's Dock after the launch of the *Minion* in 1581 or shortly after we have the earliest evidence of sgraffito ware decoration produced in Somerset. As with much that Robert Dunning has written, here is food for thought and stimulus for further archaeological fieldwork and documentary research.[36]

---

[33] SHC, D\B\bw/1305.

[34] For example, assemblages have been found in Cardiff, at Penhow Castle, at Cosmeston as well as in Bristol see D. Dawson, with J. Andersen J., and G. Rollinson, 'Characterising post-medieval pottery production centres in Somerset', *Medieval Ceramics* forthcoming; A. Forward, pers. comm..

[35] For the full impact of these changes locally see the 17th-century wares made at Wrangway – T. Pearson with D. Dawson, and M. Ponsford, 'Evidence for 17th-century pottery production at Wrangway, Somerset', *PSANHS* 158 (2014), pp. 81-103.

[36] Acknowledgements: The author would like to thank Chris Webster for the map in figure 1, Kate Iles of Bristol City Museum and Art Gallery for access to the Narrow Quay excavation archive and permission to reproduce the photographs of the material, and Amal Khreisheh of the South West Heritage Trust for access to the Crowcombe archive.

6. Kingston Iuxta Yeovil in 1633

STEVE HOBBS

On the death of Edward Stourton on 7 May 1633,[1] his successor and son William, 11th Baron Stourton, undertook a survey of his manors, domains and liberties, an extract of which is published here. Written on paper and bound in a sheet of parchment, the size of a membrane of a deed, the volume is in excellent condition. It is titled 'A Survey of my Lord Stowrtons land[e]s in the Counties of Wilt[e]s, Dorset and Som[er]set taken before William Hussey and Robert Byflete esquires'. Although centred on Stourton, Wiltshire, most of the fourteen manors were in Dorset, notably Gillingham, Lydlinch, and Stourton Caundle in the north of the county and Overmoigne near Dorchester. The Somerset manors were Kingston by iuxta Yeovil and Frome Selwood. Penleigh in Westbury was the other Wiltshire manor. Several small estates in each county were also covered.

Kingston iuxta (beside) Yeovil (hereafter referred to as Kingston), descended from the Carent family to the Stourtons whose base was Stourton Wiltshire.[2] Following the Reformation, the family suffered for being Catholic and Royalist; its house at Stourton was sacked during the Civil war and its estates were encumbered by debt.[3] It is probable that as a result of the family's vicissitudes very few of its archives survive, which makes this survey of particular importance.

The house and estate were put up for sale in the early 18th century and Stourton in Wiltshire and Stourton Caundle in Dorset were purchased by Henry Hoare, the banker, who set about creating the house and gardens of Stourhead. Kingston was sold to Samuel Rich of Holwell in 1705.[4] Soon after it passed to the Prowse family in whose ownership it reminded until the 19th century.

The book's subsequent history is unknown. It might have passed to any of the various purchasers of the manors. Its excellent condition suggests that it did not

---

[1] G.H. White, ed., The Complete Peerage G.E.C. Cokayne, vol. 12, pt. 1 (London, 1953).

[2] J. Collinson, *History and Antiquities of Somerset* (Bath, 1791), vol. 2, p. 207. William Carent married before 1418 Margaret Stourton, see J.S. Roskell, L. Clark, C. Rawcliffe, eds., *The History of Parliament: the House of Commons 1386-1421* (Stroud, 1992).

[3] *Stourhead* (National Trust 1975 edition of guide), p. 5.

[4] WSA, 967/11, Acknowledgement of the ownership by Sam Rich of Holwell, Somerset, of the manor of Kingston iuxta Yeovil and the advowson of Pitney iuxta Yeovil following its purchase by George Turner from Edward Lord Stourton on behalf of Sam Rich, Apr 1705.

remain at Stourton, since its archive is in a generally poor condition due to exposure to moisture. It was acquired by John Batten, solicitor and antiquarian, of Aldon Lodge, Yeovil, who died in 1900. On the sale of the family library, in 2015, it was purchased by Wiltshire and Swindon History Centre.[5]

The first entry in the volume is the appointment, made 26 August 1633, of Hussey and Byflete as joint stewards. All sub stewards, bailiffs, farmers, tenants and lower officers were charged to assist them. The stewards did not waste time as the first manor, Gillingham, was surveyed 30 August and by the end of October most of the manors had been covered. The remaining few were surveyed in March 1634 and the following September and October. The speed may explain why throughout details of rents of free tenants are left blank, as they are for every manor in the volume, with the possible intention that they would be added at a later date. The stewards travelled to each manor, held meetings at which the freehold, copyhold and leasehold tenants presented the written evidence of their title to their estates, which were presumably compared with the entries in the court book, or the counterparts of the leases.[6]

The free tenants owed homage, acknowledgement of the over-lordship of the lord of the manor and a relief, rent on taking over the tenement, as well as an annual quit rent, both of which were fixed and unchanging. They also owed attendance at the manor court, and could quit their tenancies. However, they are just named in the survey, with no record of their estates or rents, although each name is followed by the preposition 'for' indicating an intention to add these details at a later date.

Customary tenants, those holding by an agreement made in the manor court and said to hold by copy of court roll, were bound more tightly. Copyholders were the successors of the medieval villeins who owed the lord work days on his demesne, as well as other services, but had rights enshrined in the customs of the manor. While these services had ceased by the 16th century, the copyholders fared less well than the freeholders in that annual rent, and a fine, paid on entering a tenement, were not fixed but could be increased. They might be required to have their corn ground in the manorial mill. Like the freeholders they owed attendance to the manor court.

Leaseholders represented a relatively recent development of tenure, in that they held by individual agreement and were not bound by the customs of the manor, although they were required to attend the manor court and use the manorial mill like the copyholders. The distinction between them is emphasised in the survey by the copyhold being recorded in Latin and the leaseholds in English. Both types of tenure were for the length of the longest liver of three individuals named in each agreement. The sole exception for Kingston being Pen Mill which was held by lease for one year, a reflection of the desire of the lord to retain strict control over the maintenance and upkeep of this important building.[7]

---

[5] WSA, 4314/1. Purchased with the assistance of a grant from The Friends of the National Libraries.
[6] For a description of this procedure see E. Kerridge, ed., *Surveys of Lord Pembroke's Manors, 1631-2*, WRS 9 (1953), p. xi. For a digital version go to www.wiltshirerecordsociety.org.uk.
[7] See below p. 83.

The manor comprised 39 copyhold and 25 leasehold estates and is an important genealogical source, particularly as the lives were generally children or close relatives of the tenants. Three tenants held both copy and leasehold estates.[8] Their ages are given, as of 1633. Many of the entries have annotations indicating the deaths of lives and names of current tenants. These appear to have been made in the mid 1640's.[9]

Apart from their linguistic difference, there are important distinctions between these the copyhold and leasehold estates. There are seventeen half tenements among the former indicating division of the ancient tenements of the manor. One is described as being roofless, ie no longer having a building.[10] The leasehold estates are predominantly of land only, with just one tenement and four cottages, two of which are built on the manorial waste. A lease of 24 acres of overland (ie land brought later into cultivation) in Marsh is another sign of their later emergence.[11]

The survey is an important source of topographical detail mainly through the field names recorded. The manor extended across the north side one the town of Yeovil, from Pen mill, which appears to be the manorial mill, in the east, to Ilchester road[12] in the west, and north to Brimsmore and Yeovil Marsh. Place name evidence from the Yeovil tithe apportionment map, indicates a concentration of land around the area of Goar Knap and Pen Mill.[13] Green quarry by Sparrows lane is an early reference to this important local source of stone.[14]

The survey provides evidence of the changing landscape of the manor. There are several examples of land recently enclosed out of the common open fields, a development probably well advanced by 1633.[15] Land in named open fields comprise just seven acres in West Field, about two in Middle Field and about seven acres in East field. However, there are several references to large tracts of land in the fields of Kingston, including one of 30 acres. Such imprecision of identification is puzzling, and may indicate the weakening of the medieval open field system. Although it may be a result of the speed at which the survey was made; the stewards recording the total acreages in the common fields, relying for the details to be found in the individual copyhold and leasehold agreements. This could be an acknowledgement that presumably would be found in the manor court records, sadly no longer extant. Lands described as being closes called Picked Wich and Coppidhill provide evidence of the complicated and piecemeal enclosure of open fields, a feature not at all unique

---

[8] See below, Burford (pp.74,81); Odams (pp.76,79); and Andros (pp.76,77,79).

[9] The age of a life on 31 Oct 1644 is given in an annotation; see below Marchant (p.81).

[10] See below Master (p.77).

[11] See below Brown (p.72).

[12] A close called Picked Wich; see below Master (p.77)., subsequently marked by the Picketty Witch public house, closed 2012.

[13] St Thomas Cross, Dichelmore, Brightmorehill, identified on the Yeovil tithe apportionment map. Much useful work on the topography of Yeovil, including a transcript of a terrier of the rectory of Yeovil, 1590, has been carried out by Robert Osborn. See A-Z of Yeovil's History www.yeovilhistory.info accessed 6 June 2017.

[14] See below Hilson (p.78).

[15] See below Laver (p.74); Moleyns (p.80).

to Kingston.[16]

There are four instances of the letting of demesne land, no longer farmed by the lord.[17] Both developments are a common feature of manors in the West Country from the 16th century. Mention of Bourdeland and customary land, reveal vestiges of medieval custom and practice; the former being land held by borders (villeins).[18] Similarly there are five references to pasture rights each for six oxen, all in Fox lease and Flippinspitt.[19] These fields are described in 1590 as being in the circuit of Marsh.[20]

However, the evidence of the survey suggests that rather than being a discrete area, the manor land was entwined with that of other estates since the total acreage of its tenements do not seem to equate to overall area in which they lay. This view is strengthened by a survey 'and boundinge' of 'Fords Liveing' dated 24 October 1604 (figure 20).[21] The estate comprised 88½ acres. Closes called Preston Townesende, Brimsmore and Lide [Lyde], indicate its extent west, north and east respectively. As well as several closes the estate, included lands in West, Middle and East fields, the medieval open fields, about which little detail is provided in 1633 survey. The bounds of these lands are defined by the adjoining landholders, including Lord Stourton, Sir John Siddenham, Sir John Wyndham, Sir William Carent, Sir John Spencer, John Phelps and thirteen others. None of these were likely to be tenants of the manor and four (Siddenham (heirs), Phelps, Dier, Gaylerd) were possibly free tenants in 1633. Lord Stourton's land presumably referred to the manor of Kingston. This strongly suggests that the manor and tithing were not coterminous, and that the tithing was much larger than the manor. The survey provides two details worthy of mention: two acres in the Middle field are described as being at the beacon, presumably at the northern end on the higher land. Land at Haies end is bounded by the church path from Marsh to Yeovil.

A volume in the Hoare archives is the only other surviving record of the Stourton manors in the 17th century and it may indicate how the manorial system was being re-organised. It is a court and contract (or entry) book, inscribed 'The Right Honourable William Lord Stourton his Courte Book for Enteringe of Bargaines 1674', a title added after the death of 10th baron Stourton, for whom the 1633 survey was made, and the succession of William 11th baron Stourton.[22] The volume begins as a court book for several manors from 1644-1649. A court for Kingston held in 1644 is recorded on the first two pages. However, they are badly damaged and it not possible to draw much detail. The list of the homage, is incomplete; the business seems to be limited to dealing with the surrender of a copyhold estate.

[16] See below Coppid Hill (pp.72,74); Picked Wich (p.77).
[17] See below Everdon (p.74); Batchiler (pp.76,79,80); Andros (p.76,79); Molton (p.82).
[18] See below Everdon (p.74).
[19] See below Parker (p.75); Odams (p.76,79); Hartwell and Sterr (p.81); Hawker (p.82).
[20] Terrier of Yeovil rectory, see A-Z of Yeovil's History op cit.
[21] SHC, DD\Wy/47/3/4. The estate is described as 'Fords Liveing' and was surveyed by John Sully.
[22] William died 25 Apr 1672 (*op. cit. Complete Peerage*). WSA, 383/109.

From 1651 the volume becomes a contract or entry book in which agreements to let land and houses are recorded, and remained in use until 1692. These are noted chronologically and not by manor. Until 1666 most bear the signature, or mark, of the tenant. This change in use could be a strong sign of the breakdown of manorial administration. Certainly no other composite court books survive for lord Stourton's manors. An agreement made 15 April 1664 for the properties held in 1633 by John Symes (figure 19),[23] included the obligation that he must provide 'twise every yeare upon reasonable warninge' for lord Stourton's steward, surveyor, receiver and servants, no more than six, when they come to keep the courts of the manor 'Good & sufficient mans meate horsmeate & lodging meet and convenient for them' for a period not exceeding two days and one night.[24] This might represent an attempt to re-assert manorial custom after the hiatus of the Civil War and Interregnum; one which may well have failed.

As well as providing information on tenure over a 40 year period, the contracts also include useful additional detail to the 1633 survey. Agreements for six year leases of Pen Mill in 1660 and 1665 include the obligation of the tenants to 'discharge the ordinary duties to the Church and poor, presumably to serve as churchwarden and overseer of the poor. They were also were to maintain the mill in good order by providing 'cogges and runges', working parts that needed frequent replacement to maintain the efficiency of the mill.[25] On 4 April 1673 a contact was agreed for John Cary to hold the Sun Inn, 13 months later he took a lease on a house in Rotten Row, formerly occupied by John Hawkins.[26] This predates its famous namesake in Hyde Park, which was completed in 1690, suggesting another rather humbler derivation of the name.

Editorial note: The Freehold and Copyhold sections have been translated from the Latin. However, a few English words are used; one, 'backside', is preceded by the French definite article 'le', the convention in such bi-lingual instances. Here they are indicated by quotation marks. The first two entries of the copyhold section and first of the leasehold section have been translated in full, while subsequent ones have been edited, removing repetitive and formulaic content. Place names and surnames are printed as they appear, while Christian names have been standardized to modern equivalents. Scribal omissions are indicated by a dash. Words struck through are included in brackets > <. Subsequent annotations are in italics with the Latin retained (*mort'* meaning dead, and *modo*, now). Editorial comments are inserted in square brackets.

[23] See below Symes (p.73).
[24] WSA, 383/109 f. 52v.
[25] WSA, 383/109 ff. 45r, 57v
[26] WSA, 383/109 ff. 79v, 82r.

KINGSTON IUXTA EVILL (YEOVIL)

Survey of the manor taken Monday 16 September 9 Chas 1633

Annual rents of free tenants

Heirs of John Sydenham esq deceased under age and in the custody of the king for -, George Hacker for -, John Laver for -, Richard Collens for -, Robert Prowse for -, Thomas Whippie for -, Thomas Silly for -, John Phelps for -, Alice Starr wid for -, William Gaylard for -, William Rich for -, George Brayne for -, Ambrose Lock for -, John Dyer for -, Lionel Whittby for -

COPYHOLD TENANTS

Alexander French jun 21, John French 23, and George French 21, sons of Alexander French sen, hold by copy granted 26 Aug - by Edward lord Stowrton the reversion of a cottage, backside, garden, orchard containing 1 rod (virga) of land in Kingston formerly in the tenure of Christian French, 55, late wife of Alexander sen, for their lives, on the death of Christian. Rent 3s, fine £6. *modo Christian French wid*

Richard Browne holds by copy granted 29 Apr 1626 by Edward lord Stowrton, on the surrender by David Ford and Thomas Ford and a fine of £100, a tenement and 35 acres of land, meadow and pasture in Marsh for the lives of Richard 45 *mort,* and his sons John 12 and Christopher 10. Rent 13s 4d and a heriot when it should arise.

Richard Browne 45 holds by copy dated 26 Aug 1624 by the grant of Edward lord Stowrton, on surrendering his right and that of John Browne, and for a fine of £35, a half tenement or half place called 'the overhouse' and garden and orchard containing 1 acre, and one close of pasture called Kitchill containing 8 acres, one close called 'a parrock' adjoining the said close containing 1 acre, one close of pasture called Linch Parrock containing 1½ acres, one close of pasture called Lewes Close containing 3 acres, one close of pasture called Oxen Leaze containing 4 acres, one close of arable called Beane Close containing 2½ acres, one parrock of pasture lying near Hartwelles house containing 1 acre, 6 acres of land and pasture lying in a close above Coppidhill and 5½ acres of arable lying in the fields of Kingston and Marsh with appurtenances, to have for the same Richard 45 *mort,* Phillip 11 and Christopher his sons for their successive lives for the rent per year 6s 8d.

Joan Clothier wid, Valentine Jacobb and John Jacobb hold by copy 28 Sep 1574 granted by John lord Stowrton, on the surrender of Joan, and fine of £50, a cottage or barn and close of pasture called Court Ash 1 acre, 10 acres of land lying in the fields of Kingston, and two half tenements or places and two orchards 1½ acres, and 31 acres in Kingston, for the lives of Joan *mort,* Valentine *mort,* John 60. Rent 37s

4d and a heriot.

John Perry holds by copy granted 30 Jul 1627 by Edward lord Stowrton, on the surrender of John Wood and Elizabeth Wood his wife by the right of Elizabeth, and a fine of £70, a tenement, 4 closes of pasture lying at Brightmorehill 9 acres, a close of land and pasture at Wilkeford [recte Milkeford] 5 acres, an acre of arable at Penn, an acre of in the Middle field and Brimble furlong and a close adjoining St Thomas Crosse, for the lives of John 48 mort, Jeronimo Perry 12 mort Thomas Perry 11. Rent 10s and a heriot. Alice Perry wid, Thomas Perry.

John Symes holds by copy granted 16 Oct 1627 by Edward lord Stowrton, on the surrender of Anne Molens and a fine of £300, two tenements, 2 half tenements, a cottage and barn, 2 gardens, 3 orchards 8 acres, 2 closes of pasture 14 aces, one of which is called Ryalles and the other Meadeclose, closes of meadow 6 acres, 65 acres of arable, meadow and pasture in Kingston iuxta Evill (except 2 mansion houses called Bennettes and buildings garden and orchard adjoining 1 acre 1 rod, part of the premises formerly held by Robert Burford, rent 4s), for the lives of John mort, John Jeanes 18 mort, Christopher Jeanes 17 mort. Rent £3 17s and 4 heriots.

William Connocke holds by copy granted 11 Sep 1618 by Edward lord Stowrton on the surrender of Edward Burbidge and Elizabeth his wife formerly Elizabeth Smyth, and a fine of £18, a cottage, garden and orchard ½ acre, and 4½ acres of land in Kingston, for the lives of William mort, and his sons Giles Conock 30, John Conock 24. Rent 4s 8d.

<Henry deleted> Giles White holds by copy granted 17 Oct 1622 by Edward lord Stowrton on the surrender of Bartholemew Jacobb and Augustin Trent, and a fine of 40s, 2½ acre of land part of a half tenement formerly held by Joan Jacobb in her widowhood lying in a close called Pickedwick part of a tenement of Lionell Chaplin in Kingston, for the lives of Giles 46 mort, and his sons John 12 and Giles junior 10. Rent £12. English ? Vaman

John Selye holds by copy granted 17 Aug 1615 by Edward lord Stowrton, on the surrender of John Selye senior and William Vyvian, a cottage, garden and orchard adjoining ½ acre and a close of pasture at Brightmorehill 4 acres and 1 rod, and 3 rods in the middle field of Kingston, for the lives of John Selye sen mort, and his sons John 40 mort and William 30 Rent 7s. Fine £17 6s 8d.

Thomas Lane, Joan Ganger [or Gauger] wife of John Ganger hold by copy granted 27 Aug 1624 by Edward lord Stowrton, on the surrender of the said Thomas and Joan, and a fine of £17 a tenement with orchard 1 acre, 2 closes of meadow and 4 closes of pasture 9½ acres, and 3 acres of arable in Marsh, and a cottage and orchard ½ rod, and 1 rod of land in Kingston, for the lives of Thomas 68, Joan Ganger 30 *mort* and Thomas Ganger 14. Rent 12s.

Samuel Carter holds by copy granted 27 Aug 1622 by Edward lord Stowrton, on the surrender of Samuel, Thomas Hellard and Mary Hellard, son and daughter of John Hellard, and a fine of £30, a Cote >within the parish of Martock< and 2 half tenements and mansion houses, a barn, an 'ox house', 'backside', garden and orchard, a 'croft or parrock' adjoining 2 acres, 5 acres in a close of meadow called Bottomes mead, 8 acres of arable or pasture called Field Close, a close of pasture called Bottomes 8 acres, a close called Meadecrafte 4 acres, and 7 acres of arable and pasture in a close called Coppidhill in Marsh and in the manor of Kingston iuxta Evill, to hold for the lives of Samuel 50 *mort*, and his daughters Mary 17 and Joan 15. Rent 13s 4d and a heriot.

Henry Laver holds by copy granted 14 Nov 46 Eliz *sic* [?1603] by Edward lord Stowrton, on the surrender of Humphrey Victor and a fine of £80, a tenement, garden and orchard 1½ acres, a close of arable called Fordes Close 4 acres, and 18 acres of land in the fields of Kingston, of which 15 are newly enclosed, and a tenement in Marsh with 2 closes of pasture 8 acres, a close of arable 12 acres and 2 acres of meadow in Greene Meade, for the lives of Henry 58, and his son and daughter Henry and Mary. Rent 42s and a heriot. *modo Tho Marsh*.

John Tawswell holds by copy granted 2 Jan 1609 by Edward lord Stowrton, on the surrender of the same John and Richard Tawswell and a fine of £10, a cottage, 'backside' and orchard 3 rods, a close of pasture called Cuffes Close 3 acres, an acre of arable called Cuffes Acre in Mudford Perry, for the lives of John *mort* and his sons John 40 and Roger 35. Rent 6s 8d.

Edward Burford holds by copy granted 28 Aug 1620 by Edward lord Stowrton, on the surrender of Edward Molens gent and Anne his wife and a fine of £6 13s 4d, a mansion house called Bennettes with buildings, garden and orchard 1 acre 1 rod, for lives of the said Edward Burford 60 *mort,* and his sons Edward 23 *mort* and William 18 *mort*. Rent 4s and 10s for a heriot.

James Everdon holds by copy granted 2 Jun 1574 by John lord Stowrton, a tenement in Kingston and orchard adjoining 1 acre, a close of pasture called Brimesmore 4 acres, a close of demesne land called Wevernell 12 acres, 26 acres of customary arable and 5 acres arable called Bourdeland lying in the fields of Kingston, for the lives of James *mort,* and his sons Edward 80 *mort* and James 60. Rent 24s. *modo wid Master*

Alice Hayne holds by copy granted 23 Apr 1583 by John lord Stowrton on the surrender of Alice and William Fourd and Christian his wife and a fine of £10, a tenement called Holes Place with orchard adjoining 3 rods, a close of arable 8 acres,

3 rods of meadow lying at Galles Pitt, 6 acres and 1 rod of arable lying in the fields of Kingston, for the lives of Alice *mort,* and her sons George Haine *mort* and Jospeh 50 *mort.* Rent 10s 6d and a heriot. *Modo Giles Hayne.*

Geoffrey Miller holds by copy granted 5 Sep 1604 by Edward Moore knight and the noble lady Frances Stowrton his wife on the surrender of Geoffrey and Elizabeth his wife and a fine of £4, a half tenement and a close of pasture 5 acres lying near Court Ash, ½ acre of pasture lying in Womore, a close of land and pasture at Stonylake 9 acres, a close lying at Ashly 4 acres in Kingston, for the lives of Geoffrey 54 and his son William and daughter Sara. Rent 13s 4d. *Modo Tho Lane.*

James Newman holds by copy granted 10 Oct 1600 by Edward Moore knight and the noble lady Frances Stowrton his wife on the surrender of Ellen Newman and Joan Newman and a fine of £13 6s 8d, a cottage, garden and orchard 1 acre, 2 closes of arable 6½ acres and 1 acre of arable lying in the field of Kingston, for the lives of James *mort,* and his sons John 55 and Nicholas 48. Rent 13s.

Giles Parker holds by copy granted 23 Apr 1588 by John lord Stowrton on the surrender of Thomas Pittman and a fine of £72, a tenement, 'backside', and orchard attached 3 rods, a close of pasture 1½ acres in 2 closes of arable each containing 15 acres of arable in the field of Kingston, a half [acre] of meadow lying in Sockford, half of a tenement and a parcel of pasture called Flepinspitt and Foxleaze with right of pasture for six oxen all the year round, 2 acres in Greenemore in Kingston, for the lives of Giles *mort,* and Giles Marchant 60 and Lucy Marchant *mort,* son and daughter of John Marchant. Rent 42 and a heriot. *Wid Marchant.*

Agnes Game, William Game sen and William Game jun son of Agnes and William hold by copy granted 13 Oct 1631 by Edward lord Stowrton on the surrender of the said William Game sen and Agnes and John Hartwell and a fine of £50, the reversion in two half tenements with garden and orchard attached 1½ acres, 3 rods of meadow lying in Sockeford in Kingston, 30 acres of arable and pasture in the fields of Kingston, for the lives of Agnes 28, William 35 *mort,* and William their son 5. Rent 40s 4d and a heriot.

George Winsor holds by copy granted 17 Apr 1618 by Edward lord Stowrton on the surrender of John Tucker wid, Robert Perry and Mary his wife formerly Mary Tucker and a fine of £160, a tenement and a half tenement in Kingston 2 orchards 1½ acres, a close of meadow 1½ acres another close of meadow at Burymeade 5 rods of land, a close of pasture 6 acres, 5 closes of arable containing 9 acres, 6 acres, 5 acres, 2 acres, 2 acres, and 22 acres of arable in the fields of Kingston, for the lives of the said George Winsor sen 40, and his sons George 20 *mort* and William 14. Rent £32 and two heriots.

Nicholas Odams holds by copy granted 16 Jul 1625 by Edward lord Stowrton on the surrender of himself and a fine of 40d a close of pasture ½ acre in Kingston a dwelling house or cottage with a barn in Kingston, for the lives of Nicholas Odams *mort,* John Odams 33 and Nicholas Odams 40. Rent 4d.

Edward Richman sen holds by copy granted 13 Sep 1621 by Edward lord Stowrton on the surrender of Edward Richmond sen, Henry Willis and Thomas Willis, a cottage, orchard and garden attached 1½ acre, 1 acre of meadow at Ratcliffe Lake, a close of land 1½ acres and 5½ acres lying in the fields of Kingston for the lives of the said Richard *sic* 60 and his sons William 15 and Edward 11. *Wid Richman. Rent 12s.*

George Hacker holds by copy granted 31 May 1625 by Edward lord Stowrton on the surrender of the said George and John Hacker and a fine of £30, 2 closes of arable on the west side of Penn Hill and a close of arable 10½ acres on the east side of that land occupied by George Winsor as subtenant at Penn Hill, 1½ acres of arable above the down in the East field, for the lives of George *mort,* and his daughters Joan 15 and Elizabeth Hacker *mort.* Rent 13s.
memo: that a lane called the mill way formerly held by Mathew Hacker deceased, is now in the hands of the lord on the surrender of Elizabeth, formerly Mathew's wife.

John Flower holds by copy granted 14 Feb 1625 by Edward lord Stowrton on the surrender of Thomas Jacobb and John Jacobb and a fine — a half tenement or a half place and pasture in Kingston, a mansion house, 'backside', orchard, part of a barn and garden 1½ acre, 4 closes of arable and pasture lying together at Lide 9 acres, a close of arable and pasture called Brimscombe 4½ acres occupied by Thomas, (except that part of the barn on which John Jacobb built a cottage on as much of the garden as Joan Jacobb wid deceased the mother of Thomas and John and the said John [Flower] surrendered for the use of John), the same John 50 *mort,* and his daughters Dorothy 21 and Joan 26. Rent —

Roger Traske holds by copy granted 14 Apr 1614 by Edward lord Stowrton on a fine of £100, the reversion of 2 half tenements in Kingston held by Roger by the right of Temperance his wife, for the lives of Roger *mort,* and his sons Arthur 26 and Edward 20. Rent 14s 10d. *modo Jo. Pinnfeild*

Richard Batchiler holds by copy granted 13 Apr 1609 by Edward lord Stowrton the reversion of a dwelling house called Mileres Well, a 'backside', orchard and garden annexed containing 5 acres in Kingston, for the lives of Richard 34 *mort,* and Mary 27 his wife, on the death of John Batchiler *mort.* Rent 2s. Fine £10

William Andros holds by copy granted 2 Jun 1574 by John lord Stowrton, a tenement in Kingston, garden and orchard 3 rods, a close of arable called Curlesmore 3 acres, 11 acres of arable in the common fields of Kingston, for the lives of William *mort*, and his sons William 60 and James. Rent 7s 7d. Fine £30.

Edward Richmond holds by copy granted 4 Apr 1623 by Edward lord Stowrton, fine £60, a cottage orchard and garden ½ acre, 5 acres of arable in Kingston, for the lives of Edward >Richard< 60 and his sons Edward 11 *mort* and Roger 10. Rent 6s 8d

Giles Rogent holds by copy granted 28 Apr 1603 by by Edward Moore knight and lady Frances Stowrton his wife on the surrender of John Speere, a cottage and 3 acres of land adjoining, for the lives of Giles 45, Nicholas Speere and Priscilla Smyth 40. Rent 4s.

William Phelps holds by copy granted 17 Aug 1615 by Edward lord Stowrton on the surrender of William Phelps and Faithful Phelps, a cottage with garden and orchard annexed 3 acres, a close pasture called Nether Lease 1 acre, 3 acres 3 rods in Kingston field, for the lives of William *mort,* and his sons Edward 22 and John 20. Rent 15s 4d.

Edward Master holds by copy granted 6 May 1631 by Edward lord Stowrton on the surrender of Lionel Chaplin and a fine of £60, a half tenement 'Roveles' [roofless] on part of a half tenement on which was but a cottage or dwelling house with orchard, garden, a close of meadow 1½ acres lying in Greenemore, a close of arable at Langlandes Bush 4 acres, 5 acres of arable in a close called Picked Wich, 2 acres and 3 rods lying in the fields of Kingston, a little close of arable lying at Picked Wich 1 acre, for the lives of Edward 28, and his brothers Samuel Masters 16 and Anthony Masters. Rent 17s 2d and a heriot.

William Jenynges holds by copy granted 28 Aug 1620 by Edward lord Stowrton on the surrender of his right and a fine of £50, 3 half tenements or place in Kingston, a 'backside' and orchard ½ acre, a close of pasture called Townesende close 2½ acres, a close of pasture and arable called Pennmillham 10 acres, a close of pasture called Barrowhay 3 acres, 8 acres of pasture at Disshillmore and a cart way, 20 acres of arable lying at Bodham, 2 acres and 3 rods in Wemore, 19 acres of arable lying in the fields of Kingston, for the lives of William *mort,* and his sons Giles Jenynges *mort* and and John Jenynges 24. Rent 37s and 2 heriots *{3 written above}. Modo wid Jenninges*

Thomas Pullen holds by copy granted 17 Oct 1622 by Edward lord Stowrton, a fine of 10s, a cottage built on the lord's waste at Marsh with a garden adjoining 20 goads, for the lives of Thomas 60 and his sons Thomas and William. Rent 16d. *Modo Chappell.*

William Turner holds by copy granted 28 Aug 1620 by Edward lord Stowrton on the surrender of William Limbry and a fine of £4 4s, a cottage in Marsh with garden annexed 1 rod, for the lives of William 47, and his daughters Grace Turner 16 and Agnes Turner 13. Rent 16d. *Couper*

John Rodbert sen holds by copy granted 12 Apr 1609 by Edward lord Stowrton on the surrender of Henry Slape and Denise Nicholas and a fine of 30s, a cottage built at Marsh with garden adjoining, for the lives of John 60 *mort,* his daughter Joan Rodbert 30 and son John Robert *mort.* Rent 12d.

Mathew Hacker holds by copy granted 14 Aug 1623 by Edward lord Stowrton a fine of 10s, a half tenement or place at Townsend, a 'backside', a close of meadow and pasture lying on the east side of Penn Mill, a close of arable below lying at Penmill 13 acres and 3 rods, for the lives Mathew *mort,* John Hacker 45 *mort,* and Joan Hacker 40 wife of Thomas Taylor. Rent 13s.

Benjamin Starr 16 *mort* and Edmund Starr 25, hold by copy for lives a cottage with garden and orchard adjoining ½ rod pasture belonging to the cottage called Hardermeade, 3 acres of arable and a Peters Stitch lying in East field. Rent 3s.

Thomas Luckest -

LEASEHOLD TENANTS (In English)

Richard Browne sen gent holds by indenture dated 20 Oct 20 Jas [1622] by the grant of Edward late lord Stourton, Sir William Stowrton now lord Stowrton and dame Frances his wife, in consideration of a surrender of a former lease of the place hereafter mentioned determinable on the death of one William Cooke and a of £70 fine, all that overland containing 5 acres of meadow, 16 acres of pasture & 3 acres of arable in Marsh in the manor of Kingston iuxta Evill (except trees with liberty to carry the same away) to hold the same from the date of the indenture to the said Richard Browne the elder for 99 years if Richard Browne younger 15 *mort,* John Browne 12, Phillip Browne 11 sons of the said Richard senior or either of them so long live under the yearly rent of 33s 4d payable quarterly by even portions and one capon at Christmas or 12d at the lord's election (choice), and suit of court.

William Hilson and Richard his son hold by indenture dated 14 May 1609 granted by Edward late lord Stowrton and a fine of 40s, a plot of ground lying waste called The Greene Quarry in Kingston at the end on west side Sparrows lane, for the lives of William 70 and his sons William 32 and Richard 28. Rent 12s and suit of court.

John Pike holds by indenture dated 20 Oct 1622 granted by Edward late lord Stowrton, Sir William Stourton now lord Stourton and dame Frances his wife, and in consideration of a former lease determinable on the death of John Tulke and a fine of £5, a cottage or dwelling house built by George Tulke on the waste near St Thomas Crosse with 14 perches of ground, for the lives of John, Henry and William, sons of the said John Pike. Rent 12d and suit of court. *modo Nich Rodber.*

William Seward holds by indenture dated 1 Oct 20 1631 granted by Edward lord Stowrton, Sir William Stowrton now lord Stourton and dame Frances his wife, and in consideration of a former lease determinable on the deaths of Ambrose Lock and Joan his wife and Katherine his daughter and a fine of £55, a close of pasture 15 acres called the Redgrove and a several close of meadow called Omore 3 acres (except all timber trees and liberty to carry them away), to hold for the lives of Ambrose Seward 16, Samuel Seward 14 and Thomas Seward 7. Rent 21s and 33s 4d for a heriot.

Nicholas Odams sen and Nicholas his son hold by indenture dated 10 Nov 7 1609 granted by Edward late lord Stowrton, in consideration of the surrender of a lease for 60 years determinable on the death of Rt Hon lady Frances late wife of John late lord Stowrton, and a fine of £80, a close of pasture [in] Meaderne Downe 2 acres, 1 acre 1 rod of meadow Greene More, 2 acres of arable in Bicken Close and right of pasture for 6 oxen in Flippins Pitt and Fox Leaze (except ½ acre in a close called Hallandes and trees and liberty to carry them away), to hold for the lives of Nicholas the father *mort,* his son Nicholas 30 *mort,* and Joan 27 his daughter. Rent 20s.

John Bachiler holds by indenture dated 12 Oct 20 1622 granted by Edward late lord Stowrton, Sir William Stowrton now lord Stourton and dame Frances his wife, and in consideration of a former lease determinable on the death of John and a fine of £10, 2½ acres of pasture sometime part of the demesnes lying in the fields of Kingston at a place called Milkeford, (except all timber trees and liberty to carry them away), to hold for 99 years and the lives of his sons and daughter, John Batchiler *mort,* Richard Batchiler 34 and Mary Batchiler 27. Rent 16d.

William Andros holds by indenture dated 1 Jun1574 granted by John late lord Stowrton, in consideration of a fine of £20, a close of pasture called Brimmsmore in Kingston 4 acres and 11 acres in the lord's demesnes, to hold for the lives of William *mort,* and his sons William 60 *mort,* and Thomas *mort.* Rent 7s. *Reversion granted to Sterr*

Reynold Courtney and Joan his wife and Giles their son hold by indenture dated 14 May 1609 granted by Edward late lord Stowrton in consideration of the surrender of a lease and a fine of 40s, a cottage with garden and plot of ground in Kingston called Pennway; to hold for the lives of Reynold *mort,* Joan his wife *mort,* and Giles 40 their son. Rent 12d.

John King holds by indenture dated 12 Oct 1622 granted by Edward late lord Stowrton, Sir William Stowrton now lord Stowrton and dame Frances his wife, for the fine of 40s, a cottage built on the waste of Kingston near the pound 11 perches of ground in length and 24 in breadth; to hold for 99 years and lives of John 40, John 26 his son and John Albin *mort*. Rent 26d and suit of court. *Now Edw Willes*

William Jennings, Giles Jennings & Edith Jennings, his children hold by indenture dated 1 Jun 1574 granted by John lord Stowrton, for the fine of £26, a cottage called Howne Hill in Kingston, a little close of pasture called Fore Strete Bridge 3 yards, 4 acres of meadow lying in Dichelmore and Meade under Downe & 14 acres of arable of the lord's demenses in Kingston fields. Rent 17s 8d and suit of court. *Now Jo Jennings.*

Edward Molyns gent holds by indenture dated 28 May 1622 granted by Edward late lord Stowrton, Sir William Stowrton now lord Stourton and dame Frances his wife, for the consideration of the surrender of a lease made by the said Edward Molyns and a fine of £60, a close of land or pasture called New Close 3 acres, a close of land or pasture called Cox Close 5 acres, a close of meadow called Caplins close 4 acres, and a newly enclosed close in the common fields of Kingston on west end of New Close 10 acres, ½ acre of pasture lying upon the highway near Brimsmore (except all trees and liberty to carry them away), to hold for 99 years for the lives of the said John Molyns 22 *mort*, and Henry Molyns 13 *mort,* sons of Edward and John Jennings 24 son of Giles Jenninges. Rent 49s 6d; 1 capon at Christmas and doing suit of court. memo this lease now belongs to mr Giles Jennings by assignment from mr Edward Molyns.

John Hardinge holds by indenture dated 12 Oct 1622 granted by Edward late lord Stowrton, Sir William Stowrton now lord Stowrton and dame Frances his wife, for the consideration of the surrender of a lease determinable on the death of John Batchiler and a fine of £20, 5 acres of arable enclosed at a place called Hardermeade, 1 acre of meadow in Greene More, in Kingston (except all trees and liberty to carry them away), to hold for the lives of John Harding *mort,* and his sons Samuel Harding 38 *mort,* and John Harding 12. Rent 5s. *Tremer Rood?*

John Dampyer holds by indenture dated 1 Sep 1631 granted by Edward late lord Stowrton, Sir William Stowrton now lord Stowrton and dame Frances his wife, for the consideration of the surrender of a lease of 99 years determinable upon 2 lives and a fine of £260, a tenement with 7 closes of pasture 37 acres (except all trees and liberty to carry them away); to hold for the lives of Mary Dampier 32 his wife, and his sons John 6 and Joseph 4. Rent £3 2s 4d, doing suit of court and a heriot of best animal.

William Forward holds by indenture dated 28 May 1622 granted by Edward late lord Stowrton, Sir William Stowrton now lord Stowrton and dame Frances his wife, for the consideration of the surrender of a lease and a fine of £140, a close of meadow or pasture called Disselmore 8 acres, Hardermeade 2 acres, (except all timber trees and liberty to carry them away); to hold for 99 years or the lives of William's son Jerome Forward 40, Giles Jenninges 16 son of Giles Jennings and William Laver 24 *mort.* Rent 16s 8d, a capon at Christmas or 12d and doing suit of court.

Henry Hartwell and William Sterr hold by indenture dated 1 Oct 1631 granted by Edward late lord Stowrton, Sir William Stowrton now lord Stowrton and dame Frances his wife, for the consideration of the surrender of a lease determinable on one life and a fine of £40, 4 acres of arable on the east side of Roger Traske's land upon the Mylmes in the West Field, 6½ acres of arable in a close by itself on east of the said 4 acres, 2½ acres of arable lying in Colethorne, ½ an acre of meadow in Greene More, right of pasture for 6 oxen in Fox Leaze, 1 acre in a close called Flepinspitt (except all trees and liberty to carry them away), to hold for 99 years or the lives of Alice Sterr 22, Mary Sterr 2 her daughter and Richard Monckton 25. Rent 26s 4d and 20s for a heriot 'for every ones death dyeing in succession', and doing suit of court.

Henry Hartwell and William Sterr hold by indenture dated 1 Oct 1631 granted by Edward late lord Stowrton, Sir William Stowrton now lord Stowrton and dame Frances his wife, for the consideration of the surrender of a estate for 3 lives and a fine of £25, of right of pasture for 6 oxen in Fox Leaze and 1a of ground (except all timber trees), to hold for 99 years or the lives of Alice Sterr 22, Mary Sterr 2 her daughter and Joan 30 the wife of Francis Beacham. Rent 11s 8d and 13s 4d 'upon either death dieing in succession.'

Edward Burford holds by indenture dated 3 Jul 1613 granted by Edward late lord Stowrton, a close of pasture called Wallrons 9 acres and 1 acre of meadow in Greene More, to hold for 99 years and lives of Edward 56, and his sons Edward 23 and John 20; rent 12s 1d. *Now Ed Burford.*
Memo this lease now belongs to John Harford by assignment from John Burford therefore see the counterpart for this is only recited in the assignment.

Giles Marchant hold by indenture dated 1 Sep 1631 granted by Edward late lord Stowrton, Sir William Stowrton now lord Stowrton and dame Frances his wife, for the consideration of the surrender of one life and a fine of £60, 2 acres of pasture lying in the south part of Penn, 2 acres of arable in East Field, a close of arable 5 acres, 3 acres of meadow in Greene More (except all trees), to hold from the date if the indenture for 99 years or the lives of Katherine Parker wid 40 *mort,* John White 12 and Giles White 10, sons of Giles White. Rent 24s 4d and 34s 4d for a heriot. *Jo White 26 years on ultimate {day} of Oct 1644.*

Nicholas Patten holds by indenture dated 24 Oct 1614 granted by John late lord Stowrton for the fine of £50, a close of meadow at Meaderne Downe 4 acres, 1 acre of meadow in Greenemore, 3 acre of arable in West Field (all timber trees excepted); to hold for the lives of Nicholas *mort*, and his sons William 28 and Joseph 18. Rent 11s 8d

Thomas Punfold holds by indenture dated 20 Oct 1622 granted by Edward late lord Stowrton, Sir William Stowrton now lord Stowrton and dame Frances his wife, for the consideration of the surrender of one life and a fine of £5, a cottage and 'backside' 1 yard; to hold from the date of the indenture for 99 or the lives of Walter Robbins 52, Mary his wife 50 and Mary Bolster 20 daughter of John Bolster of Marsh. Rent 16d and doing suit of court.

Fides [Faithful] Phelippes holds by indenture dated 20 Oct 1622 granted by Edward late lord Stowrton, Sir William Stowrton now lord Stowrton and dame Frances his wife, for the consideration of the surrender of one life and a fine of 200 marks, 5 closes of land, meadow and pasture called Swyncombe 40 acres (except all timber trees), to hold from the date of the indenture for 99 or the lives of her sons Joseph Phelippes 25 *mort,* Edward Phelippes 22 and John Phelipppes 20. Rent 5s and doing suit of court. *Now Jo Phelippes Rent 10s.*
memo that Edward late lord Stowrton, Sir William Stourton now lord Stowrton and dame Frances his wife, by indenture dated 20 Oct 1622 (reciting the grant by indenture dated 28 May 1622 to Thomas Grubham of a pasture ground called Ashley 5 acres, to hold for lives of Thomas 46, Martha 40 his wife and Elizabeth 16 their daughter. Rent 2s 6d; covenant to levy a fine to confirm the same.

Thomas Hawker holds by indenture dated 20 Oct 1622 granted by Edward late lord Stowrton and dame Frances his wife (sic), for the consideration of the surrender of one life the sixth part of Flippens Pitt and Fox Leaze, and in consideration of 2 other lives surrendered and a fine of £120, a close of pasture called Flepingspitt 37 acres (except all timber trees and one acre part of Fleppenspitt lately laid to Fox Leaze); to hold from the date of the indenture for 99 years and lives of Thomas Hawker 44 *mort*, James Appletree younger 17 and John Jennings 30. Rent 35s; a capon at Christmas or 12d and suit of court.

Nicholas Molton, Faith Molton and Elizabeth Molton his daughters, hold by indenture dated 26 Jan 1615 for the fine of £21, a close off pasture 1 rod, a close of pasture 6 acres, 3 acres of arable, part of the lord's demesnes in Kingston (all timber trees excepted); to hold for the lives of Nicholas 60, Faith 21 and Elizabeth 23. Rent 10s, with a licence of attorney to make livery but none indorsed.
Memo that this lease is now by meane assignment come to Anthony Traske.

Edward Burford holds by indenture dated 25 May 1622 granted by Edward late lord Stowrton, Sir William Stowrton now lord Stowrton and dame Frances his wife, for the consideration of the surrender a lease granted to Edward Molyns gent and a fine of £40, a close of arable called Couch Close 10 acres in Kingston (except all timber trees with liberty to cut and carry away the same); to hold for 99 years from the date of the lease for lives of John Burford 23, William Burford 20 and Edward Burford 25 his sons. Rent 12s; a capon at Christmas or 12d and suit of court.

Agnes Jennings did hold Pen Mill for 1 year from 24 Jun 1634 under the yearly rent of £40 payable quarterly.

7. A Somerset Gentleman & Landowner: Thomas Smyth of Ashton Court, Long Ashton 1609-1642

JOSEPH BETTEY

When Thomas Smyth was born, in the medieval mansion of Ashton Court, he became heir to an extensive estate, a fine manor house on a hillside overlooking the busy port and rapidly-growing city of Bristol, and a large fortune. The wealth had been accumulated by his great-grandfather, the highly-successful Bristol merchant, John Smythe (d.1555). The survival of John Smythe's account book or *Ledger* for the years 1538-1550 provides a detailed picture of his business activities.[1] He exported woollen cloth which he purchased from weavers in Somerset and Wiltshire sending consignments to various ports in France, Spain, the Mediterranean and the Netherlands. He traded in leather from the Forest of Dean, lead from the Mendips and large quantities of wheat. Returning ships brought wine from Bordeaux, iron from Spain, and woad from Toulouse and the Azores. Large quantities of wheat were carried to Spain. This needed an expensive export licence and gifts to customs officials in Bristol. Much of the grain was loaded into ships from lighters or 'trows' brought down the Severn and transferred near the mouth of the Avon at Hung Road or King Road, no doubt without troubling the customs. Other items of cargo listed in the *Ledger* included oil, soap, fruit and spices. Goods were distributed throughout the west country, using the complex system of road carriers regularly operating from Bristol, as well as by the well-developed coastal shipping service. Prudently, the goods were conveyed in different ships, including his own ship the *Trinity*. His large-scale trading activities brought him great profits which he invested in land and property in south Gloucestershire, Somerset and Bristol, establishing subsequent generations of the family as major landowners. His most important purchase was the Ashton Court estate which he bought from Sir Thomas Arundell in 1545. Other purchases of surrounding lands at Long Ashton and properties in Bristol, as well as in Somerset, ensured that John Smythe was able to pass on to his sons a fine estate with a large manor house set within its own exten-

---

[1] J. Vanes, ed., *The Ledger of John Smythe 1538-1550*, BRS, XXVIII (1975).

sive park.[2]

Not only was John Smythe an able merchant, he was also public-spirited, becoming one of the forty members of the Common Council of Bristol from c.1530, serving as sheriff and as mayor in 1547 and 1554. He played a major part arranging for the city to profit from the dissolution of the religious houses and, later, the suppression of the chantries, overseeing the purchase of lands and properties which were to make Bristol one of the richest corporations in the country. He had two surviving sons, Hugh (b.1530) and Matthew (b.1539). The wealth acquired from his successful trading activities enabled him to ensure that they were raised as gentlemen and were not intended to follow their father's occupation of merchant.[3]

In 1545, both boys were sent to Oxford, although Hugh was only 15 and Matthew was a child of 12. Neither took a degree and do not appear to have been assiduous scholars. From Oxford they took the route common for the sons of wealthy country gentlemen and went on to study at the Inns of Court in London in 1550. While in London, they seem to have been in trouble for fighting and bad behaviour. This was so serious that in 1552 their father was obliged to call upon the good offices of his friend and fellow Bristolian, Dr George Owen, who was the personal physician to the king, to intercede on their behalf. It cost John Smythe £40 to settle the matter. In view of their behaviour, Hugh was ordered back to Bristol and installed as a country gentleman at Ashton Court. In 1553 he was married to Maud, the younger daughter and joint heiress of Hugh Byccombe of Crowcombe. The marriage brought lands in Bishops Lydiard, Stogumber, Timberscombe and Dunster to the estate. Meanwhile Matthew remained at the Middle Temple in London where he was to pursue a lucrative career as a lawyer and became a prominent member and treasurer of the Middle Temple.[4]

Living at Ashton Court, Hugh Smyth continued to add to the estate he had inherited on the death of his father in 1555. Among the properties he acquired were several Somerset manors around the south side of Bristol, including Bedminster, Bishopsworth, Whitchurch, Compton Dando and Brislington. In spite of his wealth and position as a justice of the peace, Hugh Smyth's violent disposition and capacity for annoying his neighbours continued throughout his life. He maintained a gang of ruffians at Ashton Court who terrorized the neighbourhood and there were constant complaints about his conduct. These came to the attention of the Privy Council and there were frequent warnings about his behaviour, but he remained unrepentant. Hugh Smyth died in London in March 1580 where he was awaiting trial for his involvement in the death of one of his servants during a night-time raid which his men had conducted on the rabbit warren belonging to his neighbour, Sir George Norton of Abbots Leigh.[5]

[2] J. Bettey, 'The Smyths of Ashton Court c1500-1642', *Oxford Dictionary of National Biography (ODNB)*, 51 (2004), pp. 426-8.
[3] BA, AC/C2/1; AC/D1/143-50; 36074/13, 14, 15, 36.
[4] J. Bettey, 'Hugh Smyth of Ashton Court 1530-81', *PSANHS* 136 (1992), pp. 141-8.
[5] *Ibid.*

Hugh Smyth had a daughter, Elizabeth, who was married to Edward Morgan of Llanternam in south Wales, but he had no son, therefore the estate passed to his brother Matthew. Matthew died three years later in 1583, leaving his widow, Jane, to manage the estate on behalf of their son, Hugh, who was eight years old when his father died and was to be the father of Thomas Smyth. His mother, Jane, proved to be an active and efficient steward of the properties adding further land and extending the park at Ashton Court. It was probably Matthew, with his lawyer's training, who established the muniment room at Ashton Court and began the tradition of careful record keeping. Certainly, from his time as owner, a formidable quantity of correspondence, estate records, surveys, wills, inventories and all sorts of personal documents survive up to the final occupation of Ashton Court by members of the family during the twentieth century. These are now in the Bristol Record Office. Hugh Smyth came of age in 1596 and in 1603 he was one of the numerous gentlemen who travelled to the Midlands to welcome James I on his progress to London, following the death of Queen Elizabeth. At Worksop, Hugh Smyth received a knighthood from the King. The rise of the family to national prominence was completed in 1604-5 by two events. As a leading Somerset landowner, Hugh Smyth was considered sufficiently important and wealthy to be married to Elizabeth Gorges, the eldest daughter of Sir Thomas Gorges of Longford Castle in south Wiltshire. This brought an alliance with a well-connected family and close links with the Court. Sir Thomas Gorges had been a gentleman usher at Court and had married Helena, the young and strikingly beautiful, Swedish-born widow of the Marquess of Northampton (figure 21). Her story is the stuff of fantasy. She had come to England in the reign of King Eric of Sweden, who was one of the suitors of Queen Elizabeth. She remained in England as one of the Maids of Honour to the Queen and in May 1571 she married William Parr, Marquess of Northampton. He was 58 years of age and she was 18. Marriage to a young Swedish lady proved too much for the Marquess, who died in October 1571, leaving an attractive wealthy widow. Her second husband was Sir Thomas Gorges and it was their daughter, Elizabeth, who married Sir Hugh Smyth (figure 22) and in 1604 became the mother of Thomas Smyth (figure 23), who was the only son, although she had five daughters.

Sir Hugh was a melancholy man, afflicted with ill-health and constantly complaining in his surviving correspondence about his affairs. He seems to have possessed only two interests, one was the breeding of horses for racing and hunting, the other was in the latest London fashion in clothes. His portrait, which is now in the Red Lodge, Bristol shows him as a fierce, brooding figure dressed in a suit of black armour which he had ordered from Baptist Fortune at the Tower of London. His wife, Elizabeth, devoted her care and attention to their only son, Thomas. This is evident from a delightful collection of letters addressed to Thomas when he was sent to St John's College, Oxford, in 1622 at the age of 13. Sir Hugh continued to add to the estate and, among other purchases, acquired the 'Great House' which had been built on the site of the former Carmelite friary on St Augustine's Back in Bristol by Sir John Young (1519-89) during the years 1566-74. Sir Hugh and his wife, Elizabeth, were occasionally resident there, and it gave the Smyth family a mansion in Bristol, re-establishing the family's close links with the city.[6] Having been brought up at Longford Castle, with a constant stream of visitors, including members of the royal family, Elizabeth Smyth was understandably frustrated by her isolated life at Ashton Court with a depressive husband. This is evident from a letter she wrote to Thomas at St John's College, Oxford, on 19 May 1626:

> Here comes not any but such as are sent for, and coler [anger or irascibility] dothe as much abound with us as ever it did, God increase my patience to endure it stille, which for the hopes I have of great comfort in you now and hereafter makes me now to suffer.[7]

Thomas Smyth's early years, education and marriage

Thomas Smyth received the conventional upbringing considered appropriate for the heir to a large estate. The earliest portrait shows him at the age of three, still dressed, as was the custom of the time, in the elaborate long clothes with a ruff, lace head-dress and cloak, all remarkably unsuitable for a small boy. The portrait now hangs on a wall of Leeds Castle in Kent. The subject is only identified by a faded inscription, evidently added later. It was spotted by the late Miss Elizabeth Ralph, the former City Archivist of Bristol, whilst on holiday in Kent. Until the age of 13, Thomas was educated at home with his sisters. His comfortable life at Ashton Court with a doting mother and sisters ended in 1622 when he was sent to Oxford. The numerous letters he received from his anxious mother have been preserved and provide an interesting personal account of his time at St John's College. Thomas had a private tutor, Dr Thomas Atkinson, whose frequent letters to Sir Hugh Smyth report the boy's progress. Naturally Atkinson was at pains to assure Sir Hugh of his diligence in supervising Thomas's education, emphasising that his main purpose was to prepare the boy for his life as a wealthy country gentleman. His aim is set out in a revealing letter to Sir Hugh on 27 May 1624:

> I was ever an enemy to plodding in any one, most of all in a Gentleman. And I know itt is not your intent to have him earne his bread by his books. When you left him here I tooke upon mee the charge of a Gentleman. I shall blush to returne him you again a mere Scholler. If God say Amen to my intentions I will better him every way to my poore power, and I wilbee guilty of nothing which may either impaire his health or understanding.[8]

Letters to Thomas from his mother, Elizabeth, show a different aspect of his sojourn in Oxford. Ground down with the strain of living with the depressive and

---

[6] R. Gorges, *The Story of a Family* (Boston, 1944); J. Bettey, 'Sir John Young, Dame Joan Young and the Great House in Bristol', *B&GAST*, 134 (2016), pp. 221-30.

[7] BA, AC/C48/4.

[8] BA, AC/C44/4.

valetudinarian husband, she threw herself into concern for the health and welfare of her son. In the first of her letters dated 14 May 1622 she exhorts Thomas to tell her of everything he did:

> ... for the delittes you dayely beholde I pray make the like observation of all things worthey of note as if you wear a travelor in a foraine country. I hope you will be carefull for your healthe, which I must put you in mynde of.[9]

She arranged for the family's London tailor, Henry Betty of Temple Bar, to make clothes for Thomas and to go regularly to Oxford for fittings. No doubt the teenaged Thomas was growing rapidly. Even in 1626 when Thomas had been at Oxford for four years, his mother was still concerned about his clothes and his health. In a letter of October 1626, she wrote:

> I hope Betty toucke measure of you, beinge with you, that when he makes your winter clothes they may be bige inoughe. I know you will have care to keepe
> your selfe as warme as you may when the cold weather comes in with such as you have. Remember your necke and feett. Thus praying to God to bless you in
> all your good causes, I reste in hast your loving Mother.
> Your sisters commends them to.[10]

Sir Hugh Smyth's ill-health, depression, refusal to leave Ashton Court or see any of his relatives continued to give cause for great concern. Several letters survive urging him to adopt a more active life-style. He did try daily taking the waters at the Hotwells, just across the river Avon from Ashton Court, but apparently with little success. Towards the end of 1626, Sir Hugh's health deteriorated even more and Thomas, then aged 17, was brought home from Oxford and a marriage was hastily arranged for him. The reason for the haste was to prevent Thomas becoming a ward of court while still a minor. In a further sign of the way in which the Smyth family had risen in society, Thomas's bride was Florence Poulett (figure 24), the eldest daughter of Lord Poulett of Hinton St George. The marriage took place early in 1627 and brought the family to the forefront of Somerset society. Shortly after-wards, Sir Hugh Smyth died and was buried in the family vault in Long Ashton parish church.

The newly-married young squire of Ashton Court was thoroughly likeable, with a gift for making warm friendships. Unlike many of the early members of the Ashton Court family, Thomas was a normal and agreeable person, singularly free of the crippling depression which had made his father's life such a misery. Thomas

---

[9] BA, AC/C48/1.
[10] BA, AC/C48/5.

developed a close friendship with his father-in-law, John, Lord Poulett and with his brother-in-law, Denys Rolle. He maintained regular correspondence with other members of the Somerset gentry families, to many of whom he was related by marriage. These included the Horners of Mells, the Nortons of Abbots Leigh, the Phelips of Montacute, the Pophams of Houndstreet (now called Hunstrete), the Gorges of Longford, Wiltshire and of Wraxall in north Somerset, the Rogers of Cannington and the Tynte family of Chelvey. His correspondents all write to Thomas in the most friendly terms with invitations for him to visit them, and he maintained contact with a wide circle of friends. His many friends address him as 'Honest Tom', 'Sweet Tom', 'Good Friend' and conclude with 'Your affectionate friend' or 'Your faithful friend'. Sadly, many of these friends were to choose to fight on a different side in the Civil War.

The marriage to Florence Poulett was evidently happy, judging from the numerous charming letters which Florence wrote to her husband and which he obviously kept carefully. She was 15 years old and Thomas was 17 when they married. The early letters from Florence are understandably formal and hesitant, but they rapidly became much warmer and affectionate. During her childhood at Hinton St George, Florence had a rudimentary education and her letters are often disorganised and badly-written with many alterations and idiosyncratic spelling, nonetheless the letters reveal a growing love between the two young partners. The marriage was to last only 15 years, but produced several children.

The bride and bridegroom could scarcely have known each other before they pledged lifelong devotion in the marriage ceremony. Almost immediately after the wedding, Thomas became an MP and was away in London so that several letters from Florence to her husband in London survive. At first she addressed him as 'Mr Smyth' and ended with 'I am your tru constan friend and wife Florance Smyth'. Soon the letters became more intimate, with endings such a 'So I rest yours til deth', assuring him of her love and hoping that he will soon come home, 'For my part tis not day or nitli that I wish for thee but ourli'. In a letter from Hinton St George on Ash Wednesday, 1629, Florence told her husband that she had sat up so long playing cards with her father that she could scarcely see 'yet if thou wart in the bed I should kepe my eyes open'.[11] In the same letter, Florence confessed that she was bothered at the thought of having been involved in witchcraft. One of the servants named Loker had lost a dish which could not be found in spite of intensive search. Unknown to Florence, another servant:

> … went to the divell for it. She sent to a woman at Bristol before I knew it which hath mutch troubelled me for of all things I hated witchcraft, but I have prayed God not to lay the sin to my charg, nor I hope he will for I was inosent of it.

---

[11] BA, AC/C60/1-16.

Whatever advice was received from 'the woman at Bristol' the dish was found, for Loker 'had lokt up the dish in his box'. It was left to Thomas to deal with Loker when he returned. Florence proved to be an admirable wife and in spite of her youth ably managed the estate and mansion at Ashton Court during Thomas's frequent absences. They had two sons, Hugh who was born in 1632, and Thomas who was born soon after his father's death in 1642; there were six daughters of whom four survived infancy.

Member of Parliament and justice of the peace

No doubt due to the influence of his father-in-law, Lord Poulett, Thomas, soon after his marriage, became one of the two members of Parliament for the borough of Bridgwater in 1627, although he was only eighteen years of age. From the first he was an active and energetic member of Parliament, assiduous in attending sittings of the House of Commons. He kept notes of some of the debates, recording speeches by Sir Edward Coke, John Pym, Sir Miles Fleetwood and Sir Thomas Wentworth. He made notes of speeches made before the Petition of Right in 1629 and must have observed the dramatic scene when the Speaker was forcibly held in the chair while the King's actions were condemned. Having become an MP at such an early age, however, he had little personal effect himself on the parliamentary proceedings. The corporation of Bridgwater, which in spite of Lord Poulett's urging had initially been hesitant at electing such a young man as one of their two MPs, were evidently pleased with the way in which he had conducted himself in London and signified their gratitude for 'the worthy pains taken for this Corporation in the late session of Parliament'. Their appreciation was further increased by the gift from Thomas of a buck from the deer-herd in his park for the burgesses to feast upon.[12] During the times he spent in London for the parliamentary sessions of 1628 and 1629, Thomas stayed with the tailor, Henry Betty, who had made his clothes while he had been at Oxford. Florence's letters are addressed to him 'At Mr Betty's the Taylor's House by Temple Bar' or 'Leave this letter at Mr Betty the taylor's house without Temple Bar near the signe of ye blue ancker'.

In 1638 Parliament was recalled and Thomas again became a member for Bridgwater, but the increasing unpopularity of the royal policy both in religious and secular matters, and Thomas's connection with Lord Poulett who was a leading supporter of the Crown, meant that he soon lost his seat. He briefly became a member for the county of Somerset in 1640, and he was successful once more in Bridgwater at a by-election in 1641, which occurred after the election of Edmund Wyndham had been declared void. Because of the many Smiths in the House of Commons, it is impossible to be sure of the contribution to debates made by Thomas Smyth, but he was evidently an active MP. His letters contain much information about the fierce political controversies of these years.[13] There is much more

---

[12] A. Thrush & J. P. Ferris, eds., *The History of Parliament: The House of Commons 1604-1629*, VI (Cambridge, 2010), pp. 357-58; BA, 36074/47; 36074/117a; 36074/120.
[13] BA, 36074/156a.

about the political history of these momentous years in the letters Thomas received from two ardent royalists, his father-in-law, Lord Poulett and a cousin Baynham Throckmorton of Tortworth, Gloucestershire.[14]

Unlike his earlier spell in Parliament when he was still very young, Thomas was now a well-respected gentleman of 32, and it is significant that in 1641 he received the freedom of the City of Bristol, continuing the close relationship between the Smyth family and the City which was to continue until the twentieth century. The certificate granting the freedom refers to:

> ... the mutual love and amitie which for many yeares past hath been by and between the Burgesses and Inhabitants of the said cittie and the right worshipful Gent. Thomas Smith of Long Ashton in the county of Somerset Esquire and other his Ancestors and Allies as also for the better contynuacion of their ancient frendshipp for the time to come.[15]

Thomas became a justice of the peace at the Quarter Sessions held in Taunton during the summer of 1631. Thereafter, he regularly attended the sessions held at Wells, Ilchester, Taunton and Bridgwater. The justices dealt with a multitude of matters including crimes, rioting, drunkenness, illegitimate children, disputes between parishes over matters such as the repair of bridges, maintenance of roads and the care of paupers. Thomas evidently impressed his fellow justices with his good sense and reliability and was appointed to several responsible posts. With Thomas Luttrell of Dunster, he was made Treasurer for Hospitals in July 1633, and he was appointed Treasurer for Maimed Soldiers at the sessions held at Bridgwater in October 1634. He served on several commissions to settle parochial disputes in the northern part of Somerset and became involved in the controversies which attended the collection of the King's new and unpopular tax known as Ship Money. It was his experience of the hardship which this tax caused to the poorer section of society which meant that Thomas was less wholehearted in his support for the royal policy than his father-in-law Lord Poulett or his step-father Sir Ferdinando Gorges.[16] In January 1637, for example, Thomas wrote to his friend William Bassett of Claverton, who was Sheriff for that year, to complain that he had received numerous complaints from the inhabitants of the hundreds of Portbury and Bedminster because of the heavy burden of Ship Tax they were called upon to pay. In a long letter Thomas argued that the tax was higher than had been accustomed and should be reduced. He pleaded for a delay so that the load could be more evenly spread:

> By which means your selfe may come the easier by the money and the differ-

[14] BA, AC/C61/3-5; 36074/136a-d.

[15] BA, 36074/77 Freedom of the City of Bristol, 28 September 1641.

[16] E. H. Bates Harbin, ed., *Somerset Quarter Sessions Records Vol. II, Charles I, 1625-1639*, SRS XXIV (1908). Elizabeth Smyth's marriage to her cousin, Sir Ferdinando Gorges in 1629 will be discussed later.

ence be composed, with lesse charge unto the poore inhabitants. Otherwise I feare you will finde the people rude and addicted unto opposicon. I leave it unto your consideration and present my service unto your selfe and your Lady

I affectionately remayne
Your freind and servant
Tho Smyth[17]

In the following year, 1638, Thomas narrowly escaped being appointed to the unpopular and onerous office of sheriff himself. As a wealthy landowner he was an ideal candidate to undertake the duties. Thomas Meautys, the Clerk to the Privy Council, listed him as a suitable person to be chosen, since he was worth £2,000 per annum and was son-in-law to Lord Poulett. In fact, Thomas wrote to Meautys pleading to be excused, and mentioning the support of Sir William Portman of Orchard Portman and two 'boosome freindes' John Coventry of Barton Grange, Pitminster and Sir Robert Phelips of Montacute, meanwhile assuring Meautys of his gratitude. The plea was successful and Thomas escaped selection.[18]

Home life and estate management

The decision by Charles I in 1629 to rule without all the criticism of royal policy by parliament meant that Thomas Smyth and Lord Poulett, like many other gentry, were able to spend their time on their estates. Throughout the 1630s, Thomas Smyth threw himself into estate management, the cultivation of friendships with relatives and acquaintances, participation in local affairs and major building work to enlarge the medieval mansion at Ashton Court. He was fortunate in having the services and guidance of his bailiff, John Edwards, who was thoroughly competent and trustworthy. While he was away from home, letters from Edwards kept him informed of changes in tenancies, deaths of tenants, heriots or death duties payable to the estate, disputes over common rights, sub-letting by tenants and other matters. A particular concern was the income derived each year from the fattening of young cattle in the park at Ashton Court and on the demesne farm. The cattle were brought from Wales by drovers and were sold at spring-time fairs for keeping on the lush Somerset grassland before sale in Bristol, Bath or being driven to London. For their maintenance during the autumn and winter the hay-crop was vitally important and there are many references to it in the correspondence. The account book kept by John Edwards during the years 1631-6, and regularly signed by Thomas, provides full details of estate affairs, employees and finances.[19] Letters from Florence also provided information about the estate. Florence had been brought up on her father's estate at Hinton St George and was thoroughly conversant with the importance of careful estate management and the running of a household. She

---

[17] BA, 36074/149.
[18] BA, 36074/150.
[19] BA, 36074/72.

did not hesitate to make it quite clear to the household servants and the farm workers that she was in charge. For example, in a letter to Thomas, who was visiting London on 13 October 1631, she told him of rebuking the labourers for allowing rats and mice to damage one of the corn ricks before it could be threshed and of reprimanding the gardener for his idleness and drunkenness:

> I have given your gardiner warning to be gon unles I find maters in beter order when I come home againe for the garden was like a wilderness. I think it ware your best corse to get a good gardiner whare you are, for I cannot abide this sotish felo. I fere God is offended with us for keping sutch felos as wee have.[20]

Following the death of Thomas's father, Sir Hugh Smyth in 1627, Thomas's mother, Elizabeth, did not long remain a widow. In 1629, she married a cousin, Sir Ferdinando Gorges. He could hardly have been more different from her first husband. Sir Ferdinando was an active soldier, explorer, courtier and promoter of schemes for the establishment of colonies in New England. He had fought in the Netherlands and had obtained a knighthood for his services at the siege of Rouen. In recognition of his encouragement of colonies across the Atlantic he was named as the first Governor of New England and Lord Proprietor of Maine by Charles I in 1639. He came from the branch of the Gorges family who held an estate at Birdcombe Court in north Somerset. When he married Elizabeth Smyth in 1629 it was his fourth marriage. They lived at the Great House on St Augustine's Back in Bristol which Sir Hugh Smyth had bought in 1613, and in the Lower Court at Ashton Phelips, one of the subsidiary manors within the parish of Long Ashton which had become part of the Smyth estate. Thomas Smyth was soon on good terms with his stepfather and they were both to fight in the royal cause during the early months of the Civil War.[21]

One matter which concerned Thomas during the late 1630s was the education of his only son, Hugh, who was eight years of age in 1640. A private tutor, Mr Foster, was employed as a teacher, but like many small boys Hugh was not a dedicated scholar. His tutor was in a difficult position. He was treated as a high-status member of the household and dined with the family, but his relationship with his pupil was carefully watched. He was criticized if too little progress was made and yet was condemned if he was thought to be too severe or imposed harsh punishments. A letter to Thomas from John Edwards in June 1641 illustrates the problem. Edwards had evidently been asked to report on estate business and on Master Hugh's progress:

---

[20] BA, AC/C60/3.
[21] For details of the eventful career of Sir Ferdinando Gorges (1568-1647), see *ODNB*, 22 (2004), pp. 992-4.

Ashton 26

June 1641

The Collier is about the Charcole and wee shall keepe him close to his business Our haymaking hath bin much hindered by means of the wett we have had this 4 or 5 daies …

I have acquainted Mr Foster with what you wrote, and first for Mr Hughe hee saith that hee loyters as much since you went as hee did whilest you weare at home, and seldome comes to praiers at nighte. I see Mr Foster is troubled at it, the child's good and his engagement soe much being at stake, and there being as much tyme spent in play as there is in following the booke … instead of going forward its well yf hee keepe that which hee hath already lerned. Mr Foster conceaves the way to remedie this is to have the childe kepte to his booke as in a tender and loving way, soe in some discreate awe too, and yet without any correction, for hee affirmeth hee enclynes not that way.[22]

As one of the wealthiest families in Somerset, the Smyth establishment at Ashton Court operated on a grand scale. A note dated 1641, in Thomas's handwriting, provides details of the household, dining arrangements and expenses. There were 17 indoor male servants. The highest paid was John Edwards, the bailiff, who received £6 per annum, the lowest wage was given to 'Austin the Foole'. Possibly Austin was employed as a jester, but it seems more likely that he was a mentally-retarded man employed to do menial jobs around the house. On formal dining occasions in the hall the male servants sat together at the Hall Table, seven hinds or outdoor servants sat at the Hind's Table, the seven chambermaids had no table assigned to them, no doubt because they waited on the others. Eight diners were accommodated on the Family Table, consisting of Thomas Smyth, Florence, their son, Hugh, their five daughters and Mr Foster who was Hugh's private tutor. Thomas calculated that the annual cost was £548 made up as follows:

First in wages	£100
22 beeves [bullocks] @£5 per beeve	£110
100 sheepe @13s 4d	£66
340 bushells of malt	£52
In bread we spend £5 per month	£60
In Acates etc. [other provisions]	£80
In wyne	£40
In spice	£20
In soape	£5
In cole	£15
	£548[23]

---

[22] BA, 36074/140c.

[23] BA, 36074/78 Note on Household Expenses 1641. The Rolle family held extensive estates in Devon.

In 1637 and again in 1640, Thomas had spent much time drawing up a formal agreement with his father-in-law, Lord Poulett and his brother-in-law, Denys Rolle, for amalgamating their households and sharing expenses. The three families got on well together and spent much time visiting each others' mansions. Nothing came of these complex negotiations, partly no doubt because they were overtaken by political events and conflict.[24]

Building work at Ashton Court

During the period 1630-34 Thomas Smyth had a major extension added to his mansion (figure 25). At the same time, Lord Poulett constructed a large addition to his mansion at Hinton St George. Both buildings are in the same classical style, which was advanced for the period, but there is no indication of an architect who was responsible for the designs. The extension at Ashton Court was 143 feet long and provided two storeys plus attics and reflects the wealth, social status and lifestyle of the Smyth family. The building work was supervised by Christopher Watts, master mason of Bristol, whose name occurs in the account book which records some of the expenditure. Some stone came from quarries on the estate and other stone was purchased from the quarry at Dundry which had earlier supplied stone for Bristol churches and the Augustinian abbey. High quality stone was brought down the river Avon from quarries around Bath and was unloaded at Rownham on the estate. The accounts refer to payments to workmen for digging foundations, masons, scaffolders and carpenters, though many others were evidently paid separately and their wages are not recorded. Other payments were made for the supply and transport of timber, lime, sand and glass. Apparently based on pattern books or buildings which Thomas had seen in London, the architecture does not match the sophistication of later classical design. The thirteen, square-headed windows with heavy pediments on each floor are not evenly spaced but arranged in 3 +2 +3 +5 configuration which is somewhat confusing to the eye. Above are nine oval lights to the attics which again are irregularly distributed. Nonetheless, this was an impressively modern building for its time, especially set against the gothic architecture of the earlier parts of the mansion.[25]

Friends and relations

It is a tribute to Thomas Smyth's warmth and charm that he had so many friends. He was connected by marriage with many of the influential families of the west country, and his correspondence shows that his friendship was valued and that his opinions were greatly respected. Many of his relatives and especially his sisters, relied on his help and advice. He was on good terms with his grandmother, the formidable Helena, Marchioness of Northampton, whose second husband was Sir

---

[24] BA, 36074/73,76.
[25] BA, 36074/72, 74, 76, 140, 156. Michael Jenner, 'A New Style 1556-1700' in A. Gomme, M. Jenner, B. Little, eds., *Bristol: An Architectural History* (London, 1979), pp. 81-3.

Thomas Gorges of Longford castle, Wiltshire. The connection with the Gorges family was further strengthened in 1629 when his widowed mother, Elizabeth, married Sir Ferdinando Gorges. Thomas approved of the marriage and became friends with Sir Ferdinando. Although a distinguished soldier and a pioneer of encouraging settlement in the New World, Sir Ferdinando had little experience of land management and depended on the advice he received from Thomas. In 1632 Thomas's mother wrote: 'Mr Gorges and I are resolved to take no more tenants but such as shall seeme beste in your judgement, for such as shall be held fittest in your esteeme shalbe harkened unto and no other.'[26]

The marriages of Thomas's sisters and other relatives involved him with other local families. His sister Helena was married to Sir Francis Rogers of Cannington and Thomas frequently visited them. His sister Mary was married to Sir Thomas Smith of Hough near Chester; she often wrote to her brother to seek his advice and he visited her in 1632. Mary had numerous problems, many of which could be ascribed to her frequent pregnancies; she was to produce 22 children. He was frequently consulted by Anne Tynte who was married to Sir Thomas Tynte of Chelvey. She was the daughter of Sir Edward Gorges of Wraxall, brother of Sir Ferdinando. Her husband died in 1629 leaving her with five young children including John aged 11 who was heir to extensive lands in Somerset. She turned to Thomas for help and he accepted the joint wardship of her son and advised on the management of the estate.[27] This proved to be a considerable burden since John Tynte became a headstrong and difficult youth who seemed to be constantly in trouble. Thomas's aunt, Bridget, who was his mother's younger sister, also sought help with her family problems. She had married Sir Robert Phelips of Montacute, but he proved to be a leading supporter of parliament against the King which brought him into conflict with Lord Poulett. The extravagant life-style of Sir Robert Phelips meant that Bridget was always short of money and unable to provide dowries for her daughters. She wrote frequently to Thomas to complain about her problems. Thomas was also connected with the Rodney family of Rodney Stoke through the marriage of Matthew Smyth's daughter, Anne, to Maurice Rodney.

Apart from his many relatives Thomas enjoyed warm friendships and regularly corresponded with many of the local gentry, even with those who took a different view of the political controversies of the time. He was on good terms with Sir Ralph Hopton of Witham, William Bassett of Claverton, John Pyne of Curry Malet, Sir John Stawell of Cothelstone and Alexander Popham of Houndstreet (now called Hunstrete) in the parish of Marksbury. Thomas was a close friend of Alexander Popham, who was to be an outstanding commander of the parliamentary forces during the Civil War. The two men supported each other in the election of 1639 and Alexander Popham, who became MP for Bath, urged Thomas to join with Ralph Hopton, who was to be a royalist commander: 'for I am sure I have not two frends

[26] BA, AC/C48/18.
[27] M. J. Hawkins, ed., *Sales of Wards in Somerset 1603-1641*, SRS LXVII (1965), pp. 73-5.

more worthy nor that I can more hartely searve in yt'.[28] He also promised that his father, Sir Francis Popham, 'intends to canvis all the west for you'.[29]

Thomas regularly met Alexander Popham at Quarter Sessions and both were frequently involved in commissions to arbitrate on parish disputes in north Somerset. As close neighbours, the Smyth and Popham families frequently visited each other and in a letter of 1640 Alexander Popham sent good wishes to Florence Smyth, who was pregnant, 'to whome I wish a happie deliverance of her litell Hance'.[30] The eventual rift between the two men was one of the many tragedies caused by the unwanted conflict. The extensive correspondence in the Smyth archive reveals the close contact Thomas maintained with many other local families, including the Horners of Mells, the Dodingtons of Combe Sydenham and Barrow Gurney, the Horseys of Clifton Maybank and the Bassetts of Claverton.

Civil War And The Death Of Thomas Smyth

When the Civil War began in 1642 such a wealthy landowner as Thomas Smyth was compelled to take sides. There is evidence to suggest that he was critical of many aspects of royal policy and opposed to the ecclesiastical ambitions of Archbishop Laud in the years leading up to the conflict and that he was not such a strong supporter of the Crown as his father-in-law or his step-father. As a J.P., he had been made well aware of the difficulties which the hated 'ship money' tax had created in local communities and he had refused to contribute to the so-called 'loan' for the war against the Scots.[31]

Nevertheless, when the fighting began, Thomas came down decisively on the side of the King. He responded immediately to a letter from Charles I from Beverley, dated 11 July 1642, appointing him one of the Commissioners of Array for Somerset and requiring him to raise troops to fight in the royal cause. On 7 August 1642, Parliament ordered that Thomas Smyth be apprehended 'for enforcing the Commission of Array' and he was declared delinquent in both Houses of Parliament.[32] His own contribution was to raise a troop of horse and join the local royalist contingent led by the Marquess of Hertford. Not all of his tenants answered his call to arms, however, and the parliamentarian, John Ashe of Freshford, claimed perhaps with some exaggeration, that 'there came to us every one of Master Smyth's tenants, 40 yeomen well armed'. [33] The royalists assembled in Wells and Thomas was present when they confronted the parliamentarians in Shepton Mallet on 30

---

[28] BA, 36074/133a.

[29] BA, 36074/133b.

[30] *Ibid.*, the reference to 'litell Hance' is a corruption of a Dutch or German phrase *'Hance-en-Kelder'* ('Hans in the Cellar') meaning an unborn child.

[31] T. G. Barnes, *Somerset 1625-1640: A Country's Government During the Personal Rule* (Oxford, 1961), p. 135; BA, 36074/149.

[32] *Calendar of State Papers (Domestic) 1641-43*, 366; BA, AC/F6/8.

[33] A. R. Bayley, *The Great Civil War in Dorset, 1642-60* (Taunton, 1910), p. 43; John Wroughton, *The Civil War in Bath and North Somerset 1642-50* (Bath, 1973), pp. 30-1.

July. The result was inconclusive, but he took part in the much more serious conflict which occurred on 5 August when a royalist force from Wells encountered a poorly-armed and ill-prepared group of parliamentarians under the command of Alexander Popham and John Pyne at Marshall's Elm near Somerton. In the ensuing battle several men were killed or died later from their wounds. The bloodshed of the Civil War had begun in earnest.[34] In spite of this temporary triumph, the royalists in Wells were greatly outnumbered and were surrounded by parliamentary sympathisers in the surrounding area. Accordingly, the Marquess of Hertford ordered his men to abandon the city and take refuge in Sherborne Castle. They remained under siege in the castle for six weeks when the strength of the opposing forces compelled them to withdraw and undertake a forced march to Minehead where they proposed to take ship for the short crossing to join the royalist sympathisers in Wales. They were able to rest briefly in Lord Poulett's mansion at Hinton St George, but were refused admission to Dunster Castle by Thomas Luttrell. They left Sherborne on 19 September and reached Minehead on 22 September. They hoped to secure passage in some of the many ships which brought young cattle to Minehead from south Wales, but the season for such trade was over and they found only two ships in the harbour. This was insufficient to accommodate the whole force and only Lord Poulett, Sir Ferdinando Gorges and Thomas Smyth and a few leading figures secured passage to Cardiff. The privations of the siege at Sherborne and hardships of the march through the hostile territory of west Somerset had evidently taken their toll and in Cardiff Thomas fell ill, possibly of small-pox. He died on 2 October 1642.[35] His body was brought back to Long Ashton church for burial in the family vault. It seems likely that Florence had been able to visit him in Cardiff before his death, since in a note of the formal expenses she incurred on behalf of her son, Hugh, aged 10, who was now heir to the Ashton Court estate there is written 'Left with my Lord when I went from Cardiff £8'. The mention of 'my Lord' probably refers to her father, Lord Poulett.[36] The total cost of the funeral came to £137 17s. 0d.

Thomas had made a will dated 27 March 1638. In it he requested a funeral 'without any unnecessary expenses', and provided bequests for his wife, Florence, his son, Hugh, and four surviving daughters – Florence, Elizabeth, Mary and Helena. Each daughter was to have a marriage portion of £2,000 and was to be given 'a complete and religious education'. There were bequests to his servants and to the deserving poor of Long Ashton, Bedminster and King's Weston.[37] At the time of his death, Florence was again pregnant and a second son was born late in 1642. He was named Thomas after his father. The Smyth family practice of preserving records and correspondence in the muniment room at Ashton Court has meant that much more can be known about their estate, sources of wealth and family relationships than

[34] D. Underdown, *Somerset in the Civil War and Interregnum* (Newton Abbot, 1973), pp. 34-43.
[35] D. Underdown, *op.cit.,* pp. 42-44.
[36] BA, AC/F9/1 Note of the costs of Thomas Smyth's funeral.
[37] BA, AC/F7/7 Thomas Smyth's will, 27 March 1638.

about many other similar gentry families. The mass of documentation which survives provides great detail about Thomas Smyth's life, his character and concerns. His untimely death brought to an end a period of peace and prosperity at Ashton Court. Thomas's heir, Hugh, was only 10 years old when his father died and the estate was to suffer greatly during the coming years when Parliament was triumphant. Even after the Restoration financial problems continued, but recovery came eventually and the family was to remain at Ashton Court until the mid-twentieth century.[38]

[38] **Sources:** The major part of the Smyth's archive upon which this account of Thomas's life is based was deposited in the Bristol Record Office when the contents of the Ashton Court mansion were dispersed after the Second World War. These documents are listed under the reference AC/-. A second collection of Smyth documents was purchased by the City of Bristol at a Sotheby's sale in 1977. This part of the collection has the reference 36074/-. Extracts from the family correspondence during the period 1548-1642 can be found in J. Bettey, *Calendar of the Correspondence of the Smyth Family of Ashton Court*, Bristol Record Society, XXXV (1982).

I have benefited from many discussions with the late Anton Bantock on our mutual interest in the Smyth family history, and I value his gift of a specially-bound copy of his book *The Earlier Smyths of Ashton Court* which was published by the Malago Society in 1982. Dr Jenny Gaschke of Bristol Museum and Art Gallery and Amal Khreisheh of Somerset Museums Service kindly gave pemission for the use of portraits in their collections. I am grateful for the help received from successive archivists at the Bristol Record Office, and to John and Kate Bettey for their assistance.

8. A Sequestrator's Lot is Not a Happy One: Edward Curll, Sequestrator of Catsash Hundred

MARY SIRAUT

It is widely recognised that, after the Civil War, Royalists had their estates seized and confiscated or in effect sold back to them for considerable sums, often after years of argument with the County Committees. But what of the estates and farms, which had to be managed during the often protracted negotiations? The forfeited estates were placed in sequestration as property of the County Committees who appointed a pair of sequestrators for each hundred to deal with the affected property. The sequestrator's job was not an easy one but few details have survived of their work. Sequestrators received a generous penny in the shilling on all estates they secured so it was undoubtedly in their interests to sequester as many as possible. The County Committee was also in desperate need of money.

In the case of Catsash hundred (figure 26), the area between Castle Cary and Queen Camel in south Somerset, two sequestrators, Edward Curll or Curle and William Gander, were appointed between 1645 and 1647, the latter probably related to the hundred bailiff Henry Gander, also appointed by the County Committee to support the sequestrators. Edward Curll kept a detailed account book for the committee, which was discovered among the papers of William Hellyar of Coker Court.[1]

It was first brought to attention in the late 19th century by John Batten who wrote two papers for the Proceedings of the Somerset Archaeological Society on the sufferings of those Royalists whose estates appear in the account.[2] He focused on the Royalist landowners and the political divide but the account book also casts considerable light on the sequestrator himself and the breadth and difficulty of his task. His scrupulous honesty over his expenses and the goods that passed through his hands portray a strong character and his dogged pursuit of missing goods, often over long distances is indicative of a conscientious officer.

Who was he? Edward Curll was from a clothing family at Batcombe in Somerset,

---

[1] SHC, DD/WHh 136h.
[2] J. Batten, 'Somerset Sequestrations during the Civil War' *PSANHS* IV (1853), pp. 60-77; J. Batten, 'Somerset Sequestrations', *PSANHS* XVI (1870), pp. 13-34.

probably an offshoot of the Bedminster family. Unfortunately, there were three Edwards in the family but one as churchwarden failed to notify the church authorities that his rector was not following the prescribed forms of worship in the 1630s and was in dispute with their Royalist neighbours, the Bisse family. One signed the 1641 Protestation but the elder Edward, possibly the sequestrator's father, avoided doing so.[3] Perhaps unsurprisingly, given his family background, the sequestrator was a zealous Puritan and supporter of Parliament but a man who was up against human nature on both sides. Neither party nor their adherents lived up to the standards he set himself. He could be very angry, raging against the enemies of Parliament, but he was seldom happy with his fellow Parliamentarians.

He was fiercely opposed to alehouses "the nurseries of hell" and especially the many unlicensed houses 'whereby drinking to drunkenness is increased and God much dishonoured in that place'. He paid appraisers to assist in distraining alehouses in several parishes and petitioned Quarter Sessions concerning the parishes in his district. He described himself as a man who had 'laboured to reform great abuses in these places occasioned by the nurseries of Hell the alehouses and their abettors maulsters'. Although he had suppressed alehouses he claimed that alehouse keepers and others had obtained licences by clandestine means. He had done his research and found out several alehouse keepers who had got licences by going to a different JP, one of whom was accused of altering a licence. He accused the Presbyterian JP William Strode of Shepton Mallet of interfering with officers imposing penalties on unlicensed alehouses.[4] Such dogged investigation was typical of the man and his work.

Edward Curll's accounts for 1645 to 1646 tell us a great deal about himself and his opinions. He pursued three types of delinquents: royalists who had been in arms against Parliament; papists; and scandalous ministers. He carefully justified each seizure by describing the reasons why each Royalist owner should forfeit his estate. His zeal often came up against opponents from all classes of society.

At Babcary, not only did the staunch Royalist Sir John Stawell have an estate but also the Overton family several of whom had fought for the king. Curll had a great deal of trouble in this parish and hired two men to help him because of the 'extraordinary malignancy of the place'. At Hazlegrove in Queen Camel he had to get troops to assist in driving the cattle off the estate. In several parishes, he had to stop tenants paying their rents to their old landlord. Hardly surprising as tenants not

[3] TNA, C8/78/23; SHC, D/D/Ca 299; Q/SR 81/49-50; T. L. Stoate, ed. and pub. (trans. A. J. Howard), *The Somerset Protestation Returns and Lay Subsidy Rolls, 1641/2* (Bristol, 1975), pp. 141-42. A typescript copy of this edition is held in the SHC Local History Library. Note, however, a letter by S. Berry, former Senior Archivist of the Somerset Archives, questioning the accuracy of this edition, is included with this typescript. A report on the relevant House of Lords Library MS is included in the *Fifth Report of the Royal Commission on Historical Manuscripts*, Part I. Report and Appendix (London, 1876), pp. 3, 120-34 (esp.131-32), also to be found in SHC.
[4] SHC, Q/SPet 1/D; E.H. Bates Harbin, ed., *Quarter Sessions Records for the County of Somerset, vol. III, Commonwealth, 1646—60*, SRS 28 (1912), p. 163.

knowing which way the wind would blow in future were afraid of having to pay twice. In Compton Pauncefoot and Blackford his men were subjected to violence when trying to collect rents on Robert Hunt's estate and Hunt threatened anyone who took a lease of his land. Curll often found it hard to find tenants for seized lands partly as new tenants would be unsure of their security of tenure.

Sir Henry Berkeley gave a lot of trouble and when Curll seized the corn grown on his land and stored it on the ground of fellow clothier and landowner Elias Hole Berkeley threatened Hole.[5] Undeterred, Curll paid for sowing wheat and maslin on Berkeley's small Babcary estate. Sir Henry complained in 1648 that Curll had seized goods worth £77 near his lands, which belong to others including a mare worth £20 belonging to one of his sons.[6] However, Curll got his revenge for that complaint when in 1650 he discovered that a debt of £500 was due to Sir Henry Berkeley from William Craddock of West Lydford before Berkeley could offer to compound for it. Sir Edward Berkeley complained in 1648 that Curll unjustly took rents from his tenants towards his composition and shrouded 300 tall young oaks so that they withered.

At Queen Camel and Keinton Mandeville William Overton had two good houses and much land whose revenues Curll's colleague William Gander used to provision a Parliamentary troop. It pleased Curll that the revenues of a man who fought against Parliament should benefit Parliament's forces. He took a similar pleasure when dealing with William Gawen, a papist who had fought for the king, from whose lands in Hatherleigh he paid 5s. towards the pulling down of Sherborne Castle. On the families of papists Curll had no mercy taking the property of their widows and children. He complained that the Receiver of Crown rents had refused to distrain the goods of one Margaret Norris saying 'shall the poor woman starve?'.

Curll made a special note of weapons seized in various houses, including swords and pistols. They could be very useful to the Parliamentary army as well as providing evidence that a Royalist may have been in arms. Henry Rose, tenant of Hazlegrove (figure 28) in Queen Camel, had stirred people up to fight for the king but his wife had a fowling piece and musket, which she claimed were to guard the house in her husband's absence but Curll complained that she had taken them away.

Scandalous ministers were another of Curll's targets. Hugh Collins, rector of Compton Pauncefoot was said to have been ejected *c.*1646 for lewd and scandalous behaviour, including fathering a bastard child and for adhering to the Royalist cause, setting a man in arms against Parliament, carrying intelligence to Oxford, and lighting a bonfire to celebrate the defeat of Parliament at Edgehill. He disappeared, said to have been murdered during a robbery at his house in 1646 but Curll maintained that the man who was robbed and killed at the rectory house was a soldier and Collins was the robber. Possibly there had been a fight for possession of the rector's

---

[5] Elias was one of the friends appointed overseer of his will.
[6] M. A. E. Green, ed., *Calendar of the Proceedings of the Committee for Compounding,* II, 1643-60, Cases 1643-46 (1890), p. 1405.

goods, but Collins would have been in his 70s at the time. Curll listed the four oxen, three cows, two calves, 15 cheeses and two pigs he claimed Collins had stolen at Hatherleigh from Sir Edward Berkeley, a fellow Royalist.[7] Curll also harvested and sold the rector's wheat and barley but had to set a watch on it until it was safely sold. The house was said to have been broken up and the goods sold. The pigeon house was broken into frequently, probably because the dung was valuable not only as fertiliser but in providing the raw material for saltpetre for gunpowder. Eventually he found a tenant for the land and meadows and a new minister. William Haskett, rector of Maperton, was said to have railed against Parliament in his sermons and stirred up the people against the Parliamentary forces. He was ejected c. 1646.

Curll could be compassionate occasionally. Another delinquent minister was Doctor Paul Godwin of Kingweston whose rectory house was occupied by his daughter and son-in law. Here Curll found the curate poor and in want and his family in need of clothes so he gave him wheat and £5. Mr Brook, curate of Weston Bampfylde, was given the living of the ejected rector. A sad case was that of Richard Clothier of Holton, who hanged himself. Curll seized his cattle but paid for his burial.

Curll did not consider Amias Hext, rector of Babcary, as scandalous but only malignant and in any case Hext was already in prison as a Royal supporter. His kitchen goods had been spirited away to his neighbours' houses. Those neighbours were also described as malignant, as was the rector's wife who had kept the glebe and tithes, even finding a clergyman to take services while her husband was detained in prison.

On at least one occasion, Curll's zeal lead him to stray beyond the borders of his jurisdiction. He intruded into the affairs of West Camel, which was outside the hundred, to get hold of the goods of Anthony Richardson a popular Royalist. His plate and goods were hidden and Curll bribed people to discover them but he wasted his money. He had to bring in soldiers to conduct a search and no doubt intimidate the parishioners, who resisted Curll's collection of tithe. Curll resented the rector's insistence that money paid to Parliament should be described as 'imposed'.

Curll had of course to be a farmer and estate manager as well as sequestrator of lands and goods. The country needed feeding and the government needed the income from cropping and livestock rearing to pay soldiers and administrators. Having seized crops, livestock and other goods, Curll then had to dispose of them and find tenants for the land. However, many local people were either sympathetic to those who had land and goods seized, or thought that they were due some reward for Parliamentary service or losses sustained in the war. They were not prepared to pay what Curll felt was the market price for stock and produce or leases. Crops and hayricks were presumably sold locally but livestock was taken to markets and fairs. A flock of 12 sheep was sold at Wincanton fair for over £5 and cattle were sold in Somerton fair. However, the prices that Curll obtained were usually low and his need

---

[7] A.G. Mathews (ed.), *Walker Revised* (Oxford, 1948), pp. 310-11.

to dispose of produce in a hostile neighbourhood may account for the fact that two hayricks fetched only £2.

At Queen Camel he even held the manor courts, repaired the pound and paid for the jury dinner £1 2*s*. according to custom. He kept the courts because this was often the occasion when rents were paid and he had heard that Humphrey Mildmay (figure 29), lord of the manor, was making his peace with Parliament. Curll was very concerned to get in as much rent as possible before Royalist landowners compounded and recovered their estates. He was annoyed at failing to get any rents for the lands of the Marquis of Hertford because he did not get the rent roll until he was ordered to forbear collection.

It is his painstaking efforts in pursuit of livestock, crops and other goods smuggled away, which is impressive. He was very keen to prevent his masters being cheated and refused to be outwitted, even tracing 16 featherbeds that had been removed from Compton Pauncefoot to Yarlington. Christopher Chapel, a substantial leaseholder at Barton St David, was an ardent Royalist. The charges against him covered nearly a sheet of paper and four soldiers were sent to arrest him. He was then a wealthy man with considerable property. His loyal servants hid his cattle and horses, but Curll searched the moors and went as far as fairs at Bridgwater and Somerton in search of them. He found two missing horses in King's moor. He took no chances with the rest of the produce and arranged for the apples to be picked and a guard to be set on the corn. His efforts were clearly effective because Chapel was unable to pay his fine and in the 1660s lived in a house with only one hearth.[8] The rector of Maperton also had loyal support and Curll tracked down £33 worth of corn taken to a brother's house in North Cadbury, and six loads of hay were traced to a barn in Wells. Henry Rose of Hazlegrove tried to dispose of goods worth over £400. Curll traced 110 sheep a mile beyond Sherborne in Dorset and brought them back to Little Marston, south of Queen Camel and, like Hazlegrove, held by Rose. Curll put a guard on them and took security from their owner. He retrieved another man's oxen from Bridgwater at great expense. He also traced £800 belonging to Sir Henry Berkeley in the hands of people from East Pennard to Durleigh.

He paid amongst other things for intelligence and himself went to Taunton to disclose a plot to take Wareham in Dorset. A Taunton man, whose house had been ransacked by Royalist soldiers, was paid 4*s*. for his part in discovering malignants' estates. In just under two years, Curll collected over £1,455 of which nearly £100 was spent on the sequestered estates and £63 5*s*. on his own expenses and those of two assistants who were paid 3*s*. 6*d*. a week each. Furthermore, they all had a horse each. Curll worked a six-day week but from Saturday night until Monday morning he lay at his own house and kept the Sabbath.

His own side were often unappreciative of his efforts and slow to provide help.

[8] M. A. E. Green, ed., *Calendar of the Proceedings of the Committee for Compounding, General Proceedings* (1889), I, p. 14; III, p. 2023; *Dwelly's National Records, Vol. 1, Hearth Tax for Somerset, 1664-5, With Indices, Copied from the Original Rolls in the Public Record Office by R. Holworthy* (Fleet, Hants, 1916), pp. 80-1.

He seized a gelding from Thomas Watts of Queen Camel and kept it until collected by Colonel Starr's troop but it died at Norton in Wiltshire because of the soldiers' 'cruel inhumane using of him'. When trying to manage the confiscated glebe at Alford he found two parliamentary supporters in the parish, a tanner and a husbandman who were persuaded to sow 7 acres of confiscated glebe lands with wheat and beans for the state but he could not get help with a further 7 acres of arable and 14 acres of meadow and pasture. The two men he employed to thresh corn were threatened by Parliamentary soldiers quartering there.

The difficulties he had endured did not discourage him. On 21 August 1649, Edward Curll wrote to the Committee for the Advance of Money stating that he had secured the estate and goods of Hugh Fry and Richard Mogg of Wells, servant of the sheriff of Somerset. The latter caused him much difficulty as Curll claimed

> on account of his false dealing; for he broke open the study and a trunk which I had sealed, on pretense that there were things of great value belonging to the high sheriff; he spoke contemptuously of your authority, and has come up to town suddenly. Do not let him compound till you have seen my particulars of his estate, for he greatly undervalued it before.[9]

He then turned his attention to what he regarded as dishonourable behaviour by other officers. Despite all his hard work on their behalf he does not seem to have been popular with the County Committee. He had a long battle in 1650 with a commissioner Captain Benjamin Mason whom he, with other sequestrators, accused of letting better bargains to papists and cavaliers than to Parliamentarians. The County Committee found in Mason's favour, hinting at personal ill feelings, and said that it was Curll's fault that a parsonage was let at too low a rate, as he had not told the committee about it. In retaliation, Mason charged Curll with not bringing his accounts and Curll, currently working in the Bristol area, was ordered to be suspended until he brought in his accounts. In August 1650, he was complaining of the injustices of the Somerset committee to him and that he had not received his charges. There were rumours that he had received money not accounted for. The County Committee for Somerset informed the Committee for Compounding that Curll was 'of no fortune and less reputation in this county, and that he has said if he could not pay it, he could but lie in prison for it.' He was also ordered by the Committee for Compounding to repay James Hanham of Holwell, a recusant, for seizing goods worth £32 11s., which had been lent to him in his need.

Curll was not easily deterred from doing his duty as he saw it and later that year he gave evidence against Captain Latimer Sampson for favouring the Royalists when he was Governor of Bristol Castle. He also wanted to see particulars of Humphrey Hooke's composition to see whether he had compounded for a £2,000 debt, which

---

[9] M.A.E. Green, ed., *Calendar of the Committee for the Advance of Money, 1645-1650*, II (London, 1888), p. 981.

he and other Bristol malignants lent the late king. Curll was clearly good at unearthing details of financial and land transactions, presumably with the help of his informers. He had an incentive and was allowed the customary 1s. in the pound from the fine of £168 15s. paid by Henry Dunford whose estate worth £45 a year he had discovered.[10]

Even the government, which set them up, regarded sequestrators as a mixed blessing. In December 1646, the House of Commons ordered that 'no Committee-man, Sequestrator, Collector, or other Officer, employed in the Sequestrations in the several respective Counties, shall, ... take to farm, or rent, any Lands or Estates sequestered where he is employed in the Sequestrations.'[11] Closer to home, the House of Lords, the same year, had to intervene in a dispute involving a sequestrator at Exford

> ... contrary to the Order of this House, George Trenchard Clerk cannot enjoy the Rectory of Exford, in the County of Som'sett, nor the Profits thereof, by reason of the Practice and Disobedience of Rob't Edbrooke, Mr. Collier the Sequestrator, Wm. Tucker, and Silvester Williams, ... [to be] brought before this House, to answer their said Contempts; and that the said George Trenchard shall peaceably and quietly enjoy the said Rectory, and be permitted to take the Benefits thereof.[12]

Perhaps it is not surprising that Edward Curll, worn out in parliament's service, retired to Batcombe and his dyehouse. He survived to see his daughter married and died in 1653 leaving one son still at school.[13]

[10] M.A.E. Green, ed., *Calendar of the Committee for the Advance of Money, 1642-1645*, I (London, 1888), pp. 260, 291, 298, 301, 303, 813; M.A.E. Green, ed., *Calendar of the Committee for the Advance of Money, 1650-1655*, III (London, 1888), p. 1630.

[11] *Journal of the House of Commons*: volume 5: 1646-1648 (1802), pp. 4-7: www.british-history.ac.uk: accessed: 10 June 2011.

[12] *Journal of the House of Lords*: volume 9: 1646 (1767-1830), pp. 677-678: www.british-history.ac.uk accessed 10 June 2011.

[13] SHC, D/P/bat 2/1/1; TNA, PROB 11/231/459.

9. Dr Westover of Wedmore, Physician and Farmer, 1686-1705

FRANCES NEALE

Introduction

Personal records of farming in the pre-enclosure era rarely survive. Usually, working lives have to be deduced from property deeds, surveys and probate inventories. John Westover II of Wedmore (1643-1706) is an exception. Born into a family of established, prosperous farmers in Wedmore and Stoughton, John Westover II inherited the family farm in Wedmore, known since the late 1800s as Porch House (figure 30). He lived there all his life, never married, and when he died the farm passed first to his brother, Henry Westover, and then to his nephew, Henry's son John Westover III. Porch House was one of several substantial 16th – 17th century farmsteads built on the edge of former medieval open fields west of Wedmore, in the area still known as West End. Just under three acres (1.2 hectares) of enclosed paddocks and orchards adjoined the house and farm buildings. John Westover II held arable land around the village, moor-edge hay meadows and, as a manorial tenant, had rights of pasture out on the moors.

Principally remembered today as a practising physician, he was a man of standing in the local community. His father, John Westover I (1616-78), had been a surgeon. This is known only from the inscription on the floor-slab marking his grave in Wedmore parish church. It features an acrostic memorial verse, the first letter of each line spelling out **JOHNWESTOVER** vertically, and it concludes, wryly, "Repent, for doctors die", a memorial unique of its kind in the parish church. Nothing is known of John Westover I's medical career, but it is likely to have influenced his son's interest in medicine, and particularly in mental health. John Westover II inherited the care of one of his father's long-term patients, John Edwards, who apparently suffered from some form of mental handicap or possibly epilepsy. John Westover I had been paid, from 1667 onwards, 'for keeping and governing' this son of a local farming family, and John Westover II continued to look after him until his own death in 1706. John Edwards died just six weeks later.[1] The son's humane treatment of patients with mental health problems may have followed his father's example. His reputation spread widely; he rode to visit patients as far away as Bristol to the north, and the Poldens to the south.[2] Some came to live

---

[1] H. Hudson, *Doctors of Wedmore Parish 1640s-1940s* (2010), pp. 15-16.
[2] *Ibid*, chapters 1-10.

as in-patients in the 'hospice' he built next to Porch House in 1680, now known as Westovers.

The greater part of John Westover II's medical work, however, was as a general physician, serving the Wedmore community with its round of rural accidents, infectious diseases, gynaecological crises and general ailments. He was appointed as the official parish doctor by the Overseers of the Poor and kept what has become known as his 'Journal',[3] an account book with diary notes, covering the years 1686-1705. He compiled other account books, but they have not survived, though medical bills recorded in the 'Journal' refer to other books in the 1690s.[4] Just one account book remains. Extensive and fairly accurate extracts from the 'Journal', however, were printed by Revd S.H.A. Hervey in his *Wedmore Chronicle* in 1898.[5] Subsequent local historians have drawn upon Hervey, partly because the original 'Journal' was for long in private hands, and the manuscript and Westover's writing is difficult to read.

Once an account was settled, John Westover usually crossed out the entries with great vigour, making them still less legible. An attempt, in 1969, to set Dr John Westover II in his local context still used S.H.A. Hervey's printed extracts.[6] Hazel Hudson, however, produced a detailed study of him in *Doctors of Wedmore Parish 1640s-1940s* (2010), for which she used the original manuscript of John Westover's 'Journal'.[7] The quotations in this present paper are also taken directly from the original manuscript.

John Westover II's activities as a doctor are primarily recovered from this 'Journal'. Alongside the medical material, however, are many references to John Westover's farming activities, which had never received the same attention, until Hazel Hudson extracted examples for two short articles in Wedmore Parish Magazine.[8] He ran his family farm beside his general medical practice, and the care of his private patients. The farming references appear sporadically and at random. Because the 'Journal' tends to organise information by patient, many of the farming references are entered as they involve that patient or their family, and are rarely in date order This study, building on Hazel Hudson's work, brings together the farming references by kind and then, as far as possible, in chronological order.

The Farm

Dr John Westover's home, with its distinctive 17th century porch room over the front door, was called Porch House by the time Revd S.H.A. Hervey was writing in 1898. In 1886 it was called Westovers Farm after the family, who had lived there

---

[3] SHC, DD\X\HKN/1.

[4] SHC, DD\X\HKN/ fos 102v, 66v, 207v.

[5] S.H.A. Hervey, *Wedmore Chronicle II* (1898).

[6] F. Neale, *A 17th century Country Doctor: John Westover of Wedmore*, The Practitioner, vol. 203 (November 1969), pp. 699-704.

[7] H. Hudson, *Doctors of Wedmore Parish 1640s-1940s* (2010), chapters 1-10.

[8] H. Hudson, 'The New Wedmore Chronicles' 175 and 176, *The Isle of Wedmore News*, nos. 397 (January 2013), pp. 51-5 and 398 (February 2013), pp. 50-3.

since the 1500s.[9] The house fronts onto the road. The 1680 block built by Dr Westover for his resident patients stands in the adjacent courtyard. A long narrow block of single-storey farm buildings, now reconstructed and converted to residential use, extended to the west of the house. The unmarried Dr John Westover provided a home for his mother Joan until she died in 1692, and for his sisters Ann and Hannah until they married. They would have helped manage the house. His brother Andrew assisted with dentistry on one occasion in 1686.[10] His nephew William Rowley lived in as an apprentice and general help, presumably with a view to inheriting the practice, but died young in 1697.[11]

In addition, there are references to three female helpers. Joan Nutty was sent on errands and delivered messages, on occasion journeying to Bristol to buy glass 'vialls' to hold medicines and ointments. Ann Wall also ran errands and was paid for doing washing.[12] With both the household and the in-patients' washing to be done, she may have featured regularly in other account books. Thirdly, Jane Ellis was his housekeeper in later years. She was literate, dealt with patients coming to the house, and between 1701-1705, when John Westover's health was failing, she made occasional entries in the Journal herself. In 1698, she went to Bristol, entrusted with quite substantial sums of money for purchases.[13] Towards the end of his life, John Westover showed Jane increasing confidence in financial responsibilities. She was reimbursed for buying a cow and calf in 1701, and for large quantities of goose feathers in 1704.[14] Flocks of geese were farmed on the moors around Wedmore, and feathers would be needed for pillows, mattresses and quilts for both household and hospice.

Timber and cut boards, whether from his own trees or purchased locally and carried home, including ash and elm, were frequently needed for building work on the house and farm. In 1692/3, he bought board from Simon Smeathes of Crickham,[15] and in 1693 had board cut from his own trees.[16] In 1695, he bought elm board from cousin John Pitt for work on an end of the house in 'new house',[17] and, in 1698 received payment of elm board in part payment for the cure of cousin Elizabeth Pitt.[18] And further such board purchased and carried from Heath House,[19] with nails from George Ven of Blackford to repair the cart house.[20]

---

[9] 1:2500 O.S. map (1886).
[10] H. Hudson, *Doctors of Wedmore Parish*, p. 8.
[11] S.H.A. Hervey, *Wedmore Chronicle II* (1898), pp. 107, 127.
[12] SHC, DD\X\HKN/1 fo. 130r, 160v.
[13] SHC, DD\X\HKN/1 fo. 207v.
[14] SHC, DD\X\HKN/1 fo. 224B. The folios have been rebound incorrectly at this point, with fo. 224B facing fo. 216A. S.H.A. Hervey refers to it as fo. 225B.
[15] SHC, DD\X\HKN/1 fo. 139v.
[16] SHC, DD\X\HKN/1 fo. 123r.
[17] SHC, DD\X\HKN/1 fo. 176v.
[18] SHC, DD\X\HKN/1 fo. 201r.
[19] SHC, DD\X\HKN/1 fo. 177r.
[20] SHC, DD\X\HKN/1 fo. 165r as quoted by S.H.A. Hervey, *Wedmore Chronicles* II, p. 132; the top of fo. 165r which contained this entry has been torn away since Hervey saw it c.1898.

There are brief references to repairs and improvements at the farm. In August 1686, William Fisher was paid for making a door to the Westover privy;[21] in 1687 Charles Fisher made hinges for the main stone-framed doors of the house or the hospice;[22] and in October 1692 and again in October 1693, Henry Chapel, blacksmith of Wells, and others, worked at Porch House making and fitting ironwork, including a gate, door and hayrack for the stable, including hooks, hinges, nails, keys and bolts.[23]

On 26 February 1693/94, John Westover paid Richards for a day's work cutting stone for the Stable windows,[24] and in 1695 he arranged with George Palmer to buy stone from two small quarries, both for his own use and for sale, with a formal agreement entered in the 'Journal':

November ye 20th 1695
Then Concluded And agreedd with George Pamar that upon the Consideration of ye sume of fower pounds to paid [*sic*] fortey shillings next Thursday being ye 28th of November And fortey shillings more at Crismas next to be paid by me John Westover the said George Pamor Doth sell Alle the Whit Lyas Cloye & thinn Pavior Stones that hee hath now Raised this 26th of November 1695 And Allsoe Alle the Stones that duth Rise in Twentey five foot square & Allsoe Alle the stones in the other quar Allredey begun being About Tenn foot square
More. Alle thes stones not Allreday raised to be Raised at the Charge of Me John Westover Wittnes to this
John Lyde   Edward Lyde
Amos Lilley   William Rowley[25]

A week later he records,

November ye 28 [1695] Then paid George Pallmer the A bove Mentioned fortey shillings being the first moetey before Edward Lyde Allesoe paid him 15^s for y^e other 3 Load & ij^s for y^e other Large Lyas stone for

y^e step	£2 17s. 0d.
Item paid his wife at Sand Towns End five shillings in part of pay of y^e Last Moety	£0 5s. 0d.
At An other time fiftean^s	£0 15s. 0d.
Item the next time paid him	£0 6s. 0d.

Item at An other time seven

21 SHC, DD\X\HKN/1 fo. 31r.
22 SHC, DD\X\HKN/1 fo. 31r.
23 SHC, DD\X\HKN/1 fos. 137r and 150r.
24 SHC, DD\X\HKN/1 fo. 138r.
25 SHC, DD\X\HKN/1 fo. 180r.

Then he returned 5ˢ backe so there was but 3ˢ Received	£0 3s. 0d.[26]
The next tim paid him 9ˢ	£0 9s. 0d.
The last payment Paid him the other Twoe shillings	£0 2s. 0d.
Soe wee ar Even for yᵉ Stones and Ground that I bought.[27]	

The large Lias slab for the step was perhaps for the front porch. The shallow Lias quarries on the southern side of Wedmore were relatively easy to excavate, backfill and return to cultivation. On 22 July 1700, John Westover paid John Pitt the carter for carriage of mortar out of Goodmeads and lime for the porch, the first reference to the distinctive feature which gives the house its present name.[28]

The Windmill

About half a mile north of Porch House, on the east side of Quab Lane and at the highest point of the gently rising ground, stood the family windmill. The history of the mill from its first mention in 1558 to its demolition c.1700-1709 has been worked out by Hazel Hudson.[29] It stood in a small enclosure in a furlong of the former open field of Quabb.[30] In 1576, it passed to the Stone family, and became known as Stone's Mill. In 1621, John Westover I leased it from the then owners, Llewellyn's Almshouse in Wells, so it became Westover's Mill. By 1709, three years after Dr John Westover II had died, it had ceased working and the Mill Batch plot is described as being where a Windmill lately stood in the tenure of Doctor John Westover.[31] In 1765, Dr John Westover's nephew and heir John Westover III sold Porch House and the Westover land, including 3 yards (¾ acre) of arable at Mill Moot in the North Field.[32] This plot was still called Mill Batch, and the two adjoining fields were both called Westover's Mill Tyning, in 1791 and 1838.[33] The mill mound can still just be made out in the corner of Mill Batch.[34]

There is no mention of milling in the 'Journal', but there is a note that Dr John Westover lent some heavy equipment (crane, pulley wheels, etc) to his kinsman (cousin William Westover) on May yᵉ 30ᵗʰ 1700.[35] Cousin William Westover was a member of the branch of the family who lived at Allerton and held Allerton Mill, which still exists today. While William could have been working on Westover's Mill, possibly to demolish it, it seems more likely that this equipment was needed for major work on the Allerton Mill.

[26] *Sic*, in error for 2s., having originally written 7s.

[27] SHC, DD\X\HKN/1 fo. 180r.

[28] SHC, DD\X\HKN/1 fo. 222v.

[29] H. Hudson, *The New Wedmore Chronicles* (2002) pp. 113-115.

[30] Quab: OE marshy, damp.

[31] SHC, D\P\w.st.c./17/1/10.

[32] SHC, DD\BV\N/48 no. 11.

[33] SHC, D\P\wed/13/10/17 Parish map of Wedmore, 1791; D\P\wed/3/2/1 Wedmore tithe map and award, 1838.

[34] SHER 10878.

[35] SHC, DD\X\HKN/1 fo. 219v.

Fields

Throughout the 'Journal' are references to Dr John Westover's fields and what he grew in them. The combined picture from these references shows a relatively small core holding of arable land and a constant turnover of small fields leased out or rented by John Westover. Most of his land was still part of the former medieval open field pattern of Wedmore. The relative isolation of the Isle of Wedmore, with the Dean and Chapter of Wells as largely absentee lord of the manors of Wedmore, Churchland and Mudgley, meant that Wedmore farmers made their own improvements to their farming practices. Enclosure by private arrangement, with individuals exchanging strips to form compact holdings that could be hedged, was certainly taking place in neighbouring Blackford at this time.[36] In the absence of surviving manorial court records at this period, however, there is no evidence whether the same thing was happening in Wedmore, although it would seem probable. John Westover and his neighbours would have been well aware of what was being done in adjacent Blackford. The evidence, in the form of small, narrow fields created from several former strips and still within the framework of open field furlongs, survives extensively across Wedmore today, although now almost all under pasture.

Many of the holdings Westover describes are very small – acres, half-acres and yards[37]– and these were un-enclosed strips in open field furlongs; they were still shown as such in 1791.[38] A particularly good example is Clements Furlong, close by Porch House, where the old open field pattern is still clear, fossilised by the hedges enclosing groups of former strips. Dr John Westover rented one acre in Clements Furlong in 1688,[39] and in 1693 purchased three acres and one yard of arable from his kinsman Henry Marten of Penard, one acre in Clements Furlong, one acre at Rushill, half an acre in Rodford (open field southwest of Clements Furlong), and three yards in the high ground of Heathhouse Field.[40] John Westover rented out some of his arable ground, usually an acre or less at a time, suggesting perhaps that these too were unenclosed strips in open fields. The entries reveal perennial problems collecting the money due.[41]

Holdings at an inconvenient distance from Porch House in Wedmore may have encouraged a policy of leasing, as with the Allerton estate, so held by John Westover's brother and cousins.[42] Otherwise, he rented land short-term, investing outside manor and parish in 25 November 1690 in low-lying meadow he needed for early pasture and the valuable hay crop, renting four acres at Westhay in Meare in 1691.[43] He copied material into his 'Journal' in 1693 in the quasi-formal registra-

[36] SHC, DD/SE 63, 64.
[37] A yard, used locally as an areal measure, = a rood, ¼ acre.
[38] SHC, D\P\wed/13/10/17 Parish map of Wedmore, 1791.
[39] SHC, DD\X\HKN/1 fo. 71r.
[40] SHC, DD\X\HKN/1 fo. 152v.
[41] SHC, DD\X\HKN/1 fo. 77v and 83r.
[42] SHC, DD\X\HKN/1 fo. 142r.
[43] SHC, DD\X\HKN/1 fo. 106r.

18. A dish with sgraffito decoration made in West Somerset from St Clement's Dock, Narrow Quay, Bristol, catalogue number 39; diameter 370mm. The feet of the cockerel forming the central motif survive. (Reproduced by kind permission of Bristol City Museum and Art Gallery.)

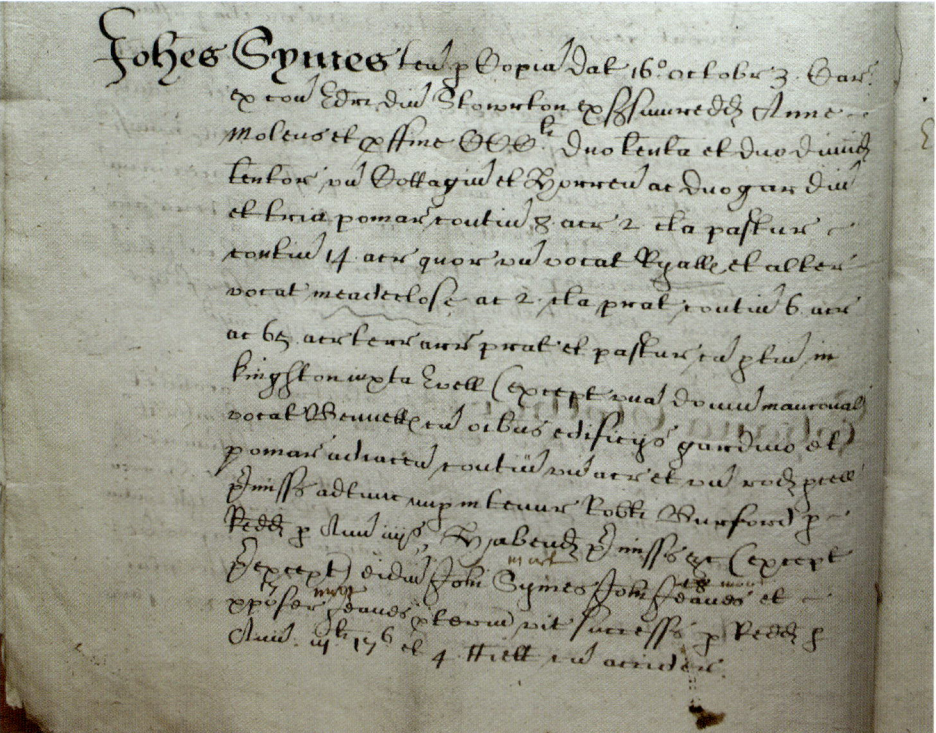

19. A description of the copyhold estate of John Symes, 1633. (Reproduced by kind permission of the Wiltshire and Swindon History Centre.)

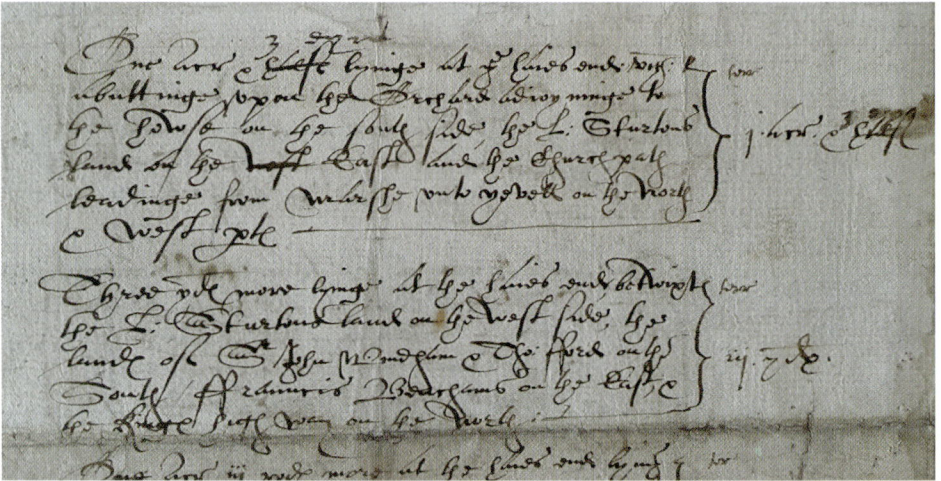

20. An extract from a survey of Fords Living in Kingston, 1604. (S.H.C., DD/WY 47/3/4.)

Above left: 21. Helena, Marchioness of Northampton (1553-1635). Her second husband was Sir Thomas Gorges and she was the grandmother of Thomas Smyth. (Wikipedia.)
Above right: 22. Sir Hugh Smyth (1572-1627). (Bristol Museum & Art Gallery.)

Above left: 23. Thomas Smyth (1609-1642) (North Somerset & South West Heritage Trust, 2017.) *Above right:* 24. Florence Smyth (d.1676), daughter of John 1st Lord Poulett and wife of Thomas Smyth (Bristol Museum & Art Gallery.)

25. The extension to Ashton Court built by Thomas Smyth during 1633-1635. (Joseph Bettey.)

26. Catsash hundred from a map of Somerset by Willem Blaeu (d. 1638). (Robin Bush Collection.)

27. The last entry in Curll's submission to his masters, boasting of his success. (S.H.C., DD/WHh 136h.)

28. The old wing of Hazlegrove House. (© Mary Siraut.)

Near this place lyeth the Body of Humphry Mildmay Esq Lord of this Mannor Second Son of Sʳ Humphrey Mildmay of Denbury in the County of Essex He sustained severall Wounds in the Warrs for his Loyaltye to his Prince King Charles the first particularly at Newbury Fight where He served as Major under his Uncle ye Earle of Cleaveland and was taken up among the slain. His first wife was Sarah the Daughter of Tho Freke Esq of Iwton Sᵗ Mary in Dorsetshire His Second wife was Sarah the Daughter of Edm and Parker Esq of Burrington in Devonshire He Dyed ye 9 day of Novem 1690 Aged 67 And haveing no Issue le t his Estate to his Kinsman Curew Mildmay Esq of Marks in the County of Essex Who in token of h s Gratitude erected this Monument

29. The monument to Humphrey Mildmay in Queen Camel church recording his suffering in the Civil War.

(© Mary Siraut.)

30. Porch House, West End, Wedmore in the 1930s. The hospice built in 1680 for resident patients is on the right. (© Hazel Hudson.)

31. An entry from Dr John Westover's Journal listing plough work and haulage in 1690. (SHC, DD\X\HKN/1 fo. 99r, reproduced courtesy of the South West Heritage Trust.)

Left: 32. A portrait of Thomas Carew by the artist Thomas Hudson (1701-1779). It appears to have been painted c.1746 as his hand is resting on an Act of 20 George II c.37 concerning Sheriffs. (Photograph courtesy of Mr Anthony Trollope-Bellew of Crowcombe.)

Below: 33. The south front and east side of Crowcombe Court. This appears to be almost the same view as that in the 1792 engraving by Thomas Bonnor used in the Reverend John Collinson's *History of Somerset.* (Photograph courtesy of Mr David Kenyon of Crowcombe and Jackson Stops of Taunton.)

34. Harrington House, 2017. Craig's Court, Westminster, was laid out by Joseph Craig in the 1690s prior to the great fire of 1698 which destroyed the Palace of Whitehall. Harrington House, which occupies the whole of one side of the Court, was built soon after the fire. Carew rented the property from Philip Craig between 1750 and 1757. (© Sue Berry.)

35. The first side of the list of Carew's debts drawn up in 1759. This includes the £2500 plus £896 interest he owed his nephew John for the mortgage he had taken out on his Pembrokeshire estate in 1748 and the £1400 plus £28 interest he owed Mrs Rishton. (S.H.C., DD\SAS\C/432/28.)

tion of meadow leases, most of the band of sought-after meadow along the moor edge below Wedmore being called Ham, enclosed early and taking its holder's name. He did not, however, just rent meadow but in 1699, for example, rented arable.[44] Some or all of these leased or rented land-holdings may also represent investment in consolidation for private enclosure. For other land, held in East Brent, separate arrangements had to be made, with special measures taken, in particular for managing water courses.[45]

In 1699, John Westover made his most expensive acquisition. He purchased Goodmeads, two matching closes of just under 4 acres each, which lie end-to-end on the north side of the road to Blackford. They have been deliberately cut out of Clements Furlong and do not conform to the layout of the surrounding ancient open field.[46] The two Goodmeads lie in the shallow valley of the infant Blackford Brook, flowing westwards to Blackford. The natural course of the brook would be down the centre of the two fields. Instead, the brook has been deliberately diverted to run at a higher level along their northern boundary, behind a retaining bank. This would provide a head of water to release, in controlled fashion, through sluices into the fields, and create a pair of small water-meadows, unusual on higher ground. In the 1980s, lengthways 'gripes' or shallow ditches were visible; these would carry the water through the fields, to an outlet in the centre of the western side from which water could be directed back to the stream. The Blackford stream then flows round Sparkmoor, the adjoining field to the west, which John Westover also held. The whole arrangement was recognised by Revd S.H.A. Hervey as a deliberate construction.[47] The site was recorded in the 1980s, prior to the development of the school sports area; the eastern field is now largely buried under tennis courts and a car park.[48] It is not possible to date the construction of the banks. The field-name 'Goodmeads' is first recorded in 1558, but this may or may not refer to these same fields.[49] Whether it was John Westover or a previous owner who diverted and embanked the stream to create the pair of water meadows, they were conveniently close to Porch House, and he used them both for arable crops and for hay, involving one day's work with four oxen, two horses, and three men to fetch nine loads of hay from Goodmead in 1692.[50]

In conclusion, it is to be noted that John Westover, as landowner, fulfilled his ecclesiastical and communal obligations. The 'Journal' records him paying Richard Dounton, vicar of Wedmore, his Allerton and Wedmore tithes for Easter in 1697 and 1699,[51] and Canon Grindal Sheafe, archdeacon of Wells, tithes for East Brent in

---

[44] SHC, DD\X\HKN/1 fo. 212v.
[45] SHC, DD\X\HKN/1 fos.172v and 205r.
[46] SHC, DD\X\HKN/1 fo. 211r.
[47] S.H.A. Hervey, *Wedmore Chronicles* II (1898), p. 129.
[48] SHER 32157.
[49] SHC, DD\SAS PR 462 fos. 22a, 41, 48a.
[50] SHC, DD\X\HKN/1 fo. 107v.
[51] SHC, DD\X\HKN/1 fo. 201r.

1698, as well as Benjamin Hill, vicar of South Brent (now Brent Knoll), in 1699.[52] And, in 1701, he continued to contribute financially towards the maintenance of Skitmore ditch, between Wedmore and Theale, both as a boundary and to prevent flooding, as had been a communal duty since the late medieval period.

Crops and carrying

The standard crops on John Westover's arable ground were peas, beans and wheat. Between 1688 and 1702 he planted beans in Clement Furlong; wheat at Allerton; wheat, beans or peas at Rodford; and wheat in Robert Coules' acre beyond our mill.[53] Cider was made from his own apples, involving sixteen bushels, nineteen bushels, nineteen bushels, and ten bushels of apples, between 1697 and 1698.[54] He also sold barley for malting and, in 1691/92 may have bought back a small quantity of malt for brewing his own beer.[55]

For ploughing and other heavy work he hired oxen (figure 31).[56] The constant work of carters reveals much farming detail: hauling timber, carting hay, peat ('turfes') for the farmhouse fires, reed for thatch, fencing material, stones, and dung to the fields. In 1690, a detailed list of such work suggests the range of such occupation: hauling timber from Stourton and Blackford, carrying hay from Meare and Burmead, carrying the bridge to Meare, fetching a load of reeds from Godney, and hauling dung at Spark Moor, and in 1691, fetching thorns from Riten meadow and stakes from Westham for fencing.[57] Similar wide-ranging lists of work survive for 1692, 1693, 1695, and 1700.[58]

Among these everyday farming activities, three entries in the 'Journal' stand out as unusual. In 1688/89 John Westover compiles a list of people to whom he has sold clover seed. The quantities of seed and the number of buyers suggest that, although it only appears in the 'Journal' once, it may be an example of a commercial venture. It may also suggest that along with enclosures by private agreement, local farmers were putting land down to pasture and actively improving its quality. Of the eighteen customers, four bought quantities of 15*lbs* and under, ten bought quantities of between 30 and 70*lbs*, and 4 bought quantities of between 100 and 150*lbs*. Prices ranged between 2½d. and 5½d. per *lb*, with the greater majority paying between 3d. and 5½d.[59] Tantalisingly, it is not clear whether John Westover produced the seed himself, or whether he was acting as a dealer, having obtained it elsewhere. The venture does not appear again.

Another unexpected enterprise is suggested by one short entry:

[52] SHC, DD\X\HKN/1 fo. 205r.
[53] SHC, DD\X\HKN/1 fos. 71r, 136v, 138v, 156v, and 212v.
[54] SHC, DD\X\HKN/1 fo. 201r.
[55] SHC, DD\X\HKN/1 fo. 124v.
[56] SHC, DD\X\HKN/1 fo. 99r.
[57] SHC, DD\X\HKN/1 fos. 99r and 107r.
[58] SHC, DD\X\HKN/1 fos. 107v, 154v, 173r, and 222v.
[59] SHC, DD\X\HKN/1 fo. 81r.

Aprill 7th 1693
Sould to ould Hindrey of Axbridg my Teaseles
the best sort at Thirty Eaight shillings & six pens the packe
the midles at Eaight pence A thousand
Received in Ernest one shilling
Received more in full fine[60]

The large quantities and the graded quality of the teasels suggest a commercial operation. A pack must have been sizeable to cost so much, and even the middling quality were packed by the thousand. It suggests a proper crop, and not just casual pickings from the edges of his lower-lying fields. While bulky, the dried teazles would have been very light. This is fully six years before the 1699 commission of enquiry into teazle-growing held at Wrington.[61] One witness at that enquiry, which was basically to ascertain whether tithes were payable on a teazle crop, said that teazle-growing had been introduced to Congresbury about 45 years earlier, using seed brought from Cheddar. Cheddar would have been a very convenient local source of seed for John Westover in Wedmore. Old Hindrey of Axbridge has not been traced, but was presumably a dealer who could sell the teazles to the clothworkers of Somerset, Bristol and Gloucestershire. Dr John Westover, it would seem, was at the forefront of an agricultural innovation in the locality – yet once again he did not pursue it. Teazles do not feature again in the 'Journal'. They were best grown as a first crop on newly ploughed pasture land, to be followed thereafter by wheat; so John Westover may have been experimenting as part of a plan to extend and improve his arable land.

The last of these three projects was foreshadowed in 1697 when on 3 November, John Westover was 'Deptor for fower score and Twelve Gribles[62] at 4[d] A peece just £1 10s. 8d.'.[63] Ninety-two rootstocks might suggest that John Westover was planning to plant a sizeable new orchard – except that two years later in 1699 he is selling gribbles himself, on a large scale:

Gribles
Sould out of y[e] nusserey at Sparkemore to John Hosie of Weshay

fower score and 15 at 4[d] [a] paes	£1 15s. 0d.
to John Taylar in 1702 fortey Eight	£0 16s. 0d.
to Cozen John Pitte fower score And tenne at 4 A paes	£1 10s. 0d.

---

[60] SHC, DD\X\HKN/1 fo. 142r. The manuscript is torn after the word 'fine'.

[61] J.H. Bettey, 'The Cultivation of Teazles in North Somerset', *Notes & Queries for Somerset and Dorset* vol. XXXIV, p. 235-6, September 1998. Anne King, 'Teazles', *A History of Blagdon* vol.3, Blagdon Local History Society (2007) pp. 153-4.

[62] Gribles or gribbles are crab-apple rootstocks, used for grafting superior orchard apples. F.T. Elworthy, *The Dialect of West Somerset*, Vol. I (English Dialect Society, London, 1875), pp. 297, 301. The term is still in use among Somerset orchard growers.

[63] SHC, DD\X\HKN/1 fo. 201r.

To John Varoe for {h]is kinsman peterham 12	£0 4s. 0d.
To Mr Robart Iveleafe 39 it being 3 duzen at 13 to yᵉ duzen	£0 12s. 0d.
To Caleb Jessey of Limsum {Lympsham] six score at 4ᵈ a peice	£2 0s. 0d.
Thomas goold 20	£0 6s. 8d.
Captin Sillvar Twentey	£0 6s. 8d.
[Robart] Browning of Vole thirtey	£0 10s. 0d.
[Capt]en Thomas Silvar the second time	£0 5s. 0d.
to one of Limsum {Lympsham] I sopose 20	6s. 8d.
to John Barow 64 or About twentey shillings.[64]	

John Westover refers to Sparkmoor, an angular wedge of former open field just west of Clements Furlong and Goodmeads, as his 'Nursery'. It suggests that he used his earlier purchase of gribbles to propagate more cuttings, for sale two years later to other landowners planting new orchards, anticipating the improved cider orchards of the 18th century. The buyers of his rootstocks are mostly from the immediate area. Cousin John Pitt gave him much help on the farm. Robert Ivyleaf was one of the substantial farmers of Blackford. The appearance of Captain Silver, buying gribbles on two occasions, is of interest: he was the husband of one of Dr Westover's resident patients and was presumably visiting her from their home in Stawell, on the Poldens.[65] The last person on the list is John Barrow, lord of the manor, presumably planning improvements to his orchards. The total number of gribbles supplied is 573, assuming that Captain Silver had 15 for his 5s. the second time, and that John Barrow had 64 as stated, rather than the 60 which would have cost 20s. It is an impressive quantity and suggests his nursery at Sparkmoor might have a future; but as with the clover and the teazles, the sale of gribbles is a one-year wonder and does not recur.

Stock

Dr John Westover kept cattle, horses and sheep, buying and selling with his neighbouring farmers and at local fairs. There is no mention either of pigs or of poultry. The latter would have been the concern of the women of the household – his mother and sisters, and later the invaluable Jane Ellis and her helpers, and accounted for separately if at all.

In 1690, he arranged with James Tucker to pasture his calves and yearlings in the 'the parke', the enclosed former deer park of Sand which lay just to the south of Porch House, before moving them out on to the open moor where he had right of common. While the number of animals is small, his note conveys the complex negotiations and stock movements involved:

James Tucker of Sand Tooke fower yearlens to keeping at Twentey shillings

---

[64] SHC, DD\X\HKN/1 fo. 214r.
[65] H. Hudson, *Doctors of Wedmore Parish*, pp. 21-2.

for one And Twentey Weackes If yᵉ More be good I may put them out in More
A Munth & Take the Munth After Mickellmas but then I must Loose the ode
[odd?] Weacke I put them in to the parke the 25ᵗʰ of Aprill.
Likewise Agreed for yᵉ keeping of the fower Calves at one shilling the Weack.
Put them in yᵉ 16ᵗʰ of May 1690.
Fecht yᵉ yearling that Made Read Water A Way yᵉ 19ᵗʰ of May.
Put yᵉ Twoe kine to parke the fowerth of June – I fecht them A way & put
them out in More a weacke After Wedmore fayer being the 28ᵗʰ of Juley. Put
them in Againe & Twoe more 16ᵗʰ of August ... [*interspersed with a medical
entry*] ...
fecht Away yᵉ Caulfes yᵉ 27ᵗʰ of September.
the 3 yearlings fecht Away at the one And Twentey Weackes End and sume
odd days fecht Away ye Cowes the 20ᵗʰ of october.[66]

The animals were brought back to the farm for the winter. When exercising his
right to pasture his cattle on the open moors, they had to be identifiable. John
Westover had a branding iron. In 1695 he had treated Robert Porch of Wedmore for
'yᵉ Cure of his face', which he had 'launct' [lanced] on 18 November, and 'received
in part of pay in worke for making of my Marking Iroen, 5s. 0d.'.[67]
  In 1694-95 he lent out two milch cows:

March yᵉ 24ᵗʰ 1693[/94]
Nickolis Sever of Marke Rented the Red Sterd[68] Cow at thirteen
shilling for yᵉ yeare In suing Ending at the 24ᵗʰ of March 1694[/95]
at which time hee must Return her without a Calfe hee Received
her with one   £0 13s.0d.[69]

The next month,

Aprill yᵉ 20ᵗʰ 1694
Nickolas Saltar of Marke Rented the Blacke Linded[70] Cow at 13ˢ
for yᵉ yeare Ending yᵉ 20ᵗʰ of Aprill 1695 At which time hee must
Returne her A gaine without a Calfe in As good Case as hee had
her Except the Cows being sicke may hindar   £0 13s. 0d.[71]

Nicholas Sever and Nicholas Saltar are probably the same person, and it is suggested

---

[66] SHC, DD\X\HKN/1 fo. 97r.
[67] SHC, DD\X\HKN/1 fo. 179v.
[68] Starred.
[69] SHC, DD\X\HKN/1 fo. 157v.
[70] Linded: a line or stripe of contrasting colour along the back of the animal.
[71] SHC, DD\X\HKN/1 fo. 158r.

that a regular milk supply was urgently needed for a motherless baby or a sick patient.[72]

On 26 April 1698 he 'put y^e 3 steares to Brint Cloase', doubtless paying someone to drive them all the way to his land at East Brent.[73] He took in another farmer's cow, for unknown reasons, on 2 May 1700, when 'William Adams put his Cowe to keeping to me in Clemans Cloase at fortean pens the weacke'.[74]

John Westover regularly bought cattle, often at local fairs. He would receive a small amount of the money at once ('in earnest'), with the rest to follow. Arrangements were made to meet and settle payment. The cattle are often identified by their colours and markings. On 6 November 1693 he 'Sould ye 2 fatt steares the Linded[75] & ye read [red] to William Gatcum A west Cuntrey Man at fifteen Pounds I am to keepe them untell fortnight before Chrismas I Received five shillings in Earnest so thear is more to Cum when he doth fech them in all fortean pounds And fiften shilling'.[76] In 1694 'John Feare And Richard Feare bought the Cow this 26th of october at five Pounds seventean shillings & six pens theay to fech her next wensday or Thursday Received in Earness five shillings'.[77] 1695 was a particularly busy year for sales. On 11 April 1695, he 'sould ye 3 steares 2 Read & one Black to Mr Melliar of Pillton Twentey three Pounds Received in Earnest five shilling him to take deliveray of them at Wells at ye signe of ye Swann & thear to Re[c]eve my money.' A fortnight later, on 24 April, he 'Sould to Mr Robart Iveleaf ye 2 Cowes ye Black Linded & ye read at Cheder fayer at Tenn pounds & A broune at holerd[78] fayre. William Rowley Sould ye Read bull at iij pounds.'[79] The next day, 25 April, he 'Sould the 2 3 yeare Age [two three-year old] heffars at Binigar fayar at Nine pounds. William Rowley sould ye read Cow and Calfe at Wells Market at five pounds five shillings to Mr Clarke of Lovington.'[80] On 3 February 1695/6, he 'soulde at Axbridg The Twoe oxen the black & ye read to Robert Hagat of froome at Twentey Twoe Pounds hee is to fetch them ye munday sennit next After & to pay ye Money. Thay Cost jist 13^s 12^d at holedey fayre[81] at Wells. Received, ye sixteenth of februarey, of Robart Hagot of frome by ye hand of William Peeterssun of Stoke 14 guines in 21 Pounds one peece of gould more in Twentey shillings.'[82] Finally, on 8 January 1699/1700 a badly torn page shows he was selling calves and steers 'About Shipham

[72] Originally suggested by Hazel Hudson, 'The New Wedmore Chronicles'175, *The Isle of Wedmore News* no. 397, January 2013, p. 51.

[73] SHC, DD\X\HKN/1 fo. 205r.

[74] SHC, DD\X\HKN/1 fo. 219v.

[75] See note 96.

[76] SHC, DD\X\HKN/1 fo. 152r.

[77] SHC, DD\X\HKN/1 fo. 165r.

[78] *I.e.* holy rood: the Feast of the Invention of the Holy Cross, 3rd May. This was one of the oldest of the fairs at Wells. Not to be confused with the Feast of the Holy Rood on 14 September.

[79] SHC, DD\X\HKN/1 fo. 169v.

[80] SHC, DD\X\HKN/1 fo. 171r.

[81] 3rd May: *cf.* note 104.

[82] SHC, DD\X\HKN/1 fo. 182v.

faye[r]', which was on 17 November each year, and dealing on behalf of 'Brother Tincknell', his brother-in-law, at an unidentified 'Cocke fayer'.[83]

References to the purchase of cattle are much fewer. On 25 April 1695, the same year in which he made frequent sales, he 'Bought of Humphrey Isgor Twoe oxen A Blacke And A read at Twelve pounds gave to good luck[84] in Earnes ij^s vj^d.' These might have been 'The Twoe oxen the black & ye read' which he sold at Axbridge on 3 February 1695/6, except that he noted those had cost him just 14s. The same day Bought Twoe 2 yeare Age heifers of William Huchens of Brint at Bridgwater at fower pounds And a 11^s. Item one Heifer more of Edward Thatcher at fifey [*sic*] shillings. Item William Rowley Bought for me ye 3th day of May 1695 Twoe oxen of George Paine of Farrington at Thirteen pounds & 12^s six pens … bought at Bridgwater 2 3 yeare Age [two three-year-old] steares of one of Chedsey at £11 7s. 6d.'.[85]

Dr Westover kept a number of horses, both for farm work and for riding often considerable distances to visit his patients. He bred from his mares, and used other farmers' stallions to service them. On 17 April 1693 'Robert Tincknell And I Agreed for the Horsing of My Mares at one shilling A mare in hand fower shillings A coult After' – clearly paying by results.[86] Two years later, he used John Gray's stallion, and noted the names and colouring of his mares:

Aprill 19th [1695] The great young Black Mare horst at John Grays. Aprill 20th The Blacke Mare Swanne horst with ye same horse.
Aprill ye 24th The stard[87] mare host At John grays. Aprill ye 25th '95 William Rowleys host. May ye 8th the young Black Mare host att John grays.
May ye 11 & 12 ye Great Black Mare & Boney[88] horst they had 2 Leapes a peece. The great Blacke Mare foled ye 17 or 18th of Aprill.[89]

No costs are given. John Gray may have been a member of the Gray family who farmed at Cocklake.[90] It was probably young 'nags' of his own breeding that John Westover sold on 14 July 1694: 'Cozen George Counsell bought y^e 2:3 yeare Age [two three-year-old] Naigs at Eaight pounds And Tenn shillings & gave ij^s vj^d in Ernis Received Eaight pounds & Tenn shillings.'[91]

---

[83] SHC, DD\X\HKN/1 fo. 218r.

[84] At £6 each, these were expensive animals. Perhaps this explains why the 2s. 6d. given immediately 'in earnest' as an undertaking to pay the rest at a later date, is also to bring 'good luck'.

[85] SHC, DD\X\HKN/1 fo. 171r.

[86] SHC, DD\X\HKN/1 fo. 139v.

[87] Starred.

[88] *I.e.* Bonny.

[89] SHC, DD\X\HKN/1 fo. 170v. The final sentence has been added later in a different ink.

[90] H. Hudson, 'The New Wedmore Chronicles' 176, *The Isle of Wedmore News* no. 398, February 2013, p.50.

[91] SHC, DD\X\HKN/1 fo. 161r.

John Westover's patients would often pay him in kind. One of the most remarkable - and touching - examples of this occurred in 1694 after Robert Leaker had suffered burns in what sounds like a gun accident: 'March y^e 6th 1693[/94] Went And visited Robert Leacker being Burnt with Powder as I under stood Went ye 9th went Againe ye 13th ons or twis mor before Being well.' In return, the doctor received from the grateful patient 'in part of pay his Labor in Cutting of five Coults £0 5s. 0d.' and furthermore on 11th March 'hee Tould mee he ould Cut Alle my Goods As Long As he And I did Live for ye my Curing him'.[92] Not only John Westover's colts, but his bull calves and ram lambs were gelded for free – a tiny but vivid record of the relationship between doctor and patient.

The only reference to John Westover buying in sheep is on 'Desember ye 4th [1697]: Then Bought forteane youe [ewe] Twooe Teath sheepe of Mr Clarke of Litten at Eaight shillings And A seven pence A peece which Came to Just £6 four shillings Tenn pens'.[93] It seems likely that most of his sheep were kept on his land at East Brent, where on 26 May 1695 'Cole of Brint' was paid the considerable sum of £10 10s. 0d. for 'shearing And Bottoming ye Rine.'[94]

Near the end of the Journal is a single entry which raises tantalising questions. In May-June 1700, at shearing-time, Dr Westover sells Ann Wall a considerable quantity of black sheep's wool. There is no mention of wool from his normal-coloured sheep anywhere else in the book, and the black wool only appears on this one occasion.

May ye 30th [1700]
Sould to Ann Wall sixtean pounds of my ould Black sheep fleese at [one s.?] ye Pound And Twoe pound & quarter of ye new blacke [sheep fleece?] and of ye blacke lockes[95] nine pounds at 4^d ye pound.[96]

Immediately preceding it in the Journal, but actually ten days later, is:

June y^e tenth 1700
Sould to Ann Walle six pound and halfe of blacke woolle at 12^d y^e pound
    £0 6s. 6d.
And five pounds of Lokes at 4^d y^e pound   £0 1s. 8d.
three pounds of blacke Lamtow[97] at 4^d y^e pound   £0 1s. 0d.

---

[92] SHC, DD\X\HKN/1 fo. 155v.
[93] SHC, DD\X\HKN/1 fo. 202v. The total should be £6 0s. 2d.
[94] SHC, DD\X\HKN/1 fo. 172v.
[95] Locks of sheep's wool: long, curly pieces detached from the main fleece and fetching a lower price – only 4d. a pound, where the quality wool and fleece is 1s. a pound.
[96] SHC, DD\X\HKN/1 fo. 220r.
[97] Lamtow: according to F.T. Elworthy, *The Dialect of West Somerset*, Vol. II, English Dialect Society (London, 1888), p. 414, lambs' shorn wool. It is the same price as locks, so is probably clippings and not quality fleece.

Received in part of pay of Ann Walle in worke at hay making Just
seven shillings Rest more to pay this 16th of Juley 1700 Just Twoe
shillings And ijd And Twoe shillings sixpens more Borowed soe in
Alle due more Just fower shillings Eaight pens   £0 4s. 8d.
more received in parte of pay of ye Abovsaid one shilling 4d in
William Walls work A but ye reecke & Ann for bruing.[98]

Ann Wall was one of John Westover's occasional helpers in the farmhouse. She is
recorded once as doing the washing; here she pays for the wool in part by haymaking and brewing, while her husband William contributes with work on a hay-
rick. Clearly they have very little money, and she has to borrow 2s. 6d. that will have
to be repaid as well. It seems probable that Ann Wall was one of the village women
who made ends meet by spinning and knitting, as a rural cottage industry; in 1700
she is spinning these black fleeces and loose wool into yarn, a distinct and attractive
contrast to the normal white. Whether she then knitted up patterned garments, or
sold the yarn on to others who did so, we cannot know. It raises the further question
of whether Dr John Westover was keeping a distinct small flock of black sheep –
they are 'my ould Black sheep fleese' and 'ye new', suggesting the wool is his own
and not something he saw at a fair and bought out of curiosity. If so, what happened
to them, since they make no other appearance in the Journal? The black sheep might
have been another of the doctor's short-lived farming ventures, but the evidence does
not survive.

Conclusion

John Westover's Journal reveals, in its myriad details, the close network of supply
and demand, of employer and worker, of money and goods that operated within the
farming community of which he was part. Payments could be complicated, and the
time-lag in settling an account could be considerable. The physical safe-keeping and
disposal of money, before banking and bank notes, needed care and organisation, of
which there are sometimes hints. John Westover was sufficiently well off to lend
money, usually to members of his extended family, but occasionally to others. In July
1688 he 'Lent James Larder of Wedmore Twentey Shillings the which he promised
to pay Me At pridey faier or their About' Added in different ink is a note, 'Received
the Twentey Shillings'.[99] The local fairs were useful meeting places for such transactions, but the quality of some coins might be doubtful: 'Received more in part of
pay by the hand of his sune Richard five And thirty shillings 2 halfe Crownes of ye
money are very small Received more in part of pay of Richard Counsell at Cheder
fayer 1692 Tenn shillings'.[100]

Patients might offer goods or services in place of cash. 'March ye 26th 1688. Joane

---

[98] SHC, DD\X\HKN/1 fo. 220r.
[99] SHC, DD\X\HKN/1 fo. 68v.
[100] SHC, DD\X\HKN/1 fo. 92r.

Adams of Wedmore had 2 Girdell for yᵉ Itch She tould Me she ould worke it out At Hay Making. Renewed them Twise. Received in full iii s.' - suggesting that in the event she found the money to pay.[101] When, on 11 March 1688/89, he settled his account with Robert Edgell, possibly for medical care, it was offset against unspecified work done by Edgell: 'thear did Apeare due to Me Just Twentey Seven Shillings Six pens Alle yᵉ Worke he hath dune for Me out setted to yˢ day A forsaid. Received of Robart Edgell in A Steare of 2 yeares ould thirty Shillings soe thear is due to Robart Edgell ijˢ jᵈ'.[102] Westover ended by paying a small amount to Edgell, but with an addition to his herd of cattle. When he 'Received in full of Alle Acounts of Cozen Iveleafe the sume of fiftean Shilliing this 4ᵗʰ of August 1697 by Me John Westover' he concludes 'She is paid for yᵉ Apells & I am payd for yᵉ cure of Cozen gabriell['s] Eye'.[103]

It is the accumulation of these daily details which make the farming notes in the 'Journal' unusual, especially given their date. They are not tidily written by a paid estate manager for an 18th century gentleman-farmer, but by a 17th century farmer himself. In addition to running the farm and a flourishing medical practice, he apparently had contact with and interest in new farming ideas, even if he did not have the time and inclination to pursue them long-term. The result gives a vivid impression of practical farming at the turn of the sixteenth and seventeenth centuries, and reveals an enterprising local farmer, open to experiment and initiative, a full hundred years before John Billingsley.[104]

Acknowledgements

This paper would not have been possible without Hazel Hudson, who first explored Westover's farming notes in *Doctors of Wedmore Parish* (2010) and in her *Isle of Wedmore News* articles in 2013, and whose local knowledge of Wedmore, its history, landscape and farming has underpinned our work together over many decades. The late Jim Skeggs helped to identify some of John Westover's farming dialect terms.

[101] SHC, DD\X\HKN/1 fo. 61r.
[102] SHC, DD\X\HKN/1 fo. 81v.
[103] SHC, DD\X\HKN/1 fo. 107r.
[104] J. Billingsley, *A General View of the Agriculture of Somerset*, 2ⁿᵈ edition (Bath, 1798).

10. Thomas Carew of Crowcombe: the Pecuniary Problems of an 18th-century Gentleman

SUE BERRY

This article is based on the correspondence, accounts, and other documents, part of the Trollope-Bellew deposit of estate and family papers of Thomas Carew (1703-1766) (figure 32), held at the Somerset Heritage Centre.[1] As an historical source, the correspondence has one great drawback which is that, with very few exceptions, the letters were all written to Carew; there are very few of his own letters in the collection and therefore it is only possible to deduce the subject(s) of his letters from the answers he received from his correspondents. Bearing this proviso in mind, the surviving letters are an excellent source of information on the financial worries that beset this particular Somerset gentleman.

Some 11 miles to the north-west of Taunton lies the parish of Crowcombe, a seemingly idyllic country village with a mainly early 16th century church, a church house built between 1515 and 1519,[2] and a village inn licensed since at least the mid-18th century.[3] Overlooking this quintessential English scene is a Queen Anne-style house begun in 1724 and described by Nicholas Pevsner as 'the finest house of its date in Somerset south of the Bath area' (figure 33).[4]

This house, Crowcombe Court, was built by Thomas Carew, a member of the family who had held the manor of Crowcombe Biccombe since 1568. Although its roots lay in Pembrokeshire, the Somerset branch had resided at Camerton since at least 1483. Camerton was where Thomas was born in 1703, the eldest son of Thomas Carew (c.1668-1719) and his wife, Elizabeth Sanford of Nynehead (1673(?)-1728).

As heir to the Carew estates in Somerset, Devon and Pembrokeshire, Carew would seem to have been born with the proverbial silver spoon in his mouth. Yet a

---

[1] SHC, DD\TB.

[2] SHC, DD\TB/5/1, Grant by Robert Biccombe to twenty named trustees of his moiety of a house 40' long and 26½' wide opposite the churchyard and abutting on the pound belonging to the prioress of Stoodleigh in trust to permit the churchwardens to dispose of it to the greatest use of the parish church, conditional upon the building or re-building of a house there within two years, 1515.

[3] SHC, Q\RLA/19, Alehousekeepers' recognisance rolls for Taunton Division, 1674-1828.

[4] J. Orbach and N. Pevsner, *South and West Somerset (The Buildings of England)* (Yale, 2002), pp. 242-4.

list of his debts, drawn up in 1759, shows he owed at least £16,741 or approximately £2,500,000 in modern terms.[5] This had increased from £10,704 14s. noted in an earlier, unfortunately undated, list of his creditors of which £6,000 was the value of the legacies owed to three of his sisters under their father's will.[6]

How had Thomas amassed this enormous liability? I believe there are three core reasons that need to be examined. First, the fact that he appears to have been a man incapable of living within his income, even when his debts threatened to overwhelm him. Secondly, a lack of sufficient manorial and estate income from his lands to cover his expenses and thirdly, his greatest extravagance, the building of Crowcombe Court and the continuing cost of its upkeep.

His extravagance was apparent from an early age when, possibly soon after leaving Westminster School,[7] he went to London and entered the Middle Temple in 1720. His account book for February-March is full of entries such as 'going to the plays' 12s. 6d., the purchase of 'oranges and other sweetmeats' and 'half pound of Smyrna figs' 2s. 10d., a silver seal and 'silk string and key to my watch' 19s. 6d., a flute 2s., three pairs of gloves 4s. 2d., 'Mr Overton[8] for a Ladys picture' 2s. 6d.[9]

Later in life, when he was already deeply in debt, he spent £862 between 1737 and 1752 just on clothing for himself and three or four of his male household servants. The account, which lists in detail the clothes bought from Charles Pearce, tailor, contains few, if any, entries for clothing for his wife, daughters or female servants.[10]

By 1744, it was apparent to John Carew that his brother could not continue spending beyond his means in this way. He wrote, in October that year, to Thomas

> collect all your debts into one sum, then make a fair calculation of your annual income allowing fully for all disburstments and deducting in full for the interest of the above sum, when you will easily see the neat remainder upon which you may live hansomely and cut your coat accordingly, by which you may always have money beforehand for as you have no house rent to pay and so generous and good a brother with you, with (I am sure) so frugal a wife, I can't see you need in the least reduce. Only pursue the above by which you will save extraordinary interest and old debts coming up on you unex-

[5] SHC, DD\SAS\C/432/28, a list of the debts of Thomas Carew, 25 April 1759.

[6] SHC, DD\TB/25/12, draft account and memoranda book of Thomas Carew, 1720-1735. At the same time as Carew was in debt to the sum of over £10,000 he was owed approximately £8,300 of which over half was due from Hudson's Bay Company stock, a mortgage by the Sherston family of Charlecombe dating from 1717 and an entry described simply as 'Navigation'.

[7] The admission records of Westminster School for this period are patchy and Thomas is not named in them. However, both his brother John and his nephew Thomas went there and it seems likely that Thomas would have as well. Information courtesy of Elizabeth Wells, Westminster School archives.

[8] Most probably Henry Overton of the White Horse without Newgate in Little Old Bailey, London. He succeeded his father John in the business in 1713.

[9] SHC, DD\TB/25/12, draft account and memoranda book of Thomas Carew, 1720-1728.

[10] SHC, DD\TB/14/21, account for clothes supplied by Charles Pearce, tailor, 1737-1752.

pectedly by which your present cash is always exhausted which, I am sensible, the want of must make a man of your generous temper uneasy and frettfull.[11]

Unfortunately for Thomas, he seems to have been incapable of following his brother's advice and his spending continued unabated. Even when in correspondence in 1757 with his solicitor Thomas Naish of Bath over the question of repaying the principal and interest on a mortgage of £1,400 due to Mrs Elianor Rishton of Bath which she had requested several times, he was at the same time looking to buy a pair of horses for his carriage. Naish wrote

[She] has sent to me several times for her interest money and as she has nothing but the interest of her moneys to live upon I beleive she much wants it, and I should be therefore much obliged to you to let her have it as soon as you can conveniently spare it . . .

Mr Prowse has desired me to buy you a pair of genteel black geldings for your coach and post chaise but cannot inform me what price you would give. It is most likely that Mr King or some of my friends here may be able to get some that will be satisfactory to you and I beg the favour of a line to let me know what price you would be pleased to give for a pair of horses and I will endeavour to purchase them for you . . .[12]

The last we hear of Mrs Riston's debt is in a letter of October 1763 when one Christopher Griffith wrote

I am directed by Messrs Sandford and Brown, executors and devisees of the last will and testament of Mrs Elianor Riston, widow, deceased, to acquaint you that as application hath been many times made to you for the payment of the fourteen hundred pounds and the interest thereof (of which there is a great arrears) which you have hitherto neglected to pay, this therefore waits on you to let you know that unless you forthwith pay the same, I shall be obliged to take all legal methods against you for the recovery thereof . . .[13]

By this time Elianor Riston had been dead for over a year and possibly for as long as two.[14]

The second cause of Carew's financial problems was that, like so many of the country gentry as opposed to the very wealthy nobility, he was land rich but income

11   SHC, DD\TB/24/9, John Carew to T. Carew, 15 October 1744.
12   SHC, DD\TB/25/21, Thomas Naish to Carew, 19 February 1757.
13   SHC, DD\TB/24/7 Christopher Griffith to Carew, 8 October 1763.
14   TNA, PROB 11/867/31, Will made 5 April 1760, proved 2 July 1761.

poor. Many of the surviving letters from Henry Lockett (1703-1778) who was Rector of Crowcombe from 1732 until his death, and who also seems to have acted as Carew's bailiff for many years, are concerned with the problem of collecting in the tenants' rents, the difficulties of letting out vacant holdings for an economic rent and the necessity of authorising repairs which would cost Carew money. These were problems that may well have affected other land owners but in addition to them, Carew seems to have been very lax in the supervision of his estates. The economic situation was summed up by Lockett in a letter of March 1745

> The chief news of the countrey are frequent seizures for rent. In short, times grow excessive bad. The tenents are on the very brink of ruin, and people of middle fortune can but barely live.[15]

He had previously reported in September 1744 that a barn had blown down at Week Farm in Clatworthy 'which the tenent made me view, and really 'tis absolutely necessary to repair it, for he assured me he could not thrash his corn so as to make up his rent as usual without it'[16] and in the following month he wrote that

> Robin Slocombe that rents Milltown Tenement of you [in Clatworthy] was with me yesterday and told me that his term would be expired at Michaelmas next but that he was willing to take it for another term. He now gives £30 per year, and for two hours together would not advance beyond 26 pound, I told him if that was his resolution I would not trouble you with the affair. At last he said he would give the present rent on condition you would repair the house which has been miserably dilapidated by Way. He says there is timber enough on the estate to do it, and stones, and the expence will not exceed sixteen or eighteen pound.[17]

In January 1745 he wrote

> Robin Slocombe was at me again about taking Miltown, tho' he sent me word a little before that he would have no more to do with it, because he had not your answer sooner, and consequently could not improve it with turnips last autumn as he intended. He was impertinent enough to offer £4 less for it. I told him I would not trouble you with it. I believe he is willing to continue in it in case the house be put in order, or if you will allow him about 40s a year for the rent of the house he now lives in, so probably will be less expence to you than rebuilding.

---

[15] SHC, DD\TB/15/2, Henry Lockett (Rector of Thorne Coffin 1729-1744, Crowcombe 1732-1779 and Clatworthy 1744-1779) to Carew, 9 March 1744/1745.

[16] SHC, DD\TB/15/2, Lockett to Carew, 10 September 1744.

[17] SHC, DD\TB/27/4, Lockett to Carew, 20 October 1744.

George Way desired me also to write to you about Week estate, his term being to expire on them at the same time. He offers you £100 a year. I answered him I would not trouble you with any proposals below the present rent for I was well satisfyed you would not comply with them. I imagine he will at last continue on the same terms, and considering the badness of the times I would advise you to close with him as soon as possible, for I am assured he is racking what he can out of the estate, and if he leaves it it will be in a poor condition. If they have not your answer soon, I am afraid they will look out for other bargains which are at present very plenty in this countrey.

I beged some time since to know the lowest price you would let Flexpool Estates [Flaxpool in Crowcombe] at, I desire your answer the first opportunity for I hope to let them to John White of Truscombe.[18]

In the summer of 1748 Lockett wrote

I have letten a meadow to your miller for five guineas a year. It measures three acres one rood four perches so that he gives you £1 12s 6 per acre for it. I did what I could to advance the rent, but to no purpose . . . surely 'tis more money than you could have made of it, if kept in your own hands.[19]

It may well be argued that the economic situation was partly where Carew's financial problems lay and that there was little he could do about that, but it can also be said he seems to have been very lax in the supervision of his estates and this inattention to their management only added to his problems. Even if he did realise the importance of maximising the return from his estates, he appears to have been so casual in his attitude towards it that not only Lockett and Thomas Naish, but also his brother-in-law John Horne, felt they had to bring it to his attention.

In November 1749, Naish was endeavouring to collect rents due to Carew in Brewham and Camerton. He wrote that he proposed to call on the cottagers at Brewham the following week to collect their chief rents but 'not having the counterparts of either of their leases shall have some difficulty to find out what they are'. He added that

I cannot find you have ever collected your whole chief rents or anything in lieu of the days' work and poultry reserved on almost every one of your leases and which amount togeather to near one third of the chief rents.[20]

[18] SHC, DD\TB/27/4, Lockett to Carew, 28 January 1744/5.
[19] SHC, DD\TB/27/4, Lockett to Carew, 6 July 1748.
[20] SHC, DD\TB/25/21, Naish to Carew, 7 November 1749.

Further evidence of his neglect of his estates can be found in a letter of April 1750, written by Horne, who was staying in Bath. At this point Carew was hoping to sell his Camerton estate to raise some much needed money and Horne went to visit it. He reported back to Carew that

> [Farmer Bennett] has cut down three very fine oaks on the estate he rents of you, and three or four of his horses are grazing on your young grass while your team is employed in carrying coals for other people. Part of the pasture is plowed up, and the ground in generall quite impoverished and worn out with constant plowing, tho' not half sown, most of the gates and hedges thrown down and the whole become in a manner common, and in very bad condition, so that it is high time you were here to look after it and to appoint a fitter person to take care of it for the future . . . You will excuse the liberty I have taken in mentioning these things as it proceeds from the regard I have for your interest, and I hope you will be able to come hither soon, when I believe you will find it necessary to stay a few days to put things into better order.[21]

By June of 1753 Henry Lockett was driven by despair to write

> In short, I think nothing but your presence here [Crowcombe] can put your affairs upon a right footing in these as well as several other respects, and I must therefore beg you for your own sake if possible to afford your unsettled accounts here a month or two at least this summer.[22]

However, to give Carew his due, this lack of supervision may have been the result of a recurring mental health problem he suffered intermittently from the age of 30. It is difficult to assess exactly what this problem was from the references to it in his correspondence; Horace Walpole wrote that he was 'a crazy zealot, who believed himself possessed by the devil . . .'.[23] Carew himself sought advice from both medical practitioners and clergymen to be told by one of the former

> You may assure yourself that the disorders of your mind are owing to those of your body, and consequently not at the command of your mind only, for which therefore you are no way answerable so that in this respect you should make yourself easy.[24]

---

[21] SHC, DD\TB/23/18, John Horne (Governor of Bombay 1734-1739 and Carew's brother-in-law) to Carew, 9 April 1750.

[22] SHC, DD\TB/24/13, Lockett to Carew, 25 June 1753.

[23] R. Sedgwick, ed., *The History of Parliament: the House of Commons 1715-1754* (London, 1970), p. 528.

[24] SHC, DD\TB/15/8, Peter Shaw to Carew 6 March 1760. Shaw was practising physic in London by 1726. In 1740 he was admitted a licentiate of the College of Physicians, being then a doctor of medicine, and became a popular physician in London, so much so that in 1752 he was appointed physician-extraordinary to the King.

And by one of the latter

Indeed, my good Sir, you hurry yourself too much, and afflict yourself with imaginary fears. God regards the heart, if that is upright, all is well. No blasphemous or filthy thoughts can dess[...]le a man, so long as they are not assented to. You abhor them from your soul, therefore they are not yours, let the author of them be answerable for them, but torment not yourself.[25]

But whatever the cause of his lack of awareness, there is no doubt that this failure to appreciate the problem only added to his financial predicament.

The third cause of Carew's insolvency was his great project, the building of his mansion, Crowcombe Court, with its gardens and park, and the continuing costs associated with its upkeep.

On the death of his father in September 1719, Thomas Carew was only 16, still a minor with his fortune under the control of trustees appointed by his father's will. He inherited Crowcombe Biccombe on the death of Katherine Carew (died 1720), the widow of his great-uncle John Carew (died 1684). By April 1724, when Thomas was just over 21, he had begun the vast project, beginning with the demolition of the existing Elizabethan manor house in Crowcombe. It was already clear to one of Thomas' former trustees, his uncle Henry Sandford, that the new mansion was going to prove far more expensive than anticipated. He wrote to his sister, Thomas' mother, in April 1724:

I was att Crowcombe last Wednesday, they have demolished all the [...] [ex]cept the hall, great parlour, Puddy's parlour and the stair case and cellar. Mr Carew sent [...] pay Parker this day £100 which I hope shall do and he will allow it out of the rent which is now do. If 'tis so in pulling downe, God alone knows what 'twill be when the house is raising.[26]

In October the same year he wrote to her from Hayne[27] where, as he said,

I have been this fortnight to avoid the constant cry of want of money att Crowcombe, tho' they have had a great deale. I have borrowed one hundred pounds out of my owne pockett which I sent a fortnight since. They sent me word it would only stop their mouths for three or four days.[28]

---

25   SHC, DD\TB/15/8, Arthur Hele (Vicar of Corston, 1755-1778, Rector of Charlecombe 1762-1778 and Rector of Porlock 1763-1778) to Carew, 29 February 1762.
26   SHC, DD\TB/24/8, Henry Sanford (Carew's uncle) to Elizabeth Carew (Carew's mother, née Sanford), 11 April 1724.
27   Most probably Hayne in Plymtree, Devon which was the home of the Harward family, connected by marriage to the Sanford family.
28   SHC, DD\TB/29/10, Sanford to Elizabeth Carew, 25 October 1724.

Three volumes of weekly accounts for the demolition of the old house at Crowcombe and the start of the building of the Court survive for the years 1724-1727.[29] In the 66 weeks between 21 March 1724 and 14 June 1725 the total money paid out was £2,469 3s. 4½d. with the weekly sums increasing as more work was done, so much so that whereas the first week's cost amounted to only £2 2s. 3d., by 25th June 1725 the week's total was £262 1s. 11d and this at a time when a gentleman could live on £300 per annum.[30] Carew did try to recoup a little of this outlay by selling off some of the materials from the demolition of the old house including bricks, timber, rafters, and even an old door for which he received 2s.. He was also selling some of his garden produce, presumably from the kitchen garden of the old house, as he received 7s. 4¾d. from the gardener for 'what he made of gowsberries, currants and cabage' but the money raised was nowhere near enough to cover the costs of the work.

Although Thomas Parker was first employed as the architect and laid the foundations for the house and finished the stable court, on his dismissal Carew employed Nathaniel Ireson of Wincanton to finish the work. Their contract, dated 8 July 1734, specified that

> Whereas the said Thomas Carew intends to erect and build a dwelling house nigh to his present dwelling house in Crocombe aforesaid upon the foundations sometime since laid and carryed up by Thomas Parker architect, Ireson would for and in consideration of the sume of one thousand two hundred thirty six pounds and three shillings to be paid at the days and times and in manner and proportion as herein after is and are mentioned . . . erect build raise and set up upon the foundations above mentioned a dwelling house after the manner and forme of the modells plans and representations well and in a work man like manner in every particular and individual respect whatsoever . . .[31]

In the detailed estimate Ireson provided, Carew was listed as paying another £370 15s. directly for extras such as lead, iron work and slate and also as having to provide the stone for coping, sills, rustic pilasters and other parts of the house on the east, west and south fronts.[32]

Quite how far Parker had got with the new house at the time of his dismissal is a vexed question which there is no space to address here. He was employed as late as 1734 and there are references in the accounts to interior work being done by his workmen. However, I believe that under Ireson's supervision much more work was

[29] SHC, DD\TB/13/1, weekly account books of disbursements on building works, 1724-1727.
[30] R. Porter, *England in the eighteenth century* (London, 1998), p. 4.
[31] SHC, DD\TB/10/9, agreement for Nathaniel Ireson's building work on Crowcombe Court with specification and estimate, 1734.
[32] SHC, DD\TB/10/9, agreement, 1734.

done. In addition to the £1,236 quoted in the 1734 contract, he later put in another account for £109 15*s*. 3½*d*. which he said was for work done 'in alterations and out of the articles' in 1734 and 1735[33] and in August 1738 he agreed to 'do the chimney piece in the hall and other works' for another £113 17*s*.[34]

Whatever interior work Parker may or may not have completed, there was still much to be done. Other members of the family appreciated that money needed to be saved where possible even if Carew himself didn't. In April 1738 his brother John wrote to him recommending he purchase the marble for the chimney pieces from Bristol and also employ a workman recommended by a friend. Not only was the man's workmanship superior but, said John, 'I am certain you would save a great deal of money by this way'.[35] Work was still being done in March five years later when Henry Lockett wrote to Carew

> Mr Phelps[36] was here yesterday to know whether the painting materials were ready. He advises, if you have not already bought them, by no means to buy them grounded and mixed there being generally a great cheat in the London mixtures, and rather to order the white lead from Bristow where 'tis as cheap and the carriage to Watchet will be trifling, and to have the oyl from the oyl mills at Ham where 'tis cheaper than in London.[37]

In June 1743 he wrote again

> The rooms and closets over the library and drawing room are near all plaistered, the floor of one is now laying, and the wainscott will be brought from Taunton to morrow; but there is no mantle for the chimney peices which I suppose you intend, and therefore was proper to be mentioned. The closet within your designed bedchamber is also begun upon. The bedchamber itself wants painting, but I beleive it will be improper to do it now; because the smell of the paint will be very offensive in summer.[38]

And in April 1744 'Your apartment is at last finished by Blake. Mr Phelps is now painting it. I beleive you will much approve of the alteration . . .'.[39] This last sentence

[33] SHC, DD\TB/13/6, single page of Ireson's accounts for extra work done at Crowcombe Court, 1734-1735.
[34] SHC, DD\TB/25/19, Ireson's detailed agreement on work to be done in the hall and staircase at Crowcombe Court, 1738.
[35] SHC, DD\TB/24/9, John Carew to Carew, 21 April 1738.
[36] Richard Phelps (*c*.1710-1785) of Porlock. He trained with Thomas Hudson and spent his career in Somerset, not only painting portraits of the local gentry but also working as an interior decorator. An album of drawings in the British Museum represents most of his surviving work, including sketches of Thomas Carew, his second wife Mary Horne, and the Reverend Henry Lockett. (BM, 1PRN:PDB30991).
[37] SHC, DD\TB/15/2, Lockett to Carew, 3 March 1742/3.
[38] SHC, DD\TB/27/4, Lockett to Carew, 15 June 1743.
[39] SHC, DD\TB/27/4, Lockett to Carew, 14 April 1744.

suggests that Carew may already have been making changes to some of the rooms.

As well as the cost of building and decorating the house, there was also the expense of the gardens. There is a note in a small account book of a contract with John Charter for 'doing the gardens' for a price of £270 to be paid in four instalments between June and December plus any remainder when the work was complete. Although the entry is undated, the following page begins in June 1729 so it seems likely that that is the date of the contract.[40] In 1733, 20 varieties of apple tree were grafted and in March 1734 Carew took delivery of some plants, spending £1 18s. on peach, nectarine, almond, apple and pear trees which had to come from Bristol by sea to Watchet because the Taunton carrier refused to bring them.[41]

We know there was at least one ornamental fish pond by 1749 as Mary Carew wrote in a letter to her husband 'I am very glad to hear the gold fish are alive and well and shall be much pleasd to find they are increasd when I see Crowcombe next'[42] and the deer park was also being finished at this time.

A volume of accounts from 25 August 1744 to 8 November 1746 reveals that £90 2s. 3d. was spent on the wages of those working in the gardens during this period at 1s. a day for men and 6d. a day for women. This does not, of course, take into account the cost of any plants purchased or materials bought for the gardens.[43] All in all, one can only agree with Carew's Uncle Henry who had expressed his despair at the cost of it all a quarter of a century earlier.

However, as Carew soon discovered, it was not only the cost of building a house like Crowcombe Court which had to be taken into consideration, but also the expenditure on its upkeep once it was completed. Even as it was being finished internally and more work was being done on the drains and in levelling the slopes in the Park, the family could no longer afford to continue living there. As a result, in 1749, his second wife Mary and her brother John Horne were looking for a property to rent in London which would both satisfy Carew's requirements and save him money. Horne wrote in September that year

> As my sister wrote you fully by the last post concerning the house in Craigs Court[44] I have nothing to add on that head, only that we have not yet heard of any other house that will do for your family[45]

---

[40] SHC, DD\TB/25/12, draft account and memoranda book of Thomas Carew, 1720-1728.

[41] SHC, DD\TB/29/15, a list of fruit trees purchased from William Cheney of Bristol, 1734.

[42] SHC, DD\TB/23/18, Mary Carew (Carew's second wife) to Carew, 5 September 1749.

[43] SHC, DD\TB/14/9, garden wages account book, 1744-1746.

[44] Little is known about the origins of Craig's Court, other than it was laid out by Joseph Craig at some point in the 1690s at the northern tip of the Palace of Whitehall. The Palace was destroyed by fire in 1698 and the property later to be called Harrington House was built shortly afterwards. Rate books exist for the period in question and show that Thomas Carew began paying rates on a property in the Court in 1750 and continued to do so until 1758. The property is known today as Harrington House. G.H. Gater and E.P. Wheeler, ed., 'Harrington House, Craig's Court', in *Survey of London: Volume 16, St Martin-in-The-Fields I: Charing Cross* (London, 1935), pp. 232-7.

[45] SHC, DD\TB/23/18, Horne to Carew, 21 September 1749.

and later the same month

> Mr Scott did not come hither 'till this morning when he showed us the
> particulars of the necessary repairs to be done to the house in Craigs Court
> which, on a stricter examination, he says will not exceed £300. We have
> desired him to go and talk with the landlord tomorrow and have empowered
> him to offer £140 per annum provided he will repair it to our liking, or else
> £120 per annum and you to be at half the expence, and in case they can come
> to an agreement, I will meet Mr Craig and settle it with him so that we may
> be able to get into the house by Christmas . . .[46]

The family spent seven years in the London house (figure 34) before eventually
returning to Crowcombe Court on a full time basis. However, when Carew did
return to Somerset in the autumn of 1757, he did so still owing some rent money to
his landlord. His 'man of affairs' in London, John Pierce, wrote to him in early
October of that year stating that

> Mr Craig has been with me today and desires I will pay him this week or at
> farthest next week, and I have promised him. Pray how much do you make
> due to him at Michaelmas?[47]

In November, Pierce had to write again concerning unpaid debts due for the
house as well as Mr Craig's bill for cleaning it and removing the rubbish left there
by Carew when he vacated the property

> There have been many people with me for rates for your house, the watchman
> says there is two years and half due, and so does the scavenger and others, and I
> cannot find their last receipts and wish that you or Mr Hughes could tell me
> how long it has been unpaid ... as the house was in a sad condition there has
> been a bill sent in to me of six pounds for cleaning the house of the rubbish &
> for scouring the wainscot, and for brushes, brooms, soap and other articles.[48]

It is quite evident from the numerous letters to Carew from his solicitor and
other men of business that he was incapable of settling all the debts he had accrued
by the late 1750s. He had borrowed extensively from numerous people over the
course of his lifetime, beginning, as we have seen, with his uncle Henry Sanford as
early as 1724.

These debts consisted of a mixture of the mortgages which he had taken out on
his properties which he was unable to pay off, or even to keep up the interest due on

---

[46] SHC, DD\TB/23/18, Horne to Carew, 28 September 1749.
[47] SHC, DD\TB/24/12, Pierce to Carew, 8 November 1757.
[48] SHC, DD\TB/24/12, Pierce to Carew, 29 November 1757.

them, monies he had borrowed on bond, or promise to repay by a certain date, from individuals and the debts he owed various tradesman and shopkeepers from whom he had purchased goods on account (figure 35).

The account of his debts drawn up in 1759 shows that he owed £9,400 on four mortgages. The largest of these, for £2,500, was of the lordship, manor and castle of Carew and other property in Pembrokeshire, which had been mortgaged to his brother John in 1748. On John's death in 1750, this had passed to his younger son, another John. Another for £1,400 was owed to Mrs Rishton as we have seen above. Money borrowed on bonds amounted to another £3,563 14s. The interest owed on all these debts totalled £1,817 10s. There was then a list of 22 individuals owed money on account and for bills; these included his cook and maidservants who were owed £58 for wages, Mr Hill, coachmaker £90, Mr March of Bristol wine merchant £57, and Mr Light of Williton, grocer, £10.[49]

How many of these debts were paid off at this time is uncertain; some of the smaller amounts such as 'Mr Lambe fishmonger of London £6' and 'Mr Winter coals £10' are marked 'Pd' on the schedule, but from later evidence it is clear some of the largest debts such as John Carew's, John Horne's and Mrs Rishton's were not.

Horne died in 1757. He left the greater part of his estate to his sister Culling Smith and her children, with only token legacies to Carew and his daughters. One at least of Thomas' acquaintances was indignant on his behalf, writing 'I can't help saying that I think he has been very ungenerous (all things considered) in his bounty to you and the young ladies and that I expected to have seen it much larger'.[50] As Carew owed Horne, according to the 1759 account, £2,124 and as he had been charging his wife's mother and brother £390 *per annum* for board, lodging, washing and the use of the coach and horses while they had been living at Crowcombe Court, it is perhaps not surprising that Horne probably felt Carew had already had quite enough of his money.

Correspondence from Horne's executors and their accountant shows that two and a half years after his will was proved in December 1757 they were still trying to get Carew to supply them with his version of what he owed Horne's estate and what he thought was due to him from it. Joseph Eyre, the accountant, wrote in November 1758:

In short, Sir, as you promised Dr Monro about Christmas last to send him an account of your demands on the Governor and have not done it, and the Governor has now been dead a year and the legacy must be paid or carry an interest, the executors are determined and particularly Mr Sullivan to use all legal methods, with civility, to get in the effects and finish the accounts of their executorship.[51]

---

[49] SHC, DD\SAS/C/432/28, a list of the debts of Thomas Carew, 25 April 1759.
[50] SHC, DD\TB/23/19, J. Coxe to Carew, 22 December 1757.
[51] SHC, DD\TB/23/19, Joseph Eyre to Carew, 4 November 1758.

and in July 1760 the executors wrote

> We further hope you will not take it amiss if we desire this [Carew's detailed
> demand on the estate] to be done without loss of time, as three years are now
> nearly elapsed since the Governor's death and we have not yet been able to get
> in money enough to discharge the legacy he bequeathed to Mrs Smith . . .[52]

James Bernard, Carew's barrister son-in-law, took on the task of trying to settle
this problem and was still meeting with Dr Monroe as late as May 1765 when Carew
was trying to offset 'French wine, tea, washing, fire, candles etc and all for extraordinary charges during the last three years of Mr Horne's illness' against the money
due to the executors.[53]

Finally, the time came when it seemed the only way Carew could clear at least
part of his debts was to sell some of his estates. By November 1760 he was already
trying to sell the Cove and West Stoodleigh estates in Devon and a year later a
private bill was being prepared in London to put before Parliament 'for the sale of
part of the settled estate'. This was passed in 1762 (2 George III c.64).

Although Francis Drewe, Carew's brother-in-law, managed to find a buyer for
Cove and with a great deal of difficulty persuaded Carew to let it go, the sale of the
West Stoodleigh estate was jeopardised by Carew's refusal to part with the advow-
son and Drewe expressed his exasperation in a letter to his niece Elizabeth in 1760,
'I really am quite out of heart to attempt to serve your Papa, for when we have done
our utmost and have some seeming prospect, his scruples of conssience mar it all'.[54]

Drewe's letters to his nieces at this time offer a great insight into Carew's
complete inability to understand the difficulty he was in financially and his constant
alterations of mind. Although the latter may be partly attributable to his ill health,
and, as Drewe put it, his daughters 'concealing from him the miserable situation of
his affairs', if Carew did 'not bestir himself, it is not in the power of any other person
to serve him'.[55]

By 1760 the expense of living at the Court was causing yet more serious problems and it was proposed that the family leave Crowcombe Court again, as they had
done in 1749, to save the expenses of living there. In January of that year John Pierce
wrote to Mary, Carew's elder daughter,

> I have wrote to your Papa pretty fully by this post, and hope it will give him
> some satisfaction, but whether he will approve of one part of it relating to his
> coming to town I do not know. But I hope it will not be dissagreeable to him
> or either of you young ladies, tho' it may seem at first a little irksome to you

[52]   SHC, DD\TB/23/19, John Monro and Thomas Smith, 22 July 1760.
[53]   SHC, DD\TB/28/19, James Bernard to Carew, 16 March 1765.
[54]   SHC, DD\TB/23/17, Francis Drewe to Elizabeth Carew, 19 November 1760.
[55]   SHC, DD\TB/25/22, Drewe to E. Carew, 1 June 1761.

if he complies with my opinion which is that in order to be free from the care and large expence of living in that great house, he would for a year or two at least quit it, and come to London in handsome chambers, or a very good lodging, as many gentlemen of distinction do, and by that means he will save many hundreds a yeare'.

The two daughters, it was suggested in the same letter, should 'submit for a while to go into some genteel apartments at some place you may like in Somersetshire or Devonshire'.[56] In April 1760, Francis Drewe wrote to Mary that 'I think Mr Pearce's advice to your Papa about leaving Crocombe is very right and I think he is no friend to himself and family, if he does not follow it'.[57] In May, it appeared to Drewe that 'he seems resolved to remove, and [I] don't doubt but you may on enquiry meet with a little house ready furnish',[58] but in December that year Carew had again changed his mind.

As Drewe rightly pointed out,

let your house keeping be ever so frugall, and under the best oeconomy, it would be far more prudent (could your father be prevailed on) to give it entirely up, for I am satisfied no creditor can possibly be easy, with such an appearance of grandeur and he to go without even his interest. Neither is it possible for you to convince the world, that so large a house, so many people and horses can be maintained for a triffle.[59]

Now, at this point, neither of Carew's surviving daughters was married. The elder, Mary, never did but the younger daughter, Elizabeth and James Bernard, a London barrister, were married in May 1764. On the 2nd July that year Nathaniel Castleton, a cousin of Carew's, wrote to him with a proposition that Bernard should buy the Studeley, Devon estate for £14,000. This was £2,000 less than it had been valued at but as Castleton said, 'who will be benefitted in the end, but your own family'.[60]

The following day, Charles Prowse wrote in the same vein

I am still in hopes that what I shall herein propose to you, as well as Mr Castleton and Mr Peirce, will be more pleasing to you as it tends yet to keep the estate in your family which you consenting to may certainly take effect. You cannot but see without going any further that it must be done by Mr Bernard . . . Good Sir, as this must centre in your own blood I perswade my

56 SHC, DD\TB/28/18, Pierce to Mary Carew, 5 January 1760.
57 SHC, DD\TB/23/17, Drewe to E. Carew, 22 February 1760.
58 SHC, DD\TB/23/17, Drewe to E. Carew, 3 May 1760.
59 SHC, DD\TB/23/17, Drewe to E. Carew, 27 December 1760.
60 SHC, DD\TB/27/6, Nathaniel Castleton to Carew, 2 July 1764.

self you will think it better than £16000 from a stranger . . .[61]

On the 28th August, Castleton wrote again

I could wish you would expedite the purchase Mr Bernard has so genteely offered to assist you in, for I apprehend the sooner the estates are conveyed to him, the sooner your affairs will be settled. I [...]ssure you I look on Mr Bernard as a man of honor and that he only engages in this purchase, with a view of serving you and yours. Suppose it should turn out advantageous and worth a little more than the £14000, who would you have benefited, but the man you have given your daughter to . . .[62]

It would appear that both Carew's man of business and his relative saw this proposal as his last chance to extricate himself from the morass of debt in which his life-long extravagance had mired him (figure 36).

Carew died in March 1766, leaving Bernard to continue the task of settling his father-in-law's outstanding debts. It is perhaps ironic that after Carew was persuaded to sell his Devon estates to Bernard to keep them in the family for a lesser sum than he might have obtained elsewhere, only the following year, in 1767, Bernard drew up a contract to sell East and West Stoodleigh to Matthew Brickdale of Bristol for £19,000.[63]

Conclusion

The evidence to be found in the correspondence and accounts of Thomas Carew shows us a man plagued by debt almost from his coming of age. I have concentrated here on what I feel were probably the greatest causes of this debt, his personal extravagance, his seeming inability to keep a tight rein on the administration of his estates, and the expenditure on building and maintaining Crowcombe Court. There were also other expenses such as the outlay on fighting the Minehead election in 1739 and subsequent costs as the Borough's MP, and the charities he was involved with which ranged from providing clothing for the pupils at Crowcombe's charity school to his work as a Governor of the Bridewell and Bethlehem Hospitals in London. Limitations of space have prevented me from exploring these in this chapter.

He hoped the sale of his estates to his son-in-law would solve his problems and perhaps they did to a certain extent; at least he could at last hand over responsibility for his debts to someone else and spend the final two years of his life as Bernard's pensioner at Crowcombe Court, the house which was to prove his enduring legacy.

[61] SHC, DD\TB/15/5, Charles Prowse to Carew, 3 July 1764.
[62] SHC, DD\TB/27/6, N. Castleton to Carew, 28 August 1764.
[63] SHC, DD\TB/31/3/13, articles of agreement concerning the sale of the manors of East and West Stoodleigh, Devon, to Matthew Brickdale, 1767.

11. New light on William Day of Blagdon, Land-Surveyor, Cartographer, and Linen Draper

ADRIAN J. WEBB

Introduction

In 1981, a landmark volume in the Somerset Record Society series was published under the honorary editorship of Dr Dunning. A facsimile version of William Day and Charles Harcourt Masters' (1782) and Christopher and John Greenwoods' (1822) maps of Somerset, totalling fifteen large sheets, was issued to members of the society in a slipcase. Accompanying the maps was a slim booklet giving information about the cartographers, their methods, and a comparison of the information they depicted, which was jointly edited by J.B. Harley and Dunning. Since then some new information has come to light about Day and Masters and their mapmaking scheme. Of particular note is the involvement of John Darch (*c*.1744-1799) and Coplestone Warre Bampfylde (1720–1791) (figure 39). Details of some of the people who subscribed to and owned the maps produced in 1782, such as Abraham Crocker (1742-1821) of Frome, are also included in this chapter.

County mapping

The eighteenth century was a golden age for mapping substantial parts, or all, of the ancient county of Somerset. It was long overdue, as until the publication of Day and Masters' survey in 1782, nearly all county maps of Somerset had been based on the work of Saxton and Speed.[1] The work of the land surveyor was increasingly in demand. John Strachey F.R.S. (1671-1743) had shown what could be achieved. Almost single-handedly he surveyed the whole county in the early 1730s, recording information in his pocket books as he went.[2] Mapmaking on a county scale was a costly business, but there were incentives. In 1759 the *Society of Arts* announced: 'The Society proposes to give a Sum not exceeding 100L as a Gratuity to any Person or Persons, who shall make an accurate actual survey of any County'.[3] Similar rewards were given throughout the following decades. How William Day managed to fund such a scheme for Somerset was something that could not be answered by Harley and Dunning in 1981. The commercial organisation behind Day's proposal

---

[1] T. Chubb, *Printed maps of Somersetshire* (Taunton, 1914), p. xi.
[2] E. Down and A.J. Webb, *Somerset mapped* (Wellington, 2016), pp. 102-5.
[3] T. Chubb, *Printed maps of Somerset*, p. x.

to the gentlemen of the county for supporting his project has now come to light.[4]

Little was known about the life and career of William Day when the facsimile was published except that by the time the survey of Somerset was complete, until his death in 1798, he was resident at Blagdon (in Pitminster). Also, only three other local surveys by Day were known to exist, suggesting that he may have had another occupation besides surveying.[5] This needs to be revised as many examples and references to Day's work in the form of maps and surveys have survived; this suggests surveying was his main occupation. He certainly possessed enough scientific instruments to suggest he had invested a good amount of money in this profession.[6]

As for his private life, on 22 September 1756, Day married Anne Locke at Pitminster by licence, when both were described as being residents of the parish. They had one child, named Nanny, baptised there on 26 August 1758. It is possible that Day was also a linen draper in the early 1760s.[7] Anne's sister Mary, who married Samuel Hallet on 6 January 1768 at Pitminster, lived at Corfe and the two sisters appeared to have remained closely connected. Little else is known, except that at the time of his wife's death they had two servants and had not become impoverished by Day's surveying activities. Their house at Blagdon had a 'green room', suggesting this room, at least, was highly decorated. His wife's will includes numerous bequests to friends, family and servants.[8] However, the property they lived in might have been rented or leased as his name does not appear in the parish rate book in 1748 or for the tithing of Blagdon in 1760, 1769 and 1783.[9] Also, there is no property transaction listed under William Day in the records of the Bishop of Winchester for the Hundred of Poundisford (figure 37).[10]

As for his work as a surveyor, in 1750 he made a survey of Barton in his home parish of Pitminster for Goodenough Earle.[11] This early work, which proves he was in business for over 47 years as a surveyor, appears to have been overlooked by researchers, being wrongly catalogued under the name 'Davy' but is by William Day.[12] This survey may also have been the catalyst Day needed to come into contact with the local elite of major landowners, Earle, friend of the artist Thomas Gainsborough (Pitminster boy), and almost certainly either directly, or through

[4] For more information on the commercialisation of cartography during this period see M. S. Pedley, *The commerce of cartography: making and marketing maps in eighteenth-century France and England* (Chicago and London, 2005).

[5] J. B. Harley and R. W. Dunning, *Somerset maps*, SRS 76 (1981), p. 7.

[6] *Sherborne Mercury*, 5 November 1798.

[7] SHC, DD/X/PED/4/14 quoting from D/P/pitm 13/3/6 examination of Elizabeth Gummer, 6 January 1769.

[8] TNA, PROB 11/1369/186 will of Mrs Ann Day, widow of Pitminster, 9 February 1802.

[9] SHC, D/P/pit/13/2/5 parish rates, 1745-1784.

[10] I am grateful to Sue Berry for establishing this fact.

[11] SHC, DD/SPY 64 survey of Barton, 1750.

[12] S. Bendall, *Dictionary of land surveyors and local map-makers of Great Britain and Ireland, 1530-1850*, 2 volumes (London, 1997).

Gainsborough, a friend of Coplestone Warre Bampfylde.[13] In 1765 he produced a map of Bradford on Tone showing land to the north and east of the church.[14] Two years later he surveyed neighbouring Norton Fitzwarren.[15] He surveyed John Durbin's estate in the parish of Cossington in 1769[16] and undertook work as a land surveyor for the Taunton Turnpike Trust[17] and a survey of the manor of Huntspill in the same year, or shortly afterwards.[18] In 1771, he must have spent a great deal of time surveying the parish of Goathurst for Sir Charles Kemeys Tynte Bart (1710-1785),[19] which was possibly a turning point in his career (figure 38). Similarly a goodly amount of time must have been taken up surveying the large parish of Pitminster in 1775;[20] the map he drew was for many years kept at Lowton House.[21] Following these commissions Harley and Dunning thought he must have started more intensively collecting information for a county survey,[22] but it was commenced in 1773[23] and not, to begin with at least, with Masters.[24] Therefore his survey of Pitminster in 1775[25] must have formed part of his contribution to the survey of the whole county. It is also possible that about 1774 he undertook a small survey for Thomas Southwood, a prosperous gentleman farmer of Pitminster.[26]

In order to take on that large and demanding task of surveying the county of Somerset, with its varying types of landscape ranging from the urban centres such as Bath and Wells, to the remote parts of Exmoor and the watery Levels, was no easy task for one man alone. Harley and Dunning asked 'why Day was attracted to such a risky venture'.[27] It is highly likely that it was the influence and patronage of two men, Sir Charles Kemeys Tynte and Coplestone Warre Bampfylde who bore most of the risk. Tynte lived at Halswell in Goathurst about five miles north of Hestercombe, Bampfylde's home. The two men were lifelong friends, so is it surprising that Tynte was a leading subscriber to a project that Bampfylde put his name to as its treasurer?[28]

Bampfylde's involvement in schemes such as this and with other matters of trust within the county places him in a strong position to have helped Day. Just a few of

[13] Information kindly supplied by Philip White of Hestercombe.

[14] SHC, DD\CH/S/2802 map of Bradford on Tone, 1765.

[15] R. Harley and R.W. Dunning, *Somerset maps*, SRS 76 (1981), p. 7.

[16] SHC, DD\DK/14 survey of the lands of John Durbin, esquire, 1769.

[17] SHC, D\T\ta/5 p.206 minutes of the Taunton Turnpike Trust, 7 Feb. 1769.

[18] SHC, D\P\hun/3/1/5 William Day's receipt, 1770.

[19] SHC, DD\S\GLY/108 'An Accurate map of the entire parish of Goathurst chiefly belonging to Sir Charles Kemeys Tynte Baronet and part of his other estates adjoining', 1771.

[20] SHC, MAP\DD\X\BLE 3 Plan of Pitminster parish, 1775.

[21] SHC, DD/X/PED/4/12 *Pitminster parish magazine*, September 1951.

[22] R. Harley and R.W. Dunning, *Somerset maps*, SRS 76 (1981), p. 8.

[23] *Bath Chronicle and Weekly Gazette*, 21 October 1773.

[24] *Bath Chronicle and Weekly Gazette*, 21 October 1773.

[25] SHC, MAP\DD\X\BLE 3 Plan of Pitminster parish, 1775.

[26] SHC, DD/MT/25/3/2-3 sketch plan, n.d.; DD/MT/26/3/9 lease of Hites Moor, 1774.

[27] R. Harley and R.W. Dunning, *Somerset maps*, SRS 76 (1981), p. 8.

[28] *Bath Chronicle and Weekly Gazette*, 3 August 1775.

his connections show a dazzling array of associations across the county and further afield. His involvement in the late 1750s as a major and later colonel in the Somerset Militia meant he was connected with six other officers and eight deputy lieutenants who were involved in the pre-publication stage of the survey; Tynte served as Lieutenant Colonel in the regiment and two subscribers, John Jeane and Thomas Horner served under Bampfylde in the Second Battalion.[29] Bampfylde was a trustee under the will of Sir John Trevelyan with Canon Southey of Fitzhead, esquire, Thomas Putt of Combe, Devon and Francis Gwyn of Forde Abbey, Dorset;[30] also as a trustee of Minehead's harbour, with five other men directly involved with the survey, plus others;[31] of Taunton Town lands from 1754 (with Sir Thomas Dyke Acland and John Lethbridge in the 1770s);[32] of Richard Fox's Grammar School in Taunton from 1770 with two other subscribers (James Bernard and Richard Combe);[33] trustee with several other subscribers of the first Somerset Hospital (in Taunton);[34] of the Taunton Turnpike Trust[35] and of Tynte's will.[36] Bampfylde also executed designs for the Lutterell family of Dunster although the latter's name does not appear amongst the early subscribers.[37] With Tynte they served as trustees of Blundell's School, Tiverton.[38] And Tynte was also a trustee of Huish's trust with four other subscribers, Acland, Trevelyan, Alexander Popham and Lethbridge in 1775.[39] As a justice of the peace he would have been in contact with dozens of influential people.[40]

But Day could not undertake the work on his own, so he turned to a fellow land surveyor, Mr John Darch (*c*.1744-1799) of Ashbrittle. Darch was the son of John Darch (*fl*.1720-d.1784) and Mary (*fl*.1744-1753) of Brushford. They had three children baptised there: Richard on 21 January 1742/3, John (the surveyor) on 5 November 1744, and James on 6 January 1753. John senior was described as a gentleman in 1756 and had connections in Devon.[41] In 1764, Mr John Darch of Brushford received a £10 premium for sowing 10 acres of carrots from the Society

[29] A.J. Webb and J. Skeggs, *The roll of the 1st and 2nd Battalions of the Somerset Militia 1758* (Weston-super-Mare, 1993), pp. 1-3.

[30] SHC, DD\WO/4/5/2 assignment, 22 August 1759.

[31] *The statutes at large, of England and of Great Britain: from Magna Carta to the union of the kingdoms of Great Britain and Ireland*, 10 (London, 1771), pp. 741-2.

[32] SHC, DD\TAC/5/5/3 leases, 1754, 1763; DD\TAC/2/3/1 minutes, 1698-1807.

[33] J. Savage, *History of Taunton In the county of Somerset originally written by the Late Joshua Toulmin, a new edition, greatly enlarged and brought down to the present time by James Savage* (Taunton, 1822), pp. 236, 317.

[34] S. Shephard, 'Three gentlemen in Arcadia', unpublished MA thesis, University of Bristol, 2003, p. 17.

[35] SHC, DD\GC/70 mortgages of Taunton Turnpike Trust tolls, 1752.

[36] Information kindly supplied by Philip White of Hestercombe.

[37] S.H.C., DD\L/1/22/7 Plans, 1755-1763.

[38] Ex inf Philip White, Hestercombe.

[39] SHC, DD/S/WH/322 Phelips to Tynte, 23 December 1775.

[40] J. Savage, *History of Taunton* (Taunton, 1822), pp. 236, 317.

[41] D.R.O., 213 M/T/322 mortgage of a messuage called Bendefin (Brendlefin), Woolfardisworthy, moor called Radisburghe, Washford Pyne, 25 May 1756.

for Encouraging the Arts.[42] Little is known about the family but John senior's wife Mary was buried on 19 August 1761 at Brushford, as he was on 13 January 1784.

In 1773, possibly earlier, Day and Darch junior (the son of a gentleman farmer), entered into partnership to survey the county and produce a map at a scale of one inch to one mile. This scale was common during the eighteenth century and they calculated the finished map would be about six feet square. To finance such a work they calculated that they needed 500 subscribers;[43] subscription was a proposition forwarded by Harley and Dunning in 1981.[44] To obtain this many people they took out an advertisement in the *Bath Chronicle and Weekly Gazette* on 21 October 1773. Messrs Day and Darch addressed the people they thought were most likely to support their venture. These were the 'Nobility, Gentlemen, and Clergy of the County of Somerset'. They appealed to them to 'encourage and support the Publication of a large and correct MAP of the said County', with the word map in capital letters. The two men, described as land surveyors in the advert, offered through the words of a third party:

MESSRS. DAY and DARCH, Land-Surveyors, humbly beg leave to offer their proposals for executing this useful work, which they will render as complete, copious, and descriptive, as any of the kind hitherto published.

They intend that this Map shall be drawn to a scale of one inch to a mile, (which they apprehend will make a complete map of about six feet square) and to describe in it the several hundreds, parishes, towns, villages, gentlemen's seats, rivers, bridges, public and private roads, remarkable places of antiquity, hills and valleys throughout the said county. The whole to be elegantly engraved, and embellished with proper ornaments.

As this will be a work of an expensive nature, they apprehend there cannot be less than 500 subscribers, at two guineas and a half each to support it.

This work is to be carried on upon such terms, as shall be proposed and agreed to by a majority of subscribers, and the surveyors, at a future meeting. Such as are inclined to support this undertaking, (which is countenanced by the liberal subscriptions of many of the nobility and most respectable gentlemen of the county) are desired to send their names, with the sums they chuse to advance, to and of the following persons, as soon as posible, that the surveyors may be thereby enabled immediately to begin their survey. Mrs. Young, at the Exchange Coffee House, Bristol; Mr. Frederick, bookseller, in the Grove, Bath; Mr. Lewis, bookseller, in Wells; Mr. Loyde, at the Swan in Fore-Street, Exeter; Mr. Nowell, at the Castle Inn, Taunton; Mr. Witherell, at the George in Bridgwater; Mr. Griffits, the Angel in Yeovil; Mr. Noble, the George in Ilminster; and Mr. Stribling, at the George, Shepton-mallet.[45]

[42] *Public Advertiser*, 10 July 1764.

[43] *Bath Chronicle and Weekly Gazette*, 21 October 1773.

[44] R. Harley and R.W. Dunning, *Somerset maps*, SRS 76 (1981), p. 11.

[45] *Bath Chronicle and Weekly Gazette*, 21 October 1773.

A similar advert was run on the 25 November[46] and 23 December in the *Bath Chronicle*.[47]

Of those who agreed with Day and Darch to deal with the advance subscription moneys, there were only two booksellers. The most prolific, Mr William Frederick (d.1776), bookseller, publisher, printer, librarian/owner of circulating library and lottery agent, had a well-established business by the time of the 1773 advertisement.[48] He also had more than a passing interest in maps, as he sold Thomas Thorpe's landmark map of five miles round Bath in 1742.[49] Mr John Evill Lewis, bookseller, in Wells was also a printer.[50] The others, who can loosely be described as innkeepers, show that there was a distinct lack of outlets for bookselling in certain parts of the county. Not to paint a picture of men and women who had no literary interests, Mr John Nowell of Taunton subscribed to Toulmin's *History of Taunton* in 1791, whereas Day did not.[51]

As for the 'future meeting', one took place over a year and a half later when some progress had been made. On 3 August 1775, a notice was published in a Bath newspaper containing a detailed proposal for Messrs Day and Darch's scheme. The notice explained quite clearly how the survey was going to be financed, when the surveyors were going to be paid, how the maps was going to be mounted on canvas and hung on rollers (figure 40). More importantly for the subscribers, Day and Darch claimed that the map would be completed in 1779. This was all very well but Day and Darch were merely land surveyors, not gentlemen, and for such a scheme to succeed they needed the patronage of a local man of some standing. Enter Coplestone Warre Bampfylde esquire of Hestercombe, near Taunton.

Exactly how Bampfylde came into contact with the two surveyors is not known. However, four distinct avenues may be considered. First is the fact that a substantial landowner such as Bampfylde would have come into contact with land surveyors such as Day and Darch. Secondly, Bampfylde's connection with Bath society might have brought him into contact with Masters, although this is unlikely. Thirdly is through Bampfylde's interests in Taunton, for which he designed the Market House (constructed in 1772) and served on numerous local trusts. As Day lived at Blagdon, in the parish of Pitminster, and Bampfylde at Hestercombe, this hypothesis is not unlikely. Fourthly is Bampfylde's links to many of the county families, through family and court business. For example, at the sessions held at Bridgwater in July 1771 Bampfylde sat with five future subscribers, any one of which could have recommended Day's skills as a surveyor.[52] Similarly, at the Quarter Sessions at Bruton on 25 April 1775, at least three subscribers were

[46] *Bath Chronicle and Weekly Gazette*, 25 November 1773.
[47] *Bath Chronicle and Weekly Gazette*, 23 December 1773.
[48] British Book Trades Index, accessed 26 November 2016.
[49] E. Down and A.J. Webb, *Somerset mapped*, pp. 106-9.
[50] British Book Trades Index, accessed 26 November 2016.
[51] Revd J. Toulmin, *The history of the town of Taunton in the county of Somerset* (Taunton, 1791).
[52] *Bath Chronicle and Weekly Gazette*, 26 August 1771.

present.[53]

The most likely possibility relates to both of their involvement with the Taunton Turnpike Trust. Bampfylde was a trustee of the Taunton Turnpike (which included Pitminster),[54] and served as chairman in 1762[55] and 1779.[56] Day undertook work as a land surveyor for the Trust in 1769,[57] 1781[58] and 1791[59] during the time Bampfylde was involved with the Trust. Therefore, it is likely that Bampfylde knew of Day and that he employed the surveyor from Blagdon to work for the Trust.

The Taunton Turnpike Trust is arguably the key to understanding the fundamental points of the county survey, that is transportation and communication. Bampfylde's involvement from 1762[60] meant he was in a position to put Day in contact with many other trustees. Men such as James Bernard of Crowcombe, Doctor Camplin, Richard Combe, John Cridland of Milverton, Benjamin Hammet esquire, William Hawker esquire, James Kirkpatrick, Reverend James Minifie clerk of Goathurst and Alexander Popham of West Bagborough who were fellow trustees, many of whom sat on specific committees dealing with matters relating to roads in the parishes where they lived.[61] Bampfylde and Popham shared an even longer connection as the two men were undergraduates together at St John's College, Oxford from 1737.[62] All of these men were involved in the pre-publication phase of the survey of Somerset. All of these men would also have realised the benefits of improved roads to reduce the costs in transporting goods and people, therefore saving money.

There were other advantages of being a trustee of Taunton Turnpike, not just those of using improved roads for communication and commerce. The benefit for Bampfylde and Hawker occurred from the sale of stone from the quarries they owned at West Monkton and Norton Fitzwarren respectively to the Trust. The amounts were not huge, being £24 and £15 17s. 6d. respectively,[63] but noteworthy. Irrespective of this, the Taunton connection was clearly important and it did not take long for the trustees' meetings to be held in Bampfylde's Market House.[64]

Thanks to Bampfylde's backing as treasurer, and the formation of a committee, a much more detailed prospectus was published on 3 August 1775:

---

[53] *Bath Chronicle and Weekly Gazette*, 1 June 1775. Elton, Camplin and Horner were present.
[54] SHC, DD\GC/70 mortgages of Taunton Turnpike Trust tolls, 1752.
[55] SHC, D\T\ta/5 p.148 minutes of the Taunton Turnpike Trust, 27 Apr. 1762.
[56] SHC, D\T\ta/6 minute of the Taunton Turnpike Trust, 16 Nov. 1779.
[57] SHC, D\T\ta/5 p.206 minutes of the Taunton Turnpike Trust, 7 Feb. 1769.
[58] SHC, D\T\ta/6 minute of the Taunton Turnpike Trust, 22 May 1781.
[59] SHC, D\T\ta/7 minute of the Taunton Turnpike Trust, 13 Dec. 1791.
[60] SHC, D\T\ta/5 p.148 minutes of the Taunton Turnpike Trust, 27 Apr. 1762.
[61] SHC, D\T\ta/5 minutes of the Taunton Turnpike Trust, 1752-1777.
[62] Information kindly supplied by Philip White of Hestercombe.
[63] SHC, D\T\ta/5 p.207 minute of the Taunton Turnpike Trust, 7 Feb. 1769.
[64] SHC, D\T\ta/6 minute of the Taunton Turnpike Trust, 1779.

1. They will take an accurate survey, of the whole county, and from thence make a correct Map thereof by the scale of an inch to a mile, which shall contain the division of the county into its several hundreds, and the cities, towns, parishes, villages, and the seats of the noblemen and gentlemen there in properly distinguished; together with the rivers, bridges, public and private roads, hills and valleys, and remarkable places of antiquity throughout the county.

2. They will deliver to every subscriber a correct copy of such map, elegantly engraved, and embellished with proper ornaments, pasted on canvas, and fitted up with rollers, at the price of two guineas and a half.
The subscribers who shall be present at Bridgewater sessions, 1775, in pursuance of an advertisement for that purpose, will be pleased to appoint a Treasurer to receive their subscriptions in the manner specified in the following articles; and they will be pleased at the same time to chuse a Committee more immediately to inspect the progress of the work from time to time, and to certify the state thereof to the treasurer at the times, and for the purposes herein after mentioned.

3. The subscribers are to pay one guinea to the treasurer at or before Michaelmas sessions, 1775, a second guinea to the treasurer at or before Michaelmas sessions, 1776, and the remaining half guinea to the undertakers themselves on the delivery of the map.

4. And because the undertakers must of necessity be at a continual expence during the progress of the work, they therefore desire that the treasurer may be empowered to pay them a part of the subscription money from time to time, in manner and upon the conditions following, viz.

5. The undertakers are to draw upon the treasurer for any sum, not exceeding two hundred pounds, between Michaelmas sessions, 1775, and Michaelmas sessions, 1776.

6. They are to draw in like manner, for any sum not exceeding two hundred pounds, in the second year, beginning from Michaelmas sessions, 1776, provided that seven at least of the Committee shall be satisfied that the undertakers have actually surveyed and mapped at least a third part of the county, and shall certify the same to the treasurer at the said sessions.

7. They are to draw for the sum of two hundred pounds in the third year, beginning at Michaelmas sessions, 1777, upon obtaining at that sessions a certificate from the committee that they have surveyed and mapped at least two thirds of the county, and provided also that the treasurer has that sum in his hands.

8. They are to draw for a further sum, not exceding four hundred pounds, if so much be then in the treasurer's hands, in the fourth year, beginning from Michaelmas sessions, 1778, if the committee or any seven of them shall then certify the treasurer that they have finished the survey of the county, and have prepared a map thereof ready for engraving.

9. Lastly, the treasurer is to pay the undertakers the residue of the subscription money in his hands, on receiving a certificate signed by at least seven of the committee, that the maps are ready to be delivered to the subscribers, completely finished and fitted up in the manner mentioned in the two first articles of these proposals, and this the surveyors promise to do by Michaelmas sessions, 1779, and are ready to give such security to the treasurer for the performance of this work as the subscribers shall require.

Bridgwater,   WM. DAY,
July 11, 1775.   JOHN DARCH.

We whose names are under-written, subscribers, amongst others, for a new Map of the county of Somerset, proposed to be made by Messrs. DAY and DARCH, being met together at Bridgwater sessions, in pursuance of an advertisement for that purpose, do hereby nominate and appoint Coppleston Warre Bampfylde, Esq; to be our treasurer, with full power and authority to receive the subscription money, and to pay over the same to the said Messrs. Day and Darch, in the manner and on the conditions mentioned in the proposals hereunto annexed.

And we do also choose Sir Thomas Dyke Acland, Sir Charles Kemeys Tynte, Sir Abraham Isaac Elton, Barts., Richard Hippisley Coxe, Edward Phelips, Coppleston Warre Bampfylde, John Smith, Thomas Horner, James Bernard, Alexander Popham, and John Lethbridge, Esqrs.; Thomas Camplin, Doctor of Laws, and John Wickham of Long Ashton, Clerk; or any seven of them, to be our committee; and do hereby intreat them to inspect the progress of the work from time to time, and to certify the state thereof at the times and for the purposes specified in the said proposals.

Sir Abraham Isaac Elton, Bt.	Dodington Hunt, Esq;
Sir Thomas Gunston Knt.	John Jeane, Esq;
Rich. Hippisley Coxe, Esq;	Charles Hippesley Coxe, Esq;
Edward Phelips, Esq;	Rev. Tho. Camplin, LL.D.
Benjamin Allen, Esq;	James Kirkpatrick, Esq;
James Bernard, Esq;	Rev. Robert Hole,
Alexander Popham, Esq;	Rev. Lancelot St. Albyn,
James Sparrow, Esq;[65]	

[65] *Bath Chronicle and Weekly Gazette,* 3 August 1775.

The fifteen subscribers were well-heeled men, whose country seats were (like the agents) also spread across the county. Of those fifteen, only eight were named in the *Bath Chronicle* as justices of the peace who attended the sessions held at Bridgwater in July 1775.[66] Having such meetings when all the great and the good of the county were in one spot for official business was a sensible idea. Choosing Bath as a location to market the map was equally sound business decision. The city possessed a large number of wealthy inhabitants, as well as sellers of books and maps. The local newspaper, *The Bath Chronicle and Weekly Gazette*, was widely circulated around the county and ran advertisements for the sale of maps. For example, in 1764 a 'curious assortment' of English and foreign maps were advertised for sale at the Printing Office in Stall Street,[67] in 1773 a school offered lessons in using maps,[68] and in January 1775 maps of the River Thames and of Boston (America) were also offered.[69] It also regularly contained advertisements calling the county's gentry and nobility to meet at the forthcoming assizes or quarter sessions.[70]

The two men must have made reasonable progress, as three years later it was reported that 183 parishes had been completed.[71] With just under 45% of the county's parishes surveyed, coupled with such noble and generous men backing the project, what could possibly go wrong? After all eleven of the subscribers were also putting their money into the Somerset Public Hospital to a much higher tune than the two and a half guineas asked for by Day and Darch.[72] Financially the scheme was being supported but, alas, Day was not. In March 1778, following a dispute between the surveyors, the partnership was dissolved by the decision of Bampfylde, the Rev. Dr Camplin and Mr Thomas Charter, arbitrators. Subsequently Day obtained new assistants for the scheme, one of whom was presumably Masters, and was able to publicly state on 12 March 1778:

SOMERSETSHIRE

THE Publick are desired to take Notice, that the Partnership between Messrs. DAY and DARCH, LAND SURVEYORS, who jointly undertook to survey the county aforesaid, and to make a complete Map thereof) is now disolved by the decision of Copplestone Warre Bampfylde, Esq; the Rev. Dr. Camplin, and Mr. Thomas Charter, who were chosen Arbitrators to settle all matters in dispute between the said Day and Darch; and the said Map is now ordered to be carried on and perfected, under the direction of the said Wm. Day, who has procured very able assistants for that purpose. – Had Mr. Day's

[66] *Bath Chronicle and Weekly Gazette*, 10 August 1775.
[67] *Bath Chronicle and Weekly Gazette*, 15 November 1764.
[68] *Bath Chronicle and Weekly Gazette*, 1 July 1773.
[69] *Bath Chronicle and Weekly Gazette*, 26 January 1775.
[70] *Bath Chronicle and Weekly Gazette*, 3 August 1775.
[71] *Bath Chronicle and Weekly Gazette*, 12 March 1778.
[72] *Bath Chronicle and Weekly Gazette*, 5 February 1778.

partner been diligent, and transacted the part he undertook, no delay would have happened; but the public may now be assured, that the work will be expedited with all possible dispatch, and will be finished before March 1779. The part already mapped (which comprehends 183 parishes) has met with the highest approbation, and will be produced at the four General Sessions and Assizes, held within the said county, for the inspection of the subscribers.

The Nobility, Gentry, and Clergy, who may be inclined to encourage this work, are desired to pay their subscriptions to Copplestone Warre Bampfylde, esq; Treasurer, or to his order, and to no other person.

WILLIAM DAY.[73]

If Darch had been disgraced for his role in this project it may explain why he is not readily obvious in any map related sources for Somerset and neighbouring Devon. It may also explain why he had to go further afield for work, as a Mr J. Darch undertook a survey of the manor of Norton in the parish of Newton St Cyres in 1792. The map on parchment has the title of 'A map of the Manor of Norton in the Parish of Newton St Cyres and County of Devon Lands of the Venerable the Dean and Chapter of St Peter in Exeter'.[74] He received 25 guineas for that work in 1791[75] and a further 10 guineas in 1792,[76] presumably when the map was delivered. His ability to find work in Devon and not in Somerset might support this suggestion. He was possibly working as a land agent in Ashbrittle in 1796.[77] He was buried at Ashbrittle on 12 March 1799 and the burial register shows his age, 55 and his occupation of land surveyor. His wife Mary was also buried there but 38 years later on 28 May 1837 aged 80 years.

With 183 parishes completed[78] this was less than half the number of parishes required to be mapped. However, if the 183 included some of the larger parishes in west Somerset, such as Wellington, Dulverton, Winsford, etc then the geographical area left to survey may not have been that great. Nevertheless Day was now going it alone. It was up to him to get the surveying completed. He wasted no time in getting on with the surveying. Exactly eight months later he was able to report to a group of 17 subscribers that 'about Three-parts in Four of the whole County is surveyed and mapped'.[79] Day also took the opportunity of claiming his second payment and to advertise a new list of agents for collecting the much needed subscriptions for his project.

---

[73] *Bath Chronicle and Weekly Gazette*, 12 March 1778.

[74] M.R. Ravenhill and M. Rowe, *Devon Maps and Map-makers: Manuscript Maps before 1840*, D&CRS, new series 43, 45 (2000), pp. 66-7, 283.

[75] ECA, D&C3574 Chapter acts, pages 28-31.

[76] ECA, D&C3574 Chapter acts, pages 90-1.

[77] *Sherborne Mercury*, 5 December 1796.

[78] *Bath Chronicle and Weekly Gazette*, 12 March 1778.

[79] *Bath Chronicle and Weekly Gazette*, 15 October 1778, 12 November 1778.

MAP of SOMERSETSHIRE.

Taunton, 8th Oct. 1778.

WE, whose Names are hereunder written, Subscribers, amongst others, to the new Map of the County of Somerset, having examined such part of the said Map as is completed by Mr. William Day, the Surveyor, are of opinion that it is correct, and that about Three-parts in Four of the whole County is surveyed and mapped: And therefore, we recommend to the Subscribers to the said Map, to make good their second payment to the Treasurer, which the said William Day is intitled to, according to his proposals; that he may be the better enabled to complete the same.

Sir Abraham Isaac Elton, Bart.
Rev. Tho. Camplin, LL.D.
Alexander Popham, Esq;
Edward Phelips, Esq;
Richard Combe, Esq;
Sir John Trevelyan, Bart.
William Hawkes, Esq;
Sir Tho. Champneys, Bart.
Henry Hobhouse, Esq;

James Kirkpatrick, Esq;
Rev. James Minifie;
Rev. William Baily;
Benjamin Allen, Esq;
Thomas Allen, Esq;
Thomas Hotchkin, Esq;
John Burland, Esq;
Benjamin Hammet, Esq;

Thereby authorize Mr. WILLIAM DAY, to receive Subscriptions towards his Map of the County of Somerset, now carrying on by him.

COP. WARRE BAMPFYLDE, Treasurer.

If the Subscribers would be pleased to pay their Subscriptions Money to either of the Gentlemen hereunder mentioned, who have kindly undertaken to receive the same, they would confer an additional obligation on their most humble servant,

WILLIAM DAY.

Jas. Kirkpatrick, Esq; Bristol,
Bath and Somersetshire Bank,
at No.6, Milson street, Bath,

J. Old Goodford, Esq; Yeovil,
Col. John Roberts, Taunton,
Wm. Provis, Esq; Shept. Mal.
Mr. Messiter, Wincanton,
Mr. Anderdon, surg. Somerton

Mr. Warry, Chard,
Mr. J. Cridland, Milverton,
Mr. Cane, surg.
Bridgwater,
Mr. Bastone, Minehead,
Mr. Yeatman, Crewkerne,
Mr. Penny, Wells,
Mr. Fry, Axbridge, and
Mr. Crocker, Ilminster.[80]

With so much support it can be presumed Day and Masters busied themselves with completing the surveying. However, a small distraction saw Day undertake a small survey for the Taunton Turnpike Trust, before 22 May 1781, for which he

---

[80] *Bath Chronicle and Weekly Gazette*, 15 October 1778, 12 November 1778.

received one guinea.[81] The next piece in the jigsaw was the engraving and publication of the maps. By 27 October 1781 the survey work was complete and a fair copy was with the engraver. Although all of the map had not been engraved, some proof sheets had been supplied to Day. As part of the agreement Day showed the proof sheets to James Kirkpatrick, and probably the rest of the committee. Kirkpatrick was actively involved in collecting subscriptions in Bristol for Day, especially from members of the Society of Merchant Venturers.[82]

The engraving must have been completed and any corrections made to the plates by the end of February 1782, as the sheets show the publication date of 1 March 1782. It took Day and Masters seven years to complete their survey, suggesting Masters was involved from 1775. Day claimed that 'the Map cost me more than a thousand Guineas, exclusive of my great labour and trouble'.[83] When it was eventually published it was produced on 9 sheets.[84] They submitted their survey for a Society of Arts award in December 1782, but it was not fully considered until the following year. Day eventually received twenty guineas and a silver medal for his efforts, while Masters was awarded a silver pallet for his contribution to the surveying. Their map became one of only thirteen county surveys to be recognised by the Society between 1765 and 1809.[85] In 1783, following the award by the Society of Arts, advertisements were run in the *Bath Chronicle* capitalising on this award. They also stated how copies were sold by Day from his home at Blagdon, by Masters from Wade's Passage, Bath and by John Wallis at his Map Warehouse, Ludgate Street, London. Day pleaded with subscribers to send for their copies and Masters advertised for work as an estate surveyor.[86]

Just Published by WILLIAM DAY,

A New MAP of the County of SOMERSET, beautifully engraved from an actual Survey, taken by the said WILLIAM DAY and CHARLES MASTERS, delineated from a scale of one inch to a mile, neatly printed on Nine Sheets of Imperial Paper, and for which the Society of Arts, &c. was pleased to present the Surveyors with a handsome premium.

Sold by the Proprietors, Wm. Day, of Blagdon near Taunton, and Charles Masters, Wade's Passage, Bath; and by John Wallis, at his Map-Warehouse, Ludgate-street, London.

Price THREE GUINEAS.

William Day begs the favour of his subscribers, that they will be so obliging as to send for their Maps.

---

[81] SHC, D\T\ta/6 minutes of the Taunton Turnpike Trust, 22 May 1781.

[82] BRO, SMV2/4/2/23/23 letter, 27 October 1781.

[83] J.B. Harley and R.W. Dunning, *Somerset maps Day & Masters 1783 Greenwood 1822*, SRS 76 (1981), p. 15.

[84] J.B. Harley and R.W. Dunning, *Somerset maps*, SRS 76 (1981), pp. 16-17.

[85] J.B. Harley and R.W. Dunning, *Somerset maps*, SRS 76 (1981), p. 9.

[86] *Bath Chronicle and Weekly Gazette*, 1, 15 and 29 May 1783.

☞ Estates accurately surveyed and neatly planned by Charles Masters. [2860[87]

Life after the survey

The publication of Day and Masters' survey was one of the best ways of advertising their talents. For Day this meant commissions in Somerset and Devon. For example, in 1785 he drew a map of the parish of East Coker for the Helyar family.[88] In 1786 he supplied information to Edmund Rack concerning the heights of Dunkery Hill and North Hill.[89] He must have spent some of his time promoting his map and arranging sales as by July 1788 he was no longer using John Wallis as his London agent. Instead he used William Faden at the corner of St Martin's Lane, Charing Cross and Mr Brown, bookseller on the Tolzey in Bristol. As the map was now six years old the price was reduced to 'a Guinea and Half in sheets', or £2 7s. 'elegantly coloured and fitted up on canvas and rollers'.[90]

Elsewhere, in 1789, he undertook a survey at Awliscombe, Devon of an estate known as 'Tracey' and another of Sidmouth, the property of Thomas Jenkins esquire (c.1722-1798).[91] Jenkins, an antiquary, was lord of the manor of Sidmouth who spent a great deal of time in Rome. He made his fortune by purchasing pictures in Italy and selling them in England. He was described as

a man of business and a lover of the arts, he is hospitable and generous. Coins, statues, pictures, are judiciously selected by Mr. J. from a vast variety of every kind exhibited continually at Rome; and what he selects with judgement he purchases with advantage to himself and friends. To him they apply on all occasions, as a guide in business and in taste.[92]

His appointment of Day was functionary rather than as a supporter of the art of cartography.

Day undertook a substantial survey for a proposed new road between Taunton and Honiton for the Taunton Turnpike Trust in 1791. The proposed road from Blagdon Green, through Priors Park to White Wall was thought to 'be of great publick utility and ought to be made'.[93] Ravenhill and Rowe suggest that Day produced a 'Plan of the Manor of Sowton in the County of Devon belonging to the Right Honorable Lord Graves', when Lord Graves purchased the estate in 1800.[94] However, this was two years after Day passed away at Blagdon. So it is highly

[87] *Bath Chronicle and Weekly Gazette*, 1 May 1783.
[88] SHC, DD\WHh/795 Map of East Coker, 1785.
[89] SHC, A/AQP/8 letter Day to Rack, 1786.
[90] SHC, DD/WGZ/2 *Western Flying Post*, 7 July 1788.
[91] Ravenhill and Rowe, *Devon maps*, pp. 66-7, 313.
[92] *Gentleman's Magazine*, 76 (1794), 732. For a short biography see
https://en.wikipedia.org/wiki/Thomas_Jenkins_(antiquary).
[93] S.H.C., D\T\ta/7 minutes of the Taunton Turnpike Trust, 13 Dec. 1791.
[94] Ravenhill and Rowe, *Devon maps and map-makers*, pp. 66-7, 317.

unlikely that this plan was by Day. His reputation was such that following his death a Bath newspaper described him as an eminent land surveyor,[95] an act probably instigated by Masters.

Day was buried on 31 July 1798 at Pitminster and was survived by his wife.[96] On 27 October 1798, she advertised in the *Sherborne Mercury* to all land surveyors her intent to sell off her late husband's surveying instruments.[97] This short advert provides the hard evidence that has so far been lacking regarding the methods used by Day in the 1770s when surveying.[98] Of particular note were two theodolites of different sizes, two perambulators, two brass protractors of different sizes, a two feet quadrant and a telescope.[99] The theodolites were used to record a network of angular observations across the county, as suggested by Harley and Dunning.[100] A perambulator was used to measure distances,[101] particularly roads, and having two meant he might have used an additional assistant, as well as Masters. A two feet quadrant shows he was using this instrument for his latitude calculations, but what was not offered for sale was a chronometer, which Harley and Dunning speculated he might have used.[102] Perhaps Mrs Day did not want to sell this on the open market, if she had one to sell. This leaves only Day's telescope used to identify objects such as buildings in the distance which he would have then plotted on his rough surveys. It could also have been used for taking astronomical observations that were used to calculate his longitude.

As for Day's engraver, Thomas Bonnor (*c.*1741-1826), he was a painter, as well as a portrait and landscape engraver. He exhibited at the Royal Academy from 1780-1807. However, in the year Day and Masters' map was published Bonnor found himself a prisoner in the King's Bench for insolvency. He recovered from this and amongst several commissions he executed landscape engravings for the Reverend John Collinson's *History and antiquities of Somerset* published in 1791.[103] It is not surprising to find that Bonnor engraved a fine view of Hestercombe, the seat of Coplestone Warre Bampfylde esquire and one of Halswell.

Two interesting aspects of this research include a reference to Mrs Day having an investment in the 'Honiton Turnpike roads'.[104] By 1796, the road from Honiton to Taunton, through Upottery and Otterford to Blagdon Hill where the Days lived,[105] was complete. With Day's interests in surveying and roads, is it possible he was also

---

[95] *Bath Chronicle and Weekly Gazette*, 16 August 1798.
[96] His will was proved at Taunton but a copy has not come to light.
[97] *Sherborne Mercury*, 5 November 1798.
[98] J.B. Harley and R.W. Dunning, *Somerset maps*, SRS 76 (1981), p. 12.
[99] *Sherborne Mercury*, 5 November 1798.
[100] J.B. Harley and R.W. Dunning, *Somerset maps*, SRS 76 (1981), p. 13.
[101] J.B. Harley and R.W. Dunning, *Somerset maps*, SRS 76 (1981), p. 14.
[102] J.B. Harley and R.W. Dunning, *Somerset maps*, SRS 76 (1981), 12.
[103] L. Worms and A. Baynton-Williams, *British map engravers: a dictionary of engravers, lithographers, and their principal employers to 1850* (London, 2011), p. 94.
[104] TNA, PROB 11/1369/86 will of Mrs Ann Day, widow of Pitminster.
[105] SHC, Q/RUP/88 map of proposed additions, 1827.

involved with the Honiton Turnpike? Another aspect relates to the sale of the nine copper plates that 'were acquired by William Faden' after Day's death.[106] By July 1788, Day was using Faden as a retail outlet for the survey.[107] It is most likely that at this time, or shortly after, Day must have made some provision for the longevity of the survey. His wife, Ann, was not buried until 9 November 1801 at Pitminster but in 1800, Faden issued the sheets with his name as the publisher the year before her death.[108] The advert for Day's instruments two years earlier makes no mention of the plates[109] and, as Masters was still alive, presumably the plates passed to Day's assistant for a short period before Faden owned them.

The purchasers and owners

It is not possible to state how many people subscribed to the project and how many purchased copies after it had been published. However, some information can be gleaned from the provenance of some of the surviving copies of Day and Masters' survey regarding the people who owned copies of it. Perhaps of those owners most relevant to the subject of maps and mapmaking was Abraham Crocker of Frome. His own copy, which came up for sale in 2016, bears his signature. There is every reason to think that a man such as Crocker, whose interests included land surveying, would have been eager to support such a venture. Therefore, it is fair to assume that as he collected subscriptions for the project in 1778[110] he would have owned a copy shortly after it was published. As his name does not appear in the known lists of subscribers it may be possible that Day came to some arrangement with the collectors of subscriptions where they might have received a commission for every subscription. If this was the case then Crocker may have cashed this payment in by means of receiving a reduction in the cost of his copy of the survey.

Crocker came from Ilminster to Frome to be Master of the Bluecoat School in 1783. He printed posters, pamphlets and books.[111] Shortly after Day and Masters' survey was published, Crocker drew the map which accompanied the Reverend John Collinson's *History and antiquities of the county of Somerset*, published in Bath in 1791. It can only be assumed that Crocker based his map of the county on the nine sheets by Day and Masters. Crocker also contributed an account of Frome and much information on the eastern part of the county to Collinson,[112] and was a reasonable artist having drawn a perspective view of Ilminster church in 1782.[113] He corresponded with Rack and provided information on heraldry, benchends, painted glass, effigies,

[106] J.B. Harley and R.W. Dunning, *Somerset maps*, SRS 76 (1981), p. 28.
[107] SHC, DD/WGZ/2 *Western Flying Post*, 7 July 1788.
[108] J.B. Harley and R.W. Dunning, *Somerset maps*, SRS 76 (1981), p. 28.
[109] *Sherborne Mercury*, 5 November 1798.
[110] *Bath Chronicle and Weekly Gazette*, 12 November 1778.
[111] Frome Museum, webpage on Crocker and Penny, https:// fromemuseum.wordpress.com/ collection/printing/crocker-and-penny/ accessed November 2016.
[112] M. McDermott and S. Berry (eds), *Edmund Rack's survey of Somerset* (Taunton, 2011), p. viii.
[113] M. McDermott and S. Berry, *Edmund Rack's survey of Somerset*, p. 7.

inscriptions, agriculture, geology, folklore and church architecture.[114]

Crocker was himself an author of some note. He authored a small tract with the title *Instruction to the children of Sunday schools, and other seminaries of learning; designed for the promotion of their welfare in this life, and their happiness in that which is to come*, dated and presumably written at the Frome School. He produced a short treatise on cider making, *The art of making and managing cyder*, before 1801.[115] He was a friend of Charles Hutton LL.D., F.R.S., author of *The compendious measurer: being a brief, yet comprehensive, treatise on mensuration, and practical geometry. With an introduction to decimal and duodecimal arithmetic. Adapted to practice, and the use of schools* published in 1807.[116] He also wrote about the weather.[117] He undertook numerous land surveys. With his sons he surveyed the manor of Nyland with Batcombe belonging to Mrs Mary Hutton in 1813; this resulted in a map and a description of the estate being produced.[118] Abraham retired from the printing business he founded in 1815.[119]

Two copies of Day and Masters' survey have survived in the Petworth House archives.[120] These are thought to have belonged to George O'Brien Wyndham, 3rd Earl of Egremont F.R.S. (1751–1837) of Petworth House in Sussex and Orchard Wyndham in Somerset. He was a British peer, a major landowner and a great art collector, interested in scientific advances, agriculture, and canals, who invested in many ventures to improve his estates. It is not surprising to find copies of Day and Masters' work in the Petworth archive, especially as Wyndham was interested in agriculture and owned a significant amount of land in Somerset. It is surprising that his name does not appear in the pre-publication documents, but as he was only in his mid-twenties he may not have been interested in such a scheme.

Richard Combe esquire (*c*.1728-1780) of Earnshill is another man of interest, as a copy of the map survives in his family papers. Fortunately, it has not been repaired and it is still mounted on the original coarse linen with what appears to be the original rollers.[121] Combe had subscribed by September 1778.[122] He was a member of the Society of Merchant Venturers of Bristol, as well as a member of parliament and was easily able to afford the two and a half guineas Day asked for. He was also one

---

[114] M. McDermott and S. Berry, *Edmund Rack's survey of Somerset*, pp. 7, 8, 14, 18, 43, 47, 55, 60, 61, 63, 64, 93-6, 98, 100-4, 107, 131-6, 138, 139, 143, 144, 148, 163-70, 172, 200, 242-4, 251.

[115] R. Griffiths (ed), *The Monthly Review; or Literary Journal enlarged: from January to April, inclusive, M,DCCCI. With an appendix*, 34 (1801), p. 104.

[116] C. Hutton, *The compendious measurer: being a brief, yet comprehensive, treatise on mensuration, and practical geometry. With an introduction to decimal and duodecimal arithmetic. Adapted to practice, and the use of schools* (London, 1807), p. 204.

[117] C. Clark, 'The heatwave over England and the great hailstorm in Somerset, July 1808' in *Weather*, 59:7 (2006), http://onlinelibrary.wiley.com/doi/10.1256/wea.04.04/pdf.

[118] SHC, DD/PO/79 Manor of Nyland with Batcombe surveys and map, 1813.

[119] Frome Museum, webpage on Crocker and Penny, https:// fromemuseum.wordpress.com/ collection/printing/crocker-and-penny/.

[120] WSRO, PHA/5129 and PHA/3465.

[121] SHC, DD/CM/137 Day and Masters' published survey, 1782.

[122] *Bath Chronicle and Weekly Gazette*, 12 November 1778.

of several supporters of the survey who served as a trustee of the Taunton Turnpike.[123] His family's collection of maps contains a wealth of different types of cartographic examples.[124] Like Camplin, he died before the survey was printed. Entries in his family accounts show two payments of £2 7s. 6d. to 'A. Crocker' in September and October 1782,[125] which may have been for the map(s) as Crocker was an agent for Day[126] and moved to Frome in 1783. The two men had known each other for years as they were both connected with the Ilminster Turnpike Trust in the early 1770s.[127]

The Reverend Doctor Thomas Camplin (1715-1780),[128] subscriber, committee member, arbitrator and examiner of the survey played a major role in the project. Son of the Reverend Thomas Camplin of Taunton, he was educated at Oxford[129] where he served as chaplain at Christ Church and rector of St Ebbe. He came back to Somerset to serve as rector of Brompton Ralph from 1752 until his death (upon the death of another Thomas Camplin). On 26 May 1761, he was appointed as Archdeacon of Bath and served until his resignation in 1767 when he became Archdeacon of Taunton, a position he held until his death on 17 August 1780. He was prebend of Combe I, Buckland Dinham then Litton in the 1760s.[130] He was also a JP from 1758 until his death, who took the sacrament at Brompton Ralph in 1761.[131] In 1778, he was licensed to preach throughout the diocese and was appointed as vicar of Chard. He was buried at Bath Abbey on 24 August following his death at his lodgings in the city on 19 August 1780.

Because of his connections with Wells, it is probably the same man, not a namesake from Bristol, who was appointed as an arbitrator in a dispute over land in Wedmore in 1774.[132] And in 1776, he submitted a plan, which was accepted, to the Corporation of Wells to rebuild the Assize Hall and Market House.[133] He was a trustee for the Minehead harbour act with other men involved in the county survey, such as James Bernard, Richard Cox, Bampfylde, Sir Thomas Dyke Acland, Sir John Trevelyan and others.[134] He was also a trustee of the Taunton Turnpike.[135] Sadly, he

[123] SHC, D\T\ta/5 minutes of the Taunton Turnpike Trust, 1752-1777.

[124] SHC, DD/CM.

[125] SHC, DD/CM 282 accounts.

[126] *Bath Chronicle and Weekly Gazette*, 12 November 1778.

[127] SHC, D/T/ilm 1 minute book, see pp. 181, 191-2, 194, 231.

[128] For his appointments and qualifications see the Church of England Clergy Database http://db.theclergydatabase.org.uk/jsp/persons/CreatePersonFrames.jsp?PersonID=11572.

[129] J. Foster, *Alumni Oxonienses: the members of the University of Oxford, 1715-1886; their parentage, birthplace and year of birth, with a record of their degrees. Being the matriculation register of the University, A-D* (Oxford, 1888), p. 214.

[130] For his appointments and qualifications see the Church of England Clergy Database http://db.theclergydatabase.org.uk/jsp/persons/CreatePersonFrames.jsp?PersonID=11572.

[131] SHC, Q/SR/329/4/23 sacrament certificate, 13 September 1761.

[132] SHC, DD\SE/69/1 appointment, 17 August 1774.

[133] *Kentish Gazette*, 28 August 1776.

[134] *The statutes at large*, 10 (London, 1771), pp. 741-2.

[135] SHC, D\T\ta/5 minutes of the Taunton Turnpike Trust, 1752-1777.

passed away before the survey he supported was published.

James Kirkpatrick (1698-1787) esquire, barrister at law of Bristol was a subscriber, examiner and agent for subscriptions. This is probably the same man who was Clerk of the Peace for Somerset from 1768,[136] President of the Anchor Society in Bristol in 1780, Town Clerk of the Corporation of Bristol from 1785,[137] a trustee of the Taunton Turnpike,[138] administrator of the Taunton Hospital scheme in 1775,[139] Recorder of the town and borough of Bridport, Dorset from 1775[140] and a Master in Extraordinary in Chancery. On 27 October 1781, he wrote from Queens Square to the Society of Merchant Venturers in Bristol regarding the project. His letter reads:

> I applied to you some time since, Sir, on behalf of the person who has measured the County of Somerset; finding the Society of Merchants meet to Day [*sic*], I have to request that you'l be so good as to intimate to them, that the Map is in ye Engraver's Hands and nearly finished; and Mr. Day would esteem himself much oblig'd to the Gentlemen if they would direct ye payment of the second Installment of their subscription, being Eight Guineas. No more is to be called for 'till the Map is delivered.
>
> As far as my private opinion goes, I think, (for I have seen ye proof sheet) it will do credit to the performer and give no small satisfaction to the subscribers.[141]

He died on 23 May 1787 in London and, like Camplin, played an important and supportive role in the project.

One other copy of the map with an interesting connection to this story is in the collection accumulated by the War Office, now residing at the National Archive of England and Wales. It was most likely one to have been gifted or purchased shortly after publication. The reason for this thinking is based upon hand stamped lettering which appears on the sheets. The lettering is not very clear, which is a familiar problem with intricate stamps of this period. The wording contains a long letter 's' and the nine sheets of maps were divided into sections possibly at the time the hand stamp was applied. The wording of the stamp reflects the publication details:

Publifhed according to Act of Parliament by
W. DAY, BLAGDON, March 1, 1783.[142]

---

[136] SHC, DD\MR/100 schedule, and Q/C/8/1 appointment, 1768.
[137] Revd A.B. Beaven, *Bristol lists: municipal and miscellaneous* (Bristol, 1899), p. 367.
[138] SHC, D\T\ta/5 minutes of the Taunton Turnpike Trust, 1752-1777.
[139] SHC, DD/WO/40/2/10 receipt, 1775.
[140] *Bath Chronicle and Weekly Gazette*, 23 February 1775.
[141] BRO, SMV2/4/2/23/23 Letter, 27 October 1781.
[142] TNA, WO 78/5723.

The date of 1783 on the stamp may possibly reflect its addition by Day's London agent, John Wallis of the Map Warehouse, Ludgate Street. The year might not be incorrect. In 1783 an advertisement for the map appeared and the person who made the stamp may have used the year of the advert instead of publication. It is worth pointing out that the advert appeared a year after the date engraved on the plate. This in itself points to the fact that the War Office copy might not have been issued until 1783.[143] However, a version of Day and Masters' published map at the Somerset Heritage Centre is stamped with the same details as above, except that the year is 1782 NOT 1783. This version is uncoloured and still in its original nine sheets.[144] To have two such stamps with different dates is intriguing. Was the hand stamp of 1783 incorrect, or was it just wishful thinking by Day that the map was published by 1 March 1782. A delay in publication was not unusual. A similar occurrence happened with the publication of Collinson's *History of Somerset*, which has 1791 on the title page but the volumes were not issued to subscribers until January 1793.[145] This is one mystery that may never be solved.

One copy that has not been passed down from its original owner is the one belonging to Thomas Horner of Mells. Although Horner, who served in the Somerset Militia with Bampfylde,[146] was a very active justice of the peace,[147] and subsequently was one a group of men from whom seven were chosen to inspect the progress of the survey in 1775,[148] no copy of Day and Masters' has survived in his family's library.[149] Neither has any evidence come to light in the voluminous archive he left behind at Mells of any payments or correspondence.[150] It may have been the case that Horner did not actually subscribe to the survey and his role was only one of an inspector. This hypothesis may well then be true of the other men who only appear in the list of inspectors and not as subscribers.

The facsimile

A final note relating to Day and Masters' facsimile is worth recording. In 1981, Mrs Rawlins retired from the committee of the Somerset Record Society. To mark this occasion, the annual general meeting was held at the Castle Hotel, Taunton on the 14th of November, at which she was presented with a copy of the facsimile by the chairman, Mr Leighton.[151] In 1995, Robert's connection to Mrs Rawlins, the grand

---

[143] *Bath Chronicle and Weekly Gazette*, 1 May 1783.

[144] I am grateful to Tom Mayberry for hunting down this copy which I saw in 2000. Since the Somerset Record Office moved to the Somerset Heritage Centre this copy has not been located. A digital version of this set is in the author's possession.

[145] *Bath Chronicle and Weekly Gazette*, 31 January 1793.

[146] A.J. Webb and J. Skeggs, *Somerset Militia*, pp. 1-3.

[147] See Michael McGarvie's excellent volume *The King's peace: the justice's notebooks of Thomas Horner of Mells, 1770-1777* (Frome, 1997).

[148] *Bath Chronicle and Weekly Gazette*, 3 August 1775.

[149] Letter from the Earl of Oxford to the author, 23 December 2016.

[150] Letter from Mr d'Arcy, Archivist to the Earl of Oxford, 27 January 2017.

[151] This information is taken from an inscription in the front of this volume in this author's possession.

lady of local history, was strengthened when he joined the committee of Somerset and Dorset Notes and Queries (SDNQ). SDNQ was founded in 1888 and still publishes a wide range of research, notes and illustrations of historical interest. In addition to editors for both counties, a small but august group of scholars comprise its committee. The committee met once a year at Newton Surmaville under the patronage of Mrs Rawlins, who herself had joined the committee in 1933.[152] Robert became chairman of SDNQ in 2013. As an aside, Mrs Rawlins was herself related to Bampfylde through his grandmother Margaret Harbin whose portrait is on display at Hestercombe House.[153]

Robert's own interest in mapping saw the generous sponsorship by the Wyndham Trust (Taunton), of which he is a trustee, of the recently published volume *Somerset Mapped*. His foresight made the difference between this volume being published or not. It is sold across the country and Robert ensured that copies were given away to all primary schools in the Taunton area. As an educational book it is the first of its kind for Somerset to be published in a century. Whether there will be another historian of Robert's ilk in the next one hundred years history will have to wait to find out.

Conclusion

Harley and Dunning wrote that the 'remapping of England between 1740 and 1800 . . . was largely accomplished by local enterprise, financed by county subscriptions'. This can now be proved to be true for Somerset for the 1780s. And Day, Darch and Masters were definitely 'novices in the production of county maps'.[154] However, by the time Day and Darch started their county survey in 1773, the former had been surveying for well over twenty years, perhaps longer. He was certainly able to take advantage of the golden age of turnpike trusts, as most of Somerset's trusts were set up from 1752 to 1759.[155]

The background to the financing of Day and Masters county mapping project is not surprising or unusual. Day was not of the wealthier class of gentlemen in Somerset. This is especially clear in his interactions with the Taunton Turnpike Trust, whereby he was servant to the trust rather than trustee.[156] Wealthy supporters were key to its success. The fact that the scheme nearly failed before it had got going, from a surveying perspective, was due to a failing partnership. Therefore the decision to make Masters a partner in 1775, albeit a very junior one, was easy to understand. Day and Masters must have been able to work together and their survey of Somerset ended up being the most detailed depiction of the county when published in 1782 (or possibly 1783). Subsequently it was used as the basis for

---

[152] *SDNQ* 33 (1933), p. 393.
[153] Information kindly supplied by Philip White of Hestercombe.
[154] J.B. Harley and R.W. Dunning, *Somerset maps*, SRS 76 (1981), p. 6.
[155] J.B. Bentley and B.J. Murless, *Somerset roads the legacy of the turnpikes phase 1 – western Somerset* (no place, 1985), p. 10.
[156] SHC, D\T\ta/5-7 minutes of the Taunton Turnpike Trust, 1752-1805.

numerous maps of the county until it was superseded by the Ordnance Survey publications issued from 1809-1817.[157]

A word of caution should be used when consulting the survey by Day and Masters. It is difficult to claim that the survey is little more than a survey of roads and principal dwellings, with brief outline depictions of Somerset's changing landscape. A closer look at Blagdon, where Day lived, shows he recorded 25 buildings plus one at Woodram to the east of the tithing. In the same decade, Rack recorded Blagdon as having 'about 30 houses, one of which is a publick houses [sic] and near 20 of the rest farms'.[158] So, roughly speaking, Day did not show every house, with those closest to the main roads being shown in more detail. Was Day's main objective to show the roads at a time when turnpikes were popular and a good source of income for surveyors like Day? This may appear to be a cynical comment but was part of Day's intention in producing a county map to further his own interests? After all, he went to great lengths to include four different types of road.

As for Day's activities after the publication of the county survey, there is a lack of evidence that he undertook many surveys in the late 1790s. This may have been due to his old age, since if he was in his twenties when he married in 1756, by the 1790s he could have been in his sixties or seventies. Having spent years walking and surveying innumerable roads, hills, valleys, fields, etc this would have taken its toll on his aging body.

Bampfylde's involvement was far more than as the 'amateur Taunton artist' described in Harley and Dunning.[159] It is likely that, thanks to Bampfylde and his close friend Tynte[160], this adventurous and expensive project gained the support it did from across the county. It should be noted, however, that pre-publication support was received from a large number of residents from the Taunton area. It seems likely therefore, that the Taunton contingent was key to the scheme's success. Who knows, that without this support and that of Camplin and Kirkpatrick, the survey by Day and Masters might never have been published.

When the survey was published, the fact that subscribers received their copies mounted on coarse linen and rollers, suggest that other examples found in atlas form (on guards), or on single sheets, may have only been issued at a later date, possibly from 1788. Nevertheless, its change of ownership and reprinting shows there was a demand for it for almost two decades after it was first published. The demand for it still exists today, partly served by the Somerset Record Society's facsimile and numerous digital versions available online.

Acknowledgements
Sue Berry, David Bromwich (SANHS Honorary Librarian), Anne Buchanan (Local Studies Librarian, Bath Central Library), Matt Coles (Bristol Record Office), John

---

[157] T. Chubb, *Somerset maps*, p. xi.
[158] M. McDermott and S. Berry, *Edmund Rack's survey of Somerset*, p. 280.
[159] J.B. Harley and R.W. Dunning, *Somerset maps*, SRS 76 (1981), p.18.
[160] Ex inf Philip White, Hestercombe.

d'Arcy (Archivist at Mells), Emma Down (The National Archive), Margit Kaye (Beinecke Library), Kim Legate (Hestercombe), George Miles (Beinecke Library), The Earl of Oxford (Mells), Andy Playll and Mervyn Richens (South West Heritage Service), Lindsay Stainton, Drew Westerman (Bath Record Office), Andy White (Taunton), Philip White and Ben Whitworth (Hestercombe).

Left: 36. A sketch of Thomas Carew in later life, possibly drawn by Richard Phelps. (© The Trustees of the British Museum, PDB30991.)

Below: 37. An extract from the survey by Day and Masters showing Blagdon, in the parish of Pitminster, where Mr and Mrs Day lived possibly for all of their married life. (Reproduced with kind permission of the Somerset Record Society.)

38. A portrait of Sir Charles Kemeys Tynte, 5th Baronet (1710-1785), attributed to William Hogarth (1697-1764) shown at Halswell. (Private Collection, England.)

39. A portrait of Coplestone Warre Bampfylde (1720–1791), c.1758 by Thomas Gainsborough (1727-1788) in the uniform of the Somerset militia. (Private Collection.)

40. Examples of Day and Masters' published survey. The top three examples are on the original 'canvas' as advertised in 1775. The bottom was mounted on a finer cloth probably much later. (S.H.C., DD/WG/MAP/29 and DD/CM/137 reproduced with kind permission of the South West Heritage Trust; S.H.C., DD/RI/4; DD/SH 8) (© Adrian J. Webb.)

41. Interior of Compton Martin church in 1835 by J. Buckler. (Reproduced with kind permission of the Somerset Archaeological and Natural History Society from the Pigott Collection).

42. Cutcombe church in 1849 by W. W. Wheatley. (Reproduced with kind permission of the Somerset Archaeological and Natural History Society from the Braikenridge Collection.)

43. The interior of Charlcombe church in 1857 by W.W. Wheatley. Although dated 1857, this image gives a flavour of the cluttered state of some of the churches seen by Rack in the 1780s. (Reproduced by kind permission of the Somerset Archaeological and Natural History Society from the Braikenridge Collection.)

44. Altar piece consisting of inscribed boards and paintings of Moses and Aaron, now in the north aisle of Minehead church. (© Mark McDermott.)

Above left: 45. Painting of King David on the front of the west gallery in Stocklinch Magdalen church. (© Julian Comrie.)

Above right: 46. Portrait of Charles Walmesley, in his Benedictine habit, showing him as a bishop by an unknown artist. (© Downside Abbey.)

47. Invitation to the execution of John Butler, 28 August 1780, who had been involved in the Gordon Riots. (© Downside Abbey.)

48. Downside Abbey photographed by Paul Barker. (© Downside Abbey.)

49. Dunn and Hansom's 1873 design for the north transept of Downside Abbey Church. (© Downside Abbey.)

12. Were Somerset Parish Churches Physically Neglected in the 18th Century? An Examination of the Evidence in Edmund Rack's Survey of Somerset

MARK MCDERMOTT

Introduction

When the Revd John Collinson was preparing the text of *The History and Antiquities of the County of Somerset*, which was eventually published in 1791, he did so in collaboration with Edmund Rack who, between 1781 and his death in early 1787, compiled a parish-by-parish survey of the historic (pre-1974) county. The survey covered a wide range of subjects, including descriptions, often very detailed, of parish churches and a few dependent chapels. Collinson omitted much of the content of the survey when selecting material for the published *History*, but most of the original MS of the survey, including descriptions of almost 400 churches and chapels, survives in the Bristol Record Office[1] and an edited transcription has been published by the Somerset Archaeological and Natural History Society.[2] All quotations from Rack in this paper are taken from this transcription.

Rack came from humble origins in Norfolk, but through marriage had run a drapery business in Essex from which he was able to retire in middle age to pursue literary and other interests in Bath. There he was closely involved with the Bath Agricultural and Philosophical Societies and the literary circles of Mrs Macaulay and Lady Miller, and his published writings included essays and poetry on a variety of subjects. His wide-ranging interests and his literary bent presumably qualified him to write the survey, but it is also evident that he had to travel around the county to observe features such as parish churches at first hand, as indicated in his correspondence with Collinson[3] and by the vivid detail of many of his descriptions of church interiors. He was, however, not an Anglican but a Quaker, which may have given him a more detached and critical approach to describing these buildings.

---

[1] BRO, MSS 32835, boxes 32b and 32c. A set of photocopies is available at SHC, A/AQP 2-38.
[2] M. McDermott and S. Berry, eds., *Edmund Rack's Survey of Somerset* (Taunton, 2011).
[3] BRO, MSS 32835, box 32a. Also photocopies at SHC, A/AQP 39.

Rack's descriptions of parish churches usually include fittings and furniture and comments on the condition of the building. Rack's descriptions of fittings and furniture have already been the subject of a paper by the present writer[4] and will be discussed more selectively here, with a focus on the question of neglect.

Fittings and furniture
Galleries

These are mentioned in more than half of Rack's descriptions of parish churches and are in most cases referred to as singers' galleries, typically situated at the west end of the nave. At Wookey, the singers' gallery was 'old and much decayed' and its front was made of 'reed and plaister' and, at East Pennard, the gallery was 'plaistered in front and but mean', but gallery fronts were frequently described by Rack as panelled or of panelled wainscot, such as the 'very handsome wainscot gallery' at Pensford, and he often mentions the use of deal and in a few instances mahogany and oak.

Some galleries dated from the previous century, as noted by Rack, but the survey also indicates that galleries were still being erected in the 18th century. The gallery at Milborne Port was erected by Sir Thomas Travell and James Medlycott in 1712, that at Pensford was erected by the churchwardens in 1727, and there were 'new' galleries at Holton, Kilve, Marksbury and Runnington, while, at West Buckland, Rack mentions a chancel screen over which was 'an old singing loft now dissused (*sic*), a new one being erected at the bottom of the church'.

Gallery fronts were frequently painted, blue being the most favoured colour in a range of colour schemes in different churches, and there were numerous examples of representational paintings, often featuring King David in reference to the Psalms. Rack was sometimes critical of such paintings, describing, for example, paintings of David with his harp at Evercreech, Ashcott and Shapwick as 'coarse', and referring to 'emblematical figures in wretched painting' at West Cranmore. Such artistic judgements do not necessarily imply neglect, and there were also favourable judgements: for example, the gallery front at Castle Cary, which included an image of David with his harp, was 'handsomely painted', and there were 'two pretty good emblematical paintings' at South Cadbury. Many descriptions do not include explicit judgements about either the artistic merit or the physical condition of the galleries, which may be taken as implying that there were no obvious signs of neglect.

Chancel screens

Rack refers to these in about a third of his descriptions of churches. Almost half are described as 'Gothic', and approximately half of the remainder are described as 'old' or 'ancient', although these terms do not necessarily indicate a medieval date or a

---

[4] M. McDermott, 'Fittings, Furniture and Decoration in Somerset Churches in the Late 18th Century: the Evidence in Edmund Rack's Survey of Somerset', *PSANHS*, 156 (2013), pp. 135-59.

poor physical condition. A few screens were evidently post-medieval, as implied by the classical architectural features described by Rack on the screens at Huntspill, Kingston St Mary and Croscombe. A number of screens were painted, the most favoured colour once again being blue.

The physical condition of the screens is sometimes mentioned explicitly by Rack. He describes the screen at Halse as 'in very good preservation', but the screen at Kilton was 'fracturd', that at Wiveliscombe was 'much decayd', and there was 'An old mutilated Gothic screen' at Greinton, 'the remains of a shabby open screen' at Wookey, and 'a very ordinary open work screen and folding doors fitter for a stable than a church' at Westbury. Such criticisms are not, however, representative of the general state of the screens described in the survey. In some instances, Rack expresses positive approval of the features he saw. He refers, for example, to a 'fine open work Gothic screen' at Dunster, a 'handsome partition of Irish oak' at Huntspill, and a 'neatly painted' screen at Puriton. Such terms may imply that the screens were not only aesthetically appealing but well maintained, and when Rack is merely descriptive and not judgemental, there is no evidence of neglect.

Pews and benches

Pews are frequently mentioned by Rack, and were evidently box pews which he distinguished from benches. The latter provided inferior seating, presumably for poorer members of the congregations, but were not necessarily of poor materials and condition, and were typically provided with backs (although there were 'plain forms' at Godney chapel in Meare). At Bickenhall, for instance, there were three pews and 'the rest of the seats good old backd benches erected 1637'. Rack also mentions carved bench-ends, as, for example, at Broomfield, Stogursey, South Brent, Trull and Crowcombe, those at the latter church being 'some of the most ancient carved oak seats in England. They were erected in 1534, and on the ends are a great many antique figures curiously carved, and some arms.' There are no indications that these bench-ends were in a poor condition, despite being over two hundred years old when Rack saw them, and many have survived until the present time.

In a few churches, such as at Priddy and Westbury, there were only benches, but the great majority of churches had a combination of pews and benches or were entirely pewed, as at Nettlecombe and Sampford Brett, for example, where in both cases 'The whole church is neatly pewed'. Pews varied considerably (and were often privately owned). At Creech St Michael, for example, 'there are scarcely two alike either in size, form or materials, being most made up of new and old stuff mixd so that they form a motley appearance'; at Wedmore, 23 of the 38 pews were 'of panneld deal newly erected. The rest are many of them old and some very ordinary'; and at Bridgwater, 'many [of the 192 pews] are large and good, but mostly of old panneld wainscot and some small and ordinary'. Oak was sometimes used, as at Norton St Philip where 15 of the 48 pews were of deal but 'the rest of oak and very ordinary', although at Dunster some of the 48 pews were 'of fine panneld oak'.

Some pews were painted. At Bathford, for example, there were '14 pews mostly good and painted'; at Stanton Prior the pews were 'all new painted'; and those at Norton Malreward were 'neatly painted'. Stone was a favoured colour, but there were other colour schemes also, as at Chew Magna (64 pews painted 'wainscot colour, with mahogony coloured mouldings at the top') and Barwick, where some of the pews were 'very good, painted mahogony colour'. At Huish Episcopi, some of the pews were 'very good and painted green', and those at Combe Hay were 'all very neat, being newly painted wainscot colour and well veind'. Benches were also sometimes painted. At South Cadbury the benches and the pews were 'newly painted of a neat light stone colour with the tops stained like mahogony', and at St Audries the benches were 'good backd benches painted stone colour'. Such descriptions hardly indicate neglect.

As an extra refinement, some pews were lined. 'Many' of the pews at Henstridge were 'very good and some lind with green cloth'; many of the 69 pews at Wellington were 'lined and most very good'; and some of the 30 pews at Milverton were 'very good, being panneld wainscot, lind and painted'.

Rack was critical of the physical condition of some of the seating which he recorded. Several of the pews at Charlton Mackrell, for example, were 'much decayd'; the seating at Clatworthy included 'old oak backd benches much work eaten'; at Doulting 'the boarded flooring, and wainscot of many of the pews is in a state of decay'; and at Evercreech there were four pews but 'The rest of the seats are back[ed] and shut in, but many of them, in the north ayle especially, are in a state of decay and the boarded floor below them very much rotted and broken up'.

Such critical comments were not, however, typical of Rack's descriptions of the seating in Somerset churches. Most of the 65 pews at Ilminster, for instance, 'are panneld deal and very good', the pews at Downhead were 'very neat and good, being of panneld wainscot, natural colour and well boarded at the bottom', and a number of other favourable comments have already been mentioned. In some churches, moreover, new pews had recently been installed. Some of the pews at Misterton, for example, were 'new panneld deal and very good'; Ansford church had been 'new pewd with 28 pews of panneld deal painted cream colour'; at Barton St David, 'Most of the seats are new'; there were '27 new pews very neatly painted' at Paulton; there were new pews at Ansford, Ashbrittle and South Petherton; and those at Wanstrow were 'of panneld deal and oak, very neat and not many years old'. Of the pews at Preston Plucknett, 'many . . . are large, handsome and almost new'; at Stratton on the Fosse Mrs Knatchbull 'new pewed the church in 1782 with neat panneld deal'; and at Compton Martin there were '45 good pews, all of deal and not painted, being erected 40 years ago' (figure 41). All these improvements had been made in the 18th century.

Pulpits

Some pulpits were made of stone, as, for example, at Ashcott, where the pulpit was 'ornamented with Gothic carvings'. The great majority, however, were constructed of wood, many being described as being of panelled wainscot: at Buckland St Mary, for example, 'The pulpit is very neat, being of fine panneld wainscot'. A few were of oak (that at Pitminster, for instance, was of 'fine old oak neatly carved') and at Kilmington the pulpit, reading desk, communion table and rail were all 'of mahogony and remarkably neat'. More elaborate decoration is sometimes referred to: there was 'fine old carved and archd wainscot' at North Petherton, for example, whilst at Somerton the pulpit is described as 'ancient but very good, and exhibits some very fine carving', and that at Kingston St Mary was 'of fine panneld wainscot, embellishd with elegant festoons'. Such descriptions do not suggest neglect.

Rack often described pulpits as 'old', 'antique' or 'ancient', as, for example, at Puckington where the pulpit was 'very old and mean'. Some pulpits described in this way may have been medieval, but Rack also used these terms to describe a number of Jacobean pulpits: at Tellisford, for instance, 'The pulpit is very ancient, small and ordinary but has some curious antique carving, and a date cut in the wood 1608'. The survival of a number of Jacobean pulpits to the present day indicates that pulpits considered to be 'old' or 'ancient' were not necessarily in a poor condition. A few pulpits are described by Rack as 'new' (Bathealton, Holton and Walton) or 'modern' (Westonzoyland and Wheathill).

In Rack's descriptions, the quality and condition of pulpits varied considerably. That at North Wootton 'is of old panneld and carved oak, very ordinary', the pulpit at Seaborough 'is old and ordinary, being of worm eaten panneld wainscot', that at Sutton Mallet was 'wretchedly mean', and at nearby Stawell the pulpit was 'very antique and tumbling to peices'. Such critical comments were not typical, however. At East Lyng, for example, the pulpit 'is very neat, being of finely carved wainscot', that at South Stoke 'is a very pretty one', and the pulpit at Nether Stowey 'is lofty and very handsome, being of very fine panneld wainscot'.

Many of the pulpits described by Rack were painted: the most favoured colours were blue, stone and brown, but also mahogany, olive, imitation marble etc., and at Combe Hay the pulpit, pews and gallery front were all 'newly painted wainscot colour and well veind'.

Pulpit cushions and cloths were also frequently described by Rack. The most favoured colours were crimson and green. Brockley, for example, had a crimson velvet cushion and cloth, fringed and tasselled, and Ilton had a green velvet cushion and cloth 'fringed yellow', whilst South Stoke had a green cushion and cloth 'laced and tasseled'. Very occasionally the colours had faded with age: Farrington Gurney had a cushion and cloth 'that once were crimson', and Northover had 'an old fringd cloth and cushion which appear once to have been blue, or green'. Such critical remarks are once again not typical of Rack's descriptions.

Sounding-boards (above pulpits) are also mentioned on more than thirty occasions (and others may have been omitted). Rack usually regarded them as old, antique or ancient, and in a few instances they carried a date: 1614 at Pitminster, 1618 at Puriton and 1634 at Blackford. At Walton, however, 'the pulpit and sounding board are new and very neat'. Rack describes a number of sounding boards as being of wainscot ('fine old carved wainscot' at Yeovil, for example), with a very occasional reference to oak: at Charlinch, for instance, the pulpit and sounding board were 'very handsome, being of fine panneld oak'. A few are referred to as painted: for example, that at North Cheriton was 'gaudily painted', and that at Pilton was, like the pulpit, 'richly embellishd with ornamental carving, gilding and painting.' Some sounding boards were quite ornate, as, for example, at Cutcombe where Rack recorded 'a large handsome sounding board on the top of which stands an angel blowing his trumpet', and at Wilton which had a 'handsome sounding board with five gilded urns'.

Although some of the sounding boards were described in various ways as old, none of the descriptions seem to indicate neglect, and some clearly express approval of their quality. The fact that sounding boards are a rare survival in Somerset today is probably due to subsequent changes in fashion rather than physical neglect.

Reading desks

Rack mentions these on more than forty occasions, approximately half being described as of panelled wainscot, and often further described as 'neat' (Nynehead and Wanstrow), 'very neat' (Milton Clevedon and Yarlington), 'good' (Penselwood), 'very good and neat'(Combe St Nicholas) and 'fine' at Over Stowey and four other parishes. A few reading desks were constructed of oak, such as the 'old oak' at Shapwick, the 'old pannelld oak' at Broomfield and the 'excellent panneld oak' at Bishops Hull. In a few instances the reading desk is described as painted.

When Rack gives an indication of age, this is once again usually 'old', 'antique' or 'ancient'. The reading desk at Minehead, however, was 'new', and that at Pawlett was 'modern'. The overall impression is not one of neglect.

Communion tables

These had replaced altars at the Reformation, and at the time of Rack's survey communion was a commemorative act which was only taken on a few occasions each year, which may explain the neglect of some of the communion tables described in the survey.

When Rack gives an indication of age, communion tables are frequently described as 'old' or 'very old'. Some tables are described as 'ordinary' or 'very ordinary', and the tables at Upton and Podimore Milton were apparently 'fit only for the fire', that at Withypool was 'worth about 4d', and that at Northover was 'very old and dislocated, being in value 2d'. At Sandford Orcas the table was 'very ancient and wormeaten' and that at Seaborough 'very ancient and almost devoured by worms'. These criticisms are outweighed, however, by the more frequent use of terms such as 'neat', 'good', 'pretty good' and 'very good'. At Stoke St Mary, for example, Rack describes the table as 'a good one, being of oak, 6ft long and near three wide', and that at Kingweston was 'a very substantial good one made 1634'.

Rack also describes many of the coverings of communion tables, sometimes critically. At Stowey he mentions 'the remains of a green cloth which the moths have nearly demolished', at Stanton Prior a green cloth 'almosd [*sic*] distroyd by moths', at West Cranmore 'an old blue cloth almost devoured by moths', and at Bawdrip a green cloth, with a yellow fringe, which was 'wormeaten'. There were also favourable comments, however, as in the case of High Littleton which had a 'good green cloth fringd', Midsomer Norton which had a 'neat sea green cloth, laced', and Meare which had a 'handsome carpet cloth'. There are also numerous descriptions which are neither critical nor favourable but seem to imply that the cloths were both colourful and properly maintained. At Luxborough, for example, there was a crimson cloth, laced and fringed with white, at Queen Camel a purple cloth fringed with gold, and at Chilcompton a scarlet plush cloth, fringed with orange coloured silk. There is no indication of neglect in such descriptions.

Communion rails

These are also frequently referred to in the survey, and their condition evidently varied. That at Charlton Adam was 'rotten and coming down' and there was a 'low old decayd railing' at Priddy, but at Barwick there was 'an elegant mahogany railing', Pilton had a 'handsome railing and wreathd bannisters', and at South Petherton there was 'an excellent oak railing and bannisters'. Most descriptions are either complimentary or purely factual (at Chelwood, for example, there was 'a rail and banister, ornamented on the top with six gilt urns') and offer no evidence of neglect.

Altar pieces

These are also frequently described, and there are numerous references to inscriptions of the Creed, Commandments and Lord's Prayer and representations of Moses and Aaron. In a very few cases, paint was applied directly to the east wall of the chancel: at Kingston Seymour, for example, 'The altar piece is [a] wretched daubing on the wall of Moses and Aaron with the two tables of the Commandments'. This must have been the cheapest way of providing an altar piece, but was far from typical. At Ston Easton, for example, there was 'an altar peice of wainscot with a neat moulding and mitrd pediment, containing the Commandments', and an example of a more ornate design is that at Wellington where 'The altar peice (over which stand Moses and Aaron in wood) is of fine Irish oak, with a neat moulding, and a raised miterd pediment in the center, 14ft high, supported by two fluted columns of the Ionic order. On the top are three elegant urns begirt with festoons of flowers'. Such descriptions do not indicate neglect.

Several paintings were by Richard Phelps (1710-85) and had evidently been commissioned in the relatively recent past. At Dunster, for example, 'The altar peice is a good painting of the crucifiction, 24 ft by 12, by Mr Phelps of this town'. Rack is sometimes very free with his artistic judgements (he refers to 'miserable daubings' of Moses and Aaron at Minehead, for instance), but such adverse (and subjective) aesthetic comments do not necessarily imply physical neglect.

Rack very occasionally identifies the donor of an altar piece. The altar piece at Timberscombe, for example, had been given by Richard Elsworth (d. 1714); an elaborate altar piece at Wilton had recently been presented by (Sir) Benjamin Hammet; and the altar piece at Wincanton was 'a very handsome one, though unfinished, and given by Nathaniel Ireson, architect, of this town'. Clearly, in these instances the fixtures and fittings of those churches were being improved during the 18th century.

Painted decoration on walls, pillars and roofs

In some churches Rack refers to various forms of painted decoration. These include scriptural texts, as, for instance, at Compton Dundon ('the walls of this church are plentifully besprinkld with texts of Scripture') and at Shapwick where the walls were 'piously decorated with the Decalogue, the Creed, the Lord's Prayer, and many texts of Scripture in coarse oval paintings, with two miserable daubings of Moses and Aaron'. Once again, an adverse artistic judgement does not necessarily imply physical neglect. In some churches there were painted pillars (representing porphyry at Dunster and 'Sienna marble' at Castle Cary, for instance) and the pillars at Carhampton and Cutcombe and several other churches were whitewashed, which was evidently a cheaper alternative to paint, but was at least a form of maintenance. Other examples of whitewashed interiors are mentioned below.

In the majority of the churches described by Rack he refers to the roofs, which were often 'arched' or 'coved', in many cases with projecting ribs and carved bosses: these were evidently medieval wagon roofs, and the decorative features were often painted, the most frequent colour being blue (clearly a popular colour in the 18th century). The implication is that these roofs, with very few exceptions, were well maintained, and at Withypool Rack mentions that the roofs of the nave, aisle and chancel were 'All open to the tyles, but at this time repairing'. Many early roofs have survived in Somerset churches until the present time.

Chandeliers

In a number of his descriptions, Rack mentions brass chandeliers. Most of the dated examples in the survey were 18th-century, as at Wincanton where, from the centre of the roof of the nave, 'a cherub reclining on a cloud suspends a handsome brass chandelier with 14 sockets, dated 1700', and Rack occasionally identifies the donors. At Bruton, for instance, a pair of chandeliers had been given by Catherine Drew in 1695 and Richard Wood in 1743, respectively; at Mells, there was 'a handsome brass chandelier, the gift of Mrs Sarah Jefferies, widow, 1721'; in the nave of Somerton church were 'two brass chandeliers of 12 sockets each, the gift of Harbin Arnold, gent' (d. 1782); and at Kingston St Mary a brass chandelier of 24 sockets had been 'put up at the expence of the parish' in 1773'.

Glazing

Rack mentions painted glass in almost thirty of his descriptions of churches. At Meare, neglect is indicated by his reference to some 'very fine ancient painted glass' which was 'much obscured by dirt', but at Kingsbury Episcopi there were windows with 'some very beautiful painted glass' (with apparently pre-Reformation imagery:

'the subjects are kings, bishops, saints, Gothic ornaments and, armorial shields'), 'many of them in very good preservation'. Some early glass was fragmentary, but Rack was aware that this was due to earlier iconoclasm: at East Brent, for instance, there was 'a great deal of old painted glass which is much injurd by time and the republican fury of the last century'. In over 70 churches Rack refers to crown glass: at Dulverton, for example, and at Widcombe and Lyncombe where there were also two 'modern sashd windows' in the chancel. Crown glass was high quality glazing which had probably been installed during the 18th century and must have made church interiors seem light and airy compared with the Victorian preference for heavy stained glass.

Tympana

These features, which infilled the upper part of a chancel arch, were recorded by Rack in a number of churches: at Kingsbury Episcopi, for example, where, above the chancel screen, 'the arch is filld up with a handsome painting of the royal arms with St Peter and St Paul in distemper'. Rack is critical of the artistic treatment of some of these tympana, as at East Pennard, where there was a 'miserable representation' of Abraham offering up Isaac and 'a horrid figure intended for Moses', but this does not necessarily indicate actual neglect. At Norton sub Hamdon 'on the upper part of the great arch (which is filled up) is an old decayed painting of the Resurrection', but in general the descriptions of these tympana do not provide evidence of neglect.

Structural issues

In a small minority of his descriptions, Rack refers to structural problems in Somerset churches. At Brean, for example, 'The whole church [is] in bad repair'; in Ashington church, 'The east end of the chancel is crackd from top to bottom, dividing the arch of the window' and 'the roof in some parts is decaying'; and at Berrow, 'The inside of this church is mean and much out of repair, the chancel especially, which has not been made any use of for some time'. Upton Noble church is described as 'a small edifice much out of repair', Kittisford church 'is in very bad repair', at Queen Charlton 'The two side ayles being in a ruinous state are made no use of', and Bradford on Tone church 'looks dull and dark and is going fast to decay'. The church at Cudworth was 'unceild, dull, gloomy, dirty and ruinous', and similarly that at Seavington St Michael was 'damp, gloomy and dirty, and much out of repair'.

Further examples include Cutcombe where 'The east end of the north ayle is very damp and in bad repair, and the north wall is bulgd out at the top near a foot from the perpendicular' (figure 42), at Wiveliscombe the pillars of the south aisle 'are more than a foot out of the perpendicular, leaning to the south', at Catcott, 'The side walls [are] bulgd out by the weight of the roof', and at Abbas Combe, 'The side walls are bulged out at the top by the weight of the roof, so as to be full a foot out of the perpendicular'.

Rack could be very critical of the way in which chancels (which were the responsibility of rectors or lay rectors rather than churchwardens) were maintained. In

Barrington church, 'The chancel, which belongs to Earl Paulet, is in a shameful condition, the walls are covered with green and black moss and the floor is entirely broken up – and every part of the church is dirty and coming to decay'; at Lopen, 'The chancel belongs to Earl Paulet and is in a very bad condition'; and at Seavington St Mary, 'The chancel, which belongs to Earl Paulet, is in a wretched condition, the tyles and roof being broken in and no floor laid at all'. At North Stoke the chancel was 'out of repair and very dirtily kept', the chancel at North Wootton 'is very badly floored and the walls are bulged out from the bottom of the roof till it is more than a foot out of the perpendicular', and at Shapwick, the chancel 'belongs to Mr [Mrs?] Strangways and wants general repair'

Towers could also be problematical: that at West Pennard 'is crackd in several places and wants much to be rebuilt', at Podimore Milton 'The church tower is crackt on the top down to the window', whilst the tower at Lympsham 'leans so much to the west as to be 2 ft 3 ins out of the perpendicular'.

In some cases attempts had been made to compensate for structural problems, but fell short of full repair. At Norton St Philip, 'The side walls of the two ayles are tied to the pillars on each side the nave with iron bars that hook together with an eye and bolt in the middle, and the side walls of the nave are tied together in the same manner', and at Minehead the pillars of the aisle 'lean out so much to the north as to be 15 ins out of the perpendicular, but strong buttresses are now built without side to prevent the wall from falling'.

Many churches, however, had evidently been subject to total or partial rebuilding during the 18th century. Rack describes the church at Woolley as 'an elegant little chapel rebuilt a few years since at the sole expence of Mrs Parkins whose property the parish then was. This chapel is built of Bath stone, having a small tower at the west end on which is a handsome cupola or dome and one bell.' At Exford, 'most of [the church] has lately been rebuilt'; and at Downhead, 'The church is a small Gothic building rebuilt in the year 1751', although 'the floor of the middle passage is badly paved and damp' and the east window of the chancel, which belonged to Thomas Horner Esq., was in a 'very bad condition'. The church at Hinton Blewett included 'a pretty stone tower ... lately rebuilt' (although the church as a whole was 'very much out of repair'), and at Clutton, 'This tower was rebuilt in the year 1728'. At High Littleton 'The church is a small but very handsome building rebuilt in the year 1735 and kept in remarkable neat order', and the church at Paulton 'is a handsome edifice rebuilt in the year 1753, and the tower in 1757, of stone brought from the quarries at Doulting on Mendip at the expence of the parish'. The tower at Stowell was 'rebuilt in the year 1748', and that at West Coker 'is newly built', whilst at Priston, 'In the center stands a handsome new built tower of stone', and the central tower at Shapwick had 'a new raised open workd bullustrade on the top with four pinnacles at the corners'.

Rack describes Pensford church as 'a neat modern edifice of stone, built by a brief about 60 years since', and the church at Brompton Ralph as 'a Gothic edifice, the greater part of it rebuilt in 1738'. Wincanton church was 'plain without but very handsome within, the chancel having been rebuilt and the church new roofd and windowd in1748'; and at Combe Hay, 'The church is a small but handsome edifice, all of it, the tower excepted, having been rebuilt about 20 years ago', and it had 'throughout an air of neatness and simple elegance seldom met with.' At Seaborough, 'The ayle is very neat, being built about 40 years since', and at East Cranmore the tower had been 'rebuilt about 40 years since'. Rack describes Marston Bigot church as 'a very mean edifice and is going to be rebuilt', and notes inserted in the survey by Abraham Crocker include the statement that 'The old church is erased, the new one going on'.

Godney chapel (in Meare) included an inscription that the chapel had been 'restored to its Ancient Use by Peter Davis Recorder of Wells Esq in the year 1737'; and at Babington, 'The church is a small neat new stone edifice rebuilt about 30 years since [*marginal insertion*: 'in the year 1750'] by Mrs Elizabeth Long, aunt to N. Knatchbull, Esq., by whose house it stands'; whilst at Stratton on the Fosse there was 'a neat north ayle newly built by Mrs Knatchbull, who also new pewed the church in 1782', and the chancel 'was rebuilt (all but the east wall) at the expence of the Revd Richard Hughes, rector'. Unusually, the chancel at Pawlett 'is built of brick, and a modern erection'. Some rectors or lay rectors evidently took their responsibilities for their chancels seriously.

In addition to these numerous instances of rebuilding, Rack speaks highly of the fabric of the buildings in many of his descriptions. For example, Charlton Horethorne church is described as 'a well built Gothic edifice', Woolavington church as 'a neat well built Gothic edifice', Publow church as a 'good substantial building' with a 'very handsome' tower, and at Kilmersdon, 'At the west end is a stately tower of excellent masonry'. The tower at North Petherton 'is of excellent masonry and one of the handsomest in the county' and Evercreech church had 'a magnificent tower of excellent symetry and masonry'. West Buckland, Durston, Dowlish Wake, Long Sutton, Yeovilton and more than a dozen other churches had 'well built' towers, and the tower at Shepton Beauchamp was also 'well built' and the church as a whole was a 'handsome . . . edifice of good stone from Ham Hill and excellent masonry'. Rack also considered Midsomer Norton church to be 'a handsome ancient stone edifice' and he refers to the 'excellent masonry' of the 'very handsome stone tower'. In such instances the impression is very far from being one of widespread structural deterioration.

Purely aesthetic judgements are made in many other descriptions. Mark church, for example, is described as 'a large handsome Gothic edifice', East Brent as 'a very handsome edifice', South Brent as 'a handsome Gothic structure', and Wrington church as 'a stately Gothic structure' with 'one of the most beautiful towers in the kingdom'. These and other examples of aesthetic approval may imply that Rack noticed no structural issues with these buildings.

General level of care

In addition to remarks relating to the structural condition of church buildings, Rack frequently refers in his descriptions of churches to their cleanliness (or otherwise), the state of the floor and whether the church was dry. What follows is by no means an exhaustive list of Rack's comments on these aspects of church interiors.

Rack's comments on a number of churches were mixed. At Thurlbear, for instance, 'The floor, except in the chancel, is very indifferent, the north wall damp and green, but the church is on the whole kept cleaner than many others'; at North Curry, 'The floor is pretty good, but not kept so clean as it ought to be'; at Charlton Mackrell, the pavement was 'pretty good' and the church 'dry but kept dirty'; and the church at Lydeard St Lawrence was 'tolerably paved and kept very decent, but the north wall, both of the ayle and chancel, is very damp and mossy'.

Some churches, however, were clearly very neglected. At Burnham, for instance, the whole church was in a dirty condition and the south aisle was 'a repository for brick, mortar, lime, boards and other materials', whilst at Stogursey, 'many parts of this church are dirty and filled with lumber', and in Spaxton church, 'The floor under the seats in the south ayle and on the north side of the nave [is] shamefully broken up and filld with rubbish'. Luccombe church was 'badly floored and damp; in the chancel the walls are almost coverd with green fungi'; at Oare, 'The floor is bad, the chancel damp and the whole church very dirty'; and in Treborough church most of the pews were 'old and ordinary, and the floor all clay in them', and 'The walls of the chancel, especially, [are] very damp and coverd with green moss, being much fitter for a stable than a place of worship' (a favourite phrase with Rack).

At Creech St Michael, 'The floor of this church is a motley mixture of large and small stones, rough stone, long and square bricks, and but dirtily kept. The chancel is damp, the walls being green and the plaister crumbling down daily. The north ayle is quite neglected and full of rubbish.' At Maperton the floor was 'damp, very dirty and shamefully broken up', Sparkford church 'is in a state of decay and very dirtily kept', and at Sutton Montis, 'The walls are exceedingly damp and coverd with black and green jelly moss. The floor dirty.'

In the church at Hinton Blewett the ceiling of the chancel 'is a considerable part of it dropt down, the rest daily mouldering away. The chancel door quite rotten and crumbling to pieces, as also is the wooden railing which divides it from the body of the church. The pavement is very bad, the stones mostly broken or sunk at one end so as to render walking dangerous, and the whole very dirty.' At Merriott the floor under some of the seating was 'quite broken up and gone' and 'The chancel and north ayle particularly are very damp and dirty, and the walls very green'; and at Crewkerne, 'The floor is very irregular, being of stones of all sizes badly laid and promiscuous jumbled together', and although the church was 'tolerably dry and airy' it was 'very dirty and incumberd with many things which ought to occupy no place in it'. In Lullington church, 'The pavement of the chancel and middle passage is very good' but 'the boards under the pews and seats [are] very much broken and crumbling to powder. The whole is very damp, the pavement and lower parts of the walls being coverd with green moss'; and at Whatley 'This church is so damp that the boards in many of the pews are crumbling to powder and the walls are coverd with green and yellow fungi'.

Further examples of neglect include the church at Milborne Port which was 'very damp and dirty, and the south end of the transept is almost filled with old boards, lumber and rubbish', and at Stowell, 'The whole church, but especially the chancel, is very damp, the floor bad, and kept in so nasty a manner that not only green moss but weeds of different kinds grow under the walls. The boards under the seats are crumbling to dust and a plentiful crop of fungi are sprouting up there.' At Middle Chinnock, 'The church is very damp and in bad repair, the walls decayd and almost covered with black and green moss, the pavement is very indifferent and the whole dirty'; and at Huish Episcopi, 'The floor of most of [the] pews is very bad, the boards being broken in and crumbling to powder; and the bottom of the walls damp and crumbling away. The pavement of the church and chancel in some parts is good though old; but the walls want cleaning and whitewashing. Under the backd oak benches the floor is in a ruinous state.'

At Luxborough one of the pews in the chancel was 'filld with lumber'; at Meare, 'many of [the pews] in the ayles are filld with dirt and lumber'; whilst in Milverton church, 'The floor [is] pretty good but kept dirty, and many parts of the church incumberd with old boards, timbers and other lumber which has no business there'; and at Stawley, 'Alley brickd, belfry [floor under the tower] rough pebbles, chancel earthen floor full of holes, boards under the seats rotted to powder'. In Hawkridge church, 'The chancel roof is droping in and in the floor are great holes quite down to the coffins' and the whole church was 'very damp and nasty, being much fitter for a stable than a place of worship'; and in the church at Hillfarrance, 'The ayle is very small and unceild, belonging to a farmer in the parish who neglects to keep it tolerably decent' and it had become 'a repository for rubbish and lumber' (figure 43).

Sutton Mallet church is described as 'a dark dismall looking place' and 'The whole church very dirty and much fitter for a stable than a place of worship'; at Wheathill, 'Within one of the seats, an elm shrub with numerous branches is grown up from between the stones in the pavement 2 ft high. It has stood there some years and consists of more than 30 stems'; and the church at Englishcombe is described as 'a damp one, and kept in very indecent dirty condition, the pavement mostly broken; and six ordinary pews, the boards at bottom are mostly rotten and crumbling to powder. Heaps of dirt are swept up and left in the corners, and the passage up the ayle scarcely safe to walk in.'

Rack's more positive comments about the general level of cleanliness and care are less dramatic, but nevertheless very significant. For example, at Hinton Charterhouse, 'In this church there is not any appearance of dampness; the pavement is pretty good and is kept cleaner than most', and Beercrocombe church 'is kept clean and decent', a phrase which Rack applied to a number of churches, including Drayton, Broomfield (which was also 'well paved'), Goathurst (where the outside of the whole building was whitewashed), Batheaston, Bathampton, Pitcombe, Carhampton, Keinton Mandeville (which was 'well floord with stone' - presumably the local lias), Kingweston, West Pennard, Whitelackington, Withiel Florey (which was 'rough cast white' and 'neatly pewed, dry, well floord'), and Freshford, where the nave, aisle and chancel roofs were 'neatly ceild and whitewashd'.

At North Cadbury, 'All the pillars, arches and walls are newly painted white, which with the number and largeness of the windows give the church a very light airy appearance. The whole church is well paved with large stones and kept very clean and decent, being pretty dry except in the chancel.' At South Cadbury, 'The walls are neatly white washd, the floor dry and good, and on the whole this is one of the neatest churches in the county', and at Ston Easton, 'Floor very good. Church dry, ceild and whitewashd.' The walls of West Cranmore church were 'plain, dry and well whitewashd, and the floor very good and dry'; and the walls at Foxcote were also 'well white washd'.

At Penselwood 'The floor is tolerable and the walls are newly whitewashd, so that this church is very decent'; Moorlinch church was 'neatly plaisterd and whitewashd, dry, and kept clean'; and Pitminster church was 'well white washd, light and airy, having 15 windows, mostly large and of Crown glass. The floor is excellent and the church kept very clean.' In the church at Barwick, 'The pavement is good and the whole church is dry, neat and clean', and at Brislington, 'The whole church seems dry and kept very clean and decent', although the churchyard was 'very much overrun with nettles and weeds'. At Marksbury, 'the whole church [is] kept more decent than many others', and at Mells 'The floor of this church is exceedingly good and pretty dry. It is also kept clean and decent'.

The stone used for paving is sometimes identified by Rack. At Kilmington, 'The whole church is whitewashd within and kept tolerably neat and clean. The floor is very good, and almost new in the chancel, being of excellent stone from Chelmark [Chilmark] in Wiltshire'; and at Shepton Beauchamp, 'The floor is of Ham stone and very good, and the church is dry and kept tolerably clean and decent', although the boards under the benches and some of the pews were 'very badly broken up'.

An analysis of all of Rack's comments on these aspects of church interiors indicates that his favourable remarks on the state of the floors outnumber his critical comments by almost two to one, and on cleanliness by about twenty per cent, and his comments on dry and damp conditions are closely balanced.

Conclusion

Very few churches in Somerset were unaffected by the widespread 'restoration' which occurred during the Victorian period, as the catalogue of faculty records in the Somerset Heritage Centre indicates.[5] It is evident from Rack's survey that many Somerset churches in the 18th century suffered from neglect in various forms. Dampness was evidently a particular problem, floors were badly maintained in many, but not a majority, of the churches in which they were described, and many churches, but once again not a majority, were not kept clean. Relatively few churches, however, were recorded by Rack as having serious structural problems

[5] SHC, D/D/Cf.

which would require major repair or rebuilding, and these were outnumbered in the survey by those churches in which restoration work had evidently taken place during the 18th century. Nor is it evident that the fittings and furniture in Somerset churches were in a general state of neglect. The various problems which Rack identified in his survey do not seem to justify the amount of restoration which took place in the following century.

With regard to the treatment of fittings and furniture during 19th-century restoration, galleries, box pews, communion tables, sounding boards, tympana and paintings of David, Moses and Aaron were largely swept away. Organs and robed choirs (in the chancel) replaced the west-gallery singers and church bands which were a feature of many Somerset churches in the 18th century; and congregations were, with few exceptions, seated in rows of uniform bench pews which faced east towards the chancel where Holy Communion was now celebrated regularly at an altar.

There was an interval of at least fifty years between the making of the survey and the beginning of Victoria's reign, during which further deterioration in Somerset churches could have taken place, but the motives for the transformation of English churches in the Victorian period went beyond the necessity for essential repair. A major factor was a desire to fulfil a vision of medievalism which owed much to the influence of the Anglican High Church movement (including the Cambridge Camden Society, which was highly critical of box pews and galleries[6]) and A. W. Pugin's campaign in favour of the Gothic style as the true Christian form of architecture.[7] In addition, bench pews had the advantage of reducing social inequality and accommodating more people than box pews at a time of population growth. The latter was also one of the motives for the enlargement of some churches during restoration.

The paintings of Moses and Aaron which Rack saw in Minehead church have survived (figure 44), and a painting of King David which he recorded at Stocklinch Magdalen survives as an integral part of a retained west gallery (figure 45), but these features are in an artistic style which was no longer in fashion in the 19th century: the Minehead paintings were relegated to the north aisle and that at Stocklinch Magdalen was hidden by a layer of brown paint until 1958.[8] A tympanum also survived at Stocklinch Magdalen until 1958 when it was removed because, significantly, it obscured the view of the chancel from the nave. Some early communion tables have survived until the present time, but have in some cases been relegated to side chapels (as at Minehead).

Rack's survey gives a mixed picture of the physical state of many Somerset

---

[6] Discussed in T. Cooper, and S. Brown, eds., *Pews, Benches and Chairs. Church seating in English parish churches from the fourteenth century to the present* (London, 2011), pp. 197-210.

[7] R. Hill, *God's Architect. Pugin and the Building of Romantic Britain* (London, 2007), *passim*.

[8] M. McDermott, 'The Restoration of Stocklinch Magdalen Church', *PSANHS*, 139 (1996), pp. 135-47.

churches in the 18th century. There was certainly much neglect of various kinds which was often described in highly judgemental language (which may make for more interesting reading), but there were very many examples of positive comments, and on balance the picture presented by Rack is a favourable one. Some restoration of Somerset churches was essential in the following century, but the motives for the widespread and often drastic 'restoration' which actually took place were mixed, and the evidence in the survey confirms that the extensive destruction of pre-Victorian fittings and furniture, in particular, should not be attributed simply to 18th-century neglect.

13. Monastic Revival in Somerset: Benedictine Monasticism from the Henrician Dissolution to the Second Vatican Council

DOMINIC AIDAN BELLENGER

'Trees yet in winter bloome, and beare their Summers greene'[1]

Michael Drayton's topographical poem, completed in 1622, evokes the decay and destruction of Glastonbury, but in this closing line suggests a hint of new life. Somerset's rich monastic tradition seemed to end with the Henrician Dissolution and the brief revival of monastic life at Westminster Abbey under Mary Tudor, which saw four former Glastonbury monks returning to the cloister, was no more than an interlude.[2] Rumours and dreams of monastic revival at Glastonbury persisted; memory and nostalgia do not pass away quickly, but the dissolution was absolute and the Protestant hegemony triumphant.[3] Nevertheless, during the four centuries that followed, monastic life, at least in its Benedictine form, was to rise again in Somerset, and in the late nineteenth century an abbey church was to be

---

[1] Michael Drayton, 'The Poly-Olbion', quoted by J. Carley, *Glastonbury Abbey* (Woodbridge, 1988), p. 170. Drayton (1563-1631) hoped to celebrate all the principal antiquarian sites in Bath.

[2] R. Dunning, *Somerset Monasteries* (Stroud, 2001), p. 127. The four Glastonbury monks John Phagan, John Neot, William Adelwold, and William Kentwyn petitioned Queen Mary for Glastonbury's restoration. This came to nothing. On the other hand, in 1557 the Carthusian house at Sheen in Surrey was restored and its foundation members included two men from former Somerset communities, John Mychell of Witham and Thurstan Hyckemans of Hinton. The Sheen charterhouse later settled at Nieuport in the Netherlands, where it remained until its suppression in 1783. At least one Somerset man, John Parsons (d. 1639), entered this monastery: D. A. Bellenger, *English and Welsh Priests, 1558-1800* (Bath, 1984), p. 187.

[3] See A. Walsham, *The Reformation of the Landscape* (Oxford, 2011), pp.166-7. William Good, born in Glastonbury in 1527, became a scholar and fellow of Corpus Christi College, Oxford, and, under Mary, was rector of Middle Chinnock and a prebendary of Wells Cathedral. Under Elizabeth he was exiled and joined the Jesuits in Italy. He died in Naples in 1586. His childhood memories of Glastonbury were important evidence in keeping alive the tradition of Joseph of Arimathea at Glastonbury: see J. Armitage Robinson, *Two Glastonbury Legends* (Cambridge, 1926), pp. 46-9. They also contributed to the cycle of historical paintings at the English College in Rome, where Good, who was spiritual director of the college, planned the cycle's narrative. The paintings, widely available in engraved form, were executed in 1582-3 by Pomerancio Circignani (1516-79), and portrayed both Joseph of Arimathea and

built at Downside which rivalled its lost medieval predecessors.[4]

In the early years of the seventeenth century a new English Benedictine Congregation slowly established itself. The medieval Congregation, made up of autonomous abbeys of men – many of which dated back to the great period of monastic flowering in England, the tenth and eleventh centuries – had been formed in the thirteenth century following the decrees of the Fourth Lateran Council in 1216, which attempted to order and regularise monastic life in the Western Church. A General Chapter of all the houses was held every three years and, from 1338, there was a single chapter for the two English ecclesiastical provinces of Canterbury and York which met regularly until the Reformation.[5] The new Congregation was distinct from the old in a number of significant ways: following the Reformation Roman Catholicism was proscribed by law, it operated in a religious and social climate inimical to its ideals, it had no autonomous abbeys (at least until the opening of Lamspringe), it included a house of nuns (Cambrai, founded in 1623), its religious communities were all outside England, and, most fundamentally, it was a missionary congregation which actively engaged with the world outside the cloister. Benefitting from the legal training and antiquarian instincts of a number of its founding fathers, the new Congregation was insistent on claiming continuity with its dissolved medieval predecessor, not least through the succession to Westminster Abbey, whose last surviving monk, Sigebert Buckley, 'affiliated' two English monks, professed in Italy, to the old Congregation on 21 November 1607.[6]

Englishmen had begun entering continental monasteries in small numbers from the end of Elizabeth's reign. They favoured the reformed monasteries found in Italy and Spain. The monks were all students of the English Colleges founded in continental Europe to train priests for the English Mission. The colleges at Douai, then in the Spanish Netherlands, Rome, and Valladolid in Spain were the most signifi-

---

the martyrdom of Richard Whiting, last abbot of Glastonbury: see A. Dillon, *The Construction of Martyrdom in the English Catholic Community 1535-1603* (Aldershot, 2002), pp. 170-242. Some relics, notably that of the Holy Thorn at Stanbrook Abbey in Yorkshire, had Glastonbury provenance: see H. Connolly, 'Relics and Plate from the Benedictine Chapel of the Rosary (c.1650-81)', *The Downside Review* 12 (1934), pp. 586-606 and T. Hopkinson-Ball, 'The story of an appearance and a disappearance: the Glastonbury Relics of Lincolns Inn Fields', *SWHC* 27 (2009), pp.10-21. The Catholic Stocker family of Chilcompton appear to have secured another relic, one of the nails used at the crucifixion, from Glastonbury but this was confiscated and has disappeared: see G. Oliver, *Collections* (1857), reprinted in *South Western Catholic History* 23 (2005), p. 33. A. Stocker (1598-1668), a Douai monk who was born in the Low Countries, may have been from this family: Bellenger, *English and Welsh Priests*, p. 111.

[4] See D. A. Bellenger, ed., *Downside Abbey, an Architectural History* (London, 2011).

[5] R. Yeo, 'The English Benedictine Congregation', in A. Berry, ed., *Belmont Abbey* (Leominster, 2012), p. 32.

[6] B. Green, *The English Benedictine Congregation* (London, 1980), p. 11. Green's account is a clear overview, but full narrative histories are provided by D. Lunn, The *English Benedictines, 1540-1688* (London, 1980), G. Scott, *Gothic Rage Undone: English Monks in the Age of Enlightenment* (Bath, 1992), and A. Hood, *From Repatriation to Renewal: Continuity and Change in the English Benedictine Congregation, 1795-1850* (Farnborough, 2014). The present author gives a personal view in *Monks with a Mission* and *Monastic Identities* (both Bath, 2014).

cant nurseries of monastic vocations. Many of the new monks were converts from the Church of England and former members of the universities of Oxford and Cambridge and the Inns of Court in London. They were all dedicated to missionary and monastic life, which they did not see as incompatible; as early as 1601 some newly professed monks, ordained before they entered religious life, were given permission to return to England. By 1606 English monks of the Spanish Congregation had started an English community at Douai, under the patronage of St Gregory the Great, and led a full conventual life by the following year. Since 1814 this monastery has been resident at Downside in Somerset. In 1608, a second English monastery was opened at Dieuoulard in Lorraine; this is now continued at Ampleforth in Yorkshire. Further foundations were made at St Malo in Brittany in 1611 (closed in 1668), dedicated to St Benedict, and in Paris, dedicated to St Edmund (of East Anglia), in 1615. This Paris house continues as Douai Abbey, Woolhampton, Berkshire. All these had the status of priories at their foundation. A final house, Lamspringe Abbey, near Hildesheim in Germany, was opened in 1644. All depended on local patronage but were generally exempt from episcopal interference and remained almost exclusively English in their personnel.

The first constitutions of the new English Benedictine Congregation were promulgated in 1619. 'What can be seen in the seventeenth-century constitutions of the English Benedictine Congregation', Richard Yeo reminds us, 'is a centralised Congregation, with a General Chapter, whose membership was largely self perpetuating, and which elected all the superiors of the Congregation not only the central government of the Congregation, but also the priors of monasteries and the superiors of the two "provinces" (of Canterbury and York), to which were assigned the monks who were involved in missionary work in England.'[7] The President General presided over the ruling council or 'regimen' and acted as chief executive in his quadrennium. This system continued until the late nineteenth century. All this activity and organisation was undoubtedly inspired by Augustine of Canterbury's mission of 597: the conversion by monks under the instruction of a monastic Pope, Gregory the Great, of the English people.[8]

In 1621, the English Benedictine General Chapter declared that 'for the preservation of the rights of the congregation to the monasteries if England, each of the communities should in future be appropriated to one of the English monasteries; and in particular that Douai should be appropriated to St Albans, Dieulouard to Westminster, S. Malo to Glastonbury, Paris to Bury St Edmunds, and so also of houses if any others be erected.'[9] The honorary use of the titles of these abbeys was not current until the nineteenth century, and the appropriation was seen as a claim of lost monastic rights rather than a means of returning alienated property. In 1629,

---

[7] R. Yeo, 'The English Benedictine Congregation', p. 33.
[8] See D. Rees, ed., *Monks of England* (London, 1997).
[9] H. Connolly and J. McCann, *The Abbots of the Ancient Monasteries and the Cathedral Priors* (privately printed, 1942), p. 50.

the Chapter appointed nine cathedral priors, 'who, each with a small body of monks, would be like a small invading army, ready to occupy its chosen objectives when England should turn Catholic'.[10] Such proprietorial ambitions were imaginable in the febrile atmosphere of early Stuart England, but the nomination of cathedral priors soon became a title of honour rather than anticipation. Bath was one of the cathedral priories supplied with a prior.[11]

In the league table of Catholic English counties shown by the number of ordinations to the priesthood in the years between 1558 and 1800, Somerset comes tenth, between Norfolk and Lincolnshire, with ninety-four ordinations in total; Lancashire and Yorkshire top the list. Sixteen of the Somerset ordinations were Benedictines; 716 Benedictines were ordained overall for England and Wales during this period.[12] The earliest to join an English community was Nicholas Fitzjames, who became the first professed monk of St Gregory's, Douai. His family, long associated with Glastonbury Abbey, was from Redlynch, near Bruton, and he was ordained priest in 1601 from the English College, Douai. He was clothed as a monk at St Gregory's on 12 May 1607 and made his monastic profession on 15 May 1608. He died at Stourton, Wiltshire, on 16 May 1652, aged ninety-two. The Benedictine annalist, Benet Weldon (1674-1713), celebrated 'his undaunted spirit in a diminutive body'.[13]

Other early Somerset monks included Thomas Hill (1564-1644), ordained in Rome in 1594, sentenced to death and reprieved in 1604, who was said to have become a monk of St Gregory's in London in 1613 and to have died in his monastery,[14] and Thomas Kemys (born 1575) of Cucklington, ordained priest in 1603, who appears in one list as a monk.[15] John Augustine Capes (1585-1628), born at Milverton and educated in Taunton, was ordained in Rome in 1612, and became a Benedictine in Spain.[16] Joseph Prater, who died in London in 1631, was probably of the Nunney family, and when he took the habit at Compostela, as early as 1599,

---

[10] Lunn, *English Benedictines*, p. 111.

[11] *Ibid.*, p. 112, quoting J. McCann on the 1634 papal bull 'Plantata', by which the new congregation not only acquired the right of succession to its medieval English predecessor, but also the privileges of the Spanish and Cassinese congregations, the friars, Jesuits and military orders. Two copies of 'Plantata' are preserved in the Downside Abbey archives and a translation of the text is available online: http://www.plantata.org.uk/docs/doc_plantata.htm (accessed 25 September 2017).

[12] Bellenger, *English and Welsh Priests*, p. 248. Most English Benedictine monks were ordained priest. Lay brothers were rare. For a wide view of those who entered the monasteries see the website of the Durham University *Monks in Motion* project: https://www.dur.ac.uk/mim/ (accessed 25 September 2017). N. Birt, *Obit Book of the English Benedictines, 1600-1912* (privately printed, 1913) and A. Allanson, *Biography of the English Benedictines* (Ampleforth, 1999) provide useful biographical information.

[13] J. McCann and H. Connolly, eds., *English Benedictines*, Catholic Record Society 33 (1934), p. 191n. This volume is seminal for the study of the early revival of the Anglo-Benedictines. It makes full use of the surviving material, including the Liber Graduum at Downside, which records the monastic progress of individual monks.

[14] G. Anstruther, *The Seminary Priests*, vol. 1 (Ware and Ushaw, 1968), pp. 167-8.

[15] J. McCann and H. Connolly, eds., *English Benedictines*, CRS 33, p. 239.

[16] Anstruther, *The Seminary Priests*, vol. 2 (Great Wakering, 1975), pp. 42-4.

he was probably the first Somerset man to become a monk since the Dissolution. He served as Provincial of Canterbury from 1621-5.[17] John Placid Muttlebury, from Wells, an alumnus of Douai College, ordained alongside Nicholas Fitzjames in 1601, became a member of the Dieulouard community, and died there in 1632.[18] His kinsman Francis Muttlebury was the son of Thomas Muttlebury of Jordans, Ashill, Somerset, and his wife Dorothy Tichborne; after his ordination, he made his monastic profession at St Edmund's, Paris, in 1658. He died in England in 1697.[19]

Robert Sherwood of Bath, born in 1558, made his profession at St Gregory's in 1613. He died at Kiddington in Oxfordshire in 1665.[20] William Sherwood was professed at Dieulouard in 1626 and died there in 1663 after many years working in England. His monastic name (monks took a new patron when entering the monastic state) was Alphege, in honour of the martyred Archbishop of Canterbury born in Bath.[21] Another member of the family, John Sherwood, was a lay brother at Lamspringe; he entered in 1656 and died in 1669. Joseph Sherwood, born in Flanders, a kinsman, was also a Lamspringe monk; he became a monk in 1653 and abbot in 1681, the first Somerset abbot since the reign of Henry VIII. He died in 1690.[22] Robert Gabriel Brett, from White Staunton, was a nephew of the English Benedictine Gabriel Gifford, Archbishop of Reims. Brett was born in 1599 and was professed at St Malo (a house founded by Gifford). He was elected prior of St Edmund's, Paris, and later of his own community. He died of the plague in London in 1665.[23] John Austin Richardson, another Somerset man, became a monk of St Gregory's in 1618 and died in 1656.[24] John Edward Byfleet (1607-1701), a Douai monk, came from Bratton Seymour, near Wincanton, and was one of three members of his family to become a Catholic priest.[25] John Martin, of Balsbury (Baltonsborough), near Glastonbury, was professed at Douai in 1661 and died at Wells just after his ordination in 1671.[26]

---

[17] J. McCann and H. Connolly, eds., *English Benedictines*, CRS 33, pp.197-8.

[18] G. Dolan, 'The Benedictines in the South West 5: Somerset', *SWCH* 30 (2012), pp. 53-75 at pp. 56-7. Dolan's article is reprinted from *The Downside Review* 22 (1903), pp. 187-99 and 293-304). See also J. McCann and H. Connolly, eds., *English Benedictines*, CRS 33, pp. 238-9.

[19] G. Dolan, 'The Benedictines in the South West 5: Somerset', *SWCH* 30, pp. 57-8.

[20] *Ibid.*, p. 57; J. McCann and H. Connolly, eds., *English Benedictines*, CRS 33, pp. 225-6.

[21] G. Dolan, 'The Benedictines in the South West 5: Somerset', *SWCH* 30, p. 57.

[22] *Ibid.* See also D. A. Bellenger, 'The Abbots of Lamspringe', in A. Cramer, ed., *Lamspringe: an English Abbey in Germany, 1643-1803* (Ampleforth, 2004), pp.21-9.

[23] J. McCann and H. Connolly, eds., *English Benedictines*, CRS 33, pp. 225-6; G. Dolan, 'The Benedictines in the South West 5: Somerset', *SWCH* 30, p. 59. William Gabriel Gifford's father John was from Weston-under-Edge in Gloucestershire and his mother was a Throckmorton from Worcestershire. After Oxford he studied at Leuven, Paris, Reims, and Rome. Ordained in 1582, he became a monk at Dieulouard in 1608. His glittering cosmopolitan career culminated in his appointment as Archbishop of Reims, although his achievement there was hampered by age and by the decayed state of the see: see J. Bergin, *The Making of the French Episcopate, 1559-1661* (Yale, 1996).

[24] J. McCann and H. Connolly, eds., *English Benedictines*, CRS 33, p. 252; G. Dolan, 'The Benedictines in the South West 5: Somerset', *SWCH* 30, p. 59.

[25] Bellenger, *English and Welsh Priests*, p. 185.

[26] G. Dolan, 'The Benedictines in the South West 5: Somerset', *SWCH* 30, p.57.

Two members of the Berriman family became monks in the middle decades of the seventeenth century: Joseph, who entered St Gregory's in 1654, and Alban who entered St Edmund's in 1661. Joseph was at Leighland from 1689-97, and died in 1715. Bede Knight joined St Gregory's in 1714, but died, before ordination, in 1718. Bede Bennett (1723-1800), from Bath, another Gregorian monk, served Leighland for three years and was procurator of his community at its most perilous period during the French Revolution. He died in 1800. Richard Peter Kendall, another Bathonian Gregorian, born 1758, professed 1779, was prior of St Gregory's during its exile at Acton Burnell in Shropshire from 1808 to 1814, when he died; he had just completed the purchase of Downside House in Somerset.[27]

After 1800 Somerset continued to provide monks: Bede Day, of Welton (1791-1870), a monk of Ampleforth and prior there from 1834 to 1838, Lawrence Burge (1810-91), from Dunster, another Ampleforth monk, and no less than ten Bathonians: Thomas Joseph Brown (1796-1880), the first to make his monastic profession at Downside, later Vicar Apostolic of Wales and first Catholic Bishop of Newport and Menevia; Bernard Short (1799-1875), Vincent Dowding (1809-77), Bernard Paillet (1810-70), Elphege Cody (1847-91), and Richard Gregory Kendal (1848-79), all Downside monks; Gregory Robinson (1780-1837), Hilary Dowding (1793-1864, brother of Vincent), Lawrence Farrant (1844-97), and Placid McAuliffe (1848-80), all Amplefordians.[28]

All these monks lived out their lives under the fear of penalty from the State on account of their identity as well as their work, so were effectively always on the run. They spent the early years of their monastic lives in their continental houses of profession as conventional monks, living in community and celebrating the canonical hours of the Church shut off from the outside world. They were protected and had the comforts of security. Once in England they relied on friends to accommodate them and keep them safe, living not as coenobites but as hermits. The new Congregation armed itself with a new spirituality suitable to changed circumstances. This was provided by Augustine Baker (1575-1641), a Welsh lawyer convert and one of the architects of the new English Benedictine Congregation, who taught the importance of mystical prayer. The new Benedictines were to be contemplatives living in the world relying on mental prayer to sustain their mission.[29]

The 'missions' on which the monks worked had nothing in common with the

---

[27] *Ibid.*, p. 58

[28] G. Dolan, 'The Benedictines in the South West 5: Somerset', *SWCH* 30, pp. 58-9; for Brown see also A. Hood, 'Bishop Thomas Joseph Brown OSB (1798-1880)', in A. Berry, ed., *Belmont Abbey* (Leominster, 2012), pp. 61-71. For Burge, Cody, Farrant and Robinson, see Birt, *Obit Book*.

[29] Baker published comparatively little in his lifetime but his teaching on the contemplative life was given definitive form in *Sancta Sophia* (Holy Wisdom), edited by his fellow monk Serenus Cressy (1605-74), which appeared in 1657. For Baker's biography see J. McCann and H. Connolly, eds., *English Benedictines*, CRS 33, and for his impact see M. Woodward, ed., *That Mysterious Man: Essays on Augustine Baker* (Abergavenny, 2001) and G. Scott, ed., *Dom Augustine Baker* (Leominster, 2012).

medieval monasteries.[30] Small hidden chapels and domestic living quarters replaced grand churches and spacious claustral buildings. Places were chosen which were out of reach of inquisitive officials of Church and State. Locations on county or diocesan boundaries were highly favoured. The two principal country missions or chaplaincies in Somerset exemplified these criteria: Leighland, near the Devon border, and Bonham, which straddled the boundaries of Dorset, Somerset and Wiltshire.[31] The monastic grange of Leigh, later known as Leigh Barton, Leighland, near Watchet and the Bristol Channel, was let by the abbot of the nearby Cistercian Cleeve Abbey to lay tenants, and from before 1606 until 1691 it was a residence of the Recusant Poyntz family.[32] Leigh Barton is situated in a very inaccessible place, approached by narrow, deeply cut lanes shaded by trees; an ideal setting for a secret chapel. Philip Powel, born in Breconshire and educated as a lawyer in London, where he came into contact with Augustine Baker, was a Douai monk who came to Leigh Barton and stayed from 1624 to 1644. When returning to his native Wales by boat from Cornwall during the Civil War, he was apprehended and was executed at Tyburn on 13 June 1646. He was to become Blessed Philip Powel when he was beatified in 1929.[33] The chapel at Leighland, remains of which may survive in the outbuildings of the present farm at Leigh Barton, remained a Benedictine mission from Powel's time until towards the end of the eighteenth century, although other Catholic priests served the place until the chaplaincy was closed in about 1808. The missioners included monks from Dieuoulard, Douai, and Lamspringe. One of them, Richard Maurus Barret of Dieulouard, died in prison at Pont-à-Mousson during the French Revolution, on 3 December 1794.

The former chapel at Bonham, near Stourhead, is now (2017) a private house but externally retains an ecclesiastical air. The parish of Stourton originally consisted of the three manors of Bonham, Gasper and Stourton; the first two were in Somerset, the third in Wiltshire. The eponymous Stourton family remained recusants and, although they left Stourton in 1785, they maintained a Catholic chapel and priest in the place. In 1714, the chapel was moved a quarter of a mile from Stourton itself to Bonham. With its proximity to the magical gardens of Stourhead, it is a place of enchantment and one of the most beautifully sited of English Catholic chapels. In the eighteenth century, the Catholic population was surprisingly numerous: the 1767 'Return of Papists' lists 107 Catholics within the parish boundaries.[34] The last

---

[30] For the English Benedictine missions see J. McCann's survey produced for the English Benedictine Chapter of 1940 and privately printed.

[31] See D. A. Bellenger, 'Religion on the Edge: Dissenting Congregations on the Somerset and Dorset Borders in the Seventeenth and Eighteenth Centuries', *Notes and Queries for Somerset and Dorset* 37, pp.170-2.

[32] A.P. Baggs, R.J.E. Bush and M.C. Siraut, 'Parishes: Old Cleeve', in R. Dunning, ed., *A History of the County of Somerset* 5 (Victoria County History), pp. 38-54.

[33] For P. Powel see D. A. Bellenger (ed.), *Downside and its Martyrs* (Bath, 2006), pp.1-13. See also Bede Camm, *Nine Martyr Monks* (London, 1931).

[34] J.A. Harding, *The Diocese of Clifton 1850-2000* (Bristol, 1999), p. 219.

resident Benedictine at Bonham, Paul Brookfield, who was there from 1945 to 1950, presented the three earliest registers of the mission to the Downside Archives; these were published in 1992–3.[35] Catholic registers have survived less well than their Anglican counterparts as they were less often institutional than personal, being kept by an individual missioner rather than by the mission. The three Bonham registers begin in 1767 and end in 1868. William Ambrose Allam, a Douai monk, who was at Bonham from 1785 to 1796, seems to have served the neighbouring mission at Marnhull in Dorset in 1786; county boundaries seemed irrelevant to the pastoral care of the thinly and widely dispersed Catholic population. The third register begins with the ministrations of Joseph Bernard Hawarden in 1802. He made his profession at Douai in 1792, was 'master of the boys' at Acton Burnell and started a small school at Bonham. In 1822, he became Provincial of Canterbury but, following a liaison with a woman and fathering a daughter, Mary Frances, who he baptised in 1822, he left Bonham and, after several reconciliations and lapses, died near Bath on 21 April 1851.[36] Benedict Wassell, another Downside monk, was to serve Bonham from 1824 to 1869, the longest of any of the Bonham priests.

Other Somerset locales sometimes had Benedictine pastors. Stratton on the Fosse had a Benedictine presence from 1814 and the chapel in the village – with dependent chapels in surrounding towns and villages – was served from neighbouring Downside, as has been chronicled by Robert Dunning and in a heavyweight parish history.[37] Elsewhere in the county, Richard Adrian Towers, the last monk professed at Lamspringe, in 1802, spent fifteen years in Taunton and died in 1844. Jerome Jenkins, of Downside, was chaplain to the Franciscans at Taunton from 1851 to 1859. Another Downside monk, Placid Hall, established a Mass centre at Frome in 1850.[38] The chapel at Midford Castle, near Bath, was served by monks from Downside or Bath from 1820 to 1863.[39]

It would be wrong to identify English Benedictine missions as being exclusively rural. In the North West of England the monks busied themselves in such developing industrial towns as Liverpool, Warrington, and Whitehaven. In Somerset, Bath was the jewel in the crown of the whole Benedictine missionary structure, the one mission in the entire country which relied as much on the English Benedictine Congregation for its welfare and endowment as on its lay benefactors. 'Run by the Chapter of the South Province who financed it ... and insisted on inspecting its accounts at every chapter',[40] it became a Benedictine mission in the last quarter of the seventeenth century and developed on the back of the many Catholic visitors

---

[35] 'Bonham Registers Transcriptions', *South Western Catholic History* 10-11 (1992-3).

[36] See Allanson, *Biography*, pp. 441-4.

[37] R. Dunning, *Fifty Somerset Churches* (Tiverton, 1996), pp.182-5; F. Daniels, G. Brine and D. A. Bellenger, *St Benedict's, Stratton-on-the-Fosse: A History* (Bath, 2014).

[38] For these various monks working on Somerset missions, see G. Dolan, 'The Benedictines in the South West 5: Somerset', *SWCH* 30, p. 47.

[39] G. Dolan, 'The Benedictines in the South West 5: Somerset', *SWCH* 30, p. 73.

[40] Scott, *Gothic Rage*, p. 48.

who resorted to Bath for health and recreation from all parts of the British Isles and continental Europe.

Bath Cathedral Priory surrendered to Henry VIII's agents of dissolution in 1539. Its last prior, William Holloway, continued to reside in Bath in comfortable retirement. Three other monks were given preferment in the city: Nicholas Jobbyn (who died in 1553) became vicar of St Mary de Stall's church and chaplain to the corporation as well as a founding benefactor to the new grammar school, established in 1552 in succession to the closed priory school; William Clements became rector of St Mary's by the North Gate; and Richard Gibbs chaplain of St Thomas Becket's in Widcombe.[41] In the years 1575-6, John Feckenham, the last abbot of Westminster, visited Bath to take the waters. Since his deprivation he had lived under house arrest in East Anglia, his final residence being at Wisbech in Cambridgeshire, where he died in 1584 and was buried in the parish church. On his visit to Bath he published a book of medicines and, with his customary benevolence based on an unknown source of income, endowed a 'lepers' hostel' providing seven beds alongside the Hot Bath for the benefit of those with skin diseases, 'the most miserable of objects who fly to Bath for relief from the hot waters'.[42] His host seems to have been the physician Dr Reuben Sherwood, whose family was to furnish several Benedictine monks, as named above.[43]

Another Benedictine celebrity, John Huddleston, came to Bath in 1687. Huddleston, born in Lancashire in 1608, was ordained priest in Rome in 1637. He became famous for the assistance he gave Charles II during the king's escape following the battle of Worcester in 1651. In the subsequent decade, he joined the English Benedictines and received King Charles into the Catholic Church on his deathbed. On the latter occasion, Huddleston was resident in London, as chaplain to Queen Catherine of Braganza. He came to Bath in the company of the openly Catholic James II and, in a much-debated episode, is said to have preached at Bath Abbey (by then reinvented as a parish church) during the ceremony of touching for the King's Evil – an expression of the sacred healing power of kingship – calling on those present to renounce Protestantism and embrace Catholicism.[44] He lived until 1698.

The Benedictines probably returned to reside in Bath before Huddleston's visit but, especially in the early years, they shunned the public gaze. Unlike Huddleston, who was excluded from persecution on account of his bravery in 1651, the monks feared reprisals against them, especially after the deposition of James II in 1688-9. The provision of the sacraments to the Bath Catholics was the monks' task and their work continued until the 1930s. It seems that, from the 1690s, the monks managed a lodging-house for Catholic visitors to Bath, The Bell-Tree House, situated on the

---

[41] J. Wroughton, *Tudor Bath* (Bath, 2006), pp. 32-8.
[42] Wroughton, *Tudor Bath*, p. 117.
[43] J. A. Williams, *Bath and Rome* (Bath, 1963), p. 12.
[44] J. Wroughton, *Stuart Bath* (Bath, 2004), pp. 178-9.

corner of Binbury Lane and Beau Street, a short walk from the Cross Bath. A chapel and the resident priest were accommodated on the second floor.[45] The earliest Benedictine missioner was Anselm Williams, who was perhaps in Bath as early as 1669 and died in harness in 1694.[46] His successor, Anselm Llewelyn, formerly Provincial of Canterbury, was in Bath until his death in 1711.[47] Llewelyn was cathedral prior of Bath, his successor in that office being William Banester, a Douai monk, who served on the Bath mission from 1714 to 1726.[48] Laurence York, another Douai monk, came in 1730, and in 1741 was consecrated bishop as coadjutor to the Vicar Apostolic of the Western District.[49] During the incumbency of Bernard Bradshaw (1746–57) the mission felt confident enough to list itself in *The Bath Guide* of 1753, at which time Catholic chapels remained illegal.[50] Placid Naylor, missioner from 1757 to 1776, and Cuthbert Wilkes (1786-91) were litigious and difficult monks much caught up in the politics of late Georgian Catholicism which, in the 'Age of Reason', was attempting to come to terms both with the Hanoverian monarchy and an appropriate balance of power between clergy and laity within the Church. With its well-heeled congregation and its freedom from the constraints of a patron, Bath was the obvious place for such conflicts. The complexities and personalities of the controversies have been discussed at length by Geoffrey Scott.[51]

One complication for the missioner was a succession of Benedictine bishops who took up residence in Bath: Laurence York, Charles Walmesley (figure 46), and Gregory Sharrock. They were vicars apostolic, prelates assigned to missionary territories in episcopal orders but without normal diocesan structures directly answerable to the Roman Congregation of Propaganda Fide. Normal dioceses were not restored to the Roman Catholics in England until 1850. There were four territorial vicars apostolic from 1688 and the western vicar (whose brief included Wales as well as the western counties, including Somerset) was invariably a member of a religious order. Laurence York, a Douai monk, was a Londoner, born in 1687, who came to Bath as missioner in 1730, having acted as a religious superior both in Paris and Douai. He was consecrated in 1741 and died in 1770. His successor, Walmesley, a tough but rarely stern Lancastrian, born in 1722, was educated at Douai and became a member of St Edmund's, Paris. He was a doctor of the Sorbonne and a distinguished mathematician and scientist who became a Fellow of the Royal Society. He was consecrated bishop in 1756 and, in turn, in 1790 consecrated John Carroll as bishop of Baltimore in Maryland, thereby becoming the 'godfather' of the American hierarchy. It was during Walmesley's episcopate that the Bath

[45] Williams, *Bath and Rome*, p. 25.
[46] S. Johnson, 'Benedictine Bath', *The Downside Review* 132 (2014), pp. 112-13.
[47] Williams, *Bath and Rome*, p. 28.
[48] Johnson, 'Benedictine Bath', p. 115.
[49] Bellenger, *Fathers*, p. 12.
[50] Williams, *Bath and Rome*, p. 28.
[51] Scott, *Gothic Rage*, pp. 48-51. See also Williams, *Bath and Rome*, pp. 18-44.

Benedictines found themselves at the centre of a local manifestation of a national phenomenon. A new chapel, designed to replace Bell-Tree House, had been built on the west side of St James' Passage, but was burnt down by a hostile crowd on 9 June 1780. This action was inspired by the Gordon Riots in London. These disturbances were precipitated by the 1778 Papists Act, which afforded some measure of relief to Catholics and was seen by Lord George Gordon (1751-93) and his Protestant Association as an affront to the nation. Popular support led to rioting and looting in London, with copycat episodes in Bath and Hull. The anti-Catholic rhetoric concealed a wider discontent. The chapel was destroyed along with the vicariate archives and much of Walmesley's library. The Bath Catholics were awarded compensation and an invitation was sent to one of the monks on 27 August 1780 to attend the execution of John Butler, the only person punished for the outrage (figure 47). Walmesley himself survived the episode unharmed and died in 1797, following the overturning of his Bath Chair.[52]

Walmesley was succeeded by another Lancastrian, the Douai monk Gregory Sharrock, his coadjutor since 1780. Born in 1742, Sharrock acted as cellarer at St Gregory's, followed by five years as prior, before his consecration. A less public figure than Walmesley, he remained vicar apostolic until his death in 1809 when he was succeeded by the Franciscan Peter Bernardine Collingridge.[53]

The gutted chapel of 1789 was not the last Benedictine chapel in Bath to be replaced. In 1863, an ambitious neo-gothic church, dedicated to St John and with a commanding spire, was opened to replace a chapel in Orchard Street, previously a theatre, which had itself replaced another in Corn Street. St John's was built during the long incumbency of Clement Worsley, an Ampleforth monk, who also had built the Catholic Perrymead cemetery and chapel.[54] The second half of the nineteenth century was a period of growth and consolidation in Catholic Bath but, as the mission took on the character of a traditional parish, the monks who served it were turning back to the inspiration of their monastic fathers: in Victorian England for the first time since the Reformation English monks wished to live in monasteries rather than missions. The building of St Alphege's, which was

[52] See D. A. Bellenger, *Fathers in Faith: The Western District, 1688-1988* (Bath, 1991), and N. Schofield and G. Skinner, *The English Vicars Apostolic, 1688-1850* (Oxford, 2009). For the Gordon Riots in Bath see I. Haywood and J. Seed, eds., *The Gordon Riots: Politics, Culture and Insurrection in late Eighteenth-Century Britain* (Cambridge, 2012), C. Haydon, 'The Gordon Riots in the English Provinces', *The Historical Journal* 63 (1990), pp. 354-59, and S. Poole, *The Politics of Regicide in England, 1760-1850* (Manchester, 2000).

[53] Bellenger, *Fathers*, pp.14-15.

[54] For the chapels see D. A. Bellenger, 'In secret and then openly, 1540-1900', in R. Dunning, ed., *Somerset Churches and Chapels* (Wellington, 2007), pp.67-76. For St John's ,designed by Charles Hansom and built in 1861-3, with the tower and spire completed separately in 1867, see M. Forsyth, *Bath* (Pevsner Architectural Guides, New Haven and London 2003), p. 211, who writes that St John's 'is demonstrative proof of how intensely the Gothicists hated the Georgian of Bath'. It might also be seen as the Benedictine riposte to Bishop Baines and Prior Park.

opened in 1929, as a chapel of ease to St John's, marked the end of an era.[55] This was the inspiration of Anselm Rutherford (1886-1952), the last Benedictine missioner in Bath, who returned to his monastery at Downside in 1932.[56]

The foundations of the monastery at Downside, on the Fosse Way, 12 miles south of Bath, and of the priory of Benedictine nuns at Cannington were the prelude to the new order in Somerset monastic life at the beginning of the nineteenth century. The nuns arrived at Cannington in 1807 and, at the invitation of the Catholic Lord Clifford, took possession of the Court House, on the site of the medieval convent.[57] The new Cannington community were the repatriated nuns of St Mary's, Paris, founded in 1652 from Cambrai and resident at Marnhull from 1795 to 1807. They were to stay at Cannington until 1836, when they transferred to Colwich in Staffordshire, where they still (2017) reside.[58] Downside House was purchased by the English Benedictines of Douai in 1814 to replace their temporary residence at Acton Burnell in Shropshire and still stands among the buildings of Downside School.[59] Alternatively called Mount Pleasant, Downside House was a substantial farmhouse, probably of the late seventeenth century, on the west side of the Fosse Way, and technically, in 1814, in the Midsomer Norton parish but actually in the small village of Stratton on the Fosse. The house stood on an elevated site on the edge of the Mendips and although the area had a rural aspect it was in the Somerset coalfield, which developed alongside the monastery. Downside and Cannington were two of a number of sizeable religious communities made up of British subjects brought back to England in consequence of the French Revolution.[60] Immediate questions of jurisdiction emerged which called into question the very survival of the communities.

[55] M. Forsyth, *Bath*, p. 291: 'modelled on Santa Maria in Cosmedin, Rome, it is a severe Early Christian Basilica of impressive simplicity', designed by Giles Gilbert Scott. See also C. Shaw, *Our Lady and St Alphege , Bath* (Bath, 2012). Scott was also employed by Downside to build the nave of the abbey church and school buildings, as well as to supervise the reconstruction of the medieval barn at Midsomer Norton as a chapel. The barn had once been the property of the Augustinian priory of Merton in Surrey.
[56] Williams, *Bath and Rome*, p. 90. Until 1891 the Bath Mission was the responsibility of the Provincial of Canterbury; from then until 1932 it came directly under Downside.
[57] Harding, pp. 53-61.
[58] See R. Eaton, *The Benedictines of Colwich 1829-1929* (London, 1929) which chronicles the prolonged dispute between the nuns and Bishop Baines during their time at Cannington.
[59] For the history of Downside see N. Birt, *Downside, a History of the School* (London, 1902), H. van Zeller, *Downside by and large* (London, 1954), and D. A. Bellenger, *Downside, a Pictorial History* (Bath, 1998).
[60] See D. A. Bellenger, ed., 'The Great Return: the English Communities in Continental Europe and their Repatriation, 1793-4', *South Western Catholic History* (1994), and T. J. Moutray, *Refugee Nuns, the French Revolution, and British Literature and Culture* (Abingdon, 2016). At Shepton Mallet, six miles from Downside, a small French Visitation Convent was opened in 1810, transferring to Westbury on Trym in 1831: Harding, pp.171-2. English Franciscan nuns from Bruges, who had been in Winchester for thirteen years, came to Taunton in 1807-8 and remained there until the 1950s. See also the website of the Queen Mary University of London research project *Who were the Nuns?*: https://wwtn.history.qmul.ac.uk/ (accessed 25 September 2017).

The English Catholics in the age of persecution had a weak and decentralised system of government in which the normal episcopal governance of the Church was marginal. The religious orders had almost complete autonomy. Individual lay patrons and missioners were rarely inspected or directed. In the years from Catholic Emancipation in 1829 to the restoration of the Catholic hierarchy in 1850 the vicars apostolic began to flex their muscles. The Benedictine President, Augustine Birdsall (1775-1837), who had been in Bath himself in 1806-9 and had been a monk at Lamspringe, saw the signs of the time when writing in 1826: 'The Vicars Apostolic consider the whole business of the mission to be placed in their hands. They consider that the Regulars are useful and available to assistance but they are only assistants. They have their privileges but these do not exalt them to an independence of the vicars apostolic, nor to an equality.'[61]

The most innovative and dominant of the vicars apostolic was Peter Augustine Baines. Born at Kirkby near Liverpool, in 1786, he was educated at Lamspringe from 1798 and, following the closure of Lamspringe, at Ampleforth, where he became a monk. In 1817, he arrived in Bath where he became a vigorous missioner and a noted preacher.[62] He became a bishop in 1823 as coadjutor to the Franciscan Collingridge, succeeding him in 1829. In 1828, Baines purchased Prior Park as his own residence, a seminary for the Western District, and a hugely visible sign of the resurgence of Catholicism. A spacious Palladian villa, Prior Park, was built in the 1740s by the entrepreneur Ralph Allen (1693-1764) to the designs of the Bath architect John Wood the Elder (1704-54), with the intention 'to see all Bath, and for all Bath to see'. The city thus became 'a spectacular stage set'.[63] Baines hoped to enhance the magnificence still further by building a great domed cathedral behind Allen's buildings. In 1836, the house was seriously damaged in a fire. By 1843, Baines was dead, many of his dreams shattered and the Western District bankrupt.[64]

Baines had hoped to use the monks of Downside to man his activities, not as monks but as secular clergy. They would not oblige. He turned to Ampleforth and divided his old community, persuading some of its ablest monks to follow his lead. Arguing that all the monastic vows made since the return to England were invalid, 'he threatened the very heart of the Congregation'.[65] A prophetic as well as a controversial figure, Baines died before he could make any long-lasting impact and the fledgling Downside community survived his attempt to divert its energies to the Prior Park scheme. It developed throughout the nineteenth century and gradually established a flourishing school and a splendid range of buildings.

[61] Quoted by Hood, *Repatriation to Renewal*, p. 89.

[62] H. Combs and A. Bax, eds., *Journal of a Somerset Rector, John Skinner, 1772-1839* (London , 1930) p. 51 records Skinner's attendance at a Corpus Christi Mass in Bath in 1823, when he heard Baines' sermon 'delivered, I must do him the credit to say, in a very impressive manner'. Skinner was highly critical of Catholicism, so this was a rare encomium.

[63] M. Forsyth, *Bath*, p. 95.

[64] For a sympathetic biography of Baines see P. Gilbert, *The Restless Prelate: Bishop Baines, 1786-1843* (Leominster, 2006).

[65] Hood, *Repatriation to Revival*, pp. 90-6.

Downside became an abbey in 1900 and, from then on, most of the monks were resident there, rather than on the mission. The new emphasis was vividly expressed in the building of a great new abbey church – begun in the 1880s and completed in its present form in the 1930s – to replace the relatively humble chapel of 1823.[66] An important library was developed, making Downside a hub of monastic scholarship. One of its monks, Aidan Gasquet (1846-1929), became a cardinal and Vatican Librarian, and was the first of a number of Downside historians who contributed to the history of the wider church.[67] Most notably, David Knowles (1896-1974), who went on to become Regius Professor of Modern History at Cambridge, transformed the study of English medieval monasticism.[68] At a more local level, Ethelbert Horne (1857-1952) was a distinguished antiquarian scholar and involved in the archaeology of Glastonbury.[69] Aelred Watkin (1918-1997) was, in his earlier years, an accomplished editor of Glastonbury texts.[70] Appropriately, Horne and Watkin were both titular abbots of Glastonbury.

When the four former Glastonbury monks petitioned Mary Tudor in 1557 for the restoration of their monastery they hoped they 'would happily prevent the ruin of much and the repair of no little part of the whole'.[71] They were to be disappointed in their immediate expectations, but in the centuries that followed many in Somerset were to follow their footsteps as disciples of the sixth-century Rule of St Benedict. The seventeenth- and eighteenth-century monks were to live their life as hermits in an England hostile to their ideals. The vow of stability taken by Benedictines at their profession has always rooted the monks in their locality; Bonham and Leigh Barton each still retain a distinct *genius loci*. The opening years of the nineteenth century witnessed a renewal of community life for both Benedictine nuns and monks at Cannington and Downside. At Downside Benedictine life continues into the twenty-first century. Robert Dunning described his own study of monasticism in Somerset as 'a matter of personal piety',[72] and this

---

[66] Bellenger, *Architectural History*, *passim*.

[67] See D. A. Bellenger, 'Cardinal Gasquet OSB (1846-1929): Monk Historian', in J. Broadley and P. Phillips, eds., *The Ministry of the Printed Word: Scholar-Priests of the Twentieth Century* (Bath, 2016), pp.145-61. Gasquet's Somerset correspondents included William Hunt (1842-1931), President of the Royal Historical Society in 1905-9, who edited the Somerset Record Society volume of Bath Cartularies and found Gasquet's 'acquaintance with the Benedictine rules and customs ... most useful' (25 June 1893). Later, Hunt reflected on Gasquet's writing: 'a monument of erudition, rather too full of the same story told over and over again' (23 January 1894). Details of these letters, which are kept in the Somerset Record Society's archives, were communicated to me by Robert Dunning in a letter of 20 October 2016.

[68] For Knowles see D. A. Bellenger and S. Johnson, eds., *Keeping the Rule: David Knowles and the Writing of History* (Bath, 2014).

[69] See D. A. Bellenger, ed., 'Horne of Mendip', *SWCH* 18 (2000), pp. 1-45. His association with Frederick Bligh Bond (1864-1945), the controversial historian of Glastonbury, can be explored in T. Hopkinson-Ball, *The Rediscovery of Glastonbury* (Stroud, 2007).

[70] See David Newsome's obituary of Watkin in *The Independent*, 9 May 1997.

[71] Dunning, *Somerset Monasteries*, p. 128.

[72] *Ibid.*, p. 11.

is true for me, too, in this tribute to him; as I write these words I cannot but reflect on the more than three decades I have spent as a Benedictine monk in Somerset. '*Succissa virescit*' is the motto on the coat of arms of Montecassino, St Benedict's own monastery: 'cut it down, and it will grow again'. This seems to be an equally appropriate summary of what happened in Somerset.

Bibliography of Robert W. Dunning's works to 2017[1]

Compiled by DAVID BROMWICH

1962

'The Wells consistory court in the fifteenth century', *PSANHS* 106(2), pp. 46-61

1963

'The administration of the diocese of Bath and Wells 1401-1491', University of Bristol Ph.D. thesis

1964

'The Muniments of Syon Abbey', *BIHR* xxxvii, pp. 103-11

1966

'Households of the bishops of Bath and Wells in the Later Middle Ages', *PSANHS* 110(2), pp. 24-39

'The members of parliament for Bath in the later middle ages', *A North Somerset miscellany* (Contributions to Local History and Archaeology, Bath and Camerton Archaeological Society), pp. 29-32

(review) 'R. M. Haines, *The administration of the diocese of Worcester in the first half of the fourteenth century* (London, 1965), pp. xviii+393', *WHR*, Vol. 3 (1966), pp. 211-13.

1967

'Rural deans in England in the fifteenth century', *BIHR* 40, pp. 207-13

(review) 'P. M. Hembry, *The Bishops of Bath and Wells, 1540-1640* (Athlone Press, 1967), pp. xii + 287', *PSANHS* 111, pp. 70-71

1968

'Some Somerset parishes in 1705', *PSANHS* 112(2), pp. 71-92

'Thomas, Lord Dacre and the West March towards Scotland', *BIHR* 41, pp. 95-99

(editor) *The Hylle Cartulary*, SRS 68

1970

'Somerset parochial clergy, 1373-1404', *PSANHS* 114(2), pp. 91-95

(review) 'Cowley, P., *The Church House* (S.P.C.K. for the Alcuin Club, 1972), pp. 92', *PSANHS* 114, p. 117

---

[1] Other items of bibliography are currently in the press and not yet published.

(review) 'Smith, M.Q., *The Medieval Churches of Bristol* (Bristol Branch of the Historical Association Local History Pamphlets, 1970), 24 pp.', *PSANHS* 114, p. 118

1971

(editor) *Bridgwater Borough Archives, vol. 5,* SRS 70

(review) 'Hallam, O., The National Farmers' Union in Somerset: a history of the County Branch, 1912 to 1962 (The Somerset Co Branch of the NFU, Taunton, 1971), 192 pp.', *PSANHS* 115, pp. 68-69

1972

'Discoveries at Combe St Nicholas', *PSANHS* 116(2), pp. 115-16

'The plasterwork at Gaulden Manor', *PSANHS* 116(2), pp. 113-14

(review) 'Neale, R.S., *Class and Ideology in the Nineteenth Century* (R & KP, 1972), pp. viii plus 200', *PSANHS* 116, p. 118

(review) 'Pearce, F.J., *A History of Wedmore* (pub. by author, 1971), pp. 76', *PSANHS* 116, p. 118

(review) 'Carew, J., *Dusty Pages: a story of two families and their homes* (pub. by author, n.d.), pp. 86', *PSANHS* 116, p. 118

(review) 'Dorothy M. Owen , *The Records of the established church in England.* (British Records Association, Archives and the User, No. 1), 1970, pp. 64, *Welsh Hist. Rev.*, Vol. 6 (1972), pp. 219-20.

1973

The church of St George, Beckington (Beckington Parochial Church Council)

Local sources for the young historian (Muller)

The Rotary Club of Taunton, 1922-72 (Rotary Club)

(review) 'Hunt, T.J., *Aspects of Somerset History* (SCC, 1973), pp. iv + 59', *PSANHS* 117, pp. 121-22

(review) 'Underdown, D., *Somerset in the Civil War and Interregnum* (David & Charles, 1973), 229 pp.,' *PSANHS* 117, pp. 121-22

1974

'Somerset towns in the Fourteenth Century', *SDNQ*, vol. 29, pp. 10-13

'Clapton Mills, Crewkerne', *SDNQ*, vol. 29, p. 20

'Netherton, A Lost Hamlet?', *SDNQ*, vol. 29, pp. 91-2

(editor and contributor) *Victoria County History of Somerset, vol. 3, Kingsbury (E), Pitney, Somerton, Tintinhull Hundreds* (London/ Oxford)

1975

(with Pearson, T.) *Taunton: History, Archaeology, and Development* (Taunton Research and Excavation Committee)

'Ilchester: a study in continuity', *PSANHS* 119, pp. 44-50

'Nineteenth-century Parochial Sources', *Studies in Church History* 11, *Materials, sources and methods of ecclesiastical history,* ed. D.Baker (Ecclesiastical History Society, Oxford), pp. 301-8 (review) 'Leech, R., *Small Medieval Towns in Avon: Archaeology and Planning* (Committee for Rescue Archaeology in Avon, Gloucester, and Somerset, 1975), iv + 60pp', *PSANHS* 119, pp. 77-8

(review) '*An Ilchester Word List and Some Folklore Notes*, by J. Stephens Cox (Ilchester and District Occasional Papers, No. 1, Toucan Press, St Peter Port, Guernsey, 1974), 24pp.', *PSANHS* 119, p. 81

1976

Beneath the Deane. Taunton Deane Research and Excavation Committee

'The Minster at Crewkerne', *PSANHS* 120, pp. 63-67

(editor and contributor) *Christianity in Somerset* (Somerset County Council)

(review) '*Light in Selwood* (Frome Society for Local Study, 1976), 80 pp.', *PSANHS* 120, p. 127

(review) '*Owain W. Jones and David Walker, eds., Links with the past: Swansea and Brecon historical essays.* (Christopher Davies, Llandybïe, Dyfed, 1974), pp. xii+251 +23. *WHR*, Vol. 8 (1976), pp. 226-27.

1977

'Croft Castle', *PSANHS* 121, pp. 129-30

(contributor) 'Revival at Glastonbury, 1530-59', *Renaissance and Renewal in Christian History*, ed. D. Baker, *Studies in Church History* 14, (Oxford), pp. 213-222

(with D. Bromwich) *Victorian and Edwardian Somerset from old photographs* (London)

(review) '*Butleigh, a thousand years of a Somerset parish*, by E. F. Synge (Butleigh PCC, 1974, rep. 1935), 50 pp.', *PSANHS* 121, p. 143

1978

A history of Somerset (Somerset County Library, and revised editions in 1987 & 2003)

(editor and contributor) *Victoria County History of Somerset, vol. 4, Crewkerne, Martock, South Petherton Hundreds* (Oxford)

(review) '*The Bounds of Selwood*, by Michael McGarvie (Frome Historical Research Group, occasional paper No. 1, Frome Society for Local Study, 1978), 28 pp.', *PSANHS* 122, p. 180

1979

(review) 'W. J. Rodwell, *Wells Cathedral: Excavations and Discoveries* (The Friends of Wells Cathedral, 1979), pp. 16', *PSANHS* 123, pp. 142-43

(review) '*Street Names in Yeovil* (Yeovil Archaeological and Local History Society, 1979), pp. I + 33', *PSANHS* 123, pp. 143-44

(review) 'A. Major, *Early Wars of Wessex* (1913:1978, Blandford Press of Poole)', *PSANHS* 123, p. 144

(review) '*Alfred's kingdom: Wessex and the south, 800-1500.* By D. A. Hinton (London, 1977), pp. xii +228, 29 plates, 40 figs', *WHR*, Vol. 9 (1979), p. 366.

1980

The laity in the church in the 1980s

Local history for beginners (Chichester, revised edition of *Local sources ...*)
Somerset and Avon (Edinburgh)

1981

(with M. Bridge) 'Abbey Barn', *PSANHS* 125, p. 120

'The building of Syon Abbey', *TAMS*, n.s., 25, pp. 16-26

'Origins of Nether Stowey', *PSANHS* 125, pp. 124-26

'Patronage and promotion in the late medieval church', *Patronage, the crown and the provinces in later medieval England,* ed. R.A. Griffiths, (Stroud), pp. 167-180

(editor, with J.B. Harley) *Somerset maps: Day & Masters 1782, Greenwood 1822.* SRS 76

(review) 'F. Bligh Bond, *An Ecclesiastical Handbook of Glastonbury Abbey* (Research into Lost Knowledge Organisation, 1981), pp. 90', *PSANHS* 125, p. 134

(review) '*Yeovil, the Changing Scene* (Yeovil Archaeological and Local History Society, 1981), 40pp.', *PSANHS* 125, p. 134

(review) 'Marion Meek, *The Book of Wells* (Barracuda Books, 1980), 128 pp.', *PSANHS* 125, p. 134

1982

'The bishop's palace', *Wells Cathedral: a history* (London), ed. L.S. Colchester, pp. 227-247

(review) 'Peter Poyntz Wright, *The Parish Church Towers of Somerset: their construction, crafts manship, and chronology, 1350-1550* (Avebury Publishing Company, Amersham, 1981), xii + 218 pp.', *PSANHS* 126, pp. 148-49

(review) 'J. H. Bettey and C. W. G. Taylor, *Sacred and Satiric: Medieval Stone Carving in the West Country* (Bristol, 1982), 64 pp.', *PSANHS* 126, p. 149

(review) 'J. R. Guy, *Milton Clevedon Church in Somerset*, 80 pp.', *PSANHS* 126, p. 144

(review) '*Long Load and Knole, Long Sutton: their houses, cottages and farms, settlement and people* (Somerset and South Avon Vernacular Building Research Group, 1982) 42 pp.'

(review) 'P. Poyntz Wright, *Hunky Punks: a Study in Somerset stone carving* (Amasham, 1982)

1983

A history of Somerset (Phillimore)

(introduction) *The history and antiquities of the county of Somerset*, by J. Collinson. (Alan Sutton microprint edition)

1984

The Monmouth Rebellion (Wimbourne)

(review) 'P. Poyntz Wright, *The Rural Bench ends of Somerset* (Avebury Publishing Company, 1983), p. x + 166', *PSANHS* 128, pp. 139-41

(review) '*Sources for English local history*. By W. B. Stephens. 2nd edition, Cambridge University Press, 1981 (The Sources of History: Studies in the Uses of Historiographical Evidence, ed. G. R. Elton); pp. xvi+342', *WHR*, Vol. 12 (1984), pp. 147-49.

1985

'The last days of Cleeve Abbey', *The church in pre-Reformation society* (Woodbridge), ed. C.M. Barron & C. Harper-Bill, pp. 58-67

Monmouth: the road to Sedgemoor (Lion)

(editor and contributor) *Victoria County History of Somerset, vol. 5, Whitley(part), Williton and Freemanors Hundreds (E part)* (Oxford)

1986

'The Abbey of the Princes, Athelney Abbey', *Kings and Nobles in the Later Middle Ages* (Gloucester), eds. R.A. Griffiths & J. Sherborne, pp. 295-303

(with B. Fletcher and I. Burrow) *St Hugh of Witham and his Priory* (Hugh of Witham Foundation)

Somerset in Domesday (Somerset County Library)

1987

'Appealing pillar of state', *Country Life* 181(37), pp. 166-67

1988

Arthur: the king in the west (Gloucester)

(contributor) R. Coleman-Smith and T. Pearson, *Excavation in the Donyatt Potteries* (Chichester), Ch. 3, 'The historic background', p. 9

1989

A history of the Old Municipal Buildings, Taunton

Wanstrow Church (Postlebury P.C.C.)

1990

(with P. Leach and R. Croft) *Ilchester* (Somerset County Council, Bridgwater)

The light remains: Glastonbury Abbey (Glastonbury Abbey Shop)

(review) 'H. Eardley-Wilmot, Yesterday's Exmoor (1990)', *PSANHS*, 134, pp. 295-96

1991

(with J. Bickersteth) *Clerks of the Closet in the royal household* (Stroud))

Some Somerset country houses (Wimbourne)

'The West-Country Carthusians', *Religious Belief and Ecclesiastical Careers in Late Medieval England*, ed. C. Harper-Bill (Woodbridge), pp. 33-42

'The Tribunal, Glastonbury, Somerset', in L. Abrams and J.P. Carley, eds., *The Archaeology and History of Glastonbury Abbey* (Woodbridge)

'Miles Salley, Bishop of Llandaff', *Journ. WEH*, vol.8, pp. 1-6

'The Glastonbury bones', *SM* 1(1), pp. 43-44

'all the fun of the fair', *SM* 1(2), p. 43

'The last archbishop', *SM* 1(3), p. 41

'Somerset's jewel', *SM* 1(4), pp. 36-37

'Beheaded at Bridgwater', *SM* 1(5), p. 37

'Emergency planning', *SM* 1(6), p. 24

'Of noyfol fowles and vermyn', *SM* 1(7), p. 29

'On the record', *SM* 1(8), p. 55

'Tippling philosophers', *SM* 1(9), pp. 34-35

'Holy, holy and Yffy, yffy', *SM* 1(10), p. 43

(review) 'K. Barker and R. Cain, eds., *Maps and History in South-West England* (University of Exeter Press, 1991), xii + 148 pp.', *PSANHS* 135, pp. 247-48

1992

Bridgwater, History and Guide (Stroud)

A Goodly Heritage. The Story of St Michael's, Galmington, 1864-1992 (privately printed)

(with M. Siraut & K. Brown) *The Quantocks: a past worth preserving* (Somerset Books)

'People count', *SM* 2(2), p. 33

'The greatest and best of the kind in England', *SM* 2(4), p. 42

'The crown jewels', *SM* 2(5), p. 19

'Somerset cricket and suspicious weather', *SM* 2(6), p. 43

'Round arm versus under arm', *SM* 2(7), p. 47

'Presidential tour', *SM* 2(8), p. 33

'The noble game', *SM* 2(10), p. 31

'Beauforts in Somerset', *SM* 2(11), p. 31

'Reorganisation again!', *SM* 2(12), p. 30

(editor and contributor) *Victoria County History of Somerset, vol. 6, Andersfield, Cannington, and North Petherton Hundreds (Bridgwater and Neighbouring Parishes)* (Oxford)

(contributor) Roskell, J.S., Clark, L., and Rawcliffe, C., eds., *The History of Parliament: The House of Commons, 1386-1421*, vols. II-IV (Stroud): biographies – Archdeacon, M. – Cornw., 1383-90; Archdeacon, T. – Devon, 1420; Arthur, Sir T. – Soms., 1397; Arundel – T., Cornw., 1417-1435; Aunger (Angre), R. – Bath, 1396; Bartlett (Bertelot), H. – Bath, 1406-10; Bathe (Bache), J. – Dorset, 1397-1402; Beauchamp, Sir T. – Soms., 1401-32; Beaupyne, T. – Bristol, 1373-93, Soms., 1390; Beville, J. – Cornw., 1386; Bonville, J. – Soms., 1366-99, Devon, 1371-1402; Boson, R. - Bridgwater, 1393; Bobreaux, Sir R. – Cornw., 1404-27; Boyton, R. – Soms., 1416; Brooke, Sir T. – Soms., 1386-1413; Burghersh, Sir J. – Soms., 1379-88; Carent, W. – Dorset, 1420-27, Soms., 1423-50; Carminowe, Sr R. – Cornw., 1383-86; Cave, T. – Bridgwater, 1414-32; Cergeaux (Sergeaux), Sir R. – Cornw., 1361-90; Chalons, Sir R. – Devon, 1420; Chaunceys, J. – Bath, 1397-99; Cheddar, R. – Soms. 1407-27; Chenduyt, J. – Cornw. 1395-1407; Cheyne, Sir W. – Dorset, 1402; Chideock, J. – Dorset, 1414; Chudleigh, Sr J. – Devon, 1381-93; Clewer, R. – Bath, 1385-90; Cole, J. IV – Devon, 1417-23; Colshull, J. I – Cornw., 1391-99; Colshull, J. II – Cornw., 1414; Copplestone, J. – Devon, 1421-39; Courtenay, Sir H – Devon, 1395-1421; Courtenay, Sir P. – Devon, 1383-1401; Derby, Sir S. – Dorset, 1372-94, Soms., 1390; Devereux, Sir J. – Dorset, 1404; Draper, R. – Bath, 1395; Fillol, W. – Dorset, 1414; FitzHerbert, Sir E. – Dorset, 1377, Sussex, 1378-86; FitzJames, J. – Bridgwater, 1421; FitzWaryn, Sir I. – Dorset, 1378-1407, Devon, 1383, Soms., 1397; Ford, E. – Bath, 1388; Fortescue, H. – Devon, 1421; Frampton, J. – Dorset, 1404; Fraunceys, S. – Bath, 1380-86; Frome, J. – Bucks, 1385, Dorset, 1386-1404; Gascoigne, W. – Bridgwater, 1406-1422; Gosse, W. – Bridgwater, 1413; Grenville, Sir J. – Devon, 1388-1402; Hakluyt, L. – Herefs, 1385-94, Soms., 1404-06; Hamely (Hamlyn), Sir J. – Liskard, 1355, Lostwithiel, 1355-58, Truro, 1355-58, Cornw, 1357-62, Launceston, 1358, Helston, 1358-61, Bodmin, 1361, Dorset, 1371-91; Hankford, R. –

Devon, 1414-16; Haygoby, J. – Bath, 1402; Herle, Sir J. – Cornw., 1410; Hill, R. – Soms., 1414-19; Hobbes, R. – Bath, 1413; Honybrigge, J. – Bath, 1386; Horsey, Sir J. – Dorset, 1421; Hunt, R. – Bath, 1417-26; Ilcombe, Sir H. – Cornw. 1388-95, Lostwithiel, 1402-07; Jacob, M. – Bridgwater, 1420-23, Taunton, 1432; Kedwelly, J. – Bridgwater, 1395-1417; Lambourne, Sir W. – Cornw., 1374-99; Luttrell, Sir H. – Soms., 1404-15, Devon, 1406; Lynde, Hugh de la – Bath, 1391-97, Chippenham, 1394; Marsh, J.L. – Bath, 1394-97; Marsh, J. II – Bath 1414-21; Martin, W. – Dorset, 1397; Mayne, R. I – Bridgwater, 1386-88; Mayne, R. II – Bridgwater, 1419, Wells, 1433; Moigne, Sir J. – Dorset, 1388-97; More, R III – Dorset, 1417; Newlyn, R. – Bath, 1421; Palmer, J. I – Bridgwater, 1377-94, Bath, 1384-88, Wells, 1385; Perle, Jn I – Dorchester, 1388, Dorset, 1394; Pitt, J. – Bridgwater, 1421-35; Pomeroy, E. – Devon, 1419; Pomeroy, Sir T. – Devon, 1404-13; Prescott, J. – Exeter, 1361-68, Totnes, 1366-73, Devon, 1390; Prideaux, Sir J. – Devon, 1383-88; Pyne, E. – Devon, 1404-11; Radstock, W. – Bath, 1414; Reskymer, Sir J. – Cornw., 1388-90; Reynell (Reynald), W. – Devon, 1404; Rich, W. – Bath, 1414-36; Rodney, Sir J. – Soms., 1391; Rodney, Sir W. – Soms., 1406; Roger, J. I – Bridport, 1395-1413, Dorset, 1421; Rous, W. – Bath, 1390; Rymour, T. – Bath, 1406; Ryton, T. – Bath, 1393?; St Aubyn, J. – Devon, 1414; Sambourn, N. I – Bath, 1391; Shropshire, W. – Bath, 1388; Skinner, R. – Bath, 1388; Stafford, Sir H. I – Warwks., 1383, Wilts., 1384, Dorset, 1388-1410, Soms., 1394; Stawell, Sir T. – Soms., 1420; Stourton, J. I – Soms., 1419-35; Stretch, J. – Devon, 1399; Stretch, Sir J. – Devon, 1385-88; Sydenham, J. – Bridgwater, 1377-97; Talbot, Sir W. – Cornw., 1402-14; Thomer (Tomere), W. – Bridgwater, 1377-1406; Touprest (Towprest), W. – Bath, 1394; Tretherf, J. – Cornw., 1420-37; Trevanion, R., – Cornw., 1407; Trevarthian, J. – Cornw., 1393-1401; Treverbyn, J. – Cornw., 1391-94; Turberville, Sir R. – Dorset, 1388; Urban (Hurban), J. – Helston, 1381-97, Truro, 1391, Cornw., 1411; Wadham, Sir J. – Exeter, 1379, Devon, 1401; Ward, R. – Bridgwater, 1407; Whalesborough, J. – Cornw., 1402; Whittocksmead, J. – Bath, 1399-1410; Widcombe (Wydecombe), R. – Bath, 1413-31; Wybbury, J. – Cornw., 1413; Wykeham, T. – Dorset, 1390-95; Wynd (Whynde), J. – Bridgwater, 1384-88.

1993

Somerset of one hundred years ago (Stroud)
'Peter Greening', *PSANHS* 137, pp. 192-93
'Straightening out the Parrett', *SM* 3(1), p. 34
'Parish clerk and sexton', *SM* 3(2), p. 29
'What have you found in your garden', *SM* 3(3), p. 23
'Loyal to the crown', *SM* 3(4), p. 31
'Brief lives', *SM* 3(5), p. 21
'That's what I was told' *SM* 3(6), p. 27
'The glory has departed', *SM* 3(7), p. 19
'Generous patron', *SM* 3(8), p. 26
'Not too much preaching', *SM* 3(9), p. 35
'I remember, I remember', *SM* 3(10), p. 35
'A visitor in Somerset', *SM* 3(11), p. 43
'The Milbornes', *SM* 3(12), p. 31

1994

'Burrow Mump: a revision', *PSANHS* 138, pp. 111-16

Glastonbury, History and Guide (Stroud)

God bless churchwardens (Diocese of Bath and Wells)

'School reports', *SM* 4(1), p. 37

'Inquisitive government', *SM* 4(3), p. 27

'The church militant', *SM* 4(4), p. 19

'One hundred years of parish councils', *SM* 4(10), p. 35

'Operation Overlord', *SM* 4(11), p. 37

(contributor), *A Guide to English County Histories* (Stroud), ed. C.R.J. Currie & C.P. Lewis, 'Somerset', pp. 348-354, *infra*

(review) '*English Episcopal Acta 1061-1203*, ed. Frances M.R. Ramsey (OUP for the British Academy, 1995), xcix + 252', *PSANHS* 138, p. 195

1995

Somerset castles (Tiverton))

'The ghost train', *SM* 5(1), p. 19

'Unknown soldiers', *SM* 5(3), p. 14

'The first English scientist', *SM* 5(4), p. 19

'Local titles for (mostly foreign) toffs', *SM* 5(6), p. 21

'Saved again', *SM* 5(8), p. 19

'The saints of Exmoor', *SM* 5(10), p. 20, 5(11), p. 16

'Christmases at Redlynch', *SM* 5(12), p. 23

(review) '*The War over Keynsham*, by M. C. Fitter (Ammonite Press, Keynsham, 1995), x + 342 pp.', *PSANHS* 139, pp. 196-97

1996

Fifty Somerset churches (Tiverton)

(contributor) *Topographical Writers in South-West England*, ed. M. Brayshay, Ch. 4, 'Somerset Topographical Writing, 1600-1900', pp. 62-76

'King Alfred under threat?', *SM* 6(1), p. 23

'Clerical crook', *SM* 6(2), p. 31

'The County Club', *SM* 6(3), p. 37

'The good lady marquess', *SM* 6(4), p. 16

'The Wells brothers or the Troteman brothers of Wells', *SM* 6(5), p. 22

'Somerset invaded', *SM* 6(6), p. 37

'Rebuilding and reseating', *SM* 6(7), p. 54

'Woodforde in Texas', *SM* 6(8), p. 41

'Ancestors and descendants', *SM* 6(9), pp. 30-31

'Two little gentlemen in black and a chimney', *SM* 6(10), p. 45

'Three royal dukes', *SM* 6(11), p. 27

'In the parson's kitchen', *SM* 6(12), p. 52

(review) 'Stokes, J., and Alexander, R.J., eds., *Records of English Drama* (University of Toronto Press, 1996) 2 vols, pp. xii + 1141pp.' *PSANHS* 140, pp. 167-68

1997
'Dr C.A. Ralegh Radford', *PSANHS* 140, pp. 180-81
(with J. and J. Penoyre) *The Glastonbury Tribunal* (Glastonbury Tribunal Ltd)
'A diplomatic journey', *SM* 7(1), p. 12
'Rebels in the West again', *SM* 7(2), p. 16
'From Castle Cary to Florida', *SM* 7(3), p. 29
'Exile in Taunton', *SM* 7(4), p. 35
'A nation of shopkeepers', *SM* 7(5), p. 33
'A family of rogues'. *SM* 7(7), p. 35
'What happened to Jones', *SM* 7(8), p. 16
'No name, no pack drill', *SM* 7(9), p. 24
'The storm', *SM* 7(11), p. 24
'A taste of Danish', *SM* 7(12), p. 20

1998
'A fantastic clergyman', *SM* 8(1), p. 55
'The defence of the realm', *SM* 8(2), p. 33
'American loyalist in exile', *SM* 8(3), p. 31
'Mummers in a nunnery', *SM* 8(5), p. 19
'From Wraxall to Belgrave in two generations', *SM* 6(7), pp. 50-51
'Expensive independence', *SM* 8(9), p. 18
'A brief chronicler of the times', *SM* 8(11), p. 21
'Treason in Somerset', *SM* 8(12), p. 92

1999
Crewkerne Grammar School (Old Crewkernians Association)
(contributor) T. Mayberry & H. Binding, eds., , *Somerset, The Millennium Book* (Tiverton),
    Ch. 4, 'Somerset Towns, 1340-1642', pp. 51-60
'Watchet blue', *SM* 9(3), p. 17
'Recruiting parson', *SM* 9(4), p. 31
'The sage of Somerset', *SM* 9(5), p. 19
'Absentee landlords', *SM* 9(6), p. 33
'Somerset cider', *SM* 9(7), p. 47
'The earldom of Wessex', *SM* 9(9), p. 38
'Or, a dragon rampant gules', *SM* 9(11), p. 55
'From nowhere to nowhere', *SM* 9(12), p. 35
(editor and contributor) *Victoria County History of Somerset, vol. 7, Bruton, Horethorne, and
    Norton Ferris Hundreds (Wincanton and Neighbouring Parishes)* (Oxford)
(review) *'The heritage crusade and the spoils of history.* By David Lowenthal (Cambridge, 1998)
    pp. xviii + 338. In *WHR*, Vol. 19 (1999), pp. 775-76.

2000
Pitminster past and present (Friends of Pitminster Church)
'Exmoor exposed', *Exmoor Review* 41, pp. 68-79
'John Stowell, freeman of Wells', *SDNQ* 34(352), 398

'Somerset and Dorset Notes and Queries', *SM* 10(1), p. 43

'Paper-maker extraordinary', *SM* 10(2), p. 35

'Dark spot in a land of religious liberty', *SM* 10(4), p. 35

'Millennium history' *SM* 10(5), p. 39

'From Glastonbury to Rome' *SM* 10(6), p. 45

'A place in the country', *SM* 10(7), p. 43

'The price of loyalty', *SM* 10(9), p. 51

'Culture on the permanent way', *SM* 10(10), p. 29

(review) *'Catalogue of seals in the National Museum of Wales*, vol. 2. Edited by David H. Williams (National Museum of Wales, Cardiff, 1998), pp. x+ 67 + 10pp. illustrations', *WHR*, Vol. 20 (2000), pp. 186-87.

(review) *'The Arthur of the English: The Arthurian legend in Medieval English life and literature.* Edited by W. R. J. Barron (University of Wales Press, Cardiff, 1999), pp. xvii + 395, *WHR*, Vol. 20 (2000), pp. 368-69.

2001

Somerset monasteries (Stroud and Charleston)

'The abbot of Glastonbury saves money', *SDNQ* 35(354), 51-52

'Christchurch, Oxford and Midsomer Norton', *Five Arches* 42, pp. 3-4

(with A.J. Scrase), 'The bishop's palace, Wells', *SDNQ* 35(354), 52-55

'Ponter's Ball', *SDNQ* 35(353), 1-2

'Scholars in our society's past', *PSANHS* 145, pp. 1-8

'Sir Thomas More, Cardinal Wolsey and Glastonbury Abbey', *SDNQ* 35(354), 88-90

'In pursuit of maidens', *SM* 11(1), p. 16

'Never mind the title, look at the flyleaf', *SM* 11(2), p. 21

'Keeping debts in the family', *SM* 11(3), p. 39

'Tiptoeing in Milborne Port', *SM* 11(4), p. 96

'A lovely day', *SM* 11(5), p. 46

'Unwontedly: how a novelist was inspired by a ... railway station', *SM* 11(6), p. 46

'The first baroness of Glastonbury', *SM* 11(10), p. 87

'Who was the king of the castle?', *SM* 11(11), p. 57

'They named a city after him', *SM* 11(12), p. 45

2002

Somerset families (Tiverton)

'Christmas at Dulverton, 1830', *Exmoor* 21, pp. 34-35

'Sir Thomas More, Cardinal Wolsey and Glastonbury Abbey', *SDNQ* 35(355), 107-108

'Gold in those hills', *Somerset Life Magazine* 12(1), 43

'Fighting churchmen', *Somerset Life Magazine* 12(2), 19

2003

(editor and contributor) *The Victoria County History of Somerset, vol. 8, The Poldens and the levels* (Woodbridge)

(review) *'Glastonbury Abbey and the Arthurian tradition.'* Edited by James P. Carley. D. S. Brewer (Cambridge, 2001), pp. xii + 648, *WHR*, Vol. 21 (2003), pp. 584-86.

2004

The parish of Heathfield with Cotford St Luke

'Twin powers', *Friends of Wells Cathedral, Annual Report*, pp. 7-11

'William Gilbert, first abbot of Bruton', *SDNQ* 35(359), 316-318

(commissioned)   12 articles in the on-line *Oxford Dictionary of National Biography*: Beckington [Bekynton], Thomas (1390?-1465);   Bere, Richard (c.1455-1525); Chinnok, John (d.1420); Collinson, John (1757-1793); Hollewey, William (d. in or before 1557?);   Hunt, William (1842-1931);   Locke, Richard (1737-1806);   Luttrell [Lutterell] family (per. c.1200-1428);   Mohun, John, first Lord Mohun (1269?-1330); Mohun, John, second Lord Mohun (1320?-1375);   Robert (d.1180);   Wells, Jocelin of (d.1242).

(review) '*King Arthur: Myth-making and history,* N. J. Higham (London, 2002), pp. xii +203, *WHR*, Vol. 22 (2004), pp. 158-59.

2005

A Somerset miscellany (Devon)

(with R. Lewis & M. Matthews) *Wells Cathedral* (Scala)

'What's in a name', *Exmoor* 33, pp. 22-23

2006

'Recreation or survival?', *Exmoor* 35, 62-63

(editor and contributor) *Victoria County History of Somerset, vol. 9, Glastonbury and Street* (Woodbridge)

(contributor) P. Hill-Cottingham, D. Briggs, R. Brunning, A. King, G. Rix, eds., *The Somerset Wetlands: An Ever Changing Environment* (Tiverton, SANHS, SCC), 'The Somerset Levels in the Last Two Millennia', pp. 57-66, *infra*

(review) '*Charters and Custumals of Shaftesbury Abbey, 1089-1216* (BA Records of Social and Economic History, 39), ed. N.E. Stacy (Oxford, 2006), 266 pp.', *PSANHS* 150, p. 195

2007

'Farleigh Hungerford Castle, 1553-4', *SDNQ* 36(366), 177-78

'Mrs S. Rawlins (née Bates-Harbin)', *SDNQ* 36(365), 89-91

(editor and contributor) *Somerset Churches and Chapels. Building Repair and Restoration* (Friends of Somerset Churches and Chapels, Wellington)

2008

Bath and Wells: a diocesan celebration (Ryelands, Wellington)

2009

'Barlinch Priory', *SDNQ* 36(369), 302-04

(introduction) *Delineations of the north-western division of the county of Somerset, and of the Mendip Caverns* by J. Rutter (facsimile edition, Stroud)

Spirit of Wells Cathedral (Wellington)

'Too near heaven for one thing', *Exmoor Review* 50, pp. 50-53

2010

(with others) *Church of St Martin of Tours, Elworthy* (Churches Conservation Trust)

King Arthur (Wellington)

(contributor and editor) *Jocelin of Wells* (Woodbridge)

(contributor) *The Victoria County History, vol. 10, Castle Cary and the Brue-Cary Watershed* (Woodbridge)

2011

Wells Cathedral Clock (Chapter of Wells Cathedral)

2012

'An auspicious beginning', *SDNQ* 37(376) 175-76

'Coke estates in Somerset and Dorset', *SDNQ* 37(376) 176-77

2013

(editor, with M.B. McDermott) *Church Accounts, 1457-1559*, SRS 95

(review) SRS 96, C. Brett, ed., *Crown Revenues from Somerset and Dorset*, 1605, *SDNQ* 37 (378), pp. 263-64

(review) H. Playfair, Jewels of Somerset: stained glass in parish churches from 1830 (Beaufort Press), *SDNQ* 37 (378), pp. 264-65

(review) SRS 95, R. W. Dunning and M. B. McDermott, eds., *Church Accounts 1443-1559*, *SDNQ* 37 (378), pp. 265-66

2015

(contributor) *The Victoria County History, vol. 11, Queen Camel and the Cadburys* (Woodbridge)

2017

'Training Teachers – The Exeter Diocesan Calendar and Clergy List', *SDNQ* 38 (385), pp. 225-26

Index

Acland, Sir Thomas Dyke, 141, 146, 155

Adams, Joane, 121-2; William, 118

Adelwold, William, 177

Aelfheah of Hampshire, 38

Aelfsige, 38

Aelswith, 38

Aescwig, Abbot, 37

Albin, John, 80

Aldfrith, 33

Aldhelm, Bishop, 32-5, 39-41

Alfwold, 39

Allam, William Ambrose, 184

Allen, Benjamin, 146, 149; Ralph, 189; Thomas, 149

All Saints, 19-21

Amos, Nicky, 28

Anderdon, Mr, 149

Andries, Guido, 62; Jasper, 62; Joris, 62; Lucas, 62

Andros, James, 77; Thomas, 79; William, 76; William jun., 77, 79; William sen., 77, 79

Appletree, James the younger, 82

Arnold, Harbin, 168

Arundell, Sir Thomas, 84

Ashe, John, 97

Atkinson, Dr Thomas, 87

Austin the Fool, 94

Auxerre, Germanus of, 29

Ayleworth, John, 45

Bachiler, John, 79

Baily, Revd William, 149

Baines, Peter Augustine, 189

Baker, Augustine, 182-3

Bampfylde, Copplestone Warre, 138, 140-1, 143-4, 146-9, 152, 155, 157-9

Banester, William, 186

Barret, Richard Maurus, 183

Barrow, John, 116

Bassett, fam., 97; William, 91, 96

Bastone, Mr, 149

Batchiler, Mary, 76, 79; Richard, 76, 79

Batten, John, 68, 100

Bayley, Humphrey, 54

Beacham, Francis, 81; Joan, 81

Becket, St Thomas, 185

Beckington, Bishop Thomas, 49

Benedict Biscop, 31-2

Bennet, Mr, 128

Bennett, Bede, 182

Bere, Abbot, 27

Berkeley, Sir Edward, 103; Sir Henry, 102, 104

Bernard, James, 135-6, 141, 144, 146, 155

Berriman, Joseph, 182

Betjeman, John, 10

Bettey, Dr Joseph, 29

Betty, Henry, 88, 90

Bevan, Elway, 53

Biccombe, Robert, 123

Bickersteth, Bishop John, 14

Billingsley, John, 122

Birdsall, Augustine, 189

Bisse, fam., 101

Bitton, Bishop William, 21-2, 26-7, 47

Blake, Mr, 131

Bolster, John, 82; Mary, 82

Bonnor, Thomas, 152

Bourne, Bishop Gilbert, 52

Bradshaw, Bernard, 186

Bramston, Richard, 50-1

Brett, Robert Gabriel, 181

Brickdale, Matthew, 137

Bromwich, David, 12

Brook, Mr Thomas, 103

Brookfield, Paul, 184

Brown, -, 125; Mr, 151; Thomas Joseph, 182

Browne, Christopher, 72; John, 72, 78; Phillip, 72, 78; Richard, 72; Richard sen., 78; Richard the younger, 78

Browning, Robert, 116

Bubwith, Bishop, 44, 46

Buckley, Sigebert, 178

Burbidge, Edward, 73; Elizabeth, 73

Burford, Edward, 82-3; Edward jun., 74, 81; Edward sen., 74, 81

Burford, John, 81, 83; Robert, 73; William, 74, 83

Burge, Lawrence, 182

Burland, John, 149

Burnell, Bishop, 47; Richard, 45

Bush, Robin, 11

Butler, John, 187

Byccombe, Hugh, 85; Maud, 85

Byfleet, John Edward, 181; Robert, 67-8

Camplin, Revd Dr Thomas, 144, 146-7, 149, 155-6, 159

Cane, Mr, 149

Capes, John Augustine, 180

Capron, William, 51

Carent, fam., 67; William, 23; Sir William, 70

Carew, Elizabeth, 123, 129, 135-6; John, 124, 129, 131, 134; Katherine, 129; Mary, 131-2, 136; Thomas, 123-37

Carroll, Bishop John, 186

Carsleygh, Canon Peter, 51

Carter, Joan, 74; Mary, 74; Samuel, 74

Cary, John, 71

Castleton, Nathaniel, 136-7

Cely, Walter, 53

Champneys, Sir Thomas, 149

Chapel, Christopher, 104; Henry, 110

Chaplin, Lionel, 77

Chappell, -, 77

Charter, John, 132; Thomas, 147

Chideok, John, 45-6

Clarke, John jun., 53; John sen., 54; Mr, 118, 120

Cleeve, Lady of, 23

Clements, William, 185

Clifford, Lord, 188

Cloppecote, Prior Robert, 37

Clothier, Joan, 72

Clunn, Nicholas, 54

Cody, Elphege, 182

Coke, Edward, 90

Collens, Richard, 72

Collier, Mr, 106

Collingridge, Peter Barnardine, 187, 189

Collins, Hugh, 102-103

Collinson, Revd John, 12, 36, 152-3, 157, 161

Combe, Richard, 141, 144, 149, 154-5

Connocke, William, 73

Conock, Giles, 73; John, 73

Cooper, John, 56

Cornish, Bishop Thomas, 45, 51

Costen, Dr Michael, 28, 40

Coules, Roberrt, 114

Counsell, Richard, 121

Couper, -, 78

Courselles, Roger of, 38

Courtenay, fam., 12

Courtney, Giles, 79; Joan, 79; Reynold, 79

Coutances, Bishop of, 39

Coventry, John, 92

Coxe, Charles Hippisley, 146; Richard Hippisley, 146, 155

Craddock, William, 102

Craig, Joseph, 132-3

Crawford, Ann, 56

Cridland, John, 144, 149

Crocker, Abraham, 138, 149, 153-5, 171

Cromwell, Thomas, 29

Crosse, Thomas, 79

Curll, Edward, 100-106; fam., 100, 106

Cuthberg, 33

Dampier, John jun., 80; Joseph, 80; Mary, 80

Dampyer, John sen., 80
Darch, James, 142; John, 138, 141-3, 146-8, 158; Mary, 141-2; Richard, 142
Davis, Peter, 171
Day, Ann, 139, 152-3; Bede, 182; Nanny, 139; William, 138-159
Dee, Richard, 62
Dier, fam., 70
Dodington, fam., 97
Douglas, David, 9
Dounton, Revd Richard, 113
Dowding, Hilary, 182; Vincent, 182
Drew, Catherine, 168
Drewe, Francis, 135-6
DuBoulay, F.R.H., 12
Dunford, Henry, 106
Dunning, Anne, 11-12; Christy, 11; Jeremy, 12; Dr Robert, 9-14, 28, 61, 66, 138, 140, 142, 152, 158-9, 184, 190-1
Durbin, John, 140
Dyer, John, 72
Earle, Goodenough, 139
Edbrooke, Robert, 106
Edgell, Robert, 122
Edwards, John, 92-3, 107
Ellis, Jane, 109
Elsworth, Richard, 167
Elton, Sir Abraham Isaac, 146, 149
Everdon, Edward, 74; James jun., 74; James sen., 74
Eyre, Joseph, 134
Faden, William, 151, 153
Farrant, Lawrence, 182
Feare, John, 118; Richard, 118
Fisher, Charles, 110; William, 110
Fitzjames, Nicholas, 180-1
Fitzwalter, fam., 26
Fleetwood, Sir Miles, 90
Flower, John, 76
Ford, David, 72; Thomas, 72
Forward, Jerome, 81; William, 80-1
Foster, Mr, 93-4
Fourd, Alice, 74-5; Christian, 74; William, 74
Frederick, Mr, 142-3
French, Alexander jun., 72; Alexander sen., 72; Christian, 72; George, 72; John, 72
Frome, John, 48
Fry, Hugh, 105; Mr, 149
Fudge, Thomas, 52
Gainsborough, Thomas, 139-40
Game, Agnes, 75; William jun., 75; William sen., 75
Gander, Henry, 100; William, 100, 102
Ganger, Joan, 73; Thomas, 74
Gardener, Ralph, 49

Gasquet, Aidan, 190
Gatcum, William, 118
Gawen, William, 102
Gaylard, William, 72
Gaylerd, fam., 70
Gibbs, Richard, 185
Gifford, Gabriel, 181
Gilmore, Joseph, 36
Godwin, Dr Paul, 103
Good, William, 177
Goodford, J. Old, 149
Goold, Thomas, 116
Gordon, Lord George, 187
Gorges, Anne, 96; Bridget, 96; Sir Edward, 96; Elizabeth, 86, 93; fam., 89, 93, 96; Sir Ferdinando, 91, 93, 96, 98; Helena, 86, 95; Sir Thomas, 86, 95
Gray, fam., 119; John, 119
Grayne, George, 72
Green, Gabriel, 56
Greening, Peter, 10
Greenwood, Christopher, 138; John, 138
Gregory, Pope, 29
Griffith, Christopher, 125
Griffits, Mr, 142
Grubham, Elizabeth, 82; Martha, 82; Thomas, 82
Gunston, Sir Thomas, 146
Gwyn, Francis, 141
Hacker, Elizabeth, 76; George, 72, 76; Joan, 78; John, 76, 78; Mathew, 76, 78
Hadley, James, 23
Hadrian, 33
Hædde, Bishop, 16, 33
Haemgisl, Abbot, 32
Hagat, Robert, 118
Haine, George, 75; Joseph, 75
Hall, Placid, 184
Hallet, Mary, 139; Samuel, 139
Hamilton, George, 56
Hammet, Benjamin, 144, 149, 168
Hanham, James, 105
Harbin, Margaret, 158
Harcourt, Charles Harcourt, see Masters, Charles Harcourt,
Harding, John jun., 80; Samuel, 80
Hardinge, John sen., 80
Harford, John, 81
Harley, J.B., 138, 140, 142, 152, 158-9
Hartwell, Agnes, 75; Henry, 81; John, 75
Haskett, William, 103
Hawarden, Joseph Bernard, 184; Mary Frances, 184
Hawker, Thomas, 82; William, 144
Hawkes, William, 149

Hawkins, John, 71
Hayne, Alice, 74; Giles, 75
Hele, Revd Arthur, 129
Hellard, John, 74; Mary, 74; Thomas, 74
Hellyar, William, 100
Helyar, family, 151
Hertford, Earl of, 51; Marquess of, 97-8, 104
Hervey, Revd S.H.S., 108, 113
Hext, Revd Amias, 103
Hill, Revd Benjamin, 114; Mr, 134; Robert, 11; Thomas, 180
Hilson, Richard, 78; William jun., 78; William sen., 78
Hindrey, -, 115
Hoare, Henry, 67
Hobhouse, Henry, 149
Hodge, Robert, 56
Hole, Elias, 102; Revd Robert, 146
Holloway, William, 185
Holy Cross, 19, 21-2, 39
Hooke, Humphrey, 105
Hooper alias Lyte, Elizabeth, 53
Hooper, Thomas, 52-4
Hopton, Sir Ralph, 96
Horne, Culling, 134; Ethelbert, 190; John, 127-8, 132-5; Mary, 131-2
Horner, fam., 89, 97; Thomas, 141, 146, 157, 170
Horsey, fam., 97
Hosie, John, 115
Hotchkin, Thomas, 149
Huchens, William, 119
Huddleston, John, 185
Hudson, Hazel, 108; Thomas, 131
Hughes, Mr, 133
Hughes, Revd Richard, 171
Hunt, Dodington, 146; Robert, 102; William, 12
Hussey, William, 67-8
Hutton, Charles, 154; Mary, 154
Hwysch, John, 44-5, 47-8, 51-2
Hyckemans, Thurstan, 177
Hygons, Richard, 50
Ireson, Nathaniel, 130-1, 168
Isgor, Humphrey, 119
Iveleafe, cosen, 122; Robert, 116, 118
Jacob, E.F., 9
Jacobb, Dorothy, 76; Joan, 73, 76; John, 72, 76; Thomas, 76; Valentine, 72
Jansen, Jacob, 62
Jeane, John, 141, 146
Jeanes, Christopher, 73; John, 73
Jefferies, Sarah, 168
Jenkins, Jerome, 184; Thomas, 151
Jenninges, Giles jun., 81; Giles sen., 81
Jennings, Agnes, 83; Edith, 80;

Edward, 80; Giles, 80; John, 80, 82; William, 80
Jenynges, Giles, 77; John, 77; William, 77
Jessey, Caleb, 116
Jesus Christ, 21-3, 25, 30
Jobbyn, Nicholas, 185
Jones, Dr Graham, 28
Jsherwood, Joseph, 181
Kemys, Thomas, 180
Kendal, Richard Gregory, 182
Kendall, Richard Peter, 182
Kentwyn, William, 177
King Aethelred of Mercia, 32
King Aldfrith of Northumbria, 33-4
King Arthur, 13
King Caedwalla, 33
King Centwine of Wessex, 32-3
King Charles I, 92, 97, 101, 106
King Charles II, 185
King Ecgfrith, 32
King Edgar, 37
King Edmund, 38
King Edward, 37
King Edward I, 37
King Edward III, 37
King Edward VI, 51
King Egbert of Kent, 31
King Eric of Sweden, 86
King Geriant of Dumnonia, 34
King Henry IV, 10
King Henry V, 11
King Henry VI, 23, 26
King Henry VII, 25-6
King Henry VIII, 10, 12, 27, 51, 62, 177
King Ine of Wessex, 33, 39-40
King James I, 86
King James II, 185
King Oswiu of Northumbria, 30-2
King Richard II, 10
King Stephen, 20-1
King Wulfhere of Mercia, 32
King, John, 79; John jun., 80; John sen., 80; Mr, 125
Kirkpatrick, James, 144, 146, 149-50, 156, 159
Knatchbull, Mrs, 164, 171; N., 171
Knight, Bede, 182
Knocston, John, 48
Knowles, David, 190
Lambe, Mr, 134
Lane, Thomas, 73, 75
Larder, James, 121; Richard, 121
Laver, Henry jun., 74; Henry sen., 74; John, 72; Mary, 74; William, 81
Layton, Richard, 29
Leaker, Robert, 120
Leighton, Gerrard, 157
Leland, John, 24, 27

Lens, Bernard, 36
Lethbridge, John, 141, 146
Lewis, John Evill, 142-3
Light, Mr, 134
Lilley, Amos, 110
Limbry, Turner, 78
Llewelyn, Anselm, 186
Lock, Ambrose, 72, 79; Joan, 79; Katherine, 79
Locke, Ann, 139; Mary, 139; Richard, 12
Lockett, Revd Henry, 126-8, 131
Loker, -, 89
Long, Elizabeth, 171
Loyde, Mr, 142
Luca Savino, Guido di, 62
Luckest, Thomas, 78
Lugwardyn, John, 45, 51
Luttrell, fam., 12; Thomas, 91, 98
Lyde, Edward, 110; John, 110
Macaulay, Mrs, 161
Maelduib, 33
Malmesbury, William of, 33, 40
March, Mr, 134; Bishop William of, 21
Marchant, Giles, 75, 81; John, 75; Lucy, 75
Marsh, Thomas, 74
Marten, Henry, 112
Martin, John, 181
Martyn, Roger, 49
Mary, 18-19
Mary of Walsingham, 15, 23
Mason, Captain Benjamin, 105
Master, Edward, 77
Masters, Anthony, 77; Charles Harcourt, 138, 140, 143, 147, 149-51, 153-4, 158-9; Samuel, 77
Matrevers, Nicholas, 44, 45-6
McAuliffe, Placid, 182
McGarvie, Michael, 39
Meautys, Thomas, 92
Medlycott, James, 162
Melliar, Mr, 118
Messiter, Mr, 149
Mildmay, Humphrey, 104
Miller, Elizabeth, 75; Geoffrey, 75; Lady, 161; Sara, 75; William, 75
Minifie, Revd James, 144, 149
Mogg, Richard, 105
Mohun, fam., 12; Reginald de, 38; William de, 37, 40
Molens, Anne, 73-4; Edward, 74
Molton, Elizabeth, 82; Faith, 82; Nicholas, 82
Molyns, Edward gent., 80, 82; Henry, 80; John, 80
Monckton, Richard, 81
Monier, Peter le, 46
Monmouth, Duke of, 13

Monro, Dr, 134-5
Moore, Sir Edward, 75, 77
Morgan, Edward, 86; Elizabeth, 86
Morris, Dr Claver, 56
Muttlebury, Francis, 181; John Placid, 181; Thomas, 181
Mychell, John, 177
Naish, Thomas, 125, 127
Naylor, Matthew, 53-4; Placid, 186
Neot, John, 177
Newman, Ellen, 75; James, 75; Joan, 75; John, 75; Nicholas, 75
Nicholas, Denise, 78
Noble, Mr, 142
Norris, Margaret, 102
Northampton, Marquess of, 86
Norton, fam., 89; Sir George, 85
Nowell, John, 142-3; Walter, 53
Nutty, Joan, 109
Odams, Joan, 79; John, 76; Nicholas, 76; Nicholas jun., 79; Nicholas sen., 79
Oker, John, 55
Orme, Professor Nicholas, 43
Osric, 32
Our Lady of Loretta, 27
Overton, fam., 101; Mr Henry, 124; William, 102
Owen, Dr George, 85
Paillet, Bernard, 182
Paine, George, 119
Palladius, Bishop, 29
Palmer, George, 110-11
Parker, Giles, 75; Katherine, 81; Thomas, 129-31
Parkins, Mrs, 170
Parr, William, 86
Parsons, John, 177
Patten, Joseph, 82; Nicholas, 81-2; William, 82
Pavy, Hugh, 12
Peeterssun, William, 118
Pempel, Dean, 44, 46, 52
Penny, Mr, 149
Perry, Alice, 73; Jeronimo, 73; John, 73; Mary, 75; Robert, 75; Thomas, 73
Pevsner, Nicholas, 123
Phagan, John, 177
Phelippes, Edward, 82; Faith, 82; John, 82; Joseph, 82
Phelips, Bridget, 96; Edward, 146, 149; fam., 85; Sir Robert, 92, 96
Phelps, Edward, 77; Faithfull, 77; fam., 70; John, 70, 72, 77; Richard, 131, 167; William, 77
Pierce, John, 133, 135-6
Piers, Canon, 56; William, 56
Pike, Henry, 79; John, 78; John jun., 79; John sen., 79; William, 79

Pincius, 22
Pinnfeild, Jo., 76
Pitt, Elizabeth, 109; John, 109, 111, 115-16
Pittman, Thomas, 75
Pomeroy, Richard, 50-1
Pontesbury, Nicholas, 44, 46, 52
Pope Celestine, 29
Pope Gregory the Great, 29, 179
Pope Sixtus II, 30
Pope Urban I, 22
Pope Vitalian, 31
Popham, Alexander, 96-8, 141, 144, 146-7, 149; fam., 89, 97; Sir Francis, 96
Porch, Robert, 117
Portman, Sir William, 92
Poulett (Paulet), Earl, 170; Florence, 88; Lord John, 88, 90-2, 94-6, 98
Powel, Philip, 183
Poyntz, fam., 183
Prater, Joseph, 180-1
Provis, William, 149
Prowse, Charles, 125, 136
Prowse, fam., 67
Prowse, Robert, 72
Pugin, A.W., 175
Pullen, Thomas jun., 77; Thomas sen., 77; William, 77
Punfold, Thomas, 82
Putt, Thomas, 141
Pyckerell, Cecily, 52
Pym, John, 90
Pyne, John, 96, 98
Queen Aelfthryth, 39
Queen Catherine of Braganza, 185
Queen Eanflaed, 30
Queen Elizabeth I, 52, 86
Queen Elizabeth II, 14
Queen Guinevere, 13
Queen Iurminburh, 32
Queen Mary, 52, 61, 177
Rack, Edmund, 151, 153, 159, 161-76
Ragneare, Martine, 66
Raignold, Herman, 62
Raineare, Martine, 66
Ralph, Elizabeth, 87
Ravenhill, Mary, 151
Rawlins, Sophia, 157-8
Renger, Martin, 60-3, 65-6
Reynolds, Herman, 62
Rich, Samuel, 67; William, 72
Richards, -, 110
Richardson, Anthony, 103; John Austin, 181
Richman, Edward jun., 76; Edward sen., 76; William, 76
Richmond, Edward, 77; Richard, 77; Roger, 77

Rishton, Elianor, 125, 134
Robbins, Mary, 82; Walter, 82
Roberts, Col. John, 149
Robertz, Richard, 52
Robinson, Gregory, 182
Rodber, Nicholas, 79
Rodbert, Joan, 78; John jun., 78; John sen., 78
Rodney, Anne, 96; fam., 96; Maurice, 96
Rogent, Giles, 77
Rogers, fam., 89; Sir Francis, 96; Helena, 96
Rolle, Denys, 88, 94
Roper, John le, 44
Rose, Henry, 102, 104
Roskell, J.S., 10
Ross, Charles, 9, 12
Rowe, Margery, 151
Rowley, William, 109-110, 118-19
Rutherford, Anselm, 188
Saint Abdon, 14
Saint Aidan, 22
Saint Albyn, Revd Lancelot, 146
Saint Aldhelm, 19-20
Saint Ambrose of Milan, 30
Saint Andrew, 18-21, 32
Saint Anne, 21, 25
Saint Anthony, 22
Saint Athelwine, 20
Saint Augustine, 19, 22, 29-30
Saint Barnabas, 19
Saint Bartholomew, 18-19
Saint Bede, 22, 27
Saint Benedict, 179, 190-1
Saint Benignus, 16, 18-20, 22
Saint Beuno, 18
Saint Blaise, 22
Saint Bridget, 16-19
Saint Cadoc, 17
Saint Calixtus, 21
Saint Carantoc, 16-20, 27
Saint Catherine, 19, 21-2
Saint Christopher, 21-3
Saint Columbanus, 26
Saint Congar, 16, 18-20
Saint Culbone, 14, 18-19, 23
Saint Cullanus, 16
Saint Cuthbert, 19-20, 44
Saint Cyricus, 19, 24
Saint David, 21
Saint David of Wales, 22
Saint Decuman, 16, 18-19
Saint Dubricius, 15, 16-19
Saint Dunstan, 19-20, 22
Saint Edmund, 19-21
Saint Edmund of Abingdon, 22
Saint Edward the Martyr, 19-20
Saint Edward, Prince of Wales, 26
Saint Erasmus, 21-3

Saint Erne, 18
Saint Fabian, 23
Saint Gabriel, 23
Saint George, 19-23
Saint Gildas, 16, 18-20, 22, 24
Saint Giles, 19-20, 24
Saint Gonthal, 26
Saint Gonzalo, 26
Saint Gregory, 19, 22, 31
Saint Hilda, 22
Saint Hugh of Lincoln, 22
Saint Indract, 16, 18, 20, 22, 26
Saint James the Great, 19
Saint John, 31, 39-40
Saint John the Baptist, 18-23
Saint John the Evangelist, 18-19
Saint Joseph of Arimathea, 22-3, 26
Saint Julietta, 19
Saint Juthwara, 26
Saint Kea, 16-17
Saint Kew, 16
Saint Kew, 17
Saint Lawrence, 19, 22, 28-42
Saint Leonard, 19-21
Saint Luke, 19
Saint Margaret, 19, 21
Saint Martin, 19-21
Saint Mary, 18-25, 32, 40
Saint Mary Magdalene, 19, 21, 23, 27
Saint Mary of Walsingham, 14, 23
Saint Matthew, 19
Saint Maurice, 22
Saint Michael, 19-22, 24, 26
Saint Nectan, 26
Saint Nicholas, 19-21, 23
Saint Olave, 19
Saint Oswald, 22
Saint Pancras, 31
Saint Patrick, 16, 18, 22
Saint Paul, 18-20, 29, 31
Saint Paulinus, 22
Saint Peter, 18-20, 22, 29, 31-2, 40
Saint Petroc, 19
Saint Philip, 19, 22
Saint Quiricus see Saint Cyricus, 24
Saint Reine, 25-6
Saint Roch, 25
Saint Salvin , 19
Saint Samson, 17
Saint Saviour, 19, 21, 23-4
Saint Sebastian, 23
Saint Sennen, 14
Saint Stephen, 19, 21, 29
Saint Swithun, 19-20
Saint Sythe, 21, 24-5
Saint Thomas of Canterbury, 14, 18, 19-21, 23
Saint Thomas of Lancaster, 26
Saint Uncumber, 25
Saint Vigor, fam., 39

Saint Vincent, 19
Saint Walter of Cowick, 22
Saint White, 25-6
Saint Wilgefortis, 25
Saint William of York, 21
Saint Willibrord, 31
Saint Wulfric, 15, 20
Saint Zita, 25
Salmon, Thomas, 54
Saltar, Nicholas, 117
Sampson, Captain Latimer, 105
Sandford, Elizabeth, 123, 129; Henry,
    125, 129, 132-3
Savage, James, 40
Saxton, Christopher, 138
Scott, Geoffrey, 186; Mr, 133
Selbourne, Nicholas, 46
Selye, John jun., 73; John sen., 73;
    William, 73
Sever, Nicholas, 117
Seward, Ambrose, 79; Samuel, 79;
    Thomas, 79; William, 79
Seymour, Edward, Duke of Somerset,
    61
Sharp, Margaret, 9
Sharrock, Bishop Gregory, 186-7
Sheafe, Canon Grindal, 113
Sherston fam., 57, 124
Sherwood, Dr Reuben, 185; John,
    181; Robert, 181; William, 181
Shorn, John, 23
Short, Bernard, 182
Shrewsbury, Bishop Ralph, 21, 44
Siddenham, Sir John, 70
Sillvar, Captain, 116
Silly, Thomas, 72
Siraut, Mary, 11
Skeggs, James, 122
Slape, Henry, 78
Slocombe, Robin, 126
Smeathes, Simon, 109
Smith, Culling, 134-5; Mary, 96;
    Thomas, 96
Smyth, Anne, 96; Elizabeth, 73, 86-
    8, 93, 98; fam., 95, 97; Florence,
    88-90, 92, 94, 97-8; Helena, 86,
    96, 98; Hugh, 90, 93-4, 98-9; Sir
    Hugh, 85-8, 93; Jane, 86; Mary,
    96, 98; Matthew, 85-6, 96; Maud,
    85; Priscilla, 77; Thomas, 90, 98;
    Sir Thomas, 84, 86-99
Smythe, John, 84-5
Somerset, Protector, 51
Southey, Canon, 141

Southwood, Thomas, 140
Sparrow, James, 146
Speed, John, 138
Speere, John, 77; Nicholas, 77
Spencer, Sir John, 70
Starr, Alice, 72; Benjamin, 78;
    Colonel, 105; Edmund, 78
Stawell, Sir John, 96, 101
Sterr, Alice, 81; Mary, 81; William,
    81
Stokes, John, 48
Stourton, Lord Edward, 67, 70, 72-
    82; Lady Frances, 75, 77-81; Lord
    John, 72, 74-6, 79-81; Lord
    William, 67, 70-1, 78-82
Strangways, Mrs, 170
Stribling, Mr, 142
Stride, Walter, 45
Strode, William, 101
Sullivan, Mr, 134
Sydenham John, 72
Symes, John, 71, 73
Tawswell, John jun., 74; John sen.,
    74; Richard, 74; Roger, 74
Taylar, John, 115
Taylor, Thomas, 78
Thatcher, Edward, 119
Theodore of Tarsus, 33
Theodore, Archbishop, 34
Thorpe, Thomas, 143
Throckmorton, Baynham, 90-1,
Tichborne, Dorothy, 181
Tincknell, Robert, 119
Toulmin, Revd Joshua, 143
Tours, Bishop John of, 28
Tout, T.F., 9
Towers, Richard Adrian, 184
Traske, Anthony, 82; Arthur, 76;
    Edward, 76; Roger, 76, 81;
    Temperance, 76
Travell, Sir Thomas, 162
Tregision, Dean Ralph, 46
Trenchard, Revd Henry, 106
Trevelyan, Sir John, 141, 149, 155
Trollope-Bellew, fam., 123
Tucker, James, 116; John, 75; Mary,
    75; William, 106
Tudor, Mary, 177, 190
Tudway, Charles, 56; Clement, 58;
    fam., 57
Tulke, George, 79; John, 79
Turner, Agnes, 78; Grace, 78;
    William, 78
Tynte, Anne, 96; Sir Charles Kemeys,

140-1, 146; fam., 89; John, 96; Sir
    Thomas, 96
Urban I, Pope, 22
Varoe, John, 116
Ven, George, 109
Victor, Humphrey, 74
Virgin Mary, 23-4
Vyvian, William, 73
Wall, Ann, 109, 120-1; William, 121
Wallis, John, 150-1, 157
Walmesley, Bishop Charles, 186-7
Walpole, Horace, 128
Wareyn, John, 44-5, 47-8, 50, 52
Warry, Mr, 149
Wassell, Benedict, 184
Watkin, Aelred, 190
Watts, Christopher, 95; Thomas, 105
Way, George, 127
Wedlake, W.J., 10
Weldon, Benet, 180
Welstead, Thomas, 54
Wentworth, Sir Thomas, 90
Westover, Andrew, 109; Ann, 109;
    fam., 107; Hannah, 109; Henry,
    107; Joan, 109; John, 107, 111;
    Dr John, 107-122; William, 111
Whippie, Thomas, 72
White, Giles jun., 73, 81; Giles sen.,
    73, 81; John, 81, 127
Whittby, Lionel, 72
Wickham, John, 146
Wilfrid, Bishop of York, 31-5
Wilhelm, Christian, 62
Wilkes, Cuthbert, 186
Willes, Edward, 80
Williams, Anselm, 186; Silvester, 106
Willis, Henry, 76; Thomas, 76
Winsor, George, 75-6; George jun.,
    75; George sen., 75; Joan, 76;
    William, 75
Winter, Mr, 134
Witherell, Mr, 142
Wood, Elizabeth, 73; John, 73; John
    the elder, 189; Richard, 168
Worcester, William, 26
Worsley, Clement, 187
Wulfric of Haselbury, 15, 20
Wulfry, 38
Wyndham, Edmund, 90; fam., 158;
    George O'Brien, 154; Sir John, 70
Yeatman, Mr, 149
Yeo, Richard, 179
York, Bishop Laurence, 186
Young, Mrs, 142